Neglect and the Peripheral Dyslexias

Guest Editor
M.J. Riddoch

A special issue of the journal
Cognitive Neuropsychology

The articles in Part 1 appeared in volume 7, 1990, number 5/6
The articles in Part 2 appeared in volume 8, 1991, number 3/4

LAWRENCE ERLBAUM ASSOCIATES, PUBLISHERS
Hove and London (UK) Hillsdale (USA)

Neglect and the Peripheral Dyslexias

Contents: Part 1

Contents: Part 2

Lawrence Erlbaum Associates Ltd., Publishers
27 Palmeira Mansions, Church Road, Hove, East Sussex, BN3 2FA, UK

ISBN: 0-86377-162-9

Printed in the United Kingdom by BPCC Wheatons Ltd., Exeter

COGNITIVE NEUROPSYCHOLOGY, 1990, 7 (5/6) 369–389

Neglect and the Peripheral Dyslexias

Jane Riddoch
Cognitive Science Research Centre, University of Birmingham, Birmingham, U.K.

INTRODUCTION

A wide variety of quantitatively different forms of reading disorder have been identified and described extensively (see Coltheart, 1981; 1985; Ellis & Young, 1987; Shallice, 1988). These may be broadly classified into the peripheral and central dyslexias, according to whether the patients have impaired prelexical or impaired lexical/post-lexical processes. The Special Issues on Neglect and the Peripheral Dyslexias are concerned with two of the peripheral dyslexias: neglect and letter-by-letter reading.

Up to now, letter-by-letter reading has been the more extensively researched disorder; a number of different accounts have been put forward and these differ particularly as regards the proposed level of impairment. For instance, low-level accounts of letter-by-letter reading have argued that the deficit is due to defective visual processing (which is not specific to words) (Friedman & Alexander, 1984), manifested as an inability to process multiple forms (Kinsbourne & Warrington, 1962a). High-level accounts have argued that there is particular disruption to the "word form" (Warrington & Shallice, 1980) or an inability to access the input lexicon via parallel letter analysis (Patterson & Kay, 1982). An alternative neurological explanation is that letter-by-letter reading reflects performance resulting from a lesion disconnecting the occipital cortex and left angular gyrus (Dejerine, 1892; Geschwind, 1965).

Hitherto, neglect dyslexia has not been so extensively researched; however, even given the paucity of reported cases, some comparisons may be made between letter-by-letter reading and neglect dyslexia. Typically, neglect dyslexia has been associated with right parietal lesions whereas

---

Requests for reprints should be addressed to Jane Riddoch, School of Psychology, University of Birmingham, Birmingham B15 2TT, U.K.

This work was supported by a grant from the Medical Research Council. I am grateful to Marlene Behrmann, Alfonzo Caramazza, Rick Hanley, Argye Hillis, Glyn Humphreys, Janice Kay, Karalyn Patterson, and Brenda Rapp for their helpful comments on this editorial.

letter-by-letter reading is associated with left occipital or occipito-temporal lesions. The disorder of neglect dyslexia is characterised by errors in reading; either areas of text on the left of the page are omitted, or within individual words the initial letters are affected so as to produce substitution, omission, or addition errors. The reading of letter-by-letter readers is perhaps less error prone but very slow.

As with letter-by-letter reading, there are a number of explanatory accounts of neglect dyslexia. A low-level account claims a particular form of defective visual processing: e.g. a disruption of attention to the contralesional hemispace (Kinsbourne & Warrington, 1962b). Other accounts have implicated higher-level representations. Costello and Warrington (1987) have argued for an abnormal distribution of attention to a *central* representation of a word (by this I take it to mean a nonretinal representation that is used to access stored lexical knowledge). This abnormal distribution of attention results in activation of an inappropriate word form. Behrmann, Moscovitch, Black, and Mozer (in press) further argue for an *interaction* between attention and higher-order lexical information (see also Siéroff, Pollatsek, & Posner, 1988).

Kinsbourne and Warrington (1962a) also proposed an attentional account for letter-by-letter reading. In this instance, it was proposed that perception is limited to single perceptual objects. With multi-item arrays such as words, impairments in performance are apparent. As indicated, there are also high-level explanations for letter-by-letter reading.

In view of the differing accounts of both disorders, several questions may be posed. For instance, to what extent are similar processes implicated in both disorders? To what extent are the disorders unitary? And what are the implications of the disorders for understanding normal reading?

NEGLECT DYSLEXIA

Currently, neglect dyslexia is enjoying a considerable degree of interest, as is reflected by the papers collected in these Special Issues of *Cognitive Neuropsychology* (Neglect and the Peripheral Dyslexias, Part 1 & Part 2. A number of new cases are described following both right-hemisphere lesions (Riddoch, Humphreys, Cleton, & Fery, Part 1; Young, Newcombe, & Ellis, Part 2) and left-hemisphere lesions (Caramazza & Hillis; Patterson & Wilson, Part 1; and Warrington, Part 2). Siéroff presents a comparison between left- and right-brain-damaged groups (Siéroff, Part 1).

Additionally, attempts are being made to relate the disorder to explicit computational accounts of reading. For instance, Behrmann, Moscovitch, and Mozer (Part 2) examine the interaction of attention and top-down knowledge in normal subjects and in a "lesioned" connectionist network

(MORSEL), which gives a qualitatively similar pattern of performance to that found in neglect patients.

The Fractionation of Neglect

In the past, neglect in reading has been regarded as part of a wider syndrome where the patient may fail to respond to contralesional information, often independently of the modality of input and across a wide range of tasks. More recently, neglect has been shown to fractionate into a number of discrete syndromes, each of which may occur in isolation in a single patient. For instance, motor neglect has been described in the absence of sensory inattention or extinction to double simultaneous stimulation. Patients with motor neglect show normal sensation, strength, and muscle tone, and they show no neglect in drawing or line bisection; yet they will fail to use the contralesional limbs spontaneously even in response to painful stimuli (Laplane & Degos, 1983; Valenstein & Heilman, 1981). A double dissociation between "near" and "far" neglect has been demonstrated in lesion studies with monkeys by Rizzolatti and his associates (Rizzolatti & Camarda, 1987; Rizzolatti, Gentilucci, & Mantelli, 1985), and "conjectural support" for equivalent dissociations in man has been presented by Bisiach and his co-workers (Bisiach, Perani, Vallar, & Berti; 1986) (see Humphreys, Riddoch, Müller, & Duncan, Note 1, for a discussion of this). Such results suggest that the neglect syndrome may fractionate into a number of separate disorders. As far as neglect dyslexia is concerned, it is true that neglect in reading has been described in isolation from "generalised" neglect (i.e. neglect on other visual tasks) (Baxter & Warrington, 1983; Patterson & Wilson; Riddoch et al., Part 1; Warrington, Part 2). However, reading may be considered to be particularly demanding on visual processing. It therefore remains possible that in all these cases, "general neglect" may have been elicited if performance had been assessed under more stringent conditions than those generally available clinically. For instance, MO (Riddoch et al., Part 1) showed no neglect in everyday life nor on typical clinical tests (such as the Rivermead Star Cancellation Test). He also showed no clinical neglect in reading words or complex passages of text. However, under reduced exposure conditions (words being presented for a limited period) he showed the typical symptoms of a right-hemisphere lesioned neglect dyslexic: that is, the initial part of the word was misread. It seems clear that more stringent tests of "general neglect" should be devised and applied before claims of a selective deficit (e.g. in reading) may be upheld.

The Fractionation of Neglect Dyslexia

Nevertheless, assuming that neglect dyslexia reflects a particular type of visual processing disorder (which may or may not be separated from other aspects of the neglect syndrome), the question arises whether neglect dyslexia itself fractionates. Evidence presented both here and elsewhere suggests that neglect dyslexia may fractionate in a number of different ways. For instance, different forms of material (e.g. text, words, single letters) may be differentially affected. Thus in some patients, single-word reading may be selectively impaired although the reading of text may be intact (Costello & Warrington, 1987; Patterson & Wilson; Riddoch et al.; Part 1), whereas other patients may show deficits in both areas of reading (Behrmann et al., in press; Ellis, Flude, & Young, 1987; Kinsbourne & Warrington, 1962b; Caramazza & Hillis; Riddoch et al., Part 1; Young et al.; Warrington, Part 2). Young et al. (Part 2) argue for a *qualitative* distinction between neglect reading errors in text and in single words, whilst the case for distinct processes involved in single word and text reading is further supported by evidence of a double dissociation, where patients have problems in reading text but not single words (see Kartsounis & Warrington, 1989).

Performance may also vary according to the nature of the symbols involved (e.g. alphanumeric vs. geometric symbols). For instance, it was noted earlier that some patients may be described whose deficit is specific to individual words rather than passages of text. However, only one case has been tested with numeric and geometric shape strings in addition to alphabetic stimuli (TB, Patterson & Wilson, Part 1). TB consistently made erors to the initial letter of word and nonword strings. In addition, when asked to name either the letters or the numbers in alternating strings (e.g. 2s5v6a or a6s5n3), errors continued to be made to the initial item and the level of performance was similar for letters and numbers. TB appears to have a deficit which is specific to alphanumeric stimuli. No omissions or indeed any form of error were made when asked to name strings of four geometric stimuli.

Additionally, "neglect" may be affected by the lexicality of the material (there may be differences in performance between words, pronounceable nonwords, and random letter strings). These effects may be due to the nature of the written material, to lexical constraint, or to other (as yet unidentified) factors. Usually performance is better with words than with pronounceable nonwords (Behrmann et al., in press; Caramazza & Hillis; Patterson & Wilson; Riddoch et al.; Siéroff; (Part 1), although not always. VB (Ellis et al., 1987) showed equivalent performance with both sets of stimuli. One typical account of this effect is that with both words and nonwords there is degradation of the letter(s) on the contralesional side. The lexical activation elicited by the intact portion of word stimuli may be sufficient to determine the identity of the word (e.g. even without adequate information about the leftmost or rightmost letter respectively, it may be relatively easy to identify -ACHT or STYL-). Further, word-like nonwords (BLANE, FAIN) may elicit similar lexical activation to words; however, given impaired letter identification, real-word responses are likely to be generated (PLANE, RAIN). Correspondingly, patients will tend to perform better with words than with nonwords. Both Patterson and Wilson and Riddoch et al. tested their patients with random letter strings. Patterson and Wilson used strings that were four letters long. Initial letter identification was significantly worse with such strings than with strings where the four letters comprised a real word, or with strings where the middle two letters had been replaced by digits. Patterson and Wilson (Part 1) propose that "first letter identification is boosted if subsequent letters offer lexical constraints on its identity; it deteriorates if other letters are present without offering such clues". Riddoch et al. tested their neglect dyslexic JB with words, pronounceable nonwords, and random letter strings. Performance was better for the initial letters for words relative to pronounceable nonwords and random letter strings (as Patterson and Wilson found); however, report of the first letter in random letter strings was significantly *better* than report of the second letter in the string. Similar effects have been found with normal subjects (Merikle, Coltheart, & Lowe, 1971), although it is not then confined to random letter strings (e.g. Carr, Lehkuhle, Kottas, & Astor-Stetson, 1976). With JB, this effect may be due to a re-orienting of attention to the left end of the string (in the instances just cited) when no sense can be made of right-sided information (see Kartsounis & Warrington, 1989; Seron, Coyette, & Bruyer, 1989). The conclusion is that not only will word identification differ from nonword identification because of top-down lexical influence, but different processes may also be implicated in identifying the different string types; neglect may interact with these different processes. However, the notion of top-down lexical influence does not rest easily with all investigators; in particular, Caramazza and Hillis account for the difference in report between words and nonwords with a strictly bottom-up processing architecture (see Caramazza & Hillis, Part 1).

Possible Explanations for the Fractionation Effects

Perhaps the most obvious account of the differences shown by patients in the ability to read text and individual words, and to read words, nonwords, and other printed symbols, is to propose that different materials may require qualitatively different processes. However, various alternative possibilities may be considered, as discussed next.

Nature of Written Material

As far as the distinction between single words and text is concerned, words may be omitted due to defective location of the line beginnings whereas initial letters may be deleted because the patient fails to make adequate compensatory eye movements for hemianopia (Young et al., Part 2). Alternatively, we may regard text as comprising a number of discrete objects (the words) bearing somewhat arbitrary spatially defined relationships to each other, whereas individual words may reflect single objects within which individual features (the letters) bear specific spatial relationships both to each other and to the composite shape they define. It has been argued elsewhere that quantitatively different processes underlie space coding between objects (e.g. words in text) and space coding within objects (letters in words) (Humphreys et al., Note 1). Patients with a selective deficit in reading single words (see earlier) may have impaired space coding within objects. Patients with both impaired single-word and text reading impairments may have deficits with both within- and between-object spatial encoding (Humphreys et al., Note 1).

In some patients, single-letter reading may also be affected (Patterson & Wilson, Part 1). Patterson and Wilson have argued that this patient has a letter level representation deficit specific to the first letter position. It may be that single letters are processed as though they occupy the initial position in a letter string and consequently are as likely to be incorrectly processed as initial letters. Alternatively, problems in letter recognition may simply be an associated impairment in some patients, or they may reflect visual field deficits, with single-letter reading being more impaired than word reading since there may be very little available information in the intact field to facilitate identification of letters. In words the contextual constraint provided by letters in the intact field may facilitate word recognition (see later).

Nature of the Symbols

Patterson and Wilson's patient appeared to have a selective deficit with alphanumeric stimuli, since his performance with strings of geometric shapes was unimpaired. Again material specificity is implicated. However, Patterson and Wilson also acknowledge that the geometric stimuli constituted a rather limited set of items relative to alphanumeric stimuli. It therefore may have been possible to elicit "neglect" of the initial member of such strings had perhaps a larger vocabulary of shapes been used.

Lexicality Effects

Differential performance with words and nonwords gives support to the notion that there are lexical constraints on the performance of patients with neglect dyslexia. An alternative account here is that a degraded visual representation causes a sufficient degree of lexical activation to allow guessing to take place. However, the data from two cases suggests that this is not so. Siéroff et al. (1988) presented patients with compound words and unrelated word *pairs* of equal length. If performance was strongly influenced by guessing, compound words should produce a greater proportion of correct responses than the unrelated word pairs. This was not found to be the case. Riddoch et al. (Part 1) compared compound words with *single* words of the same length. In this case guessing might benefit noncompounds, since the beginnings of single noncompound words tend to be more predictable from their end letters than those of compound words (see Riddoch et al. (Part 1), for supporting evidence on this point). Again, no significant difference was found between performance with compound and noncompound words. It therefore does not appear that "guessing" can account for the lexical effects observed in at least some neglect dyslexics. Interestingly, at least one case has been reported where performance was better with compound than with paired noncompound words (Behrmann et al., in press). Behrmann et al. have argued that lexical look-up effects may be strongly influenced by the degree of attentional deficit the patient may have. If the "attentional gradient" is reasonably shallow, interactions may occur between a degraded visual representation and later lexical or guessing process, producing compound–noncompound word differences. If the "attentional gradient" is steep, such interactions are compromised (see later).

Locus of Lesion and Neglect Dyslexia

Generalised neglect is most commonly found following right-hemisphere lesions, although under stringent test conditions (such as reduced stimulus exposure) symptoms commonly associated with neglect (such as extinction) may be found in both left- and right-brain-damaged groups (Siéroff et al., 1988; Siéroff, Part 1). In both groups of patients extinction of a contralesional stimulus is observed for centred pairs of stimuli.

Previously reported patients (Behrmann et al., in press; Ellis et al., 1987; Kinsbourne & Warrington, 1962b), and three cases reported in the Special Issue on Neglect and the Peripheral Dyslexias (JB and MO, Riddoch et al., Part 1; and SP, Young et al., Part 2), have generally had right-hemisphere lesions; however, as noted earlier, four cases of neglect dyslexia following a *left-sided lesion* are reported here: NG (Caramazza & Hillis, Part 1), TB (Patterson & Wilson, Part 1), PF (Siéroff, Part 1), and RNR (Warrington, Part 2). Three of these patients showed neglect for the *right* end of letter strings (NG, PF, and RNR), whereas one showed neglect for the left side of the string (TB). JOH (Costello & Warrington, 1987) is an interesting case of bilateral neglect. This patient had a lymphoma and after partial removal of the tumour, C.T.-scan demonstrated a left parieto-occipital lesion extending across the splenium of the corpus callosum into the right hemisphere. He showed a *right-sided neglect* for visuospatial tasks (such as the Benton Visual Retention Test and Line Bisection Tasks) and *left-sided* neglect in reading. He thus shows a dissociation between general visuo-spatial neglect and neglect dyslexia.

The work of Siéroff (Part 1) indicates that patients with left and right lesions may show qualitatively different patterns of performance. Patients with right parietal lesions were consistent in showing left extinction to nonwords (whether these were pairs of nonwords, or one long centred nonword); extinction in patients with left parietal lesions varied both across patients and across conditions within the same patient. One possible account here may be that the different lesion groups are demonstrating different attentional problems. For instance, right parietal patients may have particular difficulties in orienting contralesionally as a result of a chronic shift of attention towards the ipsilesional side (see Riddoch et al., Part 1). Left parietal patients may not demonstrate such a strong ipsilesional bias (Kinsbourne, 1978); however, once attention has been focused, it may prove difficult to disengage (Posner, Walker, Friedrich, & Rafal, 1984). This "disengagement" could explain Siéroff's finding that extinction in his left parietal group occurred for either left- or right-sided stimuli and that individual patients demonstrated inconsistent performance. Initial attentional capture may be provided by some particularly salient aspect of either a left- or a right-sided stimulus, it may be provided by the left side of a stimulus array (given a normal left–right scanning strategy in reading), or it may depend on initial fixation. All of these factors are open to empirical investigation.

Visual Field Defects and Neglect

It may be argued that the problems shown in reading by patients with a neglect dyslexia simply reflect the effects of visual field defects, the neglected part of the word falling into the blind field. The effects may even be apparent with single letter presentation, perhaps particularly where the informative strokes in the letter fall in the impaired field.

Of the patients described in the Special Issues on Neglect and the Peripheral Dyslexias, three are reported to have no visual field loss. These three all have left-hemisphere lesions (NG, Caramazza & Hillis; PF, Siéroff; RNR (both Part 1), Warrington, Part 2). Of the patients with right-hemisphere lesions, VB (Ellis et al., 1987), HR and AH (Behrmann et al., in press), SP (Young et al., Part 2), and MO (Riddoch et al., Part 1) all had a left homonymous hemianopia, while JB (Riddoch et al., Part 1) had a right upper quadrantanopia. The remaining patient with a left-hemisphere lesion (TB, Patterson & Wilson, Part 1) had very restricted vision, having a right homonymous hemianopia and virtually no vision in the left eye due to macular degeneration, restricting viewing to the nasal field of the right eye. We should note, however, that TB's residual visual acuity was good; he showed no evidence of "generalised visual neglect" and he was able to trace visually presented letters.

Is it possible to account for the difficulties experienced in reading by patients with right-sided lesions in terms of their visual field deficits? Two different empirical methods have been used to explore this possibility. For instance, Ellis et al. (1987) presented words tachistoscopically to VB's intact right visual field while monitoring central fixation with a camera, and Young et al. (Part 2) also presented words tachistoscopically to SP's intact right field. Initial letter misreadings continued. Riddoch et al. (Part 1) compared performance for the reporting of the initial letter of a word with reporting the initial letter when the word was flanked with a # (LAND vs. #LAND). In the first condition, report of the second letter of the string was nearly 100%. One would therefore expect that report of the L in the # condition should reach a similar level since both letters occupied the same position in the visual field. This was not found to be the case. Report of the L in #LAND was significantly worse than the report of A in LAND. These findings suggest that although a visual field deficit may contribute to the impaired processing of contralesional letters in neglect dyslexia, other factors are also implicated.

Coding of Word Length

Early accounts of neglect dyslexia noted that the errors produced maintained the length of the target stimulus (Kinsbourne & Warrington, 1962b). Ellis et al. (1987, p. 457) noted that VB largely made substitution errors rather than addition or omission errors and therefore proposed that "neglect affects the coding for the identity of initial letters but their existence was still responded to by the positional encoding system". An alternative suggestion, made by Caramazza and Hillis (Part 1) is that the correlation between stimulus and response length results directly from the assumption that graphemes are represented in word-centred coordinate systems and thus necessitate the encoding of positional information. Apparently preserved coding of word length, as evidenced by substitution errors being produced, is noted in some of the patients reported in Part 1 of this issue (TB, Patterson & Wilson; JB, Riddoch et al.). However, preserved coding of word length is not *always* evident, and it seems to vary across patients and across stimulus encoding conditions (e.g. as a function of word length).

Consider the effects of word length. RHR, reported by Warrington (Part 2), made predominately substitution errors in three- and four-letter words but she was predisposed to make *omission errors* in five- and six-letter words. JB (Riddoch et al., Part 1) made increasing numbers of omissions and additions with longer words. This suggests that, as the number of letters in a word increases, it may become less easy to code word length accurately. Furthermore, JB made an increased number of *addition errors* when a # was added to the beginning of a word relative to conditions where there was no # (suggesting that he included the # as part of the letter string, and an increased word length was computed) (Riddoch et al., Part 1). On the basis of these data we may argue that the coding of word length may not be a function of the number of letters in a word but rather a function of the number of items in a string (as would be expected if it is derived from low-level visual information). This is difficult to account for if length preservation is a by-product of coding in word-centred co-ordinates.

In neglect dyslexic patients, accurate coding of word length, revealed by a predominance of substitution errors, has been found when words are presented for unlimited durations. However, if viewing time is restricted, this coding may be impaired. For instance, MO makes an increased number of omission errors when the exposure of stimuli is reduced from 400msec. to 250msec., suggesting that under these conditions there is less time to code word length accurately (Riddoch et al., Part 1).

Accurate length coding is also not found in all patients. One interesting related point concerns what Ellis et al. (1987) proposed as a "neglect point". The neglect point is the point at which the target word and the produced error diverge. In some patients, the neglect point is reported to be in the same position across words of different lengths. For instance, Ellis et al. (1987) reported this with their patient VB. In other patients, the neglect point seems to vary. Caramazza and Hillis (Part 1), and Warrington (Part 2), report a gradient effect, in which the probability of correct report decreases for letters to the neglected side of the central letter position. In some accounts, the gradient effect is taken to reflect different degrees of perceptual impairment, with there being increased impairment as stimuli are presented further into the neglected side of space for patients showing shallow gradients (e.g. Behrmann et al., in press; Caramazza & Hillis, Part 1). Note that this space may be based on word- or string-centred co-ordinates, rather than retinal co-ordinates; thus there may be a gradient of worse report of letters to the neglected side of the centre of letter strings, rather than to the neglected side of fixation (Caramazza & Hillis, Part 1). Riddoch et al. (Part 1), in contrast, propose that gradient effects are linked to orienting problems in patients. If the spatial location of orienting varies, perhaps due to variation in the computation of word length, so the neglect point may vary over trials, producing a spatial gradient. This may be most apparent with longer words for which the computation of word length may be less accurate (see earlier). Consistent with this, their patient JB showed a steep cut-off with short words and a more gradual gradient with longer words. The relations between word length, the neglect point, and the relative prevalence of substitution, omission, and addition errors need careful consideration in future work.

Levels of Deficit in Neglect

Caramazza and his colleagues have argued that neglect dyslexia may result from a lesion at any one of a number of different representational levels (Caramazza & Hillis, Part 1; Rapp & Caramazza, Part 2). They propose at least three prelexical representations (analogous to the levels of analysis for object recognition defined by Marr, 1982). Processing will differ at each level as will the nature of the co-ordinate system involved. For instance, the representation said to be analogous to the primal sketch (the retino-centric feature level representation) is defined in terms of a retino-centric co-ordinate system. The representation said to be analogous to the 2½D sketch (the stimulus-centred letter shape level representation) is defined in terms of a non-retino-centric viewer-centred co-ordinate system, whereas the representation said to be analogous to the 3D sketch (the word-centred graphemic level representation) is defined in terms of an object-centred co-ordinate system.[1]

In order to explore the level of the impaired representation in cases of neglect dyslexia two techniques have been used: (1) manipulating the orientation of stimuli, and (2) exploring the relationship between oral and written spelling.

Vertical Presentation of Words

In some patients, vertical presentation of words appears to improve their reading performance (as indicated by the cases SP, Young et al., Part 2; and HR and RH, Behrmann et al., in press). In Caramazza et al's. terms, this suggests an impairment to processes based in either retinal and/or string-based co-ordinates, since the deficit relates to the left or right positions of the letters in the world, rather than their positions in a word. Two patients described in the Special Issues, both with left-sided lesions, found the reading of vertical words very difficult to perform (RNR and TB, Warrington, Part 2; Patterson & Wilson, Part 1). The other left-hemisphere patient, NG, continued to make the same sort of errors as had been shown with normally oriented text; i.e. errors were made to the end of the word or letter string (Caramazza & Hillis, Part 1).

---

[1]Though note that this analogy is somewhat loose. In Marr's account, both the primal sketch and the 2½D sketch are retino-centric.

Inverted Presentation of Words

A second manipulation of the orientation of the stimuli has been to present words INVERTED or as a MIRROR IMAGE. In some patients this seems to make little difference to the nature of the reading problem, in that the patients continue to misread letters on the neglected end (e.g. the left side of space for right-hemisphere patients, the right side of space for left-hemisphere patients) (see JB, Riddoch et al., Part 1). In contrast NG continued to make *left-side of word* errors (even though these letters are now on the right side of space). This suggests that her deficit is within a representation not affected by spatial coding in terms of visual or environmental co-ordinates; rather the representation may be centred on the letter string.

Spelling

In two right-hemisphere patients where spelling has been tested (VB, Ellis, Young, & Flude, 1987; and JB, Riddoch et al., Part 1), there was no evidence of neglect errors. The written output of both patients was characterised particularly by stroke additions or omissions which could be located anywhere in the word. Again, this is not true of all neglect dyslexics. TB (Patterson & Wilson, Part 1) performed at a high level with oral spelling, but with written spelling (either to aurally presented words or definitions), there was a tendency for errors to be made to the initial letters. NG's spelling (Caramazza & Hillis, Part 1) was tested extensively, using both oral and written responses, where she was required to spell words both from left to right and from right to left. In all instances she was impaired on letters in the right half of words and nonwords; i.e. NG's spelling performance mirrors her reading performance. Within Caramazza et al.'s scheme, the qualitatively similar pattern of reading and spelling problems is taken to indicate a common underlying problem, affecting processes operating on a representation coded within a word-centred co-ordinate system. Such a representation is presumed to be used as an input to the visual lexicon in reading, as a storage buffer in oral and written spelling. However, though Caramazza et al.'s account is parsimonious, it should not be forgotten that the stress here is on an association of deficits (qualitatively similar reading and spelling problems). It remains possible that, in such cases, we witness the co-occurrence of separate deficits rather than a common underlying problem (but see Caramazza, 1986; Caramazza & McCloskey, 1988; McCloskey & Caramazza, 1988).

Attentional Processes in Neglect

Unilateral neglect is often characterised as an attentional disorder. Various pieces of evidence are consistent with this. For instance, neglect may sometimes be improved by cueing patients to the neglected side (Riddoch & Humphreys, 1983); patients may have apparent problems in particular components of the attentional system (e.g. engaging vs. moving vs. disengaging attention; see Humphreys & Riddoch, 1990; Posner, Rafal, Choate, & Vaughan, 1985; Posner et al., 1984; Rafal & Posner, 1987); and neglect may be induced by double simultaneous stimulation (extinction) (Birch, Belmont, & Karp, 1967). In neglect dyslexia, some evidence indicating amelioration due to cueing and/or extinction can be found. Riddoch et al. (Part 1) report that in one patient (JB) neglect on the left end of the string was less when the string was preceded by a hash sign than when the string was presented alone. This was so even when the # did not disturb the retinal positions of the letters (at least with five-letter words; see Riddoch et al., Part 1). They interpret this in terms of the patient orienting more to the left when the # was present. Siéroff (Part 1) reports specific effects of extinction. Both results point to some attentional involvement in at least some neglect dyslexics.

One problem with the attentional account is that, in order to explain the differences between patients such as VB (Ellis et al., 1987) and NG (Caramazza & Hillis, Part 1), who respectively seem to neglect a retinocentric and a word-centred representation, attention would need to operate at different levels of representation. An attentional account cannot easily be separated from an account proposing an impairment within the representation itself (see Caramazza & Hillis, Part 1). An attempt to overcome the problem of tying attentional processes to increasingly more abstract levels of representation is made by Riddoch et al. (Part 1). They suggest that attention is chronically oriented to the contralesional side of retinocentric space. When reading, the position where subjects attend to in words is said to be determined by the computed word length, with attention being biased more to the left of centre (the "convenient viewing position", O'Regan & Levy-Schoen, 1987; O'Regan, Levy-Schoen, Pynte, & Brugaillere, 1984). In neglect dyslexia, attention may be oriented chronically to one side of the convenient viewing position. However, because the convenient viewing position varies with word length, letters may be neglected at the same position in the word, but different positions in space (e.g. the first letter in centred four- and five-letter words). This account does away with the need to propose a word-centred representation to explain neglect based on letter position in word rather than retinal space. It also predicts interesting variations in neglect according to whether word length is computed correctly (see Riddoch et al.,

Part 1). However, it is not easy to see how the account can be extended to explain cases such as NG (Caramazza & Hillis, Part 1), who negelected the right of normally oriented words and the left side of mirror-reversed words, without proposing that attentional processes are also tied to specific representations.

Lexical Interactions and Neglect in Normals

We noted earlier that, in at least some cases of neglect dyslexia, words are read more accurately than nonwords. Given that this word advantage cannot be attributed to a simple guessing bias (see earlier), it would appear to suggest some form of interaction between lexical factors and the underlying impairment producing neglect. One account of this interaction has been provided by Behrmann et al. (in press) and Mozer and Behrmann (in press). In their model, attentional processes enhance processing at particular letter positions in a separate word recognition system. Neglect is simulated by lesioning the model so there is impaired attentional enhancement at some positions. In words, top-down feedback works to some degree to overcome poor letter activation. Such feedback is weaker in nonwords than in words. Hence a lexical advantage emerges.

Behrmann et al. (Part 2) suggest that these effects may be mimicked to some degree in normal subjects by experimental manipulations which cause attention to be directed towards one part of the stimulus. The nature of the to-be-ignored portion of the stimulus is influential on the subject's responses, and in particular, there are strong lexical influences on performance. The result points to possible interactions between lexical and attentional processes in reading, both in neglect and in normal reading.

LETTER-BY-LETTER READING

Letter-by-letter reading is characterised by slowed reading performance, the patient apparently only able to recognise words once each individual letter has been identified. The deficit underlying the performance of different letter-by-letter readers has generally been considered to vary in degree, in that some patients may be more severely affected than others (e.g. RAV took 1.8 seconds on average to read 3–4 letter words compared with 16.9 seconds for CH [Warrington & Shallice, 1980; Patterson & Kay, 1982; respectively]), but the nature of the deficit has been presumed to be consistent across patients (Shallice, 1988). Typically, theoreticians have argued for a post-perceptual deficit with debate almost exclusively concerned with the *level* of impaired post-perceptual representation, whether in parallel letter analysis or an impaired "word form" (although see Friedman & Alexander, 1984; Howard, 1989; Levine & Calvanio, 1978).

Two cases of patients who may be described as "letter-by-letter" readers are presented in Part 2 of the Special Issue on Neglect and the Peripheral Dyslexias (HR, PD, TU, Rapp & Caramazza, Kay & Hanley, Farah & Wallace, respectively). The data from two patients (HR and PD) suggest that, in at least three cases, early perceptual deficits may contribute to the letter-by-letter reading impairment (Rapp & Caramazza, Kay & Hanley, respectively). In HR the deficit is thought to be within a prelexical representation (specifically at a string-level representation; see Rapp & Caramazza, Part 2). PD is thought to be unable to indentify more than one letter at a time (see Kay & Hanley, Part 2). PD has also been used to illustrate the fact that letter-by-letter readers may differ not only in the severity of their deficit but also as regards the *level* of deficit. For instance, PD appears to have an inability to identify letters in parallel as compared with another letter-by-letter reader, WL, who is thought to be impaired at a stage of visual word recognition at which abstract letter identities are determined (Reuter-Lorenz & Brunn, 1990).

On the basis of HR's performance on a number of tests, Rapp and Caramazza observe that (at least some) letter-by-letter readers show a spatial deficit which may be compared and contrasted to the spatial deficit shown in cases of neglect dyslexia. This interesting suggestion may be assessed by comparing neglect dyslexia and letter-by-letter reading (in particular with regard to the cases described in this issue) with regard to the same issues, namely lexicality effects, locus of lesion, visual field effects, and the coding of word length.

Lexicality Effects

Some patients with neglect dyslexia perform better when reading words than nonwords (see earlier). Similar word superiority effects can also occur with letter-by-letter readers, even when the stimuli are briefly presented and forced-choice procedures are used. For instance, Rapp and Caramazza employed a partial report procedure similar to that described by Averbach and Sperling (1968). More accurate performance was obtained for words and pseudowords relative to random letter strings. Interestingly, their patient HR did not show the typical W function obtained in normal subjects in this task, but rather a steep left-to-right gradient. This is also true of Kay & Hanley's patient (Part 2). However, at least one letter-by-letter patient in the literature (WL, Reuter-Lorenz & Brunn, 1990) has been reported as showing a W-shaped function in a tachistoscopic letter naming task. Either these patients differ in the nature of their deficit, or the difference is one of severity. Possibly W-shaped functions under forced-choice conditions can be found in patients with less severe deficits. It is certainly the case that the letter-by-letter readers reported in the literature differ greatly in their reading speed (see earlier).

In neglect dyslexia the word superiority effect can be attributed to top-down feedback from lexical representations to enhance processing at the neglected end of the letter string (see earlier). A similar proposal can be put forward to explain the word superiority effect in letter-by-letter readers. Alternatively, words may be advantaged because they can be more readily encoded in phonological short-term memory or because of their orthographic redundancy (see Kay & Hanley, Part 2). A redundancy account is not applicable to all letter-by-letter readers. For instance Reuter-Lorenz and Brunn's patient WL was significantly more accurate in reporting the letters in words than in pseudowords but showed only a small numerical (and not statistically significant) advantage for pseudowords over nonwords (Reuter-Lorenz & Brunn, 1990). Whichever explanation holds, these results are difficult to account for if the patients have impaired lexical representations or are unable to make use of a "word form" system that "categorises words visually" (cf. Warrington & Shallice, 1980).

Locus of Lesion

Unlike neglect dyslexia, which has been reported following both left- and right-hemisphere lesions, letter-by-letter reading has typically been reported in cases of left-hemisphere damage, classically involving the occipital lobe and the splenium of the corpus callosum. Both of the cases reported in Part 2 of the Special Issue on Neglect and the Peripheral Dylexias had left posterior lesions (Kay & Hanley; Rapp & Caramazza). This appears to be the standard pathology for this disorder (see Patterson & Kay, 1982). Given the difference in lesion sites, neglect dyslexia and letter-by-letter reading could be expected to differ functionally, given some overlap between brain function and localisation. This, of course, remains an empirical question.

Visual Field Deficits

Patients with letter-by-letter reading deficits typically have right visual field defects, and this is true of the patients described in this issue (HR and PD both had a right homonymous hemianopia with macular sparing; TU is described as having a right homonymous hemianopia). As with neglect dyslexia, it may be possible to propose that letter-by-letter reading is produced by a particular field defect. However, cases of letter-by-letter reading have been reported with intact visual fields (Greenblatt, 1976; Vincent, Sadowsky, Saunders, & Reeves, 1977). Further, at least some patients are able to read successfully the digits at either end of an 8-letter word presented for 150msec. (e.g. 7thinking4) (Warrington & Shallice, 1980). However, this sort of demonstration has not necessarily been performed on all letter-by-letter readers, and successful performance may reflect patients with less severe deficits. Also, as letter-by-letter readers may not form a homogeneous group, assessment of the contribution of the visual field defect to the disorder should always be assessed or compensation made for it (for instance Kay & Hanley, Part 2, presented stimuli to the left of fixation so that they would fall within the intact field, providing no eye movements took place; Rapp & Caramazza presented stimuli in a similar manner although additionally reducing the exposure to 250msec. to reduce the likelihood of eye movements).

Coding of Word Length

Many patients with neglect dyslexia appear to compute word length relatively accurately, at least for shorter words (see earlier). The same also appears to be true of letter-by-letter readers. While letter-by-letter readers demonstrate increased latencies in reading as the length of the word increases, they do not omit to read the final letters of the word. The errors made by PD were largely visual errors and maintained the target length (Kay & Hanley, Part 2).

TYPES OF DEFICIT

The fact that both neglect dyslexia and letter-by-letter readers can show preserved knowledge of word length and better performance on reading words than nonwords does not necessarily indicate a common form of impairment. For instance, lexical influence can be pervasive in reading, benefiting report when visual feature or letter information is deficient irrespective of the cause or even the functional level of the deficiency. Also, not all neglect dyslexics and letter-by-letter readers show a word superiority effect (Ellis et al., 1987; Kay & Hanley, Part 2), consistent with different neglect dyslexics and different letter-by-letter readers having different functional impairments.

Is there any further evidence for a common functional deficit in the two forms of reading disorder? Work presented in Part 2 of the Special Issue on Neglect and the Peripheral Dyslexias suggests that some letter-by-letter readers have a low-level deficit, either in the simultaneous processing of multiple forms or in switching attention rapidly across visual forms. For instance, Farah and Wallace report that their patient TU was impaired in the recognition of various kinds of multi-forms, irrespective of whether they were letters, number, or pictures (see also Friedman & Alexander, 1984). Rapp and Caramazza (Part 2) also showed significant and abnormal effects of display size in their letter-by-letter reader in a simple feature search task. Impaired perception of simultaneously presented forms, as evidenced by the phenomenon of extinction, is of course characteristic of visual neglect.

One further similarity between the two disorders is that both neglect dyslexics and letter-by-letter readers can show a gradient of deficit. This gradient is manifested in rather different ways in the two syndromes. In neglect dyslexia it is typically the case that patients misidentify or fail to report letters appearing in the neglected field. In letter-by-letter reading, word report typically becomes increasingly slow as words become longer. Rapp and Caramazza suggest that these differences in the nature of the gradient in the two cases could reflect the shape and slope of the underlying processing efficiency function—neglect patients show a step-like function whereas letter-by-letter readers show a less steep (even linear) gradient. An alternative account suggests that, at least in some instances of both neglect dyslexia and letter-by-letter reading, patients have impaired orienting to the convenient viewing position in words (Riddoch et al., Part 1). In letter-by-letter reading patients orient to the left of the normal convenient viewing position, and then need to scan to the right to read the word. Scanning may be impaired because of problems disengaging and shifting attention, producing abnormally slow and perhaps also error-prone reading. Nevertheless, letter-by-letter reading is characterised by a latency rather than an accuracy deficit because there is normally a left-to-right attentional and scanning bias in reading (see Humphreys & Bruce, 1989, for a review), which helps ensure that patients do scan across to the right (albeit slowly). In some instances of neglect dyslexia, patients orient to the right of the convenient viewing position. Their problems in orienting are then exacerbated by the usual left-to-right scanning bias, producing inaccurate reading.

CONCLUSIONS

Clearly, future studies must address the issue of the different processes involved in coding visual descriptions of print, and the way in which these different processes may be impaired following brain damage. The papers in the Special Issue on Neglect and the Peripheral Dyslexias suggest that peripheral reading disorders may be produced by various functional deficits, which may manifest themselves in clinical syndromes of neglect dyslexia and letter-by-letter reading. By understanding these syndromes in more detail, we come to understand better how visual lexical access normally occurs.

Manuscript received 1 July 1990
Revised manuscript received 3 August 1990

REFERENCES

Averbach, E. & Sperling, G. (1968). Short-term storage of information in vision. In R. N. Haber (Ed.), *Contemporary theory and research in visual perception*. New York: Holt, Rinehart, & Winston.

Baxter, D. M. & Warrington, E. K. (1983). Neglect dysgraphia. *Journal of Neurology, Neurosurgery, and Psychiatry*, *46*, 1073–1078.

Behrmann, M., Moscovitch, M., Black, S. E., & Mozer, M. (in press). Perceptual and conceptual mechanisms in neglect dyslexia: Two contrasting case studies. *Brain*.

Birch, H. G., Belmont, I., & Karp, E. (1967). Delayed information processing following brain damage. *Brain*, *90*, 113–130.

Bisiach, E., Perani, D., Vallar, G., & Berti, A. (1986). Unilateral neglect: Personal and extrapersonal. *Neuropsychologia*, *24*, 759–767.

Caramazza, A. (1986). On drawing inferences about the structure of normal cognitive systems from the analysis of patterns of impaired performance. *Brain and Cognition*, *5*, 41–66.

Caramazza, A. & McCloskey, M. (1988). The case for single-patient studies. *Cognitive Neuropsychology*, *5*, 517–528.

Carr, T. H., Lehkuhle, S. W., Kottas, B., & Astor-Stetson, E. C. (1976). Target position and practice in the identification of letters in varying contexts: A word superiority effect. *Perception and Psychophysics*, *19*, 412–416.

Coltheart, M. (1981). Disorders of reading and their implications for models of normal reading. *Visible Language*, *15*, 245–286.

Coltheart, M. (1985). Cognitive neuropsychology and the study of reading. In M. I. Posner & O. S. M. Marin (Eds.), *Attention and performance, XI*. Hillsdale, N.J.: Lawrence Erlbaum Associates Inc.

Costello, A. & Warrington, E. (1987). The dissociation of visuospatial neglect and neglect dyslexia. *Journal of Neurology, Neurosurgery, and Psychiatry*, *50*, 1110–1116.

Dejerine, J. (1892). Contribution à l'étude anatomoclinique et clinique des differentes variétés de cécité verbale. *Mémoires de la Société de Biologie*, *4*, 61–90.

Ellis, A. & Young, A. (1987). *Human cognitive neuropsychology*. London and Hove: Lawrence Erlbaum Associates Ltd.

Ellis, A., Flude, B. M., & Young, A. W. (1987). "Neglect dyslexia" and the early visual processing of letters in words and nonwords. *Cognitive Neuropsychology*, *4*, 439–464.

Ellis, A., Young, A. W., & Flude, B. M. (1987). "Afferent dysgraphia" in a patient and in normal subjects. *Cognitive Neuropsychology*, *4*, 465–486.

Friedman, R. B. & Alexander, M. P. (1984). Pictures, images, and pure alexia: A case study. *Cognitive Neuropsychology*, *1*, 9–23.

Geschwind, N. (1965). Disconnection syndromes in animal and man. Part II. *Brain*, *88*, 585–645.

Greenblatt, S. H. (1976). Subangular alexia without agraphia or hemianopsia. *Brain and Language*, *3*, 229–245.

Howard, D. (1989). Letter-by-letter readers: Evidence for parallel processing. In D. Besner & G. W. Humphreys (Eds.), *Basic processes in reading: Visual recognition*. Hillsdale, N.J.: Lawrence Erlbaum Associates Inc.

Humphreys, G. W. & Bruce, V. (1989). *Visual cognition: Computational, Experimental, and Neuropsychological Perspectives*. London: Lawrence Erlbaum Associates Ltd.

Humphreys, G. W. & Riddoch, M. J. (1990). Interactions between object and space systems revealed through neuropsychology. In D. E. Meyer & S. Kornblum (Eds.), *Attention and performance XIV*. Hillsdale, N.J.: Lawrence Erlbaum Associates Inc.

Kartsounis, L. D. & Warrington, E. K. (1989). Unilateral neglect overcome by cues implicit in stimulus displays. *Journal of Neurology, Neurosurgery, and Psychiatry*, *52*, 1253–1259.

Kinsbourne, M. (1978). *Asymmetrical function of the brain*. Cambridge: Cambridge University Press.

Kinsbourne, M. & Warrington, E. (1962a). A disorder of simultaneous form perception. *Brain*, *85*, 461–486.

Kinsbourne, M. & Warrington, E. K. (1962b). A variety of reading disability associated with right-hemisphere lesions. *Journal of Neurology, Neurosurgery, and Psychiatry*, *25*, 339–344.

Laplane, D. & Degos, J. D. (1983). Motor neglect. *Journal of Neurology, Neurosurgery, and Psychiatry*, *46*, 152–158.

Levine, D. N. & Calvanio, R. (1978). A study of the visual defect in verbal alexia-simultanagnosia. *Brain*, *101*, 65–81.

McClosky, M. & Caramazza, A. (1988). Theory and methodology in cognitive neuropsychology: A response to our critics. *Cognitive Neuropsychology*, *5*, 583–623.

Marr, D. (1982). *Vision*. New York: W. H. Freeman & Co.

Merikle, P. M., Coltheart, M., & Lowe, D. G. (1971). On the selective effects of a pattern masking stimulus. *Canadian Journal of Psychology*, *25*, 264–279.

Mozer, M. C. & Behrmann, M. (in press). On the interaction of selective attention and lexical knowledge: A connectionist account of neglect dyslexia. *Journal of Cognitive Neuroscience*.

O'Regan, J. K. & Levy-Schoen, A. (1987). Eye-movement strategy and tactics in word recognition and reading. In M. Coltheart (Ed.), *Attention and performance XII*. Hillsdale, N.J.: Lawrence Erlbaum Associates Inc.

O'Regan, J. K., Levy-Schoen, A., Pynte, J., & Brugaillere, B. (1984). Convenient fixation location within isolated words of different lengths and different structures. *Journal of Experimental Psychology: Human Perception and Performance*, *10*, 250–257.

Patterson, K. & Kay, J. (1982). Letter-by-letter reading: Psychological descriptions of a neurological syndrome. *Quarterly Journal of Experimental Psychology*, *34A*, 411–441.

Posner, M. I., Rafal, R. D., Choate, L. S., & Vaughan, J. (1985). Inhibition of return: Neural basis and function. *Cognitive Neuropsychology*, *2*, 211–228.

Posner, M. I., Walker, J. A., Friedrich, F. J., & Rafal, R. D. (1984). Effects of parietal injury on the covert orienting of attention. *Journal of Neuroscience*, *4*, 1863–1874.

Rafal, R. D. & Posner, M. I. (1987). Deficits in human visual spatial attention following thalamic lesions. *Proceedings of the National Academy of Science*, *84*, 7349–7353.

Reuter-Lorenz, P. A. & Brunn, J. L. (1990). A pre-lexical basis for letter-by-letter reading. *Cognitive Neuropsychology*, *7*, 1–20.

Riddoch, M. J. & Humphreys, G. W. (1983). The effect of cueing on unilateral neglect. *Neuropsychologia*, *21*, 589–599.

Rizzolatti, G. & Camarda, R. (1987). Neural circuits for spatial attention and unilateral neglect. In M. Jeanerrod (Ed.), *Neurophysiological and neuropsychological aspects of spatial neglect*. North Holland: Elsevier Science Publishers.

Rizzolatti, G., Gentilucci, M., & Matelli, M. (1985). Selective spatial attention: One centre, one circuit, or many circuits? In M. I. Posner & O. S. M. Marin (Eds.), *Attention and performance XI*. Hillsdale, N.J.: Lawrence Erlbaum Associates Inc.

Seron, X., Coyette, F., & Bruyer, R. (1989). Ipsilateral influences on central processes in neglect patients. *Cognitive Neuropsychology*, *6*, 475–498.

Shallice, T. (1988). *From neuropsychology to mental structure*. New York: Cambridge University Press.

Siéroff, E., Pollatsek, A., & Posner, M. I. (1988). Recognition of visual letter strings following injury to the posterior visual spatial attention system. *Cognitive Neuropsychology*, *5*, 427–449.

Valenstein, E. & Heilman, K. M. (1981). Unilateral hypokinesia and motor extinction. *Neurology*, *31*, 445–448.

Vincent, F. M., Sadowsky, C. H., Saunders, R. L., & Reeves, A. G. (1977). Alexia without agraphia, hemianopia, or colour-naming defect: A disconnection syndrome. *Neurology*, *27*, 689–691.

Warrington, E. & Shallice, T. (1980). Word form dyslexia. *Brain*, *103*, 99–112.

REFERENCE NOTE

1. Humphreys, G. W., Riddoch, M. J., Müller, H., & Duncan, J. Where and what: On the distinction between ventral object vision and dorsal space vision in humans. Submitted to *Cognitive Neuropsychology*.

COGNITIVE NEUROPSYCHOLOGY, 1990, 7 (5/6) 391–445

Levels of Representation, Co-ordinate Frames, and Unilateral Neglect

Alfonso Caramazza
Cognitive Science Center, The Johns Hopkins University, Baltimore, U.S.A.

Argye E. Hillis
HealthSouth Rehabilitation Corp., Baltimore, U.S.A.

We describe the performance of a brain-damaged subject, NG, who made reading errors only on the right half of words. This problem persisted even when the subject had demonstrated accurate recognition of the letters in a stimulus through naming all the letters. Furthermore, the spatially determined reading impairment was unaffected by topographic transformations of stimuli: identical performance was obtained for stimuli presented in horizontal, vertical, and mirror-reversed form. The same pattern of errors was also obtained in all forms of spelling tasks: written spelling, oral spelling, and backward oral spelling. The performance of the subject is interpreted in the context of a multi-stage model of the word recognition process. It is concluded that the locus of the deficit responsible for NG's reading impairment is at a stage of processing where word-centred grapheme representations are computed. The spatially determined pattern of performance reported for NG, as well as other patterns observed for other brain-damaged subjects, are interpreted as providing support for the proposed multi-stage model of word recognition. The more general implications of the reported results for models of visual processing and attention are also considered.

Requests for reprints should be addressed to Alfonso Caramazza, Cognitive Science Centre, The Johns Hopkins University, Baltimore, MD 21218, U.S.A.

The research reported here was supported in part by N.I.H. grant NS22201 and by grants from the Seaver Institute and the McDonnell/Pew Program in Cognitive Neuroscience. This support is gratefully acknowledged. We would especially like to thank NG for her patience and good cheer throughout our interminable experiments and probings. We are grateful to the members of the Cognitive Neuropsychology Laboratory, and in particular Brenda Rapp, for their helpful suggestions at various points of the research reported here. We thank Howard Egeth, Glyn Humphreys, Brenda Rapp, Jane Riddoch, Tim Shallice, Eric Siéroff, Paolo Viviani, and Steven Yantis for comments on an earlier version of this paper.

INTRODUCTION

In this paper we investigate several aspects of the reading process that are illuminated by consideration of the reading performance of patients presenting with a striking perceptual/cognitive disorder that disproportionately affects a spatially defined part of visually presented objects—unilateral visual neglect. We will argue that the clinical category of unilateral neglect consists of a heterogeneous set of patients with deficits at different levels of the perceptual system. One level of deficit involves damage to the perceptual mechanisms that compute retino-centric representations of visual inputs; another level of deficit involves damage to mechanisms that compute a viewer- or stimulus-centred representation of the font-specific and orientation-specific letter shapes, and a third level of deficit involves damage to mechanisms that compute word-centred (or object-centred) representations of the abstract letter identities that comprise a word. This claim about the various types of possible impairments is based on strong assumptions about the types and structure of representations that are computed in the course of recognising a string of letters as a word of the language. Our discussion of these issues is organised as follows: we begin by identifying the relevant computational problems that must be solved in reading—in the specific case considered here, the computational problems associated with the recognition of a string of letters as a word of the language; we then describe experimental results obtained with a brain-damaged subject which severely constrain plausible claims about the structure of the representations and the processes that underlie the recognition of written words; we conclude with a discussion of various problems and pseudoproblems that have arisen in the context of considerations of reading and unilateral neglect.

A Computational-level Analysis of Written Word Recognition: Levels of Representation and Co-ordinate Frames

Within an information processing framework, the computational goal in word recognition consists of determining the types and structure of representations that are computed in the course of mapping a visual stimulus onto a lexical-orthographic representation. We take it that this process is not dissimilar in its general form to that involved in visual object recognition. Following Marr (1982; Marr & Nishihara, 1978), we assume that the latter process entails computing several different types of representations, prior to actual recognition: beginning with a description of the visual array in terms of perceptual primitives, blobs, edges, and bars—the primal sketch; proceeding to a description of the visible surfaces of objects in terms of local surface orientation and distance—the 2½-D sketch; and, finally, an abstract, canonical description of the object—the 3-D model.[1] In this framework, the descriptions computed at each level of processing differ not only in terms of the types of representations that are computed, but also in terms of the co-ordinate system within which the respective representations are defined. Our working hypothesis is that the early stages of reading, up to word identification, are similarly organised (see Monk, 1985, for a discussion of this parallel). And, in fact, in the absence of evidence to the contrary, we will assume that the representational spaces involved in visual word and object recognition are the same. On this view, the visual processes involved in word recognition can be characterised in terms of three stages of analysis: (1) the computation of a retino-centric feature map; (2) the computation of a viewer- or stimulus-centred letter shape map; and (3) the computation of a word-centred grapheme description.[2,3] The grapheme descriptions computed at the latter level of analysis serve to activate lexical-orthographic representations for word identification (see Fig. 1).

The multi-stage model of word recognition adopted here makes a number of specific assumptions about the representations computed at

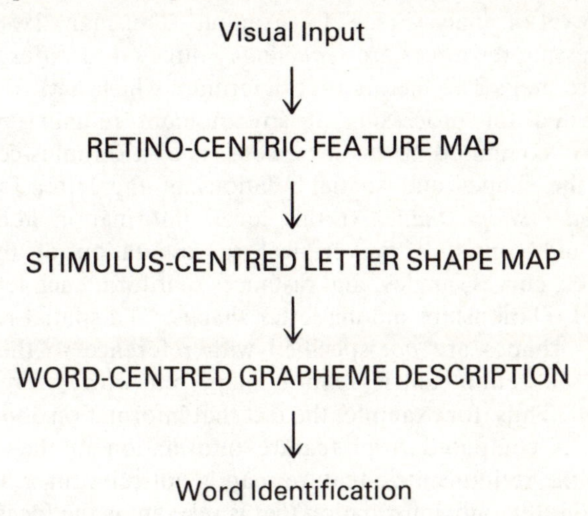

FIG. 1 Levels of representation in visual word recognition.

---

[1]See Hildreth and Ullman (1989) and Kosslyn, Flynn, Amsterdam, and Wang (1990) for recent accounts of the computational problems in visual perception.

[2]We follow Venezsky (1970) and Cummings (1988) in using the term *grapheme* to refer to the basic units of analysis in orthographic representations—abstract (case- and font-independent) letter identities.

[3]It should be noted that the term "word" in "word-centred co-ordinate system" is used to refer to a letter string, bounded by perceptually salient features, that only potentially forms a word in the linguistic sense. More on this follows.

each level of the recognition process. The major assumptions may be rendered explicit by considering the computational problem that must be solved at each of the hypothesised levels of processing. At the first level, the problem is that of extracting directly from surface-reflected light intensities the relevant discontinuities that define edges in the image (within the limits of visual acuity). It is assumed that this process is spatially parallel across the entire visual field, in the sense that edge information may be computed simultaneously at every location of the retinal image. The representation computed at this stage of processing consists of a retino-centric description of the edges in a retinally projected image—a *feature map*. Thus, for example, feature information extracted from a word presented in the upper right quadrant of the visual field will be represented in the upper right quadrant at the retino-centric feature level.

The computational problem at the second level of analysis involves recovering from a feature map the shape properties of contours and the spatial relations that obtain among parts of an image (stimulus). This process is assumed to be only locally parallel, in the sense that processing is spatially and temporally inhomogeneous across the feature map computed at the first level of analysis (see, for example, Treisman, 1988). In other words, processing resources are *sequentially* directed to different subparts of the feature map. The factors that determine which part of the feature map is selected for processing at any moment remain unclear. The representation computed at this level consists of a stimulus-centred[4] description of the shapes and spatial relations of the letter forms in the image—a *letter shape map*. At this level, information about a word stimulus would consist of a veridical representation of the spatially arranged lines, curves, angles, and distances that form each letter, as well as the spatial relationships among letter shapes. The spatial relationships among letter shapes are *not* specified with reference to their absolute position in the retino-centric feature map, but with reference to the stimulus itself. Thus, for example, the fact that information about a specific letter shape is computed from feature information in the upper right quadrant of the retino-centric feature map is not relevant at this level of representation; the only information that is relevant is the *local* position of

[4]We have chosen to use the term "stimulus-centred" instead of the more common "viewer-centred" in order to emphasise the stimulus-bound aspect of the representation computed at this level of processing. That is, we wish to emphasise the fact that we can think of the several levels of processing considered here as ordered in terms of progressive abstraction from the physical stimulus: as a process that abstracts away from irrelevant physical detail to a representation of only the perceptually relevant information. However, at this point we are agnostic on the issue of whether processing resources are directed to a *stimulus* or to a *region of space that contains a stimulus*. At the level of detail we are working the distinction is not significant.

the letter shape relative to other letter shapes in the stimulus. For example, the *leftmost* letter shape of a stimulus in the *upper right* quadrant of the retino-centric feature map would be represented on the *left* of the stimulus-centred letter shape representation. In general, then, the information that is retained at this level of representation is the local topographic relationship (e.g. vertical arrangement) of the letter shapes that comprise a stimulus.

At the third level of analysis, the computational problem consists in computing from simple shape properties the abstract letter identities—case-, font-, and orientation-independent letter representations—that comprise a letter string. It is not clear whether this process should also be assumed to be locally parallel, in the sense that simultaneous processing is restricted to a spatially defined subset of the shape description, or whether it should be thought to be strictly serial for each segregated shape (for discussion of this issue see Duncan, 1987; Egeth, Jonides, & Wall, 1972; Pashler & Badgio, 1987; Treisman & Gelade, 1980; and see Allport, 1989, for a general review of the issues and results). The representation computed at this level consists of a word-centred description of the graphemes and their relative spatial position in a word—a *grapheme description*. At this level of analysis there is no difference among the representations for the stimuli *CHAIR*, *chair*, *ChAIr*, *cHAiR*, CHAIR and so forth; in each case the representation consists of the grapheme sequence [<c>, <h>, <a>, <i>, <r>].[5] It is also assumed that the computed grapheme description is "normalised" to an orientation-invariant, canonical format, with the horizontal plane as the major axis. On this assumption, the grapheme representations for the stimuli shown in Fig. 2 would in each case have the form <chair> with the grapheme <a> occupying the central position of the grapheme description, the graphemes <c> and <h> would be to the left of centre and the graphemes <i> and <r> would be to the right of centre in the horizontal plane. Figure 3 summarises the hypothesised progression of abstraction from physical parameters to a canonical grapheme representation. The representation computed at the word-centred grapheme level is used by lexical processing mechanisms in word identification.

Various proposals have been offered concerning the processing structure of the lexical access stage of word identification (see, e.g., Coltheart, 1981; McClelland & Rumelhart, 1981; Taft, 1985). The proposal we will entertain here shares important similarities with some of these, but also differs from them in important respects. For present purposes, the aspects of the proposed lexical access procedure that need to be made explicit are the following:

---

[5]Letters in triangular brackets indicate graphemes.

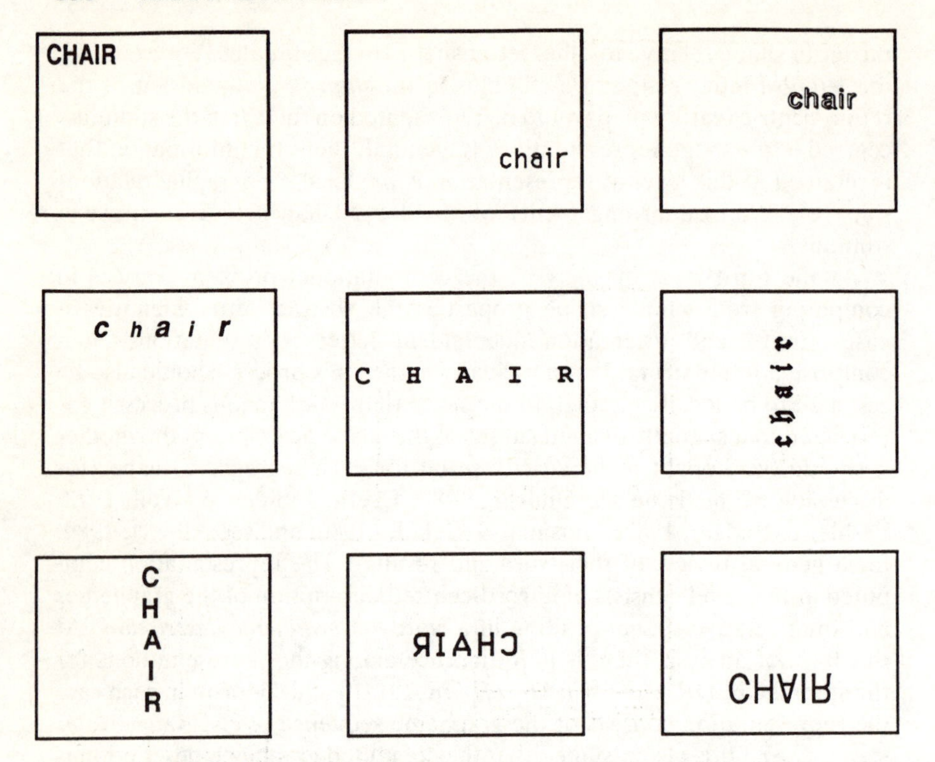

FIG. 2 Various word formats for which the graphemic description would be identical.

1. The unit of representation that serves as input to the lexical access system is a grapheme string;

2. input grapheme strings activate in parallel all access units in the lexicon that share graphemes with the input representation (e.g. the input grapheme representation <pots> activates, to varying degrees, the access units POTS, POT, PIT, NOT, TOPS, PINS, POTATO, and so forth);

3. access units in the lexicon consist of the known words *and* morphemes of the language (e.g. WALKING, WALK-, -ING, and so on);[6]

4. the activation level of an access unit in the lexicon is proportional to the degree of similarity between input grapheme string and access unit, where similarity is indexed by the degree of grapheme overlap defined in terms of both identity and relative position of graphemes (e.g. for the input

[6]Although we assume that there are both whole-word and morpheme access units in the lexical access procedure, in this report we will only refer to word access units. This choice is not intended to reflect a theoretical choice: it is adopted only for convenience. The aspects of the word identification process discussed in this report are largely unaffected by the distinction between word and morpheme access units. In the Discussion we will return to the issue of the nature of the units of analysis computed at the level of grapheme representations.

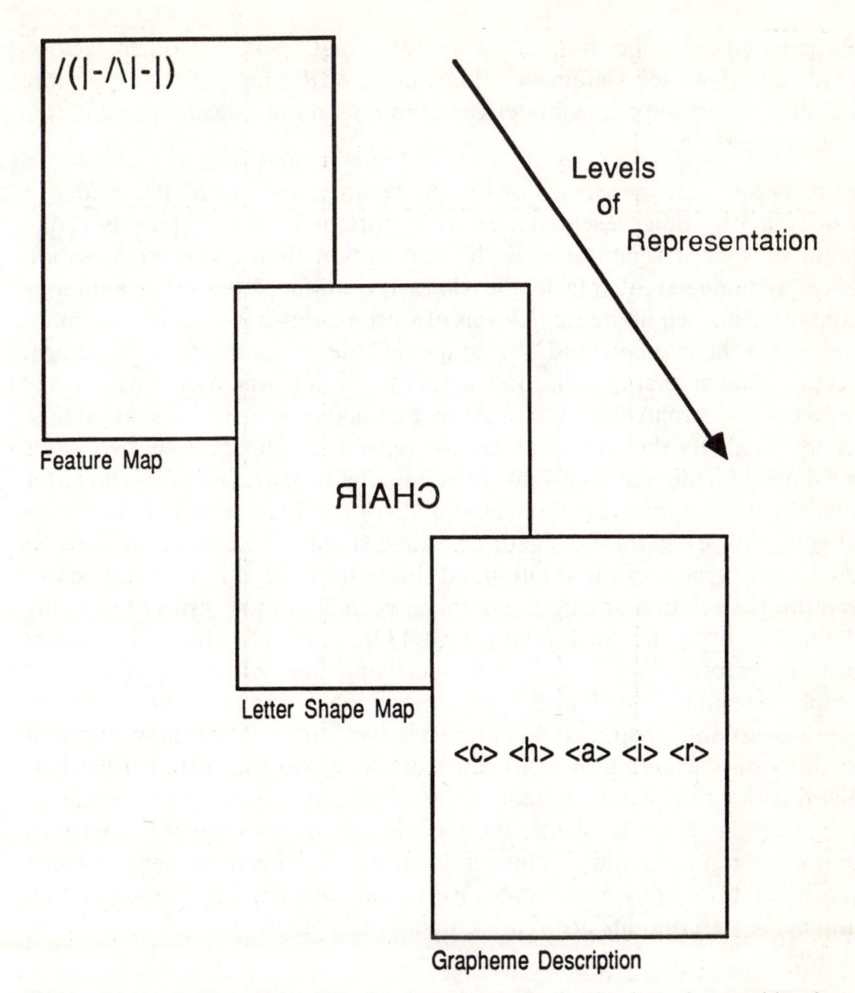

FIG. 3 Schematic illustration of levels of representation in visual word recognition for a mirror-reversed word projected to the upper right quadrant. The first level of analysis is the retino-centric feature map (upper left panel), followed by a stimulus-centred letter shape map (middle panel), and, finally, the word-centred grapheme description (lower right panel).

grapheme string <pots>, the access unit in the lexicon, POTS, would be activated more than PATS, which would be activated more than PAT, which would be activated more than STEP, and so forth; furthermore, the input grapheme string <pots> would maximally activate POTS and much less STOP, TOPS, and SPOT because even though all four access units have the same graphemes, those of the latter three do not have the same spatial arrangement/order as those of the input representation);

5. access units differ in terms of the amount of activation required to reach identification threshold—threshold settings for access units are

determined by word frequency, context, and, perhaps, other factors[7] (Morton, 1969; see Caramazza, Laudanna, & Romani, 1988, for a more detailed discussion of the model's assumptions about lexical representation and processing).

Although various aspects of the processing structure of the model of word identification presented here are important for present purposes, one point of special significance is the assumption that spatial organisation plays a fundamental role in the characterisation of the representations computed at each of the three levels of word processing—the feature map, the letter-shape map, and the grapheme description—prior to lexical access. That spatial organisation should be an intrinsic part of the representations computed at the feature and letter shape levels is almost tautological. By their very nature, the representations at these two levels must preserve the spatial arrangement among the parts (features and letter shapes) that comprise the visual stimulus (a written word). It is not so obvious, however, that spatial organisation should be a significant factor at the level of grapheme description. At this latter level, it is not necessary to capture the relation among the graphemes in a word in terms of spatially defined co-ordinates; such relations could be captured, without significant loss of information, strictly by specifying the *ordinal* positions of graphemes in a word. For example, the grapheme <r> in the grapheme representation <chair> could be specified as <r/5>. Note, however, that in this case the notion of word-centredness, which was assumed to characterise the co-ordinate system for grapheme representations, would be vacuous;[8] in this case, centredness could not be an *explicit* property of grapheme representations. Thus, if it could be documented that grapheme representations are word-centred, we would have empirical evidence that grapheme descriptions are represented in a spatially defined co-ordinate system.

---

[7]There are various other aspects of the lexical access procedure, not considered here, that must be addressed in a more complete model of word identification. Thus, for example, there is the issue of whether or not the graphemes in an input string contribute equally to the activation of an access unit in the lexicon: perhaps the initial letters contribute more than the final letters, or the initial and final letters could contribute more than the medial letters, and so forth. As another example, there is the issue of whether there might not be facilitory or inhibitory links among access units (see, e.g. Caramazza et al., 1988; McClelland & Rumelhart, 1981). Although these and other aspects of the lexical access procedure are important, they are not considered here because they do not affect the specific issues we wish to address.

[8]To be sure, it is possible to articulate an alternative representation format with ordinal positions for graphemes that gives the notion of word-centredness a non-vacuous reading. For example, the graphemic representation for chair could be specified as [<c/−2>, <h/−1>, <a/0>, <i/1>, <r/2>]. However, as will become apparent shortly, this solution fails to provide a principled account for the experimental results reported here.

The assumption that visual word identification involves a series of processing stages which compute different types of representations, each specified in a spatially defined co-ordinate system, constrains plausible claims about the form of impairment that could result from selective damage to any of the stages of processing. One obvious implication is that, although spatially defined impairments may be observed following damage to any of the three stages of processing, the units of representation affected would be different in the three cases—edges for the feature map, shapes for the letter shape map, and graphemes for the grapheme description. On this reasoning, the spatial specificity of a processing deficit would not, on its own, provide evidence as to the locus of damage responsible for the observed impairment. To determine the locus of damage we must have evidence about the type of representations affected.

In this paper, we describe the reading and spelling performance of a brain-damaged subject, NG, who presents with the clinical picture of unilateral neglect. Various aspects of her performance have been reported elsewhere (Hillis & Caramazza, 1990) and some of the results described here were summarized in Caramazza and Hillis (1990). In reading and spelling, NG only made errors in processing the right half of written words, regardless of the length of the word and independently of the topographic arrangement of the stimulus in reading, and the form of output in spelling. It is argued that these results, as well as others described here, cannot be explained by a deficit to low-level visual processing mechanisms. Instead, we must assume that the deficit is at the grapheme level. Furthermore, given that the impairment consistently involved the *"right" half* of words, irrespective of task type, we must assume that grapheme descriptions are represented in a word-centred co-ordinate system. The implications of these conclusions for models of word recognition are considered, as are the more general implications for claims about visual processing and object recognition and implications for the nature of unilateral neglect.

CASE REPORT

Social and Medical History

NG is a 79-year-old woman who completed 8th grade in a parochial school. She reports premorbid left-hand dominance for all tasks except writing; she was taught to use her right hand for writing at school. NG has always been active in the community, and was reportedly able to read and write well. She lived alone between the time of her husband's death and her stroke, but currently lives with her son, and attends a senior centre several days a week.

NG had a stroke in the fall of 1986, resulting in right hemiparesis of the arm and leg, which persists. There was no reduction of her visual field, nor were there signs of aphasia or dysarthria. A C.T.-scan revealed a large area of infarction in the left parietal white matter and a smaller area in the left anterior basal ganglia, adjacent to the head of the caudate. She has since had several T.I.A.'s that did not cause any lasting changes in her neurological status.

NG initially showed right "neglect" in virtually all tasks—she walked into people on her right side, failed to eat food on her right, made right-sided errors in line cancellation, copying, and matching tasks, and omitted words on the right side of the page in reading. She has since shown improvement in many of these areas. Thus, for example, she no longer has right-sided problems in eating, and no longer makes errors in simple left-to-right stimulus matching tasks. She also rarely omits whole words on the right in reading sentences or paragraphs. Despite these improvements in responding to stimuli presented in the right hemispace, her reading and spelling of individual words have not changed to any significant extent during the three years we have studied her performance. She continues to make errors in which the right-most letters are replaced with incorrect letters, both in reading single words—e.g. *park* read as "part"—and sentences—e.g. she read *The quick brown fox jumps over the lazy dog* as "The quiet brown fox jumped over the lazy doctor."

NG's pattern of spelling errors has also remained highly stable over the testing period. She has continued to make spelling errors on the right-most part of words in writing to dictation, written naming, and spontaneous writing. For example, her written name in response to a picture of a church was *churc* and to a picture of a guitar was *guiton*. She wrote *Hou much was the postal to mailed the packy* to convey "How much was the postage to mail the package".

Cognitive Evaluation

On retesting at 24 months post-stroke, NG made no errors in responding to sequential commands or repeating sentences on the Boston Diagnostic Aphasia Examination (Goodglass & Kaplan, 1972). Verbal description of the "Cookie Theft" picture was normal in all respects. On the Modified Token Test (De Renzi & Faglioni, 1978) she received a normal score of 33.5/36. Unlike performance on a previous administration, she made no errors that might be attributed to failure to attend to the tokens on the right. Performance on the Weschler Memory Scale (Weschler, 1972) was within normal limits for her age, except in visual reproduction (score = 5/15; errors on right) and mental control (errors in counting by 3's and completing the alphabet). Forward digit span was 7; backward span was 3. She showed persisting right-sided tactile and visual extinction with double simultaneous stimulation. In a line cancellation task she crossed out 40/46 lines (improved from 13/46); all errors were on the extreme right. She copied a flower normally, but omitted the right side of each figure in copying a scene (see Appendix). Impaired performance in line bisection, reading, and spelling will now be described in detail.

EXPERIMENTAL METHOD, RESULTS, AND DISCUSSION

Reading and Spelling

Methods

The data reported were collected between 4 and 24 months after NG's stroke. The most recent studies, involving mirror-reversed reading, backward oral spelling, line bisection, and identifying the effects of affixes on reading performance, took place between 18 and 24 months post-stroke.

NG was presented with a set of words in a variety of formats and tasks: normal (horizontal) oral reading, vertical reading, recognition of aural spelling, mirror-reversed reading, delayed copying, oral spelling, written spelling, and backwards oral spelling. A total of 976 words and 208 nonwords were presented individually (through a window card) for oral reading. The stimuli included 374 items from the Johns Hopkins University Dyslexia Battery (Goodman & Caramazza, 1986) and 602 items from the Johns Hopkins Morphology Battery (Badecker & Caramazza, 1987). The words in these batteries vary across various dimensions of experimental interest: grammatical class, frequency, concreteness, length, phonological transparency (for pronunciation), and affix type (prefix versus suffix, opaque versus transparent suffix, and so forth). The stimuli from the J.H.U. Dyslexia Battery were printed in large block print; the stimuli from the Morphology Battery were printed in lower case, medium font (12pt Times Roman). Neither case nor print size significantly affected NG's performance. Stimuli for the other tasks were drawn from this pool. Specifically, for "vertical reading", a subset of 300 words and 60 nonwords, printed vertically on the page in large block letters, were presented individually. For recognition of aural spelling, the same subset of 300 words and 60 nonwords were spelled aloud to her, and she was asked to name the word or nonword. Stimuli for mirror-reversed reading and written and oral spelling consisted of the same subset, plus additional items from the J.H.U. Dyslexia Battery, for a total of 626 words and 74 nonhomophonic nonwords, plus 34 pseudohomophones (e.g. *hunnee*) for reading tasks only. Stimuli for mirror-reversed reading were made by photocopying the words printed in block letters onto transparencies, and flipping the transparencies onto a white paper background.[9] Individual words were exposed through a window card. Delayed copying involved exposing an individual word or nonword briefly (from a subset of 84 words and 40 nonwords from the main list), and immediately asking her to write it. Each task was trained with as many practice items as needed until NG produced consistently appropriate, if not accurate, responses. At least 6 weeks intervened between tasks that involved the same stimuli.

Detailed descriptions of the effects of various stimulus parameters such as frequency and grammatical class on NG's reading and spelling performance, compared to performance of two other brain-damaged subjects with spatially specific reading problems and an age-matched control subject, are reported in Hillis & Caramazza (1990). Here, we will only briefly summarise the results obtained for NG, along with a qualitative analysis of her performance. Since performance in mirror-reversed reading and backward spelling have not previously been reported in any detail, we will provide somewhat more information for these tasks. The principal focus in this report, as in Caramazza & Hillis (in press), will be on the distribution of reading and spelling errors as a function of position within a word for different types of tasks.

Results: Normal (Horizontal) Reading

NG made reading errors in response to 222/976 (22.7%) words and 118/208 (56.7%) nonwords. The only stimulus parameters that were found to affect significantly her reading accuracy were word frequency and lexicality (i.e. word versus nonword status). She correctly read 141/145 (97.2%) high-frequency words compared to 123/145 (84.8%) low-frequency words matched for length and word class ($X^2_1 = 12.21$, $P < 0.001$). Furthermore, the mean frequency of correctly read words was significantly higher than the mean frequency of incorrectly read words (103.0 versus 43.4; $P < 0.001$ by 2-tailed *t*-test). NG correctly read 75/84 (89.3%) words versus 20/68 (29.4%) nonwords matched for length in letters. She also read functors more accurately than open-class words (100% versus 89.3%), but this effect can be accounted for by the higher frequency and perhaps shorter length of functors. Although there were no significant differences with respect to word length when this variable was tested with 14 words of each length from 4 to 8 letters, the mean length of correctly read words was significantly shorter than the mean length of incorrectly read words (6.02 letters versus 6.92; $P < 0.0001$ by 2-tailed *t*-test). However, the latter effect may simply reflect the fact that NG's error rate in reading was substantially higher for suffixed words than for

[9]Credit for this technique belongs to B. Wilson and K. Patterson.

unsuffixed words of the same length and surface frequency (56% errors on 85 suffixed words vs. 18% on 85 unaffixed controls; $X^2_1 = 34.51$; $P < 0.0001$). On a list of 46 suffixed, 46 unaffixed, and 46 prefixed words, her error rate was higher for suffixed words (61% errors) than for matched unaffixed words (24% errors) or prefixed words (11% errors; $X^2_2 = 28.45$; $P < 0.001$). Thus, the result that correctly read words were significantly shorter than incorrectly read words can be accounted for by the fact that suffixed words were longer and less accurately read than unaffixed words. Finally, it should be noted that the seeming discrepancy between the overall error rate of about 23% and the much smaller error rates for some word lists (e.g. the frequency list) merely reflects the fact that the latter lists did not contain suffixed words. The implications of affixing on reading performance are discussed below.

All of NG's reading errors, both for words and nonwords, involved the right part of the stimulus. Examples of these errors are reported in Table 1. As illustrated by these examples, the majority of her responses were approximately the same length (in letters) as the stimulus. The correlation between stimulus length and response length was highly significant ($r = 0.67$, $P < 0.0001$). The mean length of the stimuli was 6.94 (s.d. = 1.7) letters, and the mean length of the responses was 6.75 (s.d. = 2.0) letters.

In response to nonwords, NG tended to produce words that shared at least the initial half of the letters with the stimulus (e.g. *aftes* → "after", *faunch* → "fault". However, her 90 correct responses demonstrated that she understood the task and had no specific deficit in converting print to sound.[10]

NG showed precisely the same pattern of reading errors in two other tasks: when words were presented tachistoscopically in her *left* visual field, and even when she first named all the letters in a word correctly. For example, when instructed to name each letter before saying the word, NG

[10]On the assumption that the graphemes at the right end of the stimuli could not be processed normally, it is unclear how she read nonwords correctly. One possibility is that when information about letters on the left is either (1) sufficient to reject the string as a word, or (2) alone corresponds to a whole word, the letter string could be parsed into separate substrings, so that the corresponding graphemic descriptions could be individually re-centred for further processing. So, for example, the left half of the nonword *teybull* (*teyb*) would be sufficient to reject the stimulus as a word, so that the grapheme description be parsed into separate representations—<tey> and <bull>—that can be centred individually and processed further. In fact, she read essentially all two-syllable nonwords correctly or incorrectly as though they were composed of two short words (e.g. *teybull* → "tea-bull" (correct); *haygrid* → "hay grit", *haytrid* → "hay trial"; *mushrume* → "mush and rum") or one real word (e.g. *hunnee* → "human"). Also consistent with this notion of parsing and re-centring is the observation that NG read compound words made of two 4-letter words (e.g. *bookmark*) as accurately as 4-letter words, and much more accurately than 8-letter monomorphemic words.

TABLE 1
Examples of NG's Errors in Normal (Horizontal) Reading (Stimulus → Response)

Word Stimuli		
humid → human	hound → house	stripe → strip
sprinter → sprinkle	dumb → dump	study → stud
though → thoughts	emotionally → emotional	hazardous → hazard
Nonword Stimuli		
petch → petcher	dring → drill	stould → stoutly

read *journal* as "j-o-u-r-n-a-l . . . journey" and read *fing* as "f-i-n-g . . . fine". In reading 150 words in this fashion, she made 39 errors (26%—comparable to her error rate in normal reading), of which all but one were restricted to the end of the word. This result establishes that NG's right-sided errors cannot be explained as simply arising from a low-level visual perceptual disorder. Tachistoscopic reading was not studied systematically, but her spontaneous reading of words in a lexical decision task, in which stimuli were presented for 100msec. to the left of the fixation point (without a mask), revealed very similar types of errors (e.g. *allow* → "allot"; *dollrb* → "dollar", *pulsr* → "pulse"). In this lexical decision task, she correctly rejected all but 5% of nonwords in which letters on the left half of the stimulus violated graphotactic constraints (e.g. *fkirt*), but failed to reject any of the nonwords in which the violation occurred on the right half of the stimulus (e.g. *suggesb*). Performance was essentially the same in a lexical decision task in which nonwords were created by omitting the final (right) or initial (left) letter of words, and in which stimuli were presented for 200msec. randomly to the left, right, or centred at the fixation point (without a mask). Her spontaneous oral reading in this task revealed some word completions on the right (e.g. *prett* → "pretty"; *golde* → "golden"), but also many letter substitutions on the right (*bowle* → "bowls", *expect* → "express").

We have noted that NG read many words correctly. An important question we may ask is: do NG's correct responses reflect occasional normal processing of information at the right end of words, or do they simply reflect default responses that are correct by chance? It is difficult to answer this question directly. In order to do so we would need to have an estimate of how much information on the right part of the word NG was able to process, and we would also need an estimate of the responses that would be possible (and their relative subjective frequencies—Gordon, 1985) given that amount of information. In the absence of clear information about NG's effective response set for a given stimulus, and in the absence of a direct procedure for estimating the degree of usable information on the right part of a word that may be available to her, we must resort to indirect means in order to determine how correct responses are produced. For these purposes we relied on the following procedure.

NG was asked to read two lists of words, each comprised of 30 nouns. One of the lists consisted of 15 regular plural and 15 singular forms. The other list consisted of the corresponding singular or regular plural forms of the words in the first list. All plural forms had the suffix -s (rather than -es). It was hypothesised that if correct responses were the result of occasional normal processing of the full stimulus, then the expectation is that NG should show above-chance discrimination of the presence/absence of the plural suffix. Considering only items for which the stem was read correctly, NG was at chance level in producing the correct form of the word. She correctly identified, as indicated by her reading response, the presence/absence of the plural suffix for 46% (12/26) of the words on list 1 and 51.8% (14/27) of the words on list 2. For 28/30 items, she produced the same response to the word whether or not the stimulus was plural. Thus, she read both *dollar* and *dollars* as "dollars" and read both *fabric* and *fabrics* as "fabric". The exceptions were: *offenses* → "offensive" versus *offense* → "offend" and *planets* → planet versus *planet* → "plant". Most often, the form of the word produced by NG was the form with the higher surface frequency; thus, she made 22 deletions of the plural suffix, 6 suffix additions, and 6 substitutions of suffixes or letter sequences (e.g. *pursuit* → "pursue") on the 60 words. These results indicate that NG had virtually zero usable graphemic information at the ends of words. The conclusion invited by the results is that correct reading performance is the product of default responses that are correct by chance.

We have claimed that NG's errors virtually always involved the right end of the stimulus. A quantitative analysis of the distribution or errors as a function of letter position within a word provided the basis for a more precise characterisation of the spatial nature of the subject's reading impairment. Words of each length were scored separately. The letter of the stimulus word in each position from the left (e.g. first letter = 1; last letter of a 4-letter word = 4, last letter of a 5-letter word = 5) was scored. If the letter did not appear in the response, or was substituted with another letter, 1 error was recorded for that position (e.g. *stripe* → "strip" was scored as 1 error in position 5, and *swam* → "swan" was scored 1 error in position 4). Transposed letters were scored as 0.5 error in each position. Thus, *quite* → "quiet" was scored as 0.5 error in positions 4 and 5. When one or more letters were added on the end of the word, 1 error was scored in the last position. To illustrate, *though* read as "thoughts" was scored as 1 error in position 6.

The upper panel of Table 2 presents the distribution of reading errors as a function of position within a word, separately for words of different lengths. It is immediately apparent upon inspection that NG's errors occurred almost exclusively on the right end of words, irrespective of their length. It is equally apparent, however, that for longer stimuli, NG is able to get more letters correct (in absolute terms). Thus, for example, the fourth position of 4-letter words engendered 15% errors, whereas the fourth position of 9-letter words engendered no errors at all. More generally, it seems that the point in a word at which NG makes reading errors shifts leftward for longer words, with errors seemingly occurring only on the *right half* of words. This is, in fact, a correct description of the results, as may be seen from the lower panel in Table 2, where the percentage of errors at each letter position are arranged by reference to the centre of words for each word length. When so arranged, several facts become clear: (1) the vast predominance of errors occurred on the right half of words irrespective of their length; (2) errors occurred at equal rates as a function of absolute distance from the centre of a word; and (3), errors increased "linearly" as a function of distance from the centre of the word.

Discussion

There are several aspects of NG's reading performance that are relevant

TABLE 2
Rate of Reading Errors as a Function of Letter Position in Words of Different Lengths

Left Aligned

Word Length	*N*	*Position in Word:* 1	2	3	4	5	6	7	8	9
4	141	0	0	4	15					
5	219	0	0	1	8	18				
6	204	0	0	0	4	8	25			
7	82	0	0	1	4	5	16	31		
8	88	0	0	0	1	3	18	21	34	
9	5	0	0	0	0	2	10	23	28	37

Centred

Word Length								*Word Centre* x								
4					0		0		4		15					
5				0		0		1		8		18				
6			0		0		0		4		8		25			
7		0		0		1		4		5		16		31		
8	0		0		0		1		3		18		21		34	
9	0		0		0		0		2		10		23		28		37

for understanding the processing structure of the word recognition system, and for determining the locus (or loci) of functional deficit responsible for the observed reading impairment. These include: the effects of word frequency and of lexicality on reading accuracy, the high correlation between stimulus and response length, and the spatial specificity of the impairment. However, these results on their own do not allow an unambiguous decision regarding the specific locus of deficit within the word recognition system. To be sure, the spatial specificity of the impairment restricts the possible locus of impairment to a stage of processing prior to lexical access. This constraint is not sufficiently specific, however. There are at least three stages of processing in the proposed model of word recognition—the feature map, the letter shape map, and the grapheme description—which if damaged could result in the observed pattern of impairment. However, the fact that NG continued to make right-sided errors with tachistoscopic presentation of stimuli to the left visual field rules out the feature level of representation as a possible locus of deficit. This still leaves as possible loci of deficit the letter shape and the grapheme levels. Selective damage to the right part of either of the latter two levels of representation could result in the observed difficulty in processing the right end of words. To distinguish between these alternative hypotheses we need information regarding NG's reading performance with topographically transformed stimuli or other lexical processing tasks that differentially affect the letter shape and the grapheme levels of representation. This is explored next.

Results: Reading Topographically Nonstandard Text, Spaced Letters, and Recognition of Aural Spelling

In reading topographically nonstandard text—vertically presented and mirror-reversed words—NG made precisely the same types of errors as she had in reading topographically standard (horizontal) text: errors virtually only occurred at the end of words. The majority of errors in these tasks involved substitutions of letters on the right end of words—e.g. *thousand* (presented in mirror-reversed form) was read as "thought". Some letter omissions on the right were also noted—e.g. *dewt* (in mirror-reversed form) was read as "dew". Additional examples of errors in these tasks are reported in Table 3. It is important to note that, in the case of mirror-reversed reading, these word-end errors occurred in response to letters *physically (absolutely and relatively) on the left* ("good") part of the word. NG correctly read 75% (225/300) of vertically printed words, and 70% (440/626) of mirror-reversed words (compared to 72% of normally printed words). Accuracy of responses to nonwords was also similar across formats: 27% (16/60) in vertical reading and 23% (25/108) in mirror-reversed reading.

TABLE 3
Examples of Reading Topographically Nonstandard Text

Errors in Vertical Reading		
blending → blemish	vivid → vivian	rang → ran
motionless → motel	discovery → discover	habitual → habit
strist → strip	neithem → neither	sipter → sip
Errors in Mirror-reversed Reading		
common → comet	joint → joint	regulated → regular
greenish → greenery	discovery → disco	dashes → dash
cring → crime	vigid → vigor	dring → drink
Errors in Recognition of Aural Spelling		
earns → earring	sparrow → space	village → villa
basis → bass	requirement → require	planet → plane
dring → drink	fing → fine	womar → woman

TABLE 4
Rate of Errors as a Function of Letter Position in Words of Different Lengths for Vertical and Mirror-reversed Reading and Recognition of Aurally Spelled Words. (x = Word Centre)

Word Length (Number of Letters)								
	Vertical Reading (x)							
4	0	1	2	18				
5	0	0	1	10	24			
6	0	0	2	11	21	34		
7	0	0	1	10	11	21	38	
8	0	0	4	10	11	23	31	39
	Mirror-reversed Reading (x)							
4	0	2	12	22				
5	0	1	3	11	21			
6	0	1	6	10	21	33		
7	0	0	7	18	27	31	41	
8	0	2	7	14	22	30	39	42
	Recognition of Aural Spelling (x)							
4	0	0	0	16				
5	0	0	1	10	22			
6	0	0	5	13	19	31		
7	0	0	0	6	14	26	36	
8	0	0	3	6	6	19	36	39

NG also made the very same types of errors when words were spelled aloud to her. Responses included 130 completion errors and 34 responses that omitted letters in word-final positions. For example, NG's response to the stimulus "e-x-c-e-s-s" was "exceed", and her response to "p-l-a-n-e-t" was "plane". Table 3 includes additional examples.

Table 4 presents the rate of errors at each grapheme position in vertically arrayed, mirror-reversed, and aurally spelled words, displayed as a function of the distance (in grapheme positions) from the centre of the word. Although the absolute rate of errors in these tasks was higher than in reading normal (left to right) print, it is clear that NG shows the same pattern of errors with respect to their distribution across grapheme positions in the word (and, for mirror-reversed words, the reverse of the pattern of errors across letter positions in the physical stimulus). Although the data from these tasks are a bit more "noisy" than those from normal reading, due in part to the fact that there were a lesser number of stimuli of each word length in these tasks, it is quite clear that reading errors are concentrated on the *right half* of words irrespective of the topographic arrangement of the stimulus or the form of the sensory signal (provided it concerns letters).

An additional list of 108 6-letter words were administered in all 4 reading tasks—the horizontal, vertical, mirror-reversed, and aural-spelling tasks—at 24 months post stroke. This allowed us to compare directly the levels of performance across tasks and, at the same time, to compare the distribution of errors as a function of position in a word. Overall accuracy rates were as follows: 79% for normal reading, 70% for recognition of aural spelling, 67% for vertical reading, and 60% for mirror-reversed reading. (The somewhat higher accuracy in normal reading can be accounted for by the fact that she never failed to attempt reading a normally printed word, whereas she declined to attempt reading 10–15 of the items in each of the other formats.) Table 5 illustrates that in all 4 tasks

TABLE 5
Distribution of Errors as a Function of Letter Position
(Given in % of Total Errors)

	Letter Position in 6-letter Words					
Task	*1*	*2*	*3*	*4*	*5*	*6*
Regular Reading	0	0	0	9	27	64
Vertical Reading	0	0	2	10	35	52
Naming of Orally Spelled Words	0	0	7	20	28	45
Mirror-reversed Reading	0	1	9	16	29	46

errors occurred virtually only on the right half of words, and increased at comparable rates as a function of distance from the centre of the word.

NG was also asked to read a list of 82 words (5–8 letters in length) in 4 formats on 4 different days: once with no spaces between letters (e.g. *cough*), once with 2 spaces between each pair of letters (*c o u g h*), once with 3 spaces between each pair of letters (*c o u g h*). The spacing had no effect on her reading accuracy: 76%, 74%, and 77% correct responses for no spaces, 2 spaces, and 3 spaces between letters, respectively.

Discussion

There are three crucial features of the results reported in this section: (1) NG made reading errors virtually only on the right half of words irrespective of the form of input—vertical, mirror-reversed, or aural spelling; (2) she produced quantitatively similar error patterns across tasks, both in terms of overall error rates and in terms of the distribution of errors as a function of position within a word (see Tables 4 and 5); and (3) her performance was unaffected by different spacings of the letters in a word. These results undermine unambiguously the possibility that NG's disorder could result from damage to the letter shape level. This conclusion follows from the assumption that information at this level of processing is represented in a stimulus-centred co-ordinate system. In such a co-ordinate system, the absolute location of a stimulus in space is not represented, but the absolute positions of its component parts in relation to each other are. In other words, a letter shape map veridically represents the within-stimulus spatial relations among letter shapes. Thus, for example, the letter-shape representation of a vertically presented word would preserve the vertical orientation of the stimulus. The implication of the foregoing is that since the letter-shape representations for horizontal, vertical, and mirror-reversed words are not the same, there can be no single form of deficit to this level of representation that could account for the qualitative and quantitative similarity of performance across reading tasks. This conclusion is further supported by the fact that the same pattern of spatially defined errors was observed for the visual presentation tasks and for the aural spelling recognition task, despite the fact that the latter task does not involve processing at the level of the letter shape map. Finally, the absence of a spacing effect on NG's reading performance allows the inference that the locus of impairment must be at a level of representation where relative and not absolute distances are encoded. We must conclude, therefore, that the spatially specific reading impairment considered here cannot be assumed to result from damage to low-level visual processing mechanisms.

Having ruled out damage to low-level visual processing mechanisms as the basis for the reported performance, the only remaining possibility is that the deficit concerns processing mechanisms at the grapheme level. At this level of processing, the information represented consists of a canonical description of letter identities (graphemes) and their relative order. Information about orientation of stimuli and absolute distances among letters are not represented at this level of processing. This means that the representations of a word presented in horizontal, vertical, or mirror-reversed form would be identical—in each case a canonical word-centred grapheme description. Consequently, damage to the processing mechanisms that operate at this level of representation would have identical effects on all reading tasks, irrespective of the topographic arrangement of stimuli—precisely the reported result.

Additional evidence for the hypothesis presented here accrues from the analysis of NG's spelling performance. Since one of the processing stages in spelling a word involves computing a grapheme-level representation of its orthographic structure (see Caramazza & Miceli, 1989; Caramazza, Miceli, Villa, & Romani, 1987; Ellis, 1988; for detailed discussion), damage to mechanisms operating at this level of representation should result in a spelling disorder (see Fig. 4). And, on the assumption that reading and spelling depend on the same processing mechanisms in com-

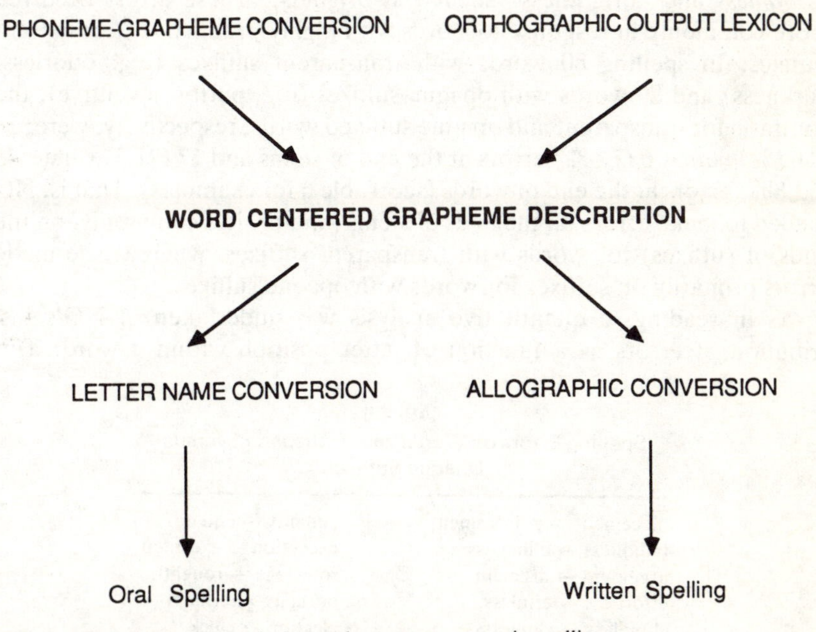

FIG. 4 The grapheme description and output processes in spelling.

puting grapheme-level representations, we would expect that damage to the grapheme level would result in qualitatively similar patterns of reading and spelling impairments.

Results: Writing to Dictation

NG's performance in writing to dictation was not significantly influenced by lexicality (word versus nonword), lexical parameters (frequency, concreteness, word class), or orthographic regularity. She correctly spelled 33% of the words and 21% of the nonwords matched for length in letters ($X^2_1 = 3.0$; n.s.). However, her spelling deteriorated steadily as a function of length, from 50% correct for 4-letter words to 7% correct for 8-letter words on a list counterbalanced for word length in letters, phonemes per word, and frequency ($X^2_1 = 5.6$; Mantel-Haentsel test for linear trend, $P < 0.03$).

Nearly all of NG's written spelling errors consisted of substitution, deletion, or insertion of letters at the end of the word or nonword. Most of the misspellings resulted in phonemically implausible nonwords, such as "advise" spelled as *advisd*, "sneeze" as *sneed* and /fout/ as *fol*. As in reading, her responses in spelling included some omissions of letters on the right (e.g. "broom" → *broo*). Suffixed words elicited some errors at the end of one or both component morphemes, such as "bottomless" spelled as *bottless* and "brightness" spelled as *brignesss*. These errors occurred more commonly in response to words with highly productive, transparent suffixes. In spelling 80 words with transparent suffixes (e.g. odorless, darkness) and 80 words with opaque suffixes (e.g. purity, inventive), the contrasts for transparent and opaque suffixed words, respectively, were: 33 (41.3%) versus 6 (7.5%) errors at the end of stems and 17 (21.3) versus 43 (53.8%) errors at the end of words (see Table 6 for examples). That is, NG tended to make errors on the ends of stems (and/or, less commonly, on the ends of suffixes) for words with transparent suffixes, whereas she made errors primarily on suffixes for words with opaque suffixes.

As in reading, a quantitative analysis was undertaken of NG's distribution of errors as a function of letter position within a word. This

TABLE 6
Spelling Errors on Words with Transparent versus Opaque Suffixes

Transparent	Opaque
placement → palacesment	equality → equald
blindness → blineness	exception → excepted
argument → argment	roughage → roughth
effortless → effuless	normal → normant
cloudless → clouless	election → eleck

TABLE 7
Rate of Spelling Errors at Each Position of Words

Length in Letters	*Position in Word* 1	2	3	4	5	6	7
Left Aligned							
4	0	2	13	25			
5	0	0	6	20	29		
6	0	0	5	15	26	39	
7	0	0	3	5	15	28	51

							Word Centre x						
Centred Words													
4				0		2		13		25			
5			0		0		6		20		29		
6		0		0		5		15		26		39	
7	0		0		3		5		15		28		51

analysis revealed that virtually all of her errors occurred at the end of words (except for the noted contrast for transparent versus opaque suffixed words). The upper panel in Table 7 reports the results of this analysis separately for 4- to 7-letter words. It is apparent upon inspection of these data that the point in a word at which NG made spelling errors moved rightward for longer words. When the data on the distribution of errors as a function of position within a word are arranged relative to the word's centre, it is observed that errors virtually only occurred on the right half of a word, irrespective of word length (see lower panel in Table 7).

Discussion

The features of NG's spelling performance that merit close attention include the relatively high rate of spelling errors when compared to reading performance, the absence of frequency and lexicality effects, the fact that errors almost invariably resulted in nonword responses, the effect of morphological structure of stimuli, and the spatial-specificity of the impairment. Although all these features of NG's performance are important, for the moment we will focus on the spatial character of her impairment. The other features of NG's spelling performance will be considered in the General Discussion.

The fact that, as in reading, NG's spelling errors were virtually restricted to the right half of words, and that, also as in reading, errors increased "linearly" as a function of distance in number of grapheme positions from the centre of a word, invites the inference that damage to a processing stage common to reading and spelling is responsible for the dyslexic and dysgraphic performance. The hypothesis we will entertain here is that this common processing stage is the grapheme description. On this hypothesis, we would expect qualitatively and quantitatively similar patterns of performance in all types of spelling tasks, irrespective of the form (written versus oral spelling) or order of output (forward versus backward oral spelling).

Results: Oral Spelling, Backward Oral Spelling, and Delayed Copying

NG's performance was essentially identical across written and oral spelling and delayed copying (for words read correctly); she respectively made 64%, 67%, and 66% errors in the three spelling tasks. The quality of errors was identical across tasks. That is, errors were restricted to the rightmost part of a word, ordinarily resulting in nonword responses. The performance in the delayed copying task contrasts with direct copying, which she performed essentially flawlessly (97% correct). Furthermore, she made precisely the same types of errors in backwards oral spelling. To illustrate, "compare" was spelled backwards as "d-r-a-p-m-o-c" (compard) and "sheets" was spelled backwards as "e-e-h-s" (shee). In backward spelling of unaffixed words 80.7% of her errors were restricted to the end of words. In spelling suffixed words, 69.7% of her errors were restricted to the end of the word, and an additional 18.2% occurred at the end of one or both morphemes (e.g. "listed" was spelled as "d-e-s-i-l" (lised) and "sickness" was spelled backwards as "e-e-n-c-i-s" (sicnee). Because these word-end errors occurred at the *beginning* of the response in backward spelling, they cannot be ascribed to a general problem maintaining "attention" to the end of a stimulus or response (see also Baxter & Warrington, 1983). Examples of errors in these spelling tasks are shown in Table 8.

Table 9 reports the distribution of errors made by NG at various positions of a word for the same set of 108 6-letter words used in all spelling (and reading) tasks. Scoring of the position of spelling errors followed scoring procedures described for reading of the same set. It is apparent upon inspection that the distributions of errors are highly similar across tasks, and that errors essentially only occurred on the right half of a word in all tasks. Overall accuracy rates for these stimuli were also similar across tasks given during the same time period: 50% for written spelling, 48% for oral spelling, 44% for delayed copying, and 37% for backward oral spelling.

TABLE 8
Examples of Errors in Various Spelling Tasks

Errors in Written Spelling		
floor → floore	sneeze → sneed	cloud → clou
unit → unite	jury → jurd	faith → fait
skart → skarr	remmun → remmey	chench → chen
Errors in Oral Spelling		
career → carred	sneeze → sneed	ground → grou
poodle → poodler	afraid → afrain	period → perio
achieme → achiemd	emplain → emplained	spond → spone
Errors in Backward Spelling		
absorb → absown	sky → skik	church → chur
garbage → garbsi	oyster → oyste	sample → sampl
Errors in Delayed Copying		
square → squard	afraid → afrain	method → meth
turkey → turket	fabric → fabrict	starve → starv

Discussion

The most important aspect of the results reported in this section is the highly consistent, spatially specific pattern of errors in all spelling tasks. The fact that spelling errors virtually only occurred on the right end of a word, irrespective of the form and order of output (written versus oral spelling, and forward versus backward spelling) strongly argues for a deficit to a common level of representation in the spelling process. We have suggested that the only level of representation common to all spelling tasks is the grapheme description. Thus, we are led to conclude that the underlying cause for NG's spelling impairment is damage to the stage of processing where grapheme representations are computed. In fact, the hypothesis entertained here is that this level of representation is common to the reading and spelling processes. Thus, it is our expectation that reading and spelling performance should, in relevant respects, be qualitatively and quantitatively similar across all reading and spelling tasks. This expectation was borne out, as may be seen from a comparison of the results reported in Tables 5 and 9. These present, respectively, the distributions of reading and spelling errors as a function of within-word position.

These results further buttress the already strong evidence for the hypothesis that damage to a common level of representation—the grapheme description—is responsible for the co-occurring impairments in reading and spelling. And, since the deficit has a distinctly spatial character, involving only the right half of words, we are further led to conclude that information at the grapheme level is represented in a word-centred co-ordinate system. As noted earlier, it would stretch credulity beyond imagination to suppose that the remarkably similar patterns of performance in reading and spelling could result from damage to distinct processing mechanisms. It would seem, then, that the evidence from reading and spelling performance converge on a common account of the nature of NG's deficit, and, therefore, on crucial aspects of the processing structure of word recognition and production. Before turning to a discussion of these issues, we present further evidence about NG's reading performance that is relevant to the problem of word identification.

TABLE 9
Distribution of Errors as a Function of Letter Position
(Given in % of Total Errors)

	Letter Position in 6-letter Words					
Task	*1*	*2*	*3*	*4*	*5*	*6*
Written Spelling	0	0	6	19	31	46
Oral Spelling	0	1	2	7	29	60
Backward Spelling	0	0	1	12	34	53
Delayed Copying	0	1	1	13	28	57

The Effects of Adding a Suffix or a Prefix on Reading Performance

We have argued that NG is unable to process normally the right half of the word-centred grapheme description that serves as input to lexical access mechanisms. The evidence adduced for the hypothesis that the deficit involves the right half of a grapheme representation is rather compelling. Less clear is the precise nature of the object that is centred at the grapheme description level of representation. Although we have called this object "word", by this term we have not meant the corresponding linguistic object identified by that term. Instead, the term "word" has been used loosely as a label for the perceptually defined object that is represented at the grapheme description level. At this level of processing, the information available to the processing system consists of grapheme strings which may or may not turn out to correspond to words of the language. However, the grapheme string selected for representation at the grapheme description level is not arbitrary. It consists, instead, of the perceptual system's computation of a *potential* word, as signalled by perceptually significant features such as spacing. Thus, one characterisation of the object represented at the grapheme description level is that it consists of a grapheme string bounded by spaces. Another perceptual parameter that might be used by the visual processing system to segregate potential words is information about possible grapheme sequences in the language. Thus, for example, a string of identical graphemes, say a series of Xs, which violate graphotactic constraints of well-formedness, might be sufficiently perceptually salient to serve as the basis for defining the boundaries of a potential word. The experiments that follow were designed to evaluate the hypothesis that spacing and letter repetition constitute salient perceptual features for defining boundaries of potential words. We consider first the effects of spacing.

On the assumption that spacing constitutes one of the perceptually salient features used by the visual processing system to define potential words, and hence the representation computed at the grapheme description level, we would expect that the effective length of a grapheme string processed at this level of representation is determined by the spacing feature. The implications of this assumption for NG's reading performance are straightforward. Consider the case where NG is asked to read the word *lead*. Given the empirically established fact that NG is unable to process normally the right half of a word, she will (with some probability) have difficulty processing the *ad* part of the stimulus. However, given that the *le* part was processed normally, this information may be sufficient to activate the lexical representations LEAD, LEAN, LEFT, LEARN, LET, and so forth. Everything else being equal, the response she produces from the set of lexical representations that were activated, will be the one with the lowest activation threshold, say, "left" in this case. Consider now the case in which the word to be read is *leading*. In the latter case, the probability that she would produce the correct stem "lead" should be much greater than in the case where the stimulus was *lead*. The reason for this expectation is that, given the assumption of word-centredness, the addition of the suffix *ing* to the stem *lead* has the effect of shifting more of the graphemes in the stem (lead) to the left half of the grapheme description. Consequently, responses such as "left", "let", "letting", "learn", "learned", and so forth, should not be produced. Instead, responses should contain at least the graphemes in the left half of the grapheme description—e.g., "leading", "leads", "leader", or "leaden". Thus, the effect of adding a suffix, whether legal or illegal (e.g. *leadest*), should be to increase the probability of correctly reading the stem of the word if not the word itself.

The expectations for the addition of a legal or illegal prefix are the opposite of those described for the addition of a suffix—it should lead to a diminution of the number of correctly read stems. Thus, for example, if the stimulus were *relead*, likely responses would include "relive", "relay", "relief", "relate", "relent", "religion", "reliant", and so forth. The basis for this expectation is that adding a prefix has the effect of shifting stem graphemes to the difficult-to-process right half of the word-centred grapheme description.

Several experiments were designed to assess the effects on reading performance of adding letters to the beginning or end of a word. For all lists, words were presented individually without time limits. For lists with "illegal" affixes (e.g. prespend, leadest), NG was told that some of the stimuli were not real words, and that she should try to pronounce the entire letter string. For lists that contained words with a series of identical letters attached—a series of Xs—she was asked to ignore the series of identical letters.

Lists 1 and 2: Prefix and Suffix Effects

Methods. Forty-one words, 3 to 7 letters in length, that could be legally prefixed and suffixed (e.g. lead → misleading) were used in this experiment. Each word was presented in 4 forms: unaffixed (e.g. lead), prefixed (mislead), suffixed (leading), and both prefixed and suffixed (misleading), for a total of 164 stimuli. Four experimental blocks were constructed with each block containing roughly one fourth of each of the 4 types of unaffixed and affixed words.

Another set of 54 words, 3 to 6 letters in length and counterbalanced for word class, frequency, and length in letters, was presented on 3 occasions. One third of the words on each occasion were presented with illegal prefixes (e.g. malnoise), one third were presented with illegal suffixes (e.g. noiseful), and one third were presented without affixes (e.g. noise).

Results and Discussion. Table 10 presents a summary of the results on the 2 lists. The main finding from list 1 was that NG was twice as likely to make an error on a suffix when there was also a prefix. She made 50% suffix errors (substitutions or deletions) in the suffixed condition, compared to 94% suffix errors in the prefix plus suffix condition ($X^2_1 = 16.1$, $P < 0.0001$). For instance, she read *readable* correctly and *unreadable* as "unreading"; and she read *writes* correctly and *rewrites* as "rewritten". There was also a slight tendency to produce more stem errors when the stem was prefixed than when it was unaffixed (e.g. *loyal* → "loyalty" versus *disloyal* → "dislodge" and *content* → "content" versus *discontent* → "discontinue"), but the effect was small (10% versus 2%) due to the low rate of stem errors. This latter tendency was confirmed by results from list 2. NG made significantly more errors on the same stems when they were prefixed than when they were unaffixed (38.9% versus 11.1% errors on prefixed and unaffixed words, respectively; $X^2_1 = 9.68$, $P < 0.01$). That is, she was less likely to read the end of a word correctly if a prefix was present. To illustrate, she read *resist* correctly, but read *deresist* as

TABLE 10
Prefix and Suffix Effects

	Number of Errors (% of Stimuli in Parentheses)	
	Errors on Stem	*Errors on Suffix*[a]
List 1		
prefixed	4/41 (10)	n/a[b]
unaffixed	1/41 (2)	n/a
suffixed	1/41 (2)	20/40 (50)
prefixed + suffixed	5/41 (12)	34/36 (94)
List 2		
prefixed	21/54 (39)	n/a
unaffixed	6/54 (11)	n/a
suffixed	2/54 (4)	22/54 (41)

[a]We scored only those suffixes for which the corresponding stem was read correctly.

[b]There were three suffix insertions on these words.

"dereal"; and she read *jury* correctly, but read *misjury* as "misjudge".

The overall pattern of results confirms the expectations derived from the hypothesised structure of the representations at the grapheme description level. Specifically, the results confirm the expectation that grapheme descriptions are word-centred in the sense that a string of graphemes bounded by spaces, whether or not it constitutes a word, is the object that is centred at this level of representation.

Lists 3 and 4: Suffix Effects

Method. The suffix effect reported for list 1 may not have been significant only because NG's error rate on the unaffixed words was not high. Two new lists were constructed with the goal of inducing a high error rate on unaffixed words, so that any position effect of adding a suffix would be evident. Both lists consisted of pairs (and 1 triplet) of words that share at least the initial 4 letters (e.g. content and contest). List 3 included 96 words that could legally be affixed with a suffix of 3 or more letters (e.g. steepest and steering). This list was presented twice; each time half of the words were suffixed, so that each word was presented once with and once without a suffix. The same procedure was used with List 4, which consisted of 287 words that were presented once with and once without an *illegal* suffix.

Results and Discussion. NG made significantly fewer errors on word stems when a legal *or* illegal suffix was present. On list 3, she made 25%

TABLE 11
Legal and Illegal Suffix Effects

	Number of Errors (% of Stimuli in Parentheses)	
	Errors on Stem	*Errors on Suffix*[a]
List 3		
unaffixed	24/96 (25)	(8 suffix insertions)
legally suffixed	4/96 (4)	66/96 (67)
List 4		
unaffixed	98/287 (34)	(11 suffix insertions)
illegally suffixed	21/287 (7)	156/287 (54.3)

[a]We scored only those suffixes for which the corresponding stem was read correctly.

stem errors in response to unaffixed words, compared to only 4.2% stem errors in response to the same words when they were suffixed ($X^2_1 = 15.10$, $P < 0.001$). For example, she read *access* as "accept" and read *accessibility* as "accessible". Similarly, on list 4, she made 43.1% stem errors in the unaffixed condition, compared to only 7.3% stem errors when each word was illegally suffixed ($X^2_1 = 61.23$, $P < 0.0001$). Table 11 summarises the results obtained with Lists 3 and 4.

Another important result from these data was that on both lists NG made approximately twice as many errors on the lower-frequency stems than on the higher-frequency stems in each pair of words with the same first 4 letters. On the combined lists, she made 80 errors on the lower-frequency words, compared to 42 errors on the higher-frequency words, when they were unaffixed; and she made 17 errors on the lower-frequency stems compared to 8 errors on the higher-frequency stems when they were suffixed. To illustrate this effect, she read *almost* correctly, and read *almond* as "almost"; and she read *review* correctly, and *revive* as "review". Table 12 demonstrates NG's tendency to produce high-frequency words in response to both high- and low-frequency stimuli. A further confirmation of this result was that the mean frequency of correctly read stems was significantly higher than the mean frequency of incorrectly read stems: 51.1 versus 13.0 ($t = 2.108$, 95 d.f., $P = <0.05$ by two-tailed t-test) for list 3, and 57.8 versus 14.4 ($t = 2.605$, 286 d.f., $P = <0.01$ by two-tailed t-test) for list 4.

NG's reading performance for lists 3 and 4 convincingly shows that the object that is centred at the grapheme description level consists of a grapheme string bounded by spaces. One implication that follows from this conclusion is that the representation computed at the level of the grapheme description does not contain morphological structure.

TABLE 12
Stem Errors as a Function of Stem Frequency

	Number Errors on Highest Frequency Stem (% in Parentheses)	*Number Errors on Lower Frequency Stem*
List 3		
unaffixed	8/48 (17)	16/48 (33)
legally suffixed	1/48 (2)	3/48 (6)
List 4		
unaffixed	34/143 (24)	64/144 (44)
illegally suffixed	7/143 (5)	14/143 (10)

Having established that spacing is a sufficient condition for defining the boundaries of the representation that is computed at the grapheme description level, we turn next to a consideration of more subtle perceptual features—repeated identical letters.

List 5: Effects of Identical Letter "Affixes"

Method. A list of 42 words was presented in 6 conditions, distributed equally across 6 forms. Each word was presented once without any affix (e.g. tempt), once with a string of 4 Xs as a "prefix", once with a string of 4 Xs as a "suffix", once with a legal suffix (e.g. temptation), once with a legal suffix and a 4-X prefix, and once with a legal suffix followed by a 4-X suffix. For example, each form of list 5 contained one of the following: *problem*, *xxxxproblem*, *problemxxxx*, *problematic*, *xxxxproblematic*, or *problematicxxxx*.

Results and Discussion. The results are summarised in Table 13. Adding a string of Xs to the beginning of the word had no effect at all on

TABLE 13
Effects of Graphotactically Ill-formed Suffixes

Affix	*Number (%) Errors on Stem*	*Suffix Errors*
No affix	5/42 (12)	3/42 (7) (insertions)
4-X prefix	5/42 (12)	2/42 (5) (insertions)
4-X suffix	1/42 (2)	11/42 (26) (insertions)
Legal suffix	0/42 (0)	26/42 (62)
Legal suffix + 4-X prefix	0/42 (0)	26/42 (62)
Legal suffix + 4-X suffix	0/42 (0)	20/42 (48)

reading. Rates of suffix and stem errors were precisely the same for 4-X prefix and no prefix conditions, for both suffixed and unsuffixed words (e.g. *problem* versus *xxxxproblem* and *problematic* versus *xxxxproblematic*). On the other hand, a string of Xs on the end of a word resulted in fewer stem errors (2% versus 12%) and more suffix insertions (26% versus 7%), for 4-X suffixed words and unaffixed words, respectively. For example, *material* was read as "mature", whereas *materialxxxx* was read as "materialise". In reading legally suffixed words, there were no stem errors, but the addition of a string of Xs at the end had the effect of reducing the number of suffix substitutions and deletions. To illustrate, *childishly* was read as "childless", whereas *childishlyxxxx* was correctly read as "childishly". Thus, repeated-X suffixes, which she was instructed to ignore, were almost as effective as graphotactically appropriate suffixes, which she was instructed to read, in reducing stem errors (2% versus 0% stem errors for 4-X and legal suffixes, respectively).

The results of this experiment are important for two reasons. First, the fact that a 4-X prefix can effectively be ignored shows that perceptual features—visual identity, in this case—may be used to segregate grapheme strings into potential words for centring (or re-centring) at the grapheme description level of representation. Second, the fact that a 4-X suffix functioned as effectively as a regular suffix to shift the centre of a grapheme representation rightward shows that NG cannot process adequately even "low-level" information, such as identity, when this information falls on the right part of the grapheme representation. The latter result is consistent with our earlier observation that there seems to be no graphemically usable information on the right end of NG's word-centred grapheme representations.

Line Bisection

Thus far, we have focused entirely on NG's reading and spelling performance. However, this emphasis must not be assumed to reflect a belief that NG's impairment is language specific. We have already noted that she made errors in various tasks not involving words or letter strings. Interestingly, this impairment in processing other visual materials is, in important respects, of the same form as that documented for words. This contention is supported by NG's performance in line-bisection tasks.

Method. NG was presented with 5 horizontal lines of each of the following lengths: 4, 6, 8, and 10 inches, for a total of 20 trials. Each line was centred on an 11-inch wide by 8½-inch high sheet of paper. Lines of various lengths were presented randomly, and were placed directly in front of her on a flat surface. She was instructed to mark the centre of the line.

TABLE 14
Line Bisection as a Function of Line Length

	Standard Task Administration		*After Marking an "X" at Each End*	
Length	*Mean Displacement (in eighths of an inch)*	*Proportion of Line*	*Mean Displacement*	*Proportion of Line*
4"	6.2	0.10	5.0	0.08
6"	9.4	0.10	6.6	0.07
8"	12.0	0.09	10.6	0.08
10"	15.0	0.09	11.2	0.07

This procedure was repeated, with the additional instruction to mark each end of the line with an "x" before marking the midline.

Results and Discussion. NG's performance on these tasks revealed a marked leftward bias in indicating the centre of a line, suggesting inability to process the right part of the line adequately. The mean deviations from the actual centre of the line for each length on the first task are shown in Table 14. Her mean responses deviated in each case by 9–10% of the stimulus. The leftward bias in marking the centre of a line was not affected significantly by first having to mark the ends of the line before bisecting it, even though she never erred in marking each end of the line (Table 14). The overall mean deviation for the standard line bisection task was 1.33ins. (s.d. = 0.83ins.), and the overall mean deviation for line bisection after placing an x at each end was 1.04ins. (s.d. = 0.5ins.) ($t = -1.332$, 38 d.f., $P = 188$, n.s. by 2-tailed t-test).

The line bisection results show that NG's spatially specific processing deficit is not restricted to processing letter strings. This is an important result. It allows the inference that the deficit concerns visual processing in general, and not just letters. Consequently, conclusions reached from the detailed analysis of reading may be generalised to object recognition. The implications of this generalisation are now discussed more fully.[11]

[11] The results of the line bisection tasks, although seemingly not inconsistent with the claim that NG has a spatially specific processing deficit at the grapheme level, do raise an important issue. There are computational reasons for expecting that a grapheme level representation must be computed in the process of recognising or producing a written word. However, it is not immediately obvious that there is any need to compute such an abstract level of representation for perception of lines. It might have been assumed that the representation computed at the level of the stimulus-centred 2½-D sketch (corresponding to the letter shape level in word recognition) should have been sufficient to support normal performance in line bisection. And, since the latter level of representation is not impaired in NG, as indicated by the fact that her errors in reading words in different topographic orientations always involved

GENERAL DISCUSSION

The results we have reported severely constrain plausible claims about the possible locus of damage to NG's visual word recognition system. In particular, the results converge in support of two specific claims: (1) the damage is in a stage of processing where word-centred grapheme representations (or object-centred 3-D model descriptions) are computed; and, (2) the deficit concerns only the right half of these representations. The evidence adduced in support of these conclusions is the following:

1. NG's reading errors involved the right part of words and nonwords, irrespective of their topographic arrangement (horizontal, vertical, or mirror-reversed) or the sensory modality of input (visually vs. aurally presented stimuli). Her word recognition and reading impairment persisted even when she successfully named all the letters in the stimulus, and when the stimulus was presented tachistoscopically to her normal left visual field. Furthermore, reading performance was unaffected by the spacing between letters in a word. These results rule out as the locus of deficit damage to retino-centric feature level and the stimulus-centred letter shape level. The first of the two levels is ruled out by the fact that the impairment was not sensory-modality specific, by the fact that the impairment persisted despite accurate reading of all the letters in the stimulus, and by the fact that the impairment was independent of the topographic location and arrangement of the stimulus. The second level is ruled out by the fact that her impairment remained unchanged under topographic transformations of the stimulus.

2. NG's distribution of reading errors as a function of letter position within a word (or nonword) were restricted to the right half of the word (nonword), irrespective of length, topographic orientation, and modality of input. Furthermore, the probability of an error increased "linearly" as a function of distance from the centre of the word. These facts unambiguously establish that the deficit concerns the right half of grapheme representations.

3. NG's spelling performance was qualitatively identical to her reading performance: she made spelling errors only on the right half of words and

---

the end of words, we would have expected normal performance in the line bisection task. How, then, do we account for the line bisection results? The interpretation we would like to offer for the line bisection results is based on two assumptions: (1) that the computation of the 3-D model level of visual representation is mandatory even for perceptually simple forms such as line segments; and (2) that low-level perceptual processes are impenetrable to cognitive operations (Fodor, 1983). Specifically, the contention is that although the representation at the level of the 2½-D sketch is normal, this representation cannot be queried by cognitively driven operations such as that of deciding the mid-point of a line.

nonwords, irrespective of modality (written versus oral spelling) and order of output (forward versus backward spelling). This fact provides strong converging evidence for the hypothesis that the deficit responsible for NG's reading and spelling disorder concerns a graphemic level of representation—the only level of representation that may plausibly be assumed to be common to all the tasks for which a spatially specific reading and spelling deficit was observed. This fact also supports the hypothesis that the deficit concerns only the right half of grapheme representations.

4. NG's systematic leftward shift in the line bisection task and her omission errors of the right part of objects in a drawing task indicate a deficit in processing the right part of *all* visually based representations, whether words or objects. This result sanctions generalisations from NG's word recognition performance to visual recognition, more generally.[12]

The fact that it is possible to explicate highly detailed features of NG's impairment by proposing damage to a stage of processing where word-centred grapheme representations are computed may not only be taken as providing evidence for the proposed level of representation, but also for the model that contains that level of representation. However, the validity of the model depends also on its ability to explicate other features of the subject's performance besides the spatially determined impairment on which we have focused thus far. In addition, the model must provide a principled account for the performance of other patients reported in the literature. A consideration of these results allows a more stringent assessment of the validity of the overall architecture of the proposed model of word recognition, as well as a greater articulation of the representational and processing structure of the hypothesised stages of processing. We begin with a discussion of results relevant to the word-centred grapheme level of representation and proceed to discuss the stimulus-centred letter shape and the retino-centric feature levels.

[12]The claim that a common deficit is responsible for NG's spatially determined impairment in processing words and objects would seem to be at variance with the results reported by Costello and Warrington (1987) for patient JOH. This patient presented with greater difficulties in processing the *left* part of words, but the *rightmost* object of series of objects and the *right* part of lines. However, JOH had bilateral parietal damage with a dense right homonymous hemianopia. Furthermore, inspection of the reading errors made by JOH revealed that he also made a nontrivial number of errors on the *right* part of words (e.g. *keep* → "knee"; *England* → "angle"). It would seem, then, that the reported dissociation between "object neglect" and "word neglect" may simply be the result of the interaction between processing mechanisms for the recognition of words and objects with different types of spatially specific deficits to the right *and* left representational spaces.

The Word-centred Grapheme Level: Further Evidence

Although NG's performance in reading and spelling words and nonwords was qualitatively identical with respect to the spatially determined nature of the impairment, it was strikingly different in terms of overall levels of performance, and in terms of the effects of (nonspatial) characteristics of stimuli on performance. Four factors are important for consideration here: (1) the fact that the overall accuracy level in reading words was in the order of 70% to 90%, depending on various factors such as frequency, whereas overall accuracy in reading nonwords was around 25% to 35%, and accuracy in spelling both words and nonwords was in the range of 20% to 40%; (2) the fact that while reading performance was affected by word frequency, spelling performance was not; (3) the fact that error responses in reading both words and nonwords were almost always words, whereas error responses in spelling both words and nonwords were almost invariably nonwords; and (4) the fact that in reading errors occurred at the end of words irrespective of their morphological structure, but in spelling errors occurred not only at the end of words but, in transparently suffixed words, also at the end of stems (e.g. brightness → "brignesss"). Factors 2 and 4 are summarised in Table 15.

These dissociations could, of course, merely reflect the co-occurrence of deficits to different components of the reading and spelling systems, resulting in different patterns of performance for the two tasks. Alternatively, and more interestingly, the observed pattern of performance could reflect characteristics of the processing structure at the level of the damaged word-centred grapheme description that is assumed to be responsible for the spatially determined impairment in this subject. In the latter case, we would have further evidence for the hypothesised model of word recognition (and production).

TABLE 15
Percentage Accuracy and Predominant Error Type in Reading and Writing Words and Nonwords

	Overall Accuracy	*Types of Errors*
Reading Words	89%	Visually similar words (e.g. *hound* → "house")
Reading Nonwords	29%	Visually similar words —Lexicalisations (e.g. *dring* → "drill")
Spelling Words	33%	Nonwords (e.g. sneeze → *sneed*)
Spelling Nonwords	21%	Nonwords (e.g. spond → *spone*)

An explanation of the observed difference in levels of accuracy between words and nonwords follows directly from two assumptions about the structure of the lexical access procedure outlined in the proposed model of word recognition: (1) the assumption that a word-centred grapheme representation activates in parallel all lexical representations in proportion to the degree of grapheme overlap between the input and lexical representations; and (2) the assumption that the lexical representation that receives the most activation, above a prespecified minimal level, or the one to reach threshold first, will be processed further and produced as a response. As discussed in detail in an earlier section of this paper, the implications of these processing assumptions is that even though the right part of the grapheme representation of a word stimulus cannot be processed normally, the usable left part may be sufficient in many cases to activate the correct lexical representation, resulting in a correct response. For nonwords, this situation does not obtain, so that default correct responses are unlikely. Consequently, the expectation is that reading accuracy for words should be superior to reading accuracy for nonwords—the obtained result.

Similar considerations account for the discrepancy in accuracy levels between reading and spelling despite the assumed commonality in the level of deficit responsible for the impairments in these tasks. The reason for the observed discrepancy in performance levels is that different constraints are at play in the use of the grapheme representations in reading and spelling: in reading the grapheme representation must be processed in parallel for lexical access, whereas in spelling the graphemes in the grapheme representation must be processed sequentially for conversion into specific letter shapes or letter names; in reading the output of the operations applied to the grapheme representation is a single object, a lexical representation, whereas in spelling the output of the operations applied to the grapheme representation is a set of independent letter shapes or letter names. Consequently, whereas in reading the normally processed part of the grapheme representation can constrain the activation of a lexical entry in the orthographic lexicon, in spelling, the normally processed part of the grapheme representation cannot constrain the independent operations of the allographic conversion mechanism which operates over individual graphemes. Thus, in the case of spelling there is no default mechanism to constrain possible *letter* responses. If the information on the right part of the word-centred grapheme representation is not usable, spelling responses for the graphemes in this part of the representation can only consist of random letter errors.[13] Thus, word spelling accuracy is expected

[13]Or, spelling responses for the graphemes in the right (impaired) part of the representation might consist of letters corresponding to the most available graphemes—for example, *x*, *z*, and *q* were rarely, if ever, produced at the end of spelling responses, whereas *s* and *t* were very common.

to be poorer than word reading accuracy. Furthermore, since lexical status is not a factor in the sequential processing of graphemes for output processes in spelling, the expectation is that words and nonwords should be spelled with comparable levels of accuracy (Caramazza et al., 1987). The results obtained for NG are consistent with these expectations.

The remaining three features of NG's performance also receive ready explanations in light of these considerations. Thus, the fact that word frequency affected reading but not spelling performance is explained by the fact that frequency is a factor in lexical access in reading—frequency affects threshold settings for activating lexical entries—but plays no role in the sequential processing of graphemes in spelling. Consequently, we expect better reading performance for high- than low-frequency words, but no effect of word frequency in spelling. In the case of the difference in error responses for reading and spelling, this is explained by the fact that the default responses of the lexical access procedure in reading involve words, whereas the default responses in spelling can only be individual letters.

The differential effect of morphological structure on reading and spelling also follows from assumptions we have made about the structure of the processes that are applied to grapheme representations in the two tasks. In the case of reading, the factors that determine the unit of representation that serves as input to the lexical access procedures (at least on a first pass), are strictly perceptual—spacing and identity, for example. The representation that is submitted for further processing at the lexical access stage is a letter string, and *not* a morpheme or word. Consequently, spatially determined errors will occur at the end of the letter string, whether it is a word, a morpheme, or a nonword. In spelling, by contrast, the representations computed prior to the grapheme level consist of lexical units—words and/or morphemes. If the production system can output morphemes as well as words, then, we might expect errors at the end of stems (or roots) and the end of suffixes when the unit of output is the morpheme. The fact that NG made errors both at the end of roots and suffixes supports the hypothesis of morphological compositionality in output (see Badecker, Hillis, & Caramazza, 1990; Miceli & Caramazza, 1988; for further discussion of this hypothesis). For present purposes, the important point is that the contrast in the spatial distribution of errors for spelling and reading follows directly from computationally motivated assumptions about lexical access in reading and lexical production in spelling.

In short, then, the proposed model of word recognition (and production) can account not only for NG's spatially determined impairment in reading (and spelling) but also for the pattern of response accuracy, the effects of frequency, and the effect of response type observed in her reading and spelling performance.

In the effort to provide an account for NG's contrasting performance on some aspects of reading and spelling, an important property of the processing structure at the grapheme level was made explicit: whether a representation at a specific level of processing is processed in parallel or serially need not be an intrinsic property of the representation level itself, but could be determined by the interactions that are possible between that representation level and the mechanisms that operate over the information represented at that level of processing. Thus, in the case of reading, the grapheme representation is processed in parallel because the information relevant to the lexical access mechanism is the whole grapheme representation. This, on its own, does not imply that representations at this level must necessarily be processed in parallel, but confers a high degree of plausibility to such a possibility. By contrast, in the case of spelling, graphemes at the word-centred grapheme level are processed serially because the mechanisms that operate over representations at this level of processing (allographic conversion and letter name conversion) are concerned with the computation of individual letter forms, and not words. This computational distinction between different forms of processing at the grapheme level of representation—parallel for lexical access in reading, serial for letter form conversion in writing—is supported by the reported results.

The Word-centred Grapheme Level: Spatial or Ordinal Co-ordinates

Throughout this report we have assumed, without explicit justification, that order information among graphemes at the word-centred grapheme level is encoded in a spatially defined co-ordinate system (see also Hillis & Caramazza, 1989; 1990). This contention is on the face of it implausible, even seemingly contradictory: graphemes are, by hypothesis, abstract objects encoding font-, case-, size-, and orientation-independent letter information. And, yet, we have reported results that unambiguously support the thesis that NG's impairment concerns the right half of a word-centred representation.

The evidence we have presented undermines the hypothesis that the deficit concerns an ordinally determined part of a grapheme representation—the distribution of NG's reading and spelling errors indicates that errors are restricted to the *right half* of a word (or nonword), irrespective of stimulus length. Thus, the deficit cannot be specified simply in terms of ordinal positions defined in terms of either the beginning or end of a word. An alternative possibility is that grapheme order is specified in terms of ordinal position from the centre of the word. Thus, for example, the order of the graphemes for the word stimulus *chair* could be specified as [<c/-2>, <h/-1>, <a/0>, <i/1>, <r/2>]. This form of representation for the order of the graphemes in a word can successfully capture the fact that NG's impairment concerns a part of the stimulus specified by reference to the mid-point of the word. However, this representational format fails to provide a motivated account for the fact that the impairment concerns the right part of the word. Of course, it could be objected that we have prejudged the issue by labelling the impaired part as the "right" part. However, this choice is not unmotivated. Recall that NG was not only impaired in processing words, but also in line bisection, object drawing, and other perceptual tasks—tasks for which a characterisation of the relations among the parts of the stimulus could not be given in any simple way in terms of ordinal relations. It is, therefore, much more parsimonious to assume that a common, spatially determined deficit is responsible for the observed processing impairment for words and objects. Nonetheless, we recognise that there are nontrivial theoretical questions introduced by the joint assumptions that representations at the level of the word-centred grapheme description consist of abstract letter identities and that the order among these objects is encoded in a spatially defined co-ordinate frame.

Finally, there is the matter of the mechanism that centres the grapheme string in the spatially defined co-ordinate system. One possibility is that the centre at the grapheme level is simply the same as the one at the letter shape level. On this view, the centre of the string of shapes at the stimulus-centred, letter shape level serves as the anchor point about which to place other graphemes at the grapheme level. This way of establishing a centre for the grapheme string does not preclude the possibility that the grapheme string may be re-centred on the basis of grapheme level information (see section on the effects of affixation).

The Stimulus-centred Letter Shape Level and the Retino-centric Feature Level

NG's reading performance is in many respects similar to that of other brain-damaged subjects who have been classified as "neglect dyslexics" (Behrmann, Moscovitch, Black, & Mozer, in press; Brunn & Farah, Note 1; Costello & Warrington, 1987; Ellis, Flude, & Young, 1987; Friedrich, Walker, & Posner, 1985; Kinsbourne & Warrington, 1962; Riddoch, Humphreys, Cleton, & Fery, this issue; Warrington & Zangwill, 1957; Young, Newcombe, & Ellis, this issue (Part 2, 1991); see Shallice, 1988, for review). Like these other patients, NG's reading impairment has a spatially determined character—errors occur only at one end (the left or the right) of the word, the right end in her case. However, there is a crucial difference between NG's performance and that of other cases described in the literature. Unlike these other cases, NG's reading impairment was invariant under topographic transformations of the stimulus (horizontal, vertical, and mirror-reversed letter strings), and she also showed a similar spatially determined impairment in all forms of spelling. The subjects reported by Ellis et al., Behrmann et al., and Riddoch et al. made errors on the same relative side of space for standardly presented and mirror-reversed words—that is, these subjects made errors on the *left part of the physical stimulus* whether or not it corresponded to the beginning of the word. For example, VB (Ellis et al.) misread the standardly presented word *yellow* as "pillow", but she misread the mirror-reversed stimulus *plant* as "plane". Furthermore, VB showed a dissociation between preserved oral spelling ability and impaired written spelling, the latter characterised by stroke errors and a tendency to write down the right side of the page (Ellis et al., 1987). Thus, there can be no doubt about the fact that the locus of impairment in VB cannot be the same as that hypothesised for NG. In fact, for VB, we must assume that the impairment involves a stage of processing prior to the word-centred grapheme level: either the stimulus-centred letter shape level or the retino-centric feature level, or, more likely, both. Although the results reported by Ellis et al. do not exclude the possibility that VB has an impairment at the level of the retino-centric feature map, they do establish clearly that she had an impairment at the level of the stimulus-centred letter shape map. The evidence for this contention is that VB made errors on the left part of stimuli even when these were presented tachistoscopically in the "intact" right visual field, and even when she had successfully read a digit to the immediate left of the word. The latter results rule out as the *only* locus of deficit the retino-centric feature level and implicate damage to the stimulus-centred letter shape level as at least one factor responsible for VB's reading impairment[14] (see also Behrmann et al., in press; Kinsbourne & Warrington, 1962; Riddoch et al., this issue; Young et al., this issue (Part 2, 1991)).

---

[14]Ellis et al. (1987) interpret their result with mirror-reversed words as providing evidence against the hypothesis that a word-centred representation level is computed in the course of visual word recognition. They argue (p. 459) that ". . . if neglect operated on word-centred co-ordinates, then initial letters would be neglected, regardless of the orientation of the word." Because this result did not obtain with their subject, VB, they conclude that order information in an abstract letter representation is encoded in terms of ordinal spatial positions (Seymour, 1979). This conclusion is inadequate for several reasons. First, it is empirically inadequate as demonstrated by the results reported for NG—there are patients whose performance is invariant under topographic transformations of stimuli (see also Hillis & Caramazza, 1990). Second, it is inadequate because it fails to account in a motivated way for the right-of-centre/left-of-centre character of the reading difficulties recorded for various "neglect" patients—as noted here, a simple representation of order information cannot capture the centredness character of the impairment of many of the patients studied, including VB. And, third, it is forced to make an unprincipled distinction between perceptual processes involved in reading words and numbers—the latter resulted most often in deletion errors whereas word errors often resulted in letter substitutions. This dissociation follows naturally from the assumption (see earlier) that word reading is constrained by possible lexical responses, whereas number reading is not subject to similar constraints.

Further evidence for spatially determined selective damage to the stimulus-centred letter shape level and the retino-centric feature level is reported by Rapp & Caramazza (this issue). These authors investigated the performance of a brain-damaged subject, HR, who presented with clinical symptoms of "letter-by-letter" reading—she identified each letter in a word either audibly or subvocally before attempting to pronounce it. Detailed investigation of the subject's ability to identify letters in a visual display documented a low-level visual processing deficit. The deficit was characterized by an increasingly severe left-to-right processing limitation for absolute spatial positions of letters. Furthermore, a relative spatial position effect was observed for horizontally arrayed stimuli, independent of absolute spatial position, with greater processing difficulties for letters on the right relative to other letters in the array. This effect of relative spatial position was not observed for vertically arrayed stimuli. These results were interpreted as reflecting spatially-determined damage for positions on the right part of representations at the level of the retino-centric feature map *and* stimulus-centred letter shape map (see Rapp & Caramazza, this issue (Part 2, 1991), for a detailed account of the possible relationship between the hypothesized form of damage in this case and her letter-by-letter reading performance).

The performance by patient MO (Riddoch et al., 1990) may be explained as resulting from selective damage to the retino-centric feature map. MO's left-sided errors in reading words occurred only when the initial letters were presented in his left visual field (perhaps within the portion of the field affected by his hemianopia). That is, MO made errors only in response to words presented tachistoscopically, which would prevent compensation by eye movements for his impairment in processing the left half of the retino-centric representation. Furthermore, when words were presented for sufficiently brief durations to prevent refixating them (250msec.), he made as many errors on the second letter of 5-letter words as on the first letter of 4-letter words (which were presented in the same retinal position). And, when 4-letter words were presented further to the right of fixation, MO made fewer errors on the first letter of each word. Together, these results are consistent with the hypothesis that MO's spatially specific deficit disrupted word recognition at the level of the retino-centric feature map.

The performance of patient TB (Patterson & Wilson, 1990) could also be accounted for by assuming damage to the retino-centric level of representation such that damage is restricted to a small segment of the feature map just at and to the left of fixation (as can result from a scotoma in one eye, at least when the other eye is nonfunctional as in TB's case). If we assume that he fixates just to the left of the second letter of 4-letter words, then he would have impaired perception of the first letter, resulting in errors like *rose* read as "nose". Further, if he were to fixate on the second letter of 5-letter words he would have impaired perception of the first and second letters, resulting in errors like *xlead* → "read" and *spear* → "wear". Adding letters, symbols, or words on the left side would shift his fixation (O'Reagan & Lévy-Schoen, 1987; O'Reagan, Lévy-Schoen, Pynte, & Brugaillère, 1984), such that more of the left letters of the word would fall within the spared retino-centric feature map, and would be read correctly—just the pattern of results reported. On longer words, only 1 or 2 letters at and to the left of fixation would be affected, so that the available information would often be sufficient to activate the correct representation in the orthographic input lexicon. For example, perception of *elephant as el_hant*, would activate the lexical representation for elephant more than any other representation. In general, the longer the word, the fewer representations would share the correctly perceived graphemes, a fact that would account for his better performance on longer words. The reported performance on stimuli like *cashland*, which elicited responses that substituted the initial letter of the first word only, would also be predicted on this account (but *not* on the McClelland & Rumelhart [1981] account as argued by Patterson & Wilson, 1990), since the entire second word would fall on the intact retino-centric map, assuming he fixated toward the beginning or in the middle of the letter string. Further, such damage would explain his perception of nonword letter strings, if they are normally fixated and perceived in a fashion similar to words. A scotoma at and to the left of fixation would also result in impaired perception of individual letters (and vertically printed words, if each letter is fixated individually). Upper-case letters might have been perceived by TB more adequately than lower-case because they are generally larger (so that more feature information would fall in the intact field). Finally, the hypothesised deficit would explain his performance in text reading—errors only on the left side of individual short words—since each word would be fixated individually. Of course, the deficit should also affect visual perception of stimuli other than alphanumeric characters, to the extent that the stimuli are comparable in size and discriminability to letters and numbers. TB's perception of such stimuli could not be tested because of his deteriorating vision. (Thus, his medical history is in line with the hypothesised impairment, since deterioration of vision to only light/dark vision, as in his left eye, would be expected in the case of macular degeneration, the most common cause of scotomas.)

In some cases, it is not possible to determine the locus of impairment with respect to the level of representation in word recognition from the data reported. For example, RNR (Warrington, this issue (Part 2, 1991) made errors that were very similar to those of NG in terms of the increase in rate of errors as a function of the distance from the centre of the word on the right side. This pattern of errors would be expected to result from right-sided damage at the level of the stimulus-centred letter-shape map *or* damage at the level of the word-centred grapheme description. Other features of RNR's reading performance are also consistent with hypothesised damage at either level of visual word recognition. Thus, RNR made errors in reading words presented for brief durations to his left (intact) visual field at a rate comparable to his error rate in untimed reading. Like NG, RNR also made some right-sided errors in vertical reading that appeared to be similar to his right-sided errors in normal (horizontal) reading. However, RNR also made many other kinds of errors in the vertical reading task (thus, less than 50% of his errors on this task occurred only on the end of the word). Similarly, his spelling errors were not restricted to the right side, presumably due, at least in part, to a premorbidly low level of spelling skill. Because of the inconclusive data from vertical reading and spelling, and absence of data on reading mirror-reversed words or recognising aural spelling, it is not possible to ascertain with any confidence the locus of damage responsible for RNR's right-sided errors in reading.

In summary, the fact that contrasting patterns of deficits to the word-centred grapheme level—NG (see also RB and HH reported in Hillis & Caramazza, 1990, and ML and DH reported in Hillis & Caramazza, 1989)—the stimulus-centred letter shape level—VB, HR, JB, SP and patients reported by Kinsbourne and Warrington (1962)—and the retino-centric feature levels, HR, MO, and TB (and perhaps JB, SP, and VB), as well as cases reported in Behrmann et al. (in press) provide strong evidence for the multi-level model of visual word recognition proposed in this paper.

On the Interpretation of Neglect: Real and Imagined Problems

A Disorder of Attention or of Representation? Thus far the focus of our discussion has been entirely on the implications of the spatially specific nature of NG's deficit for claims about the processing structure of written word recognition and production. We have avoided all discussion of whether the cause of the "neglect" impairment recorded for NG is to be specified in terms of a deficit to attentional mechanisms (e.g., Heilman, Bowers, Valenstein, & Watson, 1985; Kinsbourne, 1970; Posner, Cohen, & Rafal, 1982; Riddoch & Humphreys, 1987) or to the information represented at some stage of processing (e.g., Bisiach, Luzzatti, & Perani, 1979; DeRenzi, Faglioni, & Scotti, 1970). Although it is not possible to give a definitive answer to this question, there are several considerations that make the attentional account highly problematic. The default conclusion will be that it is more reasonable to assume that, at least for NG, the underlying cause of the observed spatially determined impairment is damage to the grapheme representation computed at the word-centred grapheme level.

The considerations that led to this conclusion are as follows. We have shown that NG's processing at the retino-centric feature level and the stimulus-centred shape level is essentially intact. This implies that the attentional mechanisms that direct processing resources to parts of the feature map and to parts of the letter shape map must be functioning sufficiently well to guarantee "normal" processing at these levels of representation. Were this not the case, we would have observed spatially determined deficits at the level of retinotopic and stimulus-centred representations. However, this was not the case. NG's spatially determined impairment concerned only the right half of a word-centred grapheme representation. This pattern of performance rules out a general deficit in directing attention to representational spaces. Consequently, either we assume that there are distinct attentional mechanisms operating at different levels of representation, or we reject the hypothesis that the deficit concerns an attentional mechanism. To save the attentional hypothesis, we could, of course, abandon the claim that there is a single, general mechanism for directing resources at all levels of representation. However, the price of this move would be to give up the possibility of having a representation-independent characterisation of attentional mechanisms. Alternatively, we could assume that the underlying cause of NG's deficit is that it directly concerns the right half of representational space at the level of word-centred grapheme (or, object-centred, 3-D model) descriptions.

It must be emphasised at this point that the hypothesis advanced here is *not* that the proposed deficit concerns stored representations of words or operations of the lexical system in general. These hypotheses are clearly inconsistent with the reported results: NG's impairment involved words *and* nonwords in qualitatively similar ways. Furthermore, NG's performance with suffixed and pseudosuffixed letter strings shows that she was able to access lexical stems which she was unable to read correctly when these were presented unsuffixed. These results show that the deficit responsible for NG's spatially determined impairment in word recognition cannot concern stored lexical representations, nor can it concern the operations of the lexical access process itself. Instead, as proposed earlier, the deficit must concern the grapheme representations that serve as input to the lexical access process. Of course, this does not exclude the possibility that other patients' spatially determined impairment in word processing may in fact be the result of a deficit to the lexical system. However, no detailed evidence or argument has been presented in favour of such a possibility.

Finally, note that the conclusion reached here is not to be understood as a general claim about the underlying cause of "neglect" in general, as has been suggested by Bisiach et al. (1979) and De Renzi et al. (1970). The claim advanced here concerns only the spatially determined impairment described for NG: it is not a claim about all patients who may be classified clinically as presenting with "neglect". The specificity of the conclusion does not make it any less important, for it establishes that at least some "neglect" symptoms may result from direct damage to the information in a spatially defined part of a representational space. This position leaves open the possibility that the clinical symptoms of "neglect" in other patients may result from damage to other perceptual or attentional mechanisms (see Riddoch et al., this issue, for putative cases of attentional deficits).[15]

On the Preservation of Positional Encoding. Ellis et al. (1987: patient VB; see also Riddoch et al., this issue: patient JB; Young et al., this issue (Part 2, 1991): patient SP) have proposed that "neglect" may affect information differentially about the identity of the letters and the length of a word. Specifically, they suggest that a patient may be unable to recover information about the identity of the letters at the beginning or end of a word while retaining the ability to encode the overall length of the word. The evidence adduced in support of this claim is the striking correlation between stimulus and response length in reading errors. Thus, all three patients discussed by these authors, VB, JB, and SP, produced reading errors that were the same or nearly the same length as the misread stimulus word. This correlation was also observed for NG, and represents a significant factor to be accounted for by theories of visual word recognition. We do not think, however, that the proposed account of independent encoding of letter identity and word length provides the correct characterisation for the observed correlation. The reasons for this contention follow.

One objection is theoretical in nature: no motivated account has been offered of how the independently encoded information about word length and letter identities are integrated in the process of word recognition.

[15]We do not think that Riddoch et al.'s conclusion, that the performance of their two patients results from deficits to attentional mechanisms as opposed to representational spaces or computed representations, is supported by the evidence they cite. Thus, the fact that JB (with left-sided processing difficulties) continued to neglect the (physical) left side of words for mirror-reversed stimuli does not imply that the deficit is to attentional mechanisms; it could just as easily be due to a deficit to the left-of-centre part of the computed stimulus-centred shape representation. The fact that JB's pattern of performance rules out a deficit to the word-centred grapheme level does not imply that the form of damage must be to an attentional mechanism (although it could be!). The situation with case MO is equally indeterminate. As argued earlier, MO's performance suggests a deficit in processing at the level of the retino-centric feature map. The fact that this patient's "neglect" could be eliminated by allowing him to fixate position 1 of the letter string suggests that the observed reading impairment may result from his hemianopia (though not necessarily!). In short, the available evidence does not allow an unambiguous conclusion on whether the reading impairment of JB and MO is most plausibly explicated by assuming a representational or an attentional deficit at one or another level of the visual word recognition process.

Thus, let us suppose that information about word length and letter identities has been encoded for a visually presented word. How are these two types of information represented? Are they represented in the same spatial representation? How are the two sorts of information used in the word recognition process? In the absence of answers to questions such as these, we must remain sceptical about the value of the proposed claim.

Empirical objections can also be raised against the claim of independent encoding of word length and letter identities. Let us suppose that the basis for the observed correlation between the length of error responses and stimuli was that the patients were able to encode word length correctly despite their inability to process some of the letters at the right or left half of words adequately. Were this to be the case, we would expect the patients in question to perform normally in line bisection or length estimation tasks where the only relevant information for performing the task concerns the length of the line. However, as documented here, NG systematically underestimated length in line bisection tasks. Consequently, it does not seem likely that the observed correlation between response and stimulus length for NG results from the independent, correct encoding of word length.

The observed correlation between the length of error responses and stimuli receives a ready explanation within the model of visual word recognition we have proposed. Briefly, the correlation between stimulus and response length is a direct consequence of the assumption that graphemes are represented in a word-centred co-ordinate system, and thus necessarily encode positional information. The implicitly encoded position information is part of the information needed for lexical access. Thus, it is important that the grapheme <p> in the stimulus *pot* is the first grapheme and not the third as in *top*. And, on the assumption that lexical representations are activated in proportion to their similarity to the input grapheme representation, this guarantees that the lexical representations receiving the maximum activation will be those that share graphemes at the same relative positions. A direct consequence of these assumptions is that the lexical representations with maximum activation will have the same length as the stimulus. Now, when a spatially determined part of a grapheme representation is damaged (say part of the right half, as is the case for NG), the undamaged part of the grapheme representation will activate lexical representations that are (approximately) the same length as the stimulus.

To illustrate this claim consider the following example. Suppose that the patient is shown the stimulus *canter*. On the assumption that the right half of the grapheme representation of this stimulus is damaged, the only fully usable information is <can>. Why, then, does the patient not just produce "can" instead of the more likely responses "cannot", "cannon", "canned", "candle", "canopy", and so forth? The reason is to be found in the fact that the undamaged graphemes <c>, <a>, and <n> occupy particular positions in the representational space of the grapheme description: the grapheme <c> occupies the third position to the left of centre, the grapheme <a> occupies the second position to the left of centre, and the grapheme <n> occupies the first position to the left of centre. When these graphemes occupy the indicated positions they will maximally activate lexical representations with graphemes in the same positions relative to their centre—the lexical entries CANNON, CANDID, CANTOR, and so forth, and not CAN, CANE, CANNIBAL, CANTALOUPE, and so forth. Consequently, everything else being equal, the patient will produce a response that is the same length as the stimulus even though its length has not been encoded explicitly. Thus, the model of visual word recognition we have proposed can account for the observed correlation between stimulus and error response length without having to make unmotivated assumptions about the independent encoding of stimulus length.

Neighbourhood Effects. The model of visual word recognition we have proposed predicts that patients with damage at any of the three levels of visual processing will show significant effects of the density of the orthographic neighbourhood of words (as reported by Riddoch et al., this issue; Patterson & Wilson, this issue). That is, on the assumptions that (1) the representation at the grapheme description level activates in parallel (proportionally to the degree of graphemic overlap) all entries in the orthographic input lexicon with which it shares graphemes in specific positions, and (2) the lexical representation that is activated for further processing depends upon the degree of activation it receives from the grapheme representation and on its own threshold level of activation, we would expect that words with many "neighbours" would have a lower chance of being read correctly than words with few or no "neighbours" (particularly if at least one of the neighbours is higher in frequency than the stimulus, as we reported for NG in lists 3 and 4).

Along the same lines, we can account for inconsistencies in reported word length effects in reading by patients who make errors restricted to the left or right side of words. We have reported that NG made more errors on longer words, and that the mean length of correctly read words was significantly shorter than the mean length of words that were read incorrectly. Ellis et al. (1987) reported similar findings for VB. By contrast, Costello and Warrington (1987) reported that JOH made more errors on shorter words; and Patterson and Wilson (this issue) reported that their patient made errors *only* on short words. The discrepancy among the reported effects of word length is just as likely to reflect differences in the nature of the stimuli used by different investigators as it is to reflect differences in the nature of damage to different components of the visual word recognition process. Thus, for example, most of the longer words incorrectly read by NG were suffixed words. In the case of these stimuli, there is always at least one word in the lexicon that shares with the stimulus the left half of the letters (thus, for example, NG might well read *accommodated* as "accommodate", "accommodates", "accommodation", "accommodations", and so on, depending on the relative accessibility of these representations). On the other hand, a patient with left "neglect" would be very likely to read *accommodated* correctly, since no other word in the lexicon ends in *-odated*. Thus, an interpretation of word length effects cannot be undertaken without considering the neighbourhood structure of the stimuli used by different experimenters.

On Supposedly Contradictory Results. It has been claimed that there are contradictory results regarding the stages at which neglect is supposed to occur—the retinotopic encoding stage or some later stage of processing (Behrmann et al., in press; Mozer & Behrmann, Note 2). However, these supposedly contradictory results can only be taken as such if one assumes that neglect is a unitary phenomenon that can only affect a specific stage of processing. Once we abandon this theoretically unmotivated restriction about possible loci at which the spatially determined deficit can occur, the seemingly contradictory results referred to by these authors are no longer paradoxical—they simply reflect damage to different levels of the visual word recognition system.

The Lexicality Effect: Automatic and Top-down Processing? One final issue we consider briefly concerns the interpretation that has been offered for the lexicality effect in reading—better performance in reading words than nonwords—that has been observed in various cases of neglect (Brunn & Farah, Note 1; Sieroff, Pollatsek, & Posner, 1988). This result has led some authors (e.g. Sieroff et al., 1988) to conclude that words are processed automatically—without visual attention—whereas nonwords require attention for normal processing (see also Brunn & Farah, 1989; Mozer & Behrmann, Note 2). This conclusion has been reached in the context of a model that fails to distinguish between the several levels of representation within the pre-lexical access part of the visual word recognition system. Consequently, the interpretation of results has been based on the simple distinction between pre-lexical, letter processes (common to word and nonwords),[16] and lexical processes (exclusively for words). In

[16]That is, no account is offered of the levels of representation that are needed to solve the computational problems in word recognition. Such a step would have involved making explicit assumptions about the nature and organisation of the information computed at each stage of processing of the word recognition system. With such an account on hand, it would have been possible to evaluate the plausibility of claims about the presumed role of attentional mechanisms at some level of processing. The absence of such an explicit account makes statements such as (Siéroff et al., 1988; p. 427) ". . . spatial attention is unnecessary for access to the lexical network that produces a visual word form" not especially informative—we simply have a juxtaposition of two poorly understood concepts: spatial attention and lexical network.

this context, and on the assumption that neglect concerns the pre-lexical level of processing, the better performance in processing words versus nonwords invites the inference that words and nonwords are processed differently at this level of the word recognition system—hence the conclusion that words are processed "automatically" and that nonwords require "attention" for normal processing. This conclusion is problematic. Even ignoring problems of interpretation of the notion of "automatic processing", it is not necessary to invoke such a notion in order to account for the superior performance with words. As discussed earlier, better performance with words may only reflect the fact that, for word stimuli, the set of possible word responses (given partial information about the grapheme string) may be highly restricted, leading to many correct responses by default. Furthermore, since no hypothesis is offered about the structure of relevant visual processes at pre-lexical access stages, the claim that processing at these stages may be automatic or attentive, depending on the type of stimulus (word versus nonword), is hardly informative.

Some aspects of the performance of some patients with spatially determined reading impairments have given rise to claims about the role of "top-down" processing in reading (e.g. Behrmann et al., in press; Mozer & Behrmann, Note 2). It has been argued that words are read better because of the influence of top-down lexical effects. The motivation for this claim has concerned the superiority of word over nonword reading performance in "neglect" patients. If by "top-down" effects is meant no more than the fact that the availability of lexical representations in the course of reading constrains possible responses, leading to superior performance for words over nonwords, then this notion is superfluous—we have shown that one can instantiate lexical constraints in a strictly bottom-up model such as the one we have proposed in this paper. If by "top-down" effects is meant that lexical knowledge affects pre-lexical perceptual processes, then the evidence cited in its support is not adequate. To defend the latter claim it would have to be shown that the letter shapes and grapheme descriptions computed for word stimuli are *different* from those computed for nonwords. No such demonstration has been provided. And, since it is possible to explicate the word/nonword contrast in reading performance in a model with strictly bottom-up processing architecture (as shown here), we must reject as premature the introduction of overly powerful notions such as "top-down" processing.

Conclusion

In this report we have presented a relatively detailed multi-stage model of visual word recognition (and spelling). Explicit assumptions were made about the processing structure of early stages of visual form analysis, about the processing structure of the mechanisms of lexical access, and about the interaction between these two sets of processes. This model received considerable support through the extensive analysis of NG's reading and spelling performance. The model could account for all the main features of NG's performance: (1) the spatially determined reading deficit, involving only the right half of words, regardless of the topographic arrangement of stimuli; (2) the spatially determined spelling deficit, involving only the right half of words, regardless of the form of output (written and oral spelling and backward oral spelling); (3) the better performance reading words compared to nonwords, and the comparably poor performance in spelling words and nonwords; (4) the presence of a word frequency effect in reading but not spelling; and (5) the prefix and suffix effects on reading performance. The fact that highly detailed aspects of NG's performance could be given a clear interpretation in the context of the proposed model provides empirical support for the model. The proposed model is further supported by the fact that it could also account for the pattern of spatially determined reading deficits in other brain-damaged subjects described in the literature.

Although we have succeeded in providing a detailed account of a wide range of facts, there remain a number of problems which we have either not been able to address satisfactorily or completely omitted from consideration because they are too difficult to yield to analysis at this time. One puzzle concerns the assumption that graphemic information is represented in a spatially defined co-ordinate system. As already noted, this assumption is not unproblematic—it remains unclear how to reconcile the assumption of abstractness of graphemic information with the assumption that this information is arrayed in a spatially defined co-ordinate frame. A long-standing, important puzzle concerns the correlation between side of damage to representational space and side of hemispheric damage. The significance of this correlation remains a mystery despite the many efforts to clarify it (see DeRenzi, 1982; and papers in Jeannerod, 1987; for discussions of this problem). And, finally, there is the poorly understood relationship between the spatial-specificity of the deficit, especially its phenomenological character, and the unity of consciousness (see Bisiach, in press, for discussion). It is to be hoped that future research will find means of addressing these important theoretical issues. For now, we can do no more than to note that significant progress on these issues is unlikely to be forthcoming without the formulation of computationally explicit accounts of the processing stages that subserve visual word and object recognition. It is our hope that the work reported here has contributed to the elucidation of at least some of the general properties of the visual word recognition system.

Manuscript received 7 March 1990
Revised manuscript received 15 June 1990

REFERENCES

Allport (1989). Visual attention. In M. I. Posner (Ed.), *Foundations of cognitive science*. Cambridge, Mass.: M.I.T. Press.

Badecker, W. & Caramazza, A. (1987). *The Johns Hopkins Morphology Battery*. Baltimore, Maryland: The Johns Hopkins University.

Badecker, W., Hillis, A. E., & Caramazza, A. (1990). Lexical morphology and its role in the writing process: Evidence from a case of acquired dysgraphia. *Cognition*, *35*, 205–244.

Baxter, D. M. & Warrington, E. K. (1983). Neglect dysgraphia. *Journal of Neurology, Neurosurgery, and Psychiatry*, *46*, 1073–1078.

Behrmann, M., Moscovitch, M., Black, S. E., & Mozer, M. C. (in press). Perceptual and conceptual factors in neglect: Personal and extrapersonal. *Brain*.

Bisiach, E. (in press). The (haunted) brain and consciousness. In A. J. Marcel & E. Bisiach (Eds.), *Consciousness and contemporary science*. Oxford: Oxford University Press.

Bisiach, E., Luzzatti, C., & Perani, D. (1979). Unilateral neglect, representational schema, and consciousness. *Brain*, *102*, 609–618.

Bisiach, E. & Vallar, G. (1989). Hemineglect in humans. In F. Boller & J. Graffman (Eds.), *Handbook of neuropsychology, Vol. 1*. North Holland: Elsevier Science Publishers, B.V., 195–222.

Caramazza, A. & Hillis, A. E. (1990). Internal spatial representation of written words: Evidence from unilateral neglect. *Nature*, *346*, 267–269.

Caramazza, A., Laudanna, A., & Romani, C. (1988). Lexical access and inflectional morphology. *Cognition*, *28*, 297–332.

Caramazza, A., Miceli, M., Villa, A., & Romani, C. (1987). The role of the graphemic buffer in spelling: Evidence from a case of acquired dysgraphia. *Cognition*, *26*, 59–85.

Caramazza, A. & Miceli, M. (1989). Orthographic structure, the graphemic buffer, and the spelling process. In C. von Euler, I. Lundberg, & G. Lennerstrand (Eds.), *Brain and reading*. London: MacMillan/Wenner-Gren International Symposium Series, 257–268.

Coltheart, M. (1981). Disorders of reading and their implications for models of normal reading. *Visible Language*, *15*, 245–286.

Costello, A. D. & Warrington, E. K. (1987). The dissociation of visuospatial neglect and neglect dyslexia. *Journal of Neurology, Neurosurgery, and Psychiatry*, *50*, 1110–1116.

Cummings, D. W. (1988). *American English spelling*. Baltimore: The Johns Hopkins University Press.

De Renzi, E. (1982). *Disorders of space exploration and cognition*. New York: Wiley.

De Renzi, E. & Faglioni, P. (1978). Normative data and screening power of a shortened version of the Token Test. *Cortex*, *14*, 41–49.

De Renzi, E., Faglioni, P., & Scotti, G. (1970). Hemispheric contribution to the exploration of space through the visual and tactile modality. *Cortex*, *6*, 191–203.

Duncan, J. (1987). Attention and reading: Wholes and parts in shape recognition. In M. Coltheart (Ed.), *Attention and performance*, *Vol. 12*. London: Lawrence Erlbaum Associates Ltd.

Egeth, H., Jonides, J., & Wall, S. (1972). Parallel processing of multi-element displays. *Cognitive Psychology*, *3*, 647–698.

Ellis, A. W. (1988). Normal writing processes and peripheral acquired dysgraphias. *Language and Cognitive Processes*, *3*, 99–127.

Ellis, A. W., Flude, B., & Young, A. (1987). "Neglect dyslexia" and the early visual processing of letters in words and nonwords. *Cognitive Neuropsychology*, *4*, 439–464.

Ellis, A. W., Flude, B., & Young, A. (1987). "Afferent dysgraphia" in a patient and in normal subjects. *Cognitive Neuropsychology*, *4*, 465–486.

Fodor (1983). *The modularity of mind*. Cambridge, Mass.: M.I.T. Press.

Friedrich, F. J., Walker, J. A., & Posner, M. I. (1985). Effects of parietal lesions on visual matching: Implications for reading errors. *Cognitive Neuropsychology*, *2*, 253–264.

Goodglass, H. & Kaplan, E. (1972). *The Boston Diagnostic Aphasia Examination*. Philadelphia, Penn.: Lea & Febiger.

Goodman, R. & Caramazza, A. (1986). *The Johns Hopkins Dyslexia Battery*. Baltimore, Maryland: The Johns Hopkins University.

Gordon, B. (1985). Subjective frequency and the lexical decision latency function: Implications for mechanisms of lexical access. *Journal of Memory and Language*, *24*, 631–645.

Heilman, K. M., Bowers, D., Valenstein, E., & Watson, R. T. (1985). Hemispace and hemispatial neglect. In M. Jeannerod (Ed.), *Neurophysiological and neuropsychological aspects of spatial neglect*. North Holland: Elsevier Science Publishers.

Hildreth, E. C. & Ullman, S. (1989). The computational study of vision. In M. I. Posner (Ed.), *Foundations of cognitive science*. Cambridge, Mass.: M.I.T. Press.

Hillis, A. E. & Caramazza, A. (1989). The graphemic buffer and attentional mechanisms. *Brain and Language*, *36*, 208–235.

Hillis, A. E. & Caramazza, A. (1990). The effects of attentional deficits on reading and spelling. In A. Caramazza (Ed.), *Cognitive neuropsychology and neurolinguistics: Advances in models of language processing and impairment*. Hillsdale, N.J.: Lawrence Erlbaum Associates Inc.

Jeannerod, M. (Ed.) (1987). *Neuropsychological and physiological aspects of spatial neglect*. New York: Elsevier Science Publishers, 69–86.

Kinsbourne, M. (1970). A model for the mechanism of unilateral neglect of space. *Transactions of the American Neurological Association*, *95*, 143.

Kinsbourne, M. & Warrington, E. (1962). A variety of reading disability associated with right hemisphere lesions. *Journal of Neurology, Neurosurgery, and Psychiatry*, *25*, 334–339.

Kosslyn, S. M., Flynn, R. A., Amsterdam, J. B., & Wang, G. (1990). Components of high-level vision: A cognitive neuroscience analysis and accounts of neurological syndromes. *Cognition*, *34*, 203–277.

Marr, D. (1982). *Vision*. New York: W. H. Freeman & Co.

Marr, D. & Nishihara, H. K. (1978). Representation and recognition of the spatial organisation of three-dimensional shapes. *Proceedings of the Royal Society of London*, *B200*, 269–294.

McClelland, J. L. & Rumelhart, D. W. (1981). An interactive activation model of context effects in letter perception: Part I. An account of basic findings. *Psychological Review*, *88*, 375–407.

Miceli, G. & Caramazza, A. (1988). Dissociation of inflectional and derivational morphology. *Brain and Language*, *35*, 24–65.

Monk, A. F. (1985). Co-ordinate systems in visual word recognition. *Quarterly Journal of Experimental Psychology*, *37(A)*, 613–625.

Morton, J. (1969). The interaction of information in word recognition. *Psychological Review*, *76*, 165–178.

O'Reagan, J. K. & Lévy-Schoen, A. (1987). Eye-movement strategy and tactics in word recognition and reading. In M. Coltheart (Ed.), *Attention and performance XIII: The psychology of reading*. Hillsdale, N.J.: Lawrence Erlbaum Associates Inc.

O'Reagan, J. K., Lévy-Schoen, A., Pynte, J., & Brugaillère, B. (1984). Convenient fixation location within isolated words of different length and structure. *Journal of Experimental Psychology: Human Perception and Performance*, *9*, 912–922.

Pashler, H. & Badgio, P. C. (1987). Attentional issues in the identification of alphanumeric characters. In M. Coltheart (Ed.), *Attention and performance XIII: The psychology of reading*. Hillsdale, N.J.: Lawrence Erlbaum Associates Inc.

Patterson, K. & Wilson, B. (1990). A ROSE is a ROSE or a NOSE: A deficit in initial letter identification. *Cognitive Neuropsychology*, *7*, 447–477.

Posner, M. I., Cohen, Y., & Rafal, R. D. (1982). Neural systems control of spatial orienting. *Philosophical Transactions of the Royal Society, London*, *298B*, 60–70.

Rapp, B. & Caramazza, A. (1991). Spatially determined deficits in letter and word processing. *Cognitive Neuropsychology*, this issue (Part 2).

Riddoch, M. J. & Humphreys, G. W. (1987). Perceptual and action systems in unilateral visual neglect. In M. Jeannerod (Ed.), *Neuropsychological and physiological aspects of spatial neglect*. New York: Elsevier Science Publishers, 151–181.

Riddoch, M. J., Humphreys, G. W., Cleton, P., & Fery, P. (1990). Interaction of attentional and lexical processes in neglect dyslexia. *Cognitive Neuropsychology*, *7*, 479–517.

Seymour, P. H. K. (1979). *Human visual cognition*. West Drayton: Collier Macmillan.

Siéroff, E., Pollatsek, A., & Posner, M. I. (1988). Recognition of visual letter strings following injury to the posterior visual spatial attentional system. *Cognitive Neuropsychology*, *5*, 427–450.

Shallice, T. (1988). *From neuropsychology to mental structure*. Cambridge: Cambridge University Press.

Taft, M. (1985). The decoding of words in lexical access: A review of the morphological approach. In D. Besner, T. G. Waller, & G. E. MacKinnon (Eds.), *Reading research: Advances in theory and practice, Vol. 5*. London: Academic Press.

Treisman, A. (1988). Features and objects: The fourteenth Bartlett Memorial Lecture. *Quarterly Journal of Experimental Psychology*, *40A*, 201–237.

Treisman, A. & Gelade, G. (1980). A feature-integration theory of attention. *Cognition and Psychology*, *12*, 97–136.

Venezky, R. L. (1970). *The structure of English orthography*. The Hague: Mouton.

Warrington, E. (1991). Right neglect dyslexia: A single case study. *Cognitive Neuropsychology*, this issue (Part 2).

Warrington, E. K. & Zangwill, O. L. (1957). A study of dyslexia. *Journal of Neurology, Neurosurgery, and Psychiatry*, *20*, 208–215.

Weschler, D. (1972). *The Weschler Memory Scale*. New York: The Psychological Corp.

Young, A. W., Newcombe, F., & Ellis, A. W. (1991). Different impairments contribute to neglect dyslexia. *Cognitive Neuropsychology*, this issue (Part 2).

REFERENCE NOTES

1. Brunn, J. L. & Farah, M. J. (1988). *The role of spatial attention in word reading: Further evidence from neglect patients*. Paper presented at the 26th Annual Meeting of the Academy of Aphasia; Montreal.
2. Mozer, M. C. & Behrmann, M. (1989). *On the interaction of selective attention and lexical knowledge: A connectionist account of neglect dyslexia*. Unpublished manuscript. Department of Computer Science, University of Colorado at Boulder.

APPENDIX A

NG's Direct Copying

COGNITIVE NEUROPSYCHOLOGY, 1990, 7 (5/6) 447–477

A ROSE is a ROSE or a NOSE: A Deficit in Initial Letter Identification

Karalyn Patterson
Medical Research Council, Cambridge, U.K.
Barbara Wilson
University of Southampton, Southampton, U.K.

We describe the letter and word identification performance of a patient with a posterior left-hemisphere lesion, a right homonymous hemianopia, and unimpaired performance on tests for visuo-spatial neglect. His frequent errors in single word reading were almost all of the variety suggested by the title, i.e. *rose* → "nose". The likelihood of his correctly identifying a word was significantly affected by lexical constraints on the initial letter, with words like *rose* (*_ose* can be many different words) yielding lower performance than words with a unique first letter (*_oap* can only be *soap*). The patient also made errors in identifying single isolated letters, and was particularly likely to misidentify the initial character in random strings of letters. By striking contrast, he identified letters in positions 2-N of words or strings with good accuracy. A variety of reading tasks and stimulus types were employed in an attempt to characterise and understand this pattern of performance.

INTRODUCTION

This is a case study of a patient with a highly specific peripheral reading disorder. Cases of this sort reflect on mechanisms of letter perception and identification, and on how these processes operate in word recognition.

Requests for reprints should be addressed to K. E. Patterson, M.R.C. Applied Psychology Unit, 15 Chaucer Road, Cambridge CB2 2EF, U.K.

We are grateful to Dr. John Wade (Charing Cross Hospital, London) for providing neurological details regarding TB. We also thank Max Coltheart, John Duncan, Andrew Ellis, Janice Kay, John Morton, and Peter van Sommers for engaging in many helpful discussions, and Alfonso Caramazza and two anonymous referees for providing thorough and insightful reviews of the original manuscript.

A preliminary version of this paper was presented to a meeting of the Experimental Psychology Society, London, January 1988.

They are also germane to a major question in psychology and neuropsychology, concerning the separability of cognitive processes that share some components. Reading is a linguistic task but it is also a visual one; in its early, visual stages, we would expect the involvement of brain modules utilised in other visual tasks. The extent to which deficits early in the reading process are either restricted to reading or apply also to other tasks requiring visual processing and attention will therefore be informative with respect to the organisation of brain modules.

It is clear that unilateral neglect can be a pervasive phenomenon, affecting reading as well as other sorts of visual tasks (Kinsbourne & Warrington, 1962). Ellis, Flude, and Young (1987) presented a thorough case study of such neglect dyslexia: VB, a patient with a right-hemisphere lesion (probably parieto-occipital), was very likely to misidentify initial letters of written words, for example reading RIVER as "liver" and UPGRADE as "parade". Although Ellis et al. appropriately interpreted VB's reading deficit in the context of her more general left-sided neglect, it is now clear that this likely association is not a necessary one. Costello and Warrington's (1987) paper entitled *The dissociation of visuospatial neglect and neglect dyslexia* is a case study of a patient, JOH, with a large, mainly left parieto-occipital lesion that also extended across the corpus callosum into the right hemisphere. JOH showed a right-sided impairment in tasks typically used to assess unilateral visual neglect such as line bisection and copying of drawings, but a left-sided neglect dyslexia; thus he made reading errors of predominantly the same type as those described by Ellis et al. (1987), e.g. LEAST → "beast". Even more recently, Katz and Sevush (1989) have presented two patients with exclusively left-hemisphere lesions whose reading errors also clustered mainly at the beginnings of printed words. Katz and Sevush coined the term "positional dyslexia" to describe this pattern.

TB, the case presented here, showed a particularly dramatic form of initial letter deficit in reading. As suggested by the title of the paper, TB's responses when asked to name a written word like ROSE were almost exclusively of two types: correct responses, and words differing from the target by the initial letter. By testing TB on a variety of reading tasks and stimulus types, we hoped to advance our understanding of this pattern of peripheral dyslexia and its implications for the processes of letter and word recognition.

CASE REPORT

TB, a right-handed man whose main job prior to retirement had been as a courier for the Royal Air Force, suffered a left-hemisphere C.V.A. in 1985 at the age of 70, following a history of hypertension and myocardial infarction. In 1978 he had also sustained ischaemic macular damage to the left eye for which he retains only light-dark vision.

A C.T.-scan in 1987 indicated an infarct in the territory of the left posterior cerebral artery, plus infarcts in the left thalamus and putamen. A neurological examination at the same time indicated a right homonymous hemianopia (RHH). Sensory examination was normal, and there was no facial or motor weakness, but reflexes were brisker on the right than the left side.

At the time of the patient's C.V.A., medical notes report a rapidly recovering expressive dysphasia with a Broca pattern. However, a speech therapist's report accompanying TB's referral to one of the authors (BW) described him as showing good verbal comprehension even of complex tasks, fluent expressive language with a wide range of grammatical constructions, and only occasional word-finding difficulty. There was no evidence of marked dysphasia (Broca's or otherwise) in any tests or interactions with the patient during this study, and good language skills are confirmed by TB's W.A.I.S. performance: a verbal I.Q. of 112, a performance I.Q. of 90, and a full-scale I.Q. of 103. The only sub-test yielding a substantially subnormal scaled score (= 5) was the digit symbol. TB's digit span was 7 forwards and 4 backwards. He did show mild word-finding difficulties in object or picture naming, scoring 14/15 in naming from description and 12/15 in object naming (both tests from Coughlan & Warrington, 1978). Further tests of naming with pictures from the "Cambridge set" (Patterson, Purell, & Morton, 1983) yielded similar levels of performance, with a majority of circumlocutory errors, e.g. a picture of a hose → "a gardening thing"; a picture of a jug → "kitchen thing, boiling milk or water or cold things only".

Visual Processing

It is necessary to rule out the possibility that TB's reading impairment was simply attributable to a failure to see the reading materials adequately. TB's combination of RHH and macular damage in the left eye means that he relies on the nasal field of his right eye to see. Acuity in that field for that eye is, however, good (6/9), and certainly sufficient to support letter discrimination and recognition; indeed, as we show later, TB rarely misidentified letters beyond about the second letter position in a word. Asked to trace visually presented letters with a pencil, he did so a little slowly but quite accurately, suggesting that he had no difficulty perceiving their visual form. Furthermore, a posterior left-hemisphere lesion and resulting RHH would, if anything, predict visual problems at the right-hand end of a horizontally printed word (see for example Siéroff, Pollatsek, & Posner, 1988). It therefore seems implausible that either of TB's visual impairments could account for his pattern of reading performance.

Visuo-spatial Processing

TB showed no significant unilateral neglect on clinical tests designed to detect this phenomenon (Wilson, Cockburn, & Halligan, 1987). (1) Although TB's copying of drawings was slow and unskilled in execution (see Fig. 1 for some examples), these certainly show no neglect of or reduced accuracy on the left side of the drawing. (2) In line cancellation, TB missed out no items anywhere in the display. (3) In line bisection, his performance was just within the range of normal control subjects reported by Wilson et al. (1987). He was somewhat inaccurate in line bisection; however the majority of his errors, and all of the ones that approach the limits of normal performance, represent errors to the left of true centre. If anything, then, TB showed a nonsignificant trend towards right-sided neglect, consistent with his left-hemisphere lesion but not with his left-sided reading errors.

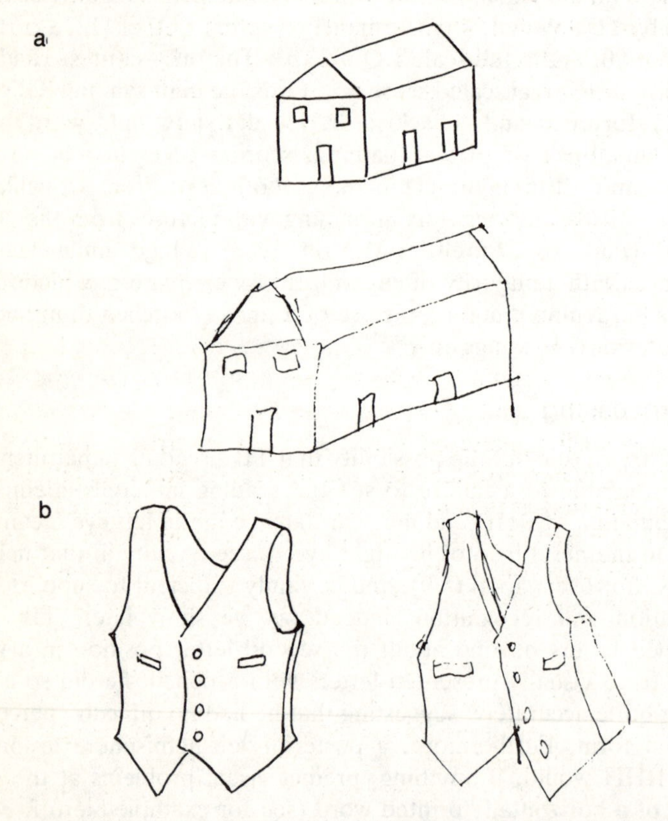

FIG. 1 (a) TB's copy (underneath) of a drawing of a house. (b) TB's copy (to the right) of a drawing of a waistcoat.

In TB's text reading, there was no hint of the pattern of performance associated with "florid" neglect. He was asked to read aloud the paragraph used by Ellis et al. (1987) to assess the text reading of their patient, VB. Whereas VB almost invariably omitted the first few words of each line (see Fig. 2, p. 444 in Ellis et al.), TB omitted no words anywhere in the paragraph. He made one error on the first word of a line, but this error (*was* → "has; no, was") is characteristic of his usual reading errors; another example occurred in the middle of the same line (*were* → "there; no, were").

Asked to name geometrical shapes arranged in a horizontal array, TB never made errors on or failed to respond to the item(s) at the left. On a set of 24 displays consisting of all possible order permutations of 4 shapes (a square, a circle, a triangle and a star, printed on cards close together rather like the letters of a 4-letter word), TB correctly named all 4 shapes in every display. The features required to discriminate amongst 4 geometric shapes are perhaps minimal by comparison with those required to identify one of 26 letters of the alphabet; therefore TB's perfect performance on the shape-naming test does not license strong claims that his deficit was restricted to reading. It merely demonstrates that his difficulty in reading is not part of a dramatic deficit in the ability to detect and identify *any* element at the left of a horizontal display.

TB's WORD READING: GENERAL DESCRIPTION

There are a variety of ways to describe TB's pattern of performance in reading words. Two of the more arresting, because so counter-intuitive, are (a) that he was more successful at reading long words than short ones (e.g. he correctly read aloud *idiosyncrasy* but misread *sit*); and (b) that he was more successful at reading orthographically strange words than words with a common spelling pattern (correct on *yacht*, in error on *light*). Both of these apparently perverse features are, however, explicable in terms of the following criterion: if the initial letter of a word were obscured, what is the likelihood that a competent reader could guess the word's identity? For *idiosyncrasy* and *yacht*, the probability of a correct guess is very high, for *sit* and *light* it is substantially lower. And indeed, TB named *sit* as "kit" and *light* as "right".

These two responses represent TB's quintessential variety of reading error. The feature of note is not just that it is the first letter which is in error, but that the error consists of a substitution for rather than a deletion of the initial letter. Predominance of a substitution error, which therefore preserves the length of the target word, is characteristic of several of the patients with this same general pattern of reading impairment; see Riddoch, Humphreys, Cleton, & Fery (this issue) for a discussion of implications for the coding of word length. Of course, deletion of the initial letter would result in another real word for only one of the target words amongst the examples listed (*sit*). Since patients and other readers expect the letter strings that they are reading to be words (unless instructed otherwise), a crucial test of the claim that a patient does not delete initial letters requires a set of words like *sit*, *frail*, *bounce*, *scamper*, etc, all of which would still be familiar words following deletion of the first letter. Asked to read aloud 50 such words, TB produced not a single response like *frail* → "rail". His errors were of 2 types, substitutions (e.g. *fright* → "bright") and additions (e.g. *pout* → "spout") at the beginnings of words.

Patterns of performance are rarely without exception. In oral reading of 400 single-syllable words, 3–6 letters in length (many though not all of which become other real words without their first letters), TB did make initial deletion errors on 4 words. He read 274/400 or 69% of these words correctly, and his 126 errors are characterised as to type and frequency in Table 1. Two-thirds of his errors consist solely of substituting a different initial letter; 86% involve substitution or addition (or both) just at the beginning of the target word. This is one of the purest, most dramatic versions of the word-initial deficit thus far described in the literature.

One additional measure demonstrates how well TB's performance is captured by the simple description of a deficit in identifying the letter in position 1 of a string. There were 199 4-letter words in the set of 400 words

TABLE 1
A Description of TB's 126 Errors in Oral Reading of 400 Monosyllabic Words, 3–6 Letters in Length

Error Type	*Examples*	*Number*	*Percent*
Substitution on initial letter	frail → "trail" safe → "cafe"	84	67%
Addition before/ after initial letter	pout → "spout" boom → "broom"	10	8%
Substit'n of + add'n to initial letter	fall → "shall" cove → "above"	14	11%
Deletion of or del'n of + substit'n of initial letter	pear → "ear" shear → "rear"	4	3%
Other (typically errors of initial letter and also elsewhere in word)	haste → "vast" purse → "horse" yearn → "earth"	14	11%
Total		126	100%

mentioned earlier. We examined TB's responses to these, and asked what proportion of responses reflect the correct letter in the correct position (counting from right to left, so that an error like *fall* → "shall" would yield correct entries for positions 4, 3, and 2 rather than incorrect entries for all positions). Table 2 shows the dramatic results of this analysis for the 199 words, as well as for a much smaller number of orthographically regular 4-letter nonwords (e.g. *neen*, *tink*, *plen*).

TABLE 2
Proportion of TB's Reading Responses Reflecting Correct Letter in Correct Position in 4-letter Words and Nonwords (Counting from Right to Left)

		Position in String			
	No.	*1*	*2*	*3*	*4*
Words	(199)	0.68	0.98	0.97	0.98
Nonwords	(19)	0.47	1.00	1.00	0.94

Finally, as we embark on the more detailed description of TB's reading, it should be emphasised that his deficit in word identification is specific to visually presented words. A set of 70 words (whose main characteristic is that each could be made into a variety of other words by a letter substitution on the initial letter—e.g. *brown* has the orthographic neighbours *crown*, *drown*, *frown*, and *grown*) was presented to TB on 2 different occasions, once printed in lower-case letters and once spelled aloud by their letter names. He identified only 44/70 (63%) of the words correctly from their written form, but 68/70 (97%) of the words from their spoken letter names. Identifying orally spelled words is exceptionally difficult for most Broca's dysphasics (Goodglass & Kaplan, 1983), and is certainly harder (for most normal readers) than identifying printed words. The fact that TB was substantially better at the harder of these tasks emphasises both (a) the extent to which he had recovered from his reported dysphasia and (b) the specificity of his deficit in visual word recognition.

LEXICAL CONSTRAINTS

The previous section suggested that TB correctly identified *idiosyncrasy* and *yacht* but not *sit* or *light* because of a single factor, namely the likelihood that one could guess the word's identity without accurate information about the word's initial letter. Guessing in this sense does not necessarily mean the employment of a conscious guessing strategy, but rather that lexical knowledge imposes constraints which will assist word identification when the identity of the second letter largely specifies the identity of letter 1. If this is correct, then in fact it should not be necessary to resort to words as long as *idiosyncrasy* or as orthographically unusual as *yacht* in order to boost TB's word identification above the level of 69% correct just reported for 3–6 letter words. It should only be necessary to select words which have no orthographic neighbours identical in all but initial letter. Compare the words *patch* and *perch*. They are of identical length and appear to have rather similar orthographic structure; but whereas *patch* has a number of orthographic neighbours with the same word "body" (Patterson & Morton, 1985) or "rime" (Treiman, 1986; Treiman & Chafetz, 1987)—that is, everything following the initial consonant (or consonant cluster) of a monosyllable—*perch* is a unique exemplar of its word body. The *p* of *perch* cannot be changed to another letter and result in a real English word. We therefore predicted that TB would be more successful at identifying words like *perch* than words like *patch*.

To test this prediction, we selected 40 words at each of 3 levels of neighbourliness defined on word bodies:

1. "Many body" words, like *patch*, share their bodies with 4 or more other words (in this case, counting only single initial consonant replacements—i.e. ignoring words like *scratch*—there are 6 neighbours: *batch*, *catch*, *hatch*, *latch*, *match*, *watch*).
2. "Few body" words, like *porch*, share their bodies with only one or 2 other words (*porch* has 2 neighbours, *torch* and *scorch*, if consonant clusters are included).
3. "One body" words, like *perch*, have unshared bodies.

The 3 sets were well matched for word length, all words being of 4 or 5 letters. It was difficult to match the sets exactly for frequency because of the body constraints, and in fact the "few body" words were somewhat lower in frequency (mean = 18.2 per million, median = 7; Kučera & Francis, 1967) than the other 2 sets. However these 2 were sufficiently close in frequency ("many": mean = 67.4, median = 18; "one": mean = 60.5, median = 21) that this variable could not plausibly account for any observed difference in performance.

One additional set of 40 words was included in this test. If, as predicted, "many body" words engendered the most difficulty for TB, we wanted to be certain that this was the result of unpredictability of initial letter within a substantial body neighbourhood, not something in the sequences of letters per se. Therefore each "many body" word was chosen such that there exists another longer word in which the critical word is embedded at the end. For example, the embedding words for *patch*, *real*, and *mane* were *dispatch*, *cereal*, and *humane*.

These 160 words, printed one to a card in lower-case letters, were presented in random order to TB for self-paced reading aloud. TB sometimes gave an initial wrong response followed by a self-correction. As none of the major effects in this or subsequent tests are altered by considering self-corrections, only scores based on TB's first response to each stimulus item will be reported.

Results are displayed in the top section of Table 3. The difference between "one" and "many" words is significant (χ^2, 1 d.f. = 6.3, $P = 0.01$); a chi-squared test based on all three conditions also yields a significant value, but the two-way comparison between "one" and "many" seems more justifiable because of frequency matching. The fact that "few" performance was numerically closer to "many" than to "one" suggests that whether a word has neighbours is more critical than the size of the neighbourhood. Table 3 also confirms that TB's relatively poor performance on "many body" words requires their initial letters to occur at the beginning of the presented string. His success in naming the longer words embedding the "many body" items was comparable to his performance on the "one body" words.

The next section examines TB's single letter identification, and demonstrates (amongst other things) a significant superiority for upper-case over lower-case letters. While still on the subject of word reading, therefore, we note that the same upper-case advantage applies to words. This is to be expected, because TB's word reading deficit arises from a letter identification deficit. Several months after the experiment on lexical constraint just reported, TB was re-tested on reading just the "one" and "many" body words, this time printed in upper-case letters. As shown in the lower section of Table 3, he made no errors on upper-case words with unique bodies. His six errors on upper-case "many" words were all of the ROSE → "nose" variety.

TABLE 3
Lexical Constraints on Accuracy of Oral Reading: TB's Proportion of Correctly Named Words of Various Types

Word Type	*(No.)*	*Example*	*Proportion Correct*
Words in Lower Case			
"One" body	(40)	soap	0.85
"Few" body	(40)	deaf	0.68
"Many" body	(40)	real	0.60
Embedding	(40)	cereal	0.83
Words in Upper Case			
"One" body	(40)	SOAP	1.00
"Many" body	(40)	REAL	0.85

SINGLE LETTER IDENTIFICATION

On two different testing sessions separated by about a fortnight, TB was asked to name the 26 letters of the alphabet, presented individually in random order, 4 times with upper-case letters and 4 with lower-case in each session. To explain this apparent overkill, we should note that we originally wondered whether size might affect TB's success in recognising letters and therefore tested him with letter sizes ranging from normal type up to large hand-printed letters about 6mm. in height. As size had absolutely no effect, his performance (shown in section 1 of Table 4) is averaged over the 8 tests within each case. TB is very poor at naming single lower-case letters, and better but by no means perfect with upper-case letters.

We have nothing insightful to say on the subject of the case difference, except to note that an advantage for upper-case letters appears to be a frequent feature in patients with letter identification deficits. For example, three of the four letter-by-letter readers (pure alexics) studied by Patterson & Kay (1982) made errors in the task of naming individual letters, and all three showed worse performance with lower- than with upper-case letters. We are primarily interested in TB's lower-case performance: all of the reading tasks that we gave him employed lower-case letters on the grounds that typical reading material appears mainly in lower case.

TABLE 4
(a) Single Letter Identification[a] (Naming)
(b) Probability of Correct Identification (Naming)

(a)

	Mean No. Correct/26	*(s.d.)*	*Proportion Correct*
Upper case	20.1	(1.96)	0.77
Lower case	15.0	(2.62)	0.58

(b)

Letter Position	*1*	*2*	*3*	*4*	*5*
Single letter[b]	0.62	0.62	0.65	0.73	0.54
Letter string[c]	0.26	0.91	0.98	0.97	0.92

[a]Entire alphabet tested (in random order) eight times each in upper and lower case.

[b]Single lower-case letter in one position of an array of five boxes (every letter of the alphabet tested in every position).

[c]Lower-case letters in the various positions of random letter strings (lengths 3–5), N = 43 strings.

TB's poor naming of single letters reflects a deficit in letter identification, not letter naming. This claim is substantiated by a test of matching 32 pairs of upper- and lower-case letters, one letter printed above the other, where TB was asked to say "yes" to letter pairs like G-g and "no" to pairs like G-q. He was correct on 26/32 pairs (0.81). This is precisely the level of performance to be expected if TB made an informed and correct match on those trials where he was able to identify the lower-case letter (which should, according to our letter naming data, be about 19/32) and guessed on the remaining trials (which should yield correct performance on half of these, about 6 or 7 out of 13).

Are particular letters either specially difficult or specially easy for TB to identify? Only one lower-case letter, *a*, was correctly named on all 8 presentations; no letter was always wrong, though *b* yielded only one correct response and 4 letters (*l*, *n*, *p*, *y*) each gave rise to only 2/8 correct responses.

When reading words or text, TB's letter identification errors are significantly constrained by his lexical knowledge and/or the context; what about errors in identifying single letters, where no such constraints exist? For instance, the letter-by-letter readers in Patterson and Kay's (1982) study showed strong visual similarity effects: the majority of their letter confusions occurred within rather than across visually similar clusters such as the ascenders, the descenders, the letters composed of a "loop on a stick" (b, d, p, g, q), and the "little roundish letters" (a, o, c, e). Furthermore, the same sorts of confusions characterise the errors of normal subjects asked to identify letters either at a distance or in eccentric vision (Bouma, 1971). TB's performance also follows this pattern, but rather weakly. His only highly consistent error was a unidirectional confusion between the visually similar letters *n* and *u*: he was correct on *n* only twice, and all 6 misidentifications were *n* → "u". He named *u* correctly 7/8 times, and called it "c" once. No specific error other than *n* → "u" occurred more than twice; a number of the 10 twice-occurring confusions seem to have a major component of visual similarity (e.g. *m* → "n", *p* → "d", *g* → "q"), but others less so (*b* → "t"); and no clear pattern whatsoever seems to characterise the 57 singly occurring confusions. Visual similarity also played a moderate role in the characterisation of letter confusions by JM and LS, the "positional" dyslexic patients described by Katz and Sevush (1989).

Does it matter where in a visual frame a single letter to be identified is positioned? This question was assessed in a further test of lower-case letter naming. On each of a set of 26 × 5 = 130 stimulus cards, a row of 5 square boxes was drawn in a horizontal array; on each card, one lower-case letter was printed in one of the 5 boxes. Every letter of the alphabet occurred once in each position. TB was given the 130 cards in randomised order and asked to name the single letter on each card. His performance is shown in section 2 of Table 4 as a function of the position occupied by the single letter. Spatial position within a frame has no significant impact on TB's letter report (χ^2, 4 d.f. = 2.18, $P = 0.7$). Over all positions, his proportion correct was 0.63, a figure comparable to the 0.58 reported earlier for individual letter identification without the array of boxes.

By contrast with the absence of an effect of spatial position on single letter identification, the position of a letter within a random letter string to be identified has massive consequences for TB's performance. Section 3 of Table 4 shows the proportion of correct letter identifications per position in the string when he was asked to name all of the letters in random strings (mainly 4 letters in length but including a few 3- and 5-letter strings). All of the errors on letters in position 1 were misidentifications; there were no omissions.

TB's severely impaired performance in single letter identification clearly has important implications for the interpretation of his reading. If his letter identification deficit in words is largely restricted to the initial position, and if a single letter can be considered to occupy the initial position (of some hypothetical string), then perhaps we should predict comparable levels of success in identifying single letters and the initial letters of strings. But what sort of strings? TB's ability to identify a lower-case letter in isolation (0.58–0.63) is at about the same level as his ability to identify the initial letter of a lower-case string with familiar orthographic structure but without much help from lexical constraint, i.e. in words with "many" bodies (0.60). As lexical constraints increase, his level of performance increases (0.85 for "one" body words); but of equal importance, as lexical and orthographic constraints decrease, TB's initial letter performance actually dips below his single letter identification (0.26 for random letter strings). This is the first indication that it might be useful to consider TB's reading deficit in terms of the phenomenon of "attentional" dyslexia investigated by Shallice and Warrington (1977).

TB: ATTENTIONAL DYSLEXIA?

Two patients with left parietal lesions studied by Shallice and Warrington (1977) could identify single items (whether letters, words, or line drawings of objects) essentially without error but began to make errors as soon as other elements of the same type were introduced into the display. In one particular demonstration of this phenomenon, Shallice and Warrington asked the patients to name a single red letter presented in one of three conditions: on its own, or flanked either side by two black numbers, or flanked either side by two black letters. The first two conditions (single letters and number flanking) gave rise to good and equivalent letter identification, but the third condition caused a significant drop in performance. There was a tendency for errors to be intrusions from the sets of flanking letters. Katz and Sevush (1989) also report that letter naming errors of their "positional" dyslexic patient JM, at least in one test, tended to be imports from elsewhere in the string.

It is clear that TB does not display a global version of the attentional disorder described by Shallice and Warrington. As reported earlier, he made no errors when naming horizontal displays of geometric shapes. More importantly, his ability to identify letters appearing in a position other than the first of a string, far from being worse than identification of a single letter, is substantially better! Since TB identifies only 58% of individually presented lower-case letters, his consistently >90% identification of letters in positions 2-N of an array (bottom of Table 4) seems to present the exact opposite of the phenomenon described by Shallice and Warrington (1977). Having ruled out general attentional dyslexia, however, we must still ask whether TB displays position-specific attentional dyslexia, as suggested by the fact that his recognition of a single letter, while substantially worse than identification of letters in positions 2-N of a random letter string, is better than identification of the letter in position 1. In other words, does the presence of other similar but uninformative elements in the field exacerbate the initial-letter deficit? If so, then Shallice & Warrington's analysis of attentional dyslexia provides two predictions: (1) TB should be better at naming the first letter of a random string if the right-flanking characters are numbers rather than other letters; (2) his errors in naming initial letters right-flanked by other letters should, at a significantly greater than chance level, reflect the identity of one of the flanking letters.

Three sets of 26 4-character strings were created; within each set, one string began with each of the 26 letters in the alphabet. One set consisted of familiar 4-letter words (e.g. *aura*, *bask*, *chin*, *drab*, *east*); the second set consisted of random letter strings (e.g. *aoya*, *btqk*, *cmsn*, *dzlb*, *eoht*); in the third set, the initial and final characters were letters but the middle two elements were numbers (e.g. *a62a*, *b74k*, *c93n*, *d48b*, *e57t*). All letters were lower case. Note that, in the examples given, the corresponding strings across sets (e.g., *bask*, *btqk*, *b74k*) not only begin with the same letter but also end with the same letter: this was true for the entire sets. TB was presented with all 78 strings (each printed on a card) twice, within the same session but separated by more than an hour filled with other tasks. The first time, he was asked to go through the cards naming the last letter of each string; the second time, he went through attempting to name the first letter of each string. As well as recording TB's accuracy on the different types of strings, in order to obtain a rough estimate of his speed we presented blocks of 8 or 9 cards from one set (2 blocks of 9 plus one of 8

= 26 items) and measured with a stop watch the time required for TB to complete a block. The order of blocks of the various types was randomised.

Table 5 shows, for the initial and final letters of each of the three types of string, the proportion of letters named correctly, the mean time per block (in seconds) and the range of times over the three blocks of each type. The composition of the strings means that, within either initial or final letter identification, exactly the same responses were required of TB in each set type; therefore any differences between types in accuracy or speed should be due to the nature of the other elements in the string. Looking first at initial letter performance, the main contrast for which the experiment was designed yields a positive result: TB named twice as many initial letters correctly when these were right flanked by numbers than when they were right flanked by other (random) lower-case letters (χ^2, 1 d.f. = 4.95, $P = 0.02$). He was also substantially slower with letter than with number flanking. Although TB was not informed that some of the blocks consisted of familiar words, his performance (as well as a comment from him during testing) indicated that this fact did not escape him: his accuracy in naming *g*, *q*, *w* etc. was higher in *gait*, *quip*, *woof* than in *g36t*, *q63p*, *w35f*, though there was no corresponding advantage in speed.

Turning to final letter performance, it is clear that there were no significant effects of string type on either accuracy or speed. By comparison with final letter identification in the data of Table 2 and the bottom section of Table 4, TB's performance on final letters in the present task yields a slightly lower estimate. Although this difference is small, it raises the possibility that there may be a detrimental effect on the first element to which TB attends (which is typically, of course, the leftmost element of an array).

Finally, although the comparison between initial and final letters is not perfectly balanced (because the initial letters did but the final letters did not include all 26 letters of the alphabet), TB was clearly more successful

TABLE 5
Accuracy (Proportion Correct) and Speed (Mean and Range, in Seconds, Over Three Blocks of Each Type) for Naming the Initial or the Final Letter in Three String Types

	Initial			*Final*		
String Type	*Propor'n Correct*	*$\bar{X}$ Time/ Block(s)*	*Range of Times*	*Propor'n Correct*	*$\bar{X}$ Time/ Block(s)*	*Range of Times*
bask	0.81	44.0	30–52	0.88	23.3	19–26
b74k	0.62	42.0	30–59	0.88	24.0	21–28
btqk	0.31	70.7	49–94	0.85	26.0	23–28

when asked to name final than initial letters. An initial/final difference in accuracy was apparent for string types other than familiar words; a difference in speed was present for all string types. In fact, there was no overlap in the distributions of times to name blocks of initial and final letters.

The first of the two predictions from the characterisation of TB as a position-specific attentional dyslexic has received clear support from this flanking experiment. The second prediction, however, does not: virtually none of TB's letter naming errors in this experiment were intrusions from other positions in the string. As in the error analysis for single letter naming, TB's errors in reporting the first letter of a random letter string show a moderate tendency towards visual similarity with the target letter (e.g. *o* → "c"; *j* → "g"). Sometimes the errors also seem to have a perseverative component: in the second block of random letter strings, TB named the first letter of 4/9 strings as "r", though no string in the block began with an *r* and only one string in the block had an *r* anywhere in it.

The results of this experiment confirm that the presence of other letters in the visual field affect TB's initial letter recognition. Not only is first letter recognition boosted if subsequent letters offer lexical constraints on its identity; it deteriorates if other letters are present without offering such clues. This effect in TB differs from the attentional dyslexia described by Shallice and Warrington (1977) both in its restriction to the initial position of a string and in its precise character. The explanation offered by Shallice and Warrington for their cases (see also Shallice, 1988) suggests a selection deficit in the transmission from a spatially parallel perceptual classification system to a more serial interpretative system. Thus the identity of a different element from the same category present in the field is likely to get selected. TB, on the other hand, seems able to keep the identities of the various elements "in their places", so that right-flanking elements do not get erroneously selected when he attempts to identify the initial letter.

MORE ON SELECTION

All of the results thus far reflect TB's efforts to identify which letter he is looking at, in circumstances where he knows (i.e. is instructed) that the element to be identified is a letter. Does he always know that a letter is a letter? A test designed to provide evidence on this question should also be revealing about two other aspects of TB's deficit. First of all, is his impairment mainly restricted to letters or does it also afflict the characters most similar to letters, namely numbers? Secondly, just how position-specific is TB's deficit? Is it the first position in an array of elements that is vulnerable or the first letter?

Six-character sequences were constructed consisting of a mixture of digits and lower-case letters. There were 45 sequences in all, but the 36 of interest contained letters and numbers in alternation, half beginning with a number and half with a letter. The remaining sequences, which had either 2 numbers and 4 letters or the reverse in completely random order, were included only to prevent TB from expecting 3 of each character type in alternation. Only 8 items from each category were used across all sequences: the numbers 0 and 1 were excluded because they are confusable with the letters *o* and *l*, which were also excluded; all letters with descenders were excluded to remove this as a potential clue to category (Arabic numerals do not have descenders). With only eight digits available (2–9), and a reduced subset of letters available, it seemed simplest to make the number of stimulus and response alternatives equivalent for the 2 categories. Furthermore, the letters and numbers were hand printed on cards in roughly the same size so that size would not provide a clue to category. The 45 sequences were presented, in random order, to TB on 2 occasions; once he was asked to name the numbers and once to name the letters. He was only instructed that each sequence contained some letters and some numbers.

Table 6 shows, for the 36 alternating arrays (18 beginning with a letter, 18 with a number), the proportion of correct identification of the first letter or the first number in the string as a function of whether it occupied the first or the second position in the string. Thus an array like *2s5v6a* provides an observation for number in position 1 and for letter in position 2 (though from different tests, as TB was asked in each test to name the numbers *or* the letters). It is clear from these results that TB's impairment is almost entirely position specific: a letter in position 2 of a string, even though it is the first letter in the string, is identified with the same high (though not quite perfect) level of success as letters in positions 2-N of words or letter strings. It is also clear that numbers are vulnerable in precisely the same way as letters.

TABLE 6
Proportion Correct Identification of the First Letter or First Number in Alternating Strings (e.g. 3c8n5e or a6s5n3)

	Position in String	
	1	*2*
Letters	0.50	0.94
Numbers	0.61	0.89

Finally, with regard to the first query motivating this test, there were several clear instances of failure on TB's part to classify a letter or a number as belonging to its appropriate category. On eight of the trials where TB was meant to be reporting the category with which the string began, he omitted the initial character in the string and reported only two numbers or letters. Since he essentially never omits the character at the beginning of a string that he knows to be all letters or all numbers, the omissions in the present situation presumably reflect occasions on which he had classified the initial character as belonging to the alternative, not-to-be-reported category. Only two trials where he was meant to be reporting the category represented by positions 2,4,6 gave rise to an error of commission on the character in position 1, such that he reported four rather than three numbers (both of these did occur in the session with number report). If the element in position 1 is hard to identify, it is perhaps not surprising that TB's classification system should more often err in the direction of assigning this troublesome object to the alternative category (which means that it can be ignored) than in the direction of including the element in the relevant category (which means that it must be identified)!

WHAT HELPS?

Table 6 suggests that TB can identify the first letter in a string with reasonable accuracy if it happens to be preceded by a number. Presumably that number occupies the initial and troublesome spatial position, and the first letter (in the second spatial position) can then receive adequate attention and processing just like any subsequent position. Will such a manipulation work to improve TB's word reading? That is, if one were to provide an irrelevant character just to the left of a word (say, a "many body" word like *land*) in which TB frequently misidentifies the initial letter, would this aid his word recognition? Early on in the investigation of TB's deficit, the technique of placing a thick black line just to the left of a word had been tried and shown to provide no benefit; but of course a bar would tend not to be perceived or categorised as a character, and therefore the control processes that assign squiggles to letter positions in word recognition might ignore the bar and assign the *l* of *land* to the first troublesome position.

Table 7 shows TB's reading performance on "many body" words like *land* (always in lower-case horizontal print) under 6 different conditions. These tests were conducted in a variety of sessions and with varying N/condition; however, every condition included at least 40 words with identical characteristics to the "many body" words from the lexical constraint experiment reported earlier: 4/5-letter words with bodies shared by a number of other lexical entries. Therefore results will be presented for these comparable 40 items from each condition. The first condition, simply repeating data already presented in Table 3, is unadorned presentation of the words to be named (*land*, *real*, etc.). The second, third, and fourth conditions all involved a single extra character printed just to the left of the word's first letter with no intervening space; TB was instructed to ignore the first character which, in the 3 conditions, was either a number, or an *x*, or a letter that made the word into another legitimate word. In the fifth condition, nothing was added to the word to be named but its initial letter was printed in red. (The remaining letters of each word, as well as all of the words in the other 5 conditions, were printed in black.) In the final condition, 80 many body words were formed into 40 unrelated pairs and printed on cards without a space between the 2 words (e.g. *cashland*, *grainduck*, etc.). In this condition, TB was told that each letter string consisted of 2 words and he was to name both words.

TABLE 7
TB's Performance in Reading "Many Body" Words (e.g. land) in Six Different Conditions

Condition		*No. Correct (out of 40)*	*Proportion Correct*
(1)	land	24	0.60
(2) 2	land	26	0.65
(3) x	land	31	0.78
(4) b	land	30	0.75
(5) (red l)	land	31	0.78
(6) cash	land	36	0.90

As revealed in Table 7, a digit preceding the word did not increase TB's performance relative to the baseline unadorned condition (χ^2, 1 d.f. = 0.21, $P = 0.64$). Although the next 3 conditions all gave rise to larger numbers of correct responses, none of these differences from the baseline condition quite reaches significance: chi-squared tests yield P values from 0.09 to 0.15. In conditions 2–4, TB had no substantial difficulty following the instruction to ignore the initial character. Even in the *bland* condition, only once in the 40 trials did he include the irrelevant character in his response: *flame* (which should have been read as "lame") → "flame". He occasionally dropped an extra element (e.g., *2linch* → "inch"); surprisingly, the majority of these omissions occurred in condition 2. Almost all of his other errors in conditions 2–4 were just as one would expect if the extraneous character had not been present (e.g. *xlead* → "read", *spear* → "wear", etc.).

The only condition producing performance significantly superior to the baseline was condition 6 (*land* in *cashland*) (χ^2, 1 d.f. = 9.60, $P = 0.002$). Further evidence of this contrast comes from TB's performance on the first word of each scrunched pair (*cash* in *cashland*): he correctly named only 22/40 = 0.55 of these words. All of the errors were of his typical variety. It was rather dramatic to observe TB carrying out this task. The required segmentation clearly provided no bother; he went through the cards reading *darkfold* → "mark, fold", *comedare* → "some, dare", *grainduck* → "train, duck", and so on. There was no significant tendency for the initial letter errors on the first word of the pair to be "imports" from the second word. Once again, TB is different in this regard from the attentional dyslexic patient FM (reported by Shallice & Warrington, 1977) who, when trying to report multiple word arrays, often showed position-specific cross-talk, e.g. *win fed* → "fin, fed".

How is the beneficial effect on the *l* of *land* in *cashland* to be interpreted? Amongst all of the conditions represented in Table 7, this is the only one where something precedes the *l* and that something is a thing which TB must attend to and identify. This point will receive further attention in the general discussion.

In conclusion, both highlighting the initial letter of a word by printing it in red and providing an extraneous single character to "use up" the troublesome initial position provide a nonsignificant hint of benefit. Perhaps a larger number of items would have achieved significance (scores in the *xland* and the *bland* conditions taken together just scrape into a statistically significant difference from the baseline); but the effects of these manipulations are not dramatic. The difference between an extraneous letter (conditions 3 and 4) and a number (condition 2), though not significant, is a puzzle; this inconsistency is reminiscent of results reported by Katz and Sevush (1989). Their "positional" dyslexic patient JM benefitted from an extraneous Q to the left of words to be named, but not from an extraneous X.

The fact that a character to ignore has no marked effect supports the notion that TB has no impairment in the perceptual system which notices squiggles in the visual field and assigns these to positions in an array to be analysed. Unless instructed otherwise, this system assigns the first squiggle to the first position. Instructed to do so, it is (mostly) successful in discarding the first squiggle and assigning the second one to the first position in the array of interest.

TASKS OTHER THAN ORAL REPORT

Although there has been nothing in TB's pattern of performance to suggest that his deficit in initial letter identification is in any way related to or a result of the requirement to name words or letters overtly, it nonetheless seemed appropriate to establish that the same impairment would be present no matter what task TB was asked to do with printed letter strings. A set of 84 words was constructed consisting of 28 triplets each sharing a word "body", e.g. *brown-crown-drown*, *bold-cold-fold*, *candy-dandy-handy*, etc. For the purposes of the sorting task to be described next, the 84 words contained 21 words beginning with *b*, 21 beginning with *c*, 21 beginning with *d*, and 21 beginning with some other letter. This set of words, each printed in lower-case letters on a card, was presented to TB in randomised order on 4 different occasions in the context of 4 different tasks:

1. TB was asked to name the first letter of each word.
2. TB was asked to sort the words into piles corresponding to their initial letters. It seemed unwise to label the piles visually: lower-case letter labels would offer the potential for a visual match, and upper-case letter labels might also assist TB's performance since he identifies single upper-case letters more successfully than lower-case letters. To obviate the need for visual labelling, the word set had been designed to offer four simple categories of initial letter: *b*, *c*, *d* (the second, third and fourth letters of the alphabet) and "other". TB was given some practice in assigning words to these unlabelled piles, and he had no difficulty remembering the categories.
3. TB was asked to read the 84 words aloud.
4. TB was asked not to say the words aloud but to define them. A subset of only 28 of the words (one from each body triplet) was presented for defining, for 2 reasons: (a) defining words takes longer than the other tasks; (b) unlike the rather shallow processing tasks of letter and word identification and naming, the more memorable task of defining a word might produce "cross-talk" between words with the same body. Thus if TB defined *brown* as something a royal person wears on her/his head and then subsequently encountered the word *crown*, the likelihood of his identifying *crown* might be altered (either positively *or* negatively).

Since all of these words are obviously "many body" words, we predicted that TB's performance would be poor. Since his deficit appears to reflect a stage of letter identification which precedes other processes such as computing a pronunciation or a meaning for the word, we predicted that his performance would be equivalently poor in all 4 conditions. Table 8 demonstrates that both of these predictions were correct. It may appear that defining words led to slightly lower performance than the other tasks, but recall that this is also a less secure estimate of ability because it is based on a smaller number of observations. In fact there are no statistically reliable differences between conditions. TB is good at defining words: it is just that, as in the other conditions, he clearly misidentified initial letters.

TABLE 8
Proportion of Responses Reflecting Correct Identification of the Initial Letter of a Word in Four Different Tasks[a]

Task	(No.)	Proportion Correct
Naming initial letter	(84)	0.68
Sorting by initial letter	(84)	0.68
Reading word	(84)	0.63
Defining word	(28)	0.57

[a]The words are the same in all tasks but defined words constitute only a subset of the items.

A few examples of his definitions demonstrate this point:

bark → "A piece of the roadway where vehicles stand, or open land" (clearly *park*)
fold → "If you've let somebody have something for money, you've sold it" (although we asked him only to define the word and not to say it, he sometimes neglected this instruction)
bead → "A strap for holding a dog" (clearly *lead*)
candy → "That's a rude word, I'd prefer not to say" (probably *randy*)

The fact that TB's initial letter misidentifications are as frequent when he is defining words as when he is naming either them or their initial letters confirms that anomia for words or letters cannot be responsible for his impaired performance in naming tasks.

Additional tests of TB's comprehension of printed words provide a similar picture. For example, he was presented with 84 words for a simple yes–no category judgement. Half of the items were correct category instances (e.g. "is it a tree?" *willow*); his hit rate on these was 37/42 = 0.88. Of the 42 incorrect category instances, half differed from a correct category instance in initial letter (e.g. "Is it a carpenter's tool?" *tile*; correct instance *file*), and half differed only in terminal letter (e.g. "Is it a unit of time?" *weed*; correct instance *week*). His false positive rate to the first type was 8/21 = 0.38 and to the latter type was 0/21. TB clearly has a deficit of initial letter identification that is independent of the task in aid of which he is processing the letter string.

NONSTANDARD STIMULUS OR RESPONSE CONDITIONS

In all of the tasks described thus far, the beginning of the word (or string) and the left-hand side of the visual array have been confounded. We already know that TB has no difficulty with word beginnings per se when the modality of presentation is nonvisual (i.e. in identifying words from oral spelling); but within the visual modality, it seemed useful to unconfound the left side of space and the initial letter of a word. This was accomplished with two different manipulations: vertically printed words, in which the beginning letter is no longer to the left of the subsequent letters, and mirror-reversed words, in which the beginning letter is to the right of all "subsequent" letters.

Furthermore, the beginning of the word or string has typically been confounded with the first thing to which TB was asked (explicitly or implicitly) to attend and response. As well as exploring nonstandard format of input, it seemed useful to unconfound the leftmost letter and the first letter that TB is asked to report. This was done by asking him to name random letter strings in a right-to-left order.

Right-to-left Letter Naming

Stimulus materials from an earlier experiment (reported in the section on attentional dyslexia) included 26 4-letter strings, with no orthographic or phonological structure, indeed random except for the fact that one string began with each letter of the alphabet. This earlier experiment provides data on TB's letter identification when he was asked to name just the first or just the last letter of each string. These same 26 stimuli had also been included in tests where he was asked to name all of the letters in random strings, in the normal left-to-right order. Here we asked him to name these 26 strings from right to left, yielding a total of 4 different performance measures on these stimulus items, all of which are shown in Table 9.

Requiring TB to adopt the abnormal right-to-left order of report alters his pattern of performance markedly. His success for position 4 (now first reported letter) is closely comparable to the condition where he was asked to name only the letter in position 4; and his success rate is still numerically

TABLE 9
TB's Performance on 26 Meaningless Strings of 4 Letters (aoya, btqk, etc.) in Four Different Tasks: Proportions Correct

	Position			
	1	*2*	*3*	*4*
Naming all letters				
From left to right	0.27	0.88	0.96	0.96
From right to left	0.42	0.58	0.62	0.88
Naming first letter only	0.31			
Naming last letter only				0.85

lowest for position 1; but in fact his performance was very poor in all positions other than 4. Positions 2 and 3 under these conditions yield identification rates (0.58, 0.62) identical to TB's naming of isolated letters (0.58, 0.63 from earlier experiments). Abnormal movement of attention from right to left across the string clearly changes the nature of the letter identification task for this patient. His performance under these conditions bears little resemblance, and therefore probably little relevance, to his word reading and his left-to-right letter recognition.

Reading Vertical and Mirror-reversed Words

For the first test, 25 words, 3–6 letters in length, were printed vertically in lower-case letters on cards. These words were taken from sets that TB had previously read under conditions of normal horizontal print, and they included both "one body" words like *soap* and "many body" words like *sing*. TB was given the cards in random order and asked to name the words. For the second test, 16 words, 4–5 letters in length, were printed with lower-case letraset in normal horizontal format on a plastic transparency. For presentation to TB, this transparency was simply turned over and placed on a blank white sheet; the effect of this, of course, is a left–right reversal of words (and their letters). Once again the words included both "one" (e.g. *noun*) and "many" (e.g. *dine*) body words that TB had read on previous occasions.

In both tests, TB's speed of reading was roughly timed with a stopwatch. With vertically printed words, his fastest latency was about 10secs. and to some words he required up to 60secs. to respond; with mirror reading, the fastest response was at about a minute, some were much longer and, as indicated in Table 10, TB was unable to produce a response at all to 6/16 words. Omissions, which occurred in both of these conditions, never occur when TB is asked to read normally printed words.

Although it is not clear how (or indeed whether) to interpret such slow,

TABLE 10
TB's Reading Performance with Vertically Printed and Mirror-reversed Words

Words	*(No.)*	*Correct*	*Omissions*	*Examples of Errors*
Vertical print	(25)	0.36	0.16	narrow → "warren" doubt → "douse" cook → "cock" dig → "rig"
Mirror-reversed	(16)	0.25	0.38	twice → "twine" loom → "loot" dine → "bird"

inaccurate, effortful performance, it may be worth noting that, under these conditions, first letter errors are no longer responsible for the majority of TB's reading errors. If a vertically printed word can be likened to a word composed entirely of "initial" letters (in the sense of letters appearing at the extreme left of the word), then we might expect TB to misidentify letters anywhere in a vertically printed word; as the error examples in Table 10 indicate, this was indeed the case. And if TB's deficit is most severe for the leftmost letter in a word, then we might expect his mirror-reading errors still to fall mainly at the left, which is now the end of the word; once again, Table 10 suggests that this was so, although it may not be a particularly revealing outcome. As his hugely augmented response times suggest, mirror-reversed words reduced TB to a letter-by-letter reader; and just as many letter-by-letter readers do with normally printed words, with mirror-reversed words TB tended to identify (with great effort) the first few letters of the word and then guess. This strategy will of course yield errors mainly at word ends.

In conclusion, TB's performance with nonstandard response conditions, and even more dramatically with nonstandard stimulus conditions, was markedly discrepant from that of normal subjects and even from his own performance under more normal conditions. These nonstandard conditions make reading harder for normal subjects, too, but not orders of magnitude harder. Experiments by Young and Ellis (1985) suggest that vertically printed words yield somewhat lower naming accuracy than normally horizontally printed words, and experiments by Ellis, Young, and Anderson (1988) suggest that misaligned words yield somewhat slower lexical decision latencies than does horizontal print; but the performance of normal subjects does not simply "break down" under these conditions. TB's performance did. Accordingly, we hesitate to give much weight to these results, preferring to concentrate on results where, despite his initial letter deficit, it can be argued that TB is using procedures of the normal letter and word recognition systems.

SPELLING, WRITING, AND THE END OF THE DATA

Our investigations of TB centred on reading processes, with only minor forays into other domains. One domain which should be mentioned, despite a relative paucity of data, is writing and spelling. TB's internal orthographic representations of words seemed largely intact: not only was he virtually perfect (as reported earlier) at recognising words from oral spelling, he was also highly accurate (50/53 = 0.94) at oral spelling to dictation. His only first letter error in this task was on the word "psychology", which he made two attempts to spell aloud: "C,Y,C,O,L,O,G,Y" and "S,C,Y,C,O,L,O,G,Y". Written spelling, however, is perhaps more pertinent: like oral spelling, it recruits internal (possibly abstract) orthographic representations; but like reading, written spelling also involves actual letter forms.

TB wrote with his right hand, rather slowly and awkwardly, in small cursive script that was just about legible. In written naming of 10 objects in the room, he made no errors (although he failed to cross the t's in words like curtain and watch). More interestingly, in a test where he was given 45 written word bodies (like _*ind* and _*orth*) and asked to fill in the blank to make a word, there were 8 items that yielded a discrepancy between what he wrote and what he said (he had not been asked to name the resulting words, but he always did so). On the majority of these (7/8), although what he said corresponded to a legitimate word, what he wrote did not (e.g. given _ole, he filled in the blank with L and said "mole"). These could just be seen as further examples of TB's initial letter *reading* deficit; but by contrast with his highly accurate oral spelling, these errors raise the possibility that the impairment on word beginnings in the visual/orthographic domain applies to writing as well as reading. In support of this, we briefly mention one final result: in our last testing session with TB,[1] he made a number of errors in writing 32 words to dictation. His writing was particularly hard to decipher at this stage; but errors clear enough to analyse included a few bizarre ones (even one semantic error! "boat" → *yacht*), 4 single letter substitutions at a position between 2 and N (e.g. "stout" → *shout*, "swig" → *swid*), and 5 instances of an incorrect letter in position 1 (e.g. "land" → *hand*, "boy" → *woy*).

GENERAL DISCUSSION

Consider a general framework for letter and word perception such as McClelland and Rumelhart's (1981) interactive activation model (I.A.M.). The investigation of TB was not guided by, and was certainly not intended as any test of, the I.A.M.; the model is being used here merely as a

[1]After a gap of some months, TB was tested again in February 1990. Perspicacious referees had queried a number of points, for example, the adequacy of evidence that the deficit was restricted to alphanumeric stimuli. Unfortunately, none of these queries can receive a full answer because, at this stage, TB appeared to have suffered a major deterioration in his vision. He claimed not to be able to see most of the test materials, and indeed his performance on all visual tasks was poor. He correctly identified only 7/26 = 0.27 of upper-case single letters (cf. 0.77 on previous testing), and was much more perseverative in responding (10/26 upper-case letters were named as R). Although his attempts at word reading (normal horizontal format) still suggested a major initial letter impairment, these attempts were now very slow and halting, and also produced both omissions and errors unlike any ever seen in previous testing (e.g. *limp* → "snap"; *tag* → "raw"). Sadly for both him and us, our testing sessions (which he always enjoyed) had come to an end.

coherent account to impose order on a large collection of data. Figure 2 displays (with trivial alterations) a sketch of the model taken from McClelland (1985, Fig. 1, p. 115). The I.A.M. postulates position-specific letter recognition units which both send activation to and receive activation back from word recognition units. A logical corollary of letter recognition units unique to each position is the possibility of position-specific susceptibility to neurological damage. Let us start with the simplest hypothesis: TB's only deficit is that letter recognition units at position 1 function in a disrupted or noisy fashion. First of all, on what basis could one claim that other components of the system represented in Fig. 2 are unimpaired for TB?

1. A claim for intactness of the control mechanism which assigns letters in the stimulus array to positions is supported by (a) the fact that he often misidentifies but almost never deletes initial letters, (b) the fact that initial letter misidentifications are almost never intrusions from other positions in the array, and (c) the ease with which he follows the instruction to ignore the first character in a string.

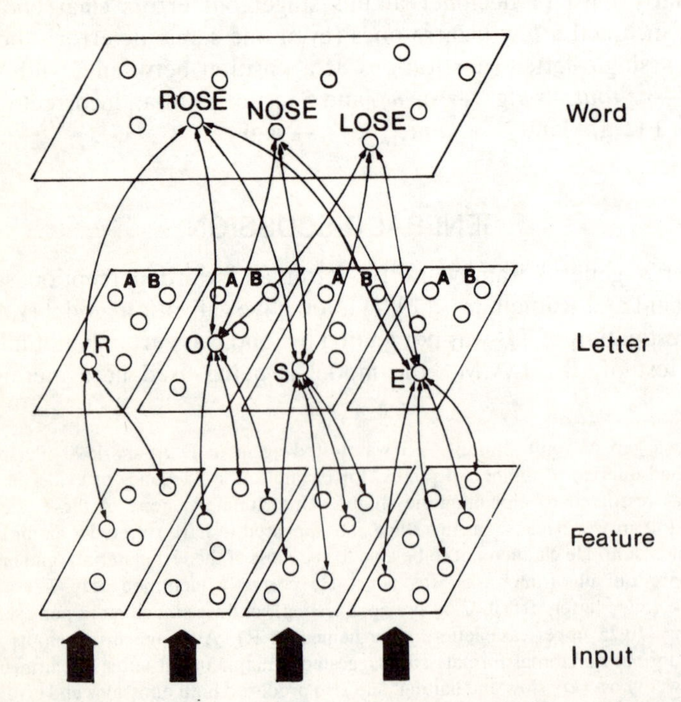

FIG. 2 A slightly modified version of Fig. 1 from McClelland (1985, p. 115) illustrating the McClelland/Rumelhart interactive activation model.

2. One can argue that both feature and letter levels for positions 2-N are in moderately good working order: TB's identification of letters in these positions of a word or string, although not perfect, was consistently good (between 0.88 and 0.98 in various tests).

3. A claim that the feature level operates reasonably well even at position 1 is at least consistent with (a) his accurate tracing of written letters and (b) the usual (though not invariable) visual similarity between a target letter and TB's misidentification of it.

4. The word level (and its feedback to the letter level) appears to be intact, although forced to rely on unreliable information about initial letters. Word-level representations account for (a) the neighbourhood effect ("many" versus "one" body words), (b) the lexicality effect (better performance on words than nonwords, and (c) the fact that the first letter in a familiar word like *chin* is identified more accurately than the first letter in a string like *c34n*. Operation of the word level might also help to explain TB's otherwise puzzling word-initial addition errors. Although the majority of his word-reading errors maintained target length, and although he performed essentially perfectly when asked to report the number of letters in a word, a certain number of his reading errors involve a word-initial addition (e.g. *tout* → either "stout" or "trout"). At the word level, it is possible that precise information about word length is no longer maintained; and representations for *stout* and *trout* are of course consistent with much of the information coming from letter-level analysis of *tout*.

5. Finally, although the I.A.M. does not go beyond the word level, TB's relatively good text reading is explicable in terms of another interactive model: the interactive compensatory reading model (Stanovich, 1980; 1984; Stanovich, West, & Feeman, 1981) describes how context can, if necessary, compensate for poor recognition skills.

What in TB's pattern of performance either requires further explication or is at odds with this account?

1. There might at first glance seem to be a paradox in the following fact: TB's identification of the first letter in a string as, say, "l" was significantly improved (a) when he was trying to name the letters in a string like *3l8j2q*, and (b) when he was trying to read the word *land* in *cashland*, but not (c) when he was trying to read the word *land* in *2land* or *xland* or *bland*. There is, however, no paradox here: in both of the facilitating cases, he was required to attend to what preceded the *l*. With *3l8j2q* under instructions to report letters, he had to make at least a category judgement about what preceded the *l* in order to know not to report it; with *cashland*, he had to identify the letters preceding the *l* because they formed part of the first word which did have to be reported. In the experiment on words preceded by an irrelevant character, on the other hand, he was instructed to ignore

the initial character and report just the word that followed it. It is clearly the first character in the array to which TB is attending that is vulnerable. The interesting thing is that, in an array like *cashland*, the *l* must of course be treated as the first letter of the word *land* at the word level of the model; but, at the letter level, it seems to be treated essentially as a character in the middle of a continuous string. It is not clear how the I.A.M. would accomplish this bipartite treatment of the *l* in *cashland*.

2. Why does TB's deficit afflict lower-case more than upper-case letters? The I.A.M. has nothing to say about case; unfortunately, neither have we. This issue remains to be resolved, not just for TB but for other patients (e.g. a number of letter-by-letter readers) who also show an upper-case advantage.

3. If TB's deficit is restricted to the letter recognition units in position 1, then his impaired identification of isolated letters requires the assumption that single letters get assigned to position 1. There is no obvious argument against this assumption, but it is post hoc and supported only by the data that it is meant to explain.

4. Why, if single letters get assigned to position 1 in the recognition system, are they recognised more successfully than the initial letter of a random letter string? There would seem to be two possibilities here. (a) TB has very position-specific attentional dyslexia (though see point 5 following), which means that the position 1 deficit is aggravated when other items from the same category are present in the display. This is little more than a re-description of the data, but attentional dyslexia is at least a known phenomenon with some independent empirical and theoretical status (Shallice, 1988; Shallice & Warrington, 1977). (b) Suppose that even random letter strings (weakly) activate word representations; this source of feedback might actually hurt position 1 of a string, relative to a single letter, because it could increase the number of candidates. Consider the isolated letter *b* and the string *btqm*. In both cases, TB's letter recognition units at position 1 receive featural information relevant to *b* but are uncertain as to whether the character is, say, *b* or *d* or *p*. For the single letter *b*, these will be the only candidates at position 1 letter level; but *btqm* would produce some activation in 4-letter words with a *t* at position 2 (e.g. *stop*) and also in words with an *m* at position 4 (e.g. *from*); and these words, even though minimally aroused, would send some activation back to the candidates *s* and *f* at position 1 letter level.

5. Why should a patient show one feature of attentional dyslexia (better performance on letters right flanked by numbers than by other letters) but not the other feature (errors reflecting intrusions from other positions in a display of similar elements)? According to Shallice and Warrington's (1977) account of attentional dyslexia, number flanking benefits letter identification because interference only occurs within a category. If TB

shows the benefit, shouldn't he suffer from the interference? We do not have an answer to this puzzle.

6. What is responsible for TB's appalling performance either when given printed words in a nonstandard format, or when asked to analyse and respond to letter strings in a nonstandard manner (from right to left)? Again, no well-motivated answers are forthcoming. Nonstandard visual displays do seem to provoke a partially different mode of word processing. For example, normal subjects given such displays show significant word length effects for items presented in the right visual field; with normal horizontal print, word length effects are only obtained with left-field presentation (Bub & Lewine, 1988; Ellis et al., 1988; Young & Ellis, 1985). As for right-to-left scanning, TB may have some more general deficit in control of attention which was not revealed by our limited domain of testing. When required to scan from right to left, TB seems to attend to each letter (except for the "first", rightmost one, where attention has not yet been forced to move in an abnormal manner) as a separate element rather than as part of a normal horizontal array.

7. Finally, perhaps the most difficult question of all: is it legitimate to consider TB's deficit as restricted to the domain of letters and words? The deficit certainly afflicts numbers; but perhaps letter and number recognition are handled by similar systems (or even the same one), with numbers only lacking the equivalent of word units (and maybe not even entirely lacking those: what about familiar dates like 1066 or 1939?). Is it even accurate to describe the deficit as confined to alphanumeric characters? Here we are hampered by inadequate data as well as a shortage of independently motivated explanatory concepts. TB's unimpaired performance in identifying arrays of small geometric shapes does rule out a major, ubiquitous deficit for things in position 1 of a horizontal array; but as noted earlier, the 4 shapes used were more discriminable than the sets of 26 letters or 10 digits. We asked TB to name arrays of symbols like #$%&+=;!?. Although his errors did not cluster at position 1, he found this task very difficult (in fact, he had a pronounced anomia for such symbols). It is not clear what test(s) would be appropriate to settle this question. In any case, further clues will have to come from other patients.

One final comment: does the postulate of a letter-level deficit specific to position 1 entail the possibility of a letter-level deficit in any position? Not necessarily. It seems clear that the initial letter of a string is both visually and orthographically distinctive. Even the various "offspring" of the original McClelland and Rumelhart (1981) model, models which have tried to improve on the inelegance of re-duplicating letter recognition machinery at all positions (e.g. McClelland, 1985; 1986; Seidenberg & McClelland, 1989), all retain some special way of coding the initial (and final) letter position in a word. Therefore, while a final letter version of TB's deficit might not be especially surprising, position-specific deficits anywhere else in a string seem unlikely.

Manuscript received 7 March 1990
Revised manuscript received 15 June 1990[2]

REFERENCES

Bouma, H. (1971). Visual recognition of isolated lower-case letters. *Vision Research*, *11*, 459–474.

Bub, D. N. & Lewine, J. (1988). Different modes of word recognition in the left and right visual fields. *Brain and Language*, *33*, 161–188.

Costello, A. de L. & Warrington, E. (1987). The dissociation of visuospatial neglect and neglect dyslexia. *Journal of Neurology, Neurosurgery, and Psychiatry*, *50*, 1110–1116.

Coughlan, A. K. & Warrington, E. K. (1978). Word-comprehension and word-retrieval in patients with localised cerebral lesions. *Brain*, *101*, 163–185.

Ellis, A. W., Flude, B. M., & Young, A. W. (1987). "Neglect dyslexia" and the early visual processing of letters in words and nonwords. *Cognitive Neuropsychology*, *4*, 439–464.

Ellis, A. W., Young, A. W., & Anderson, C. (1988). Modes of word recognition in the left and right cerebral hemispheres. *Brain and Language*, *35*, 254–273.

Goodglass, H. & Kaplan, E. (1983). *The assessment of aphasia and related disorders* (2nd Edition). Philadelphia: Lea & Febiger.

Katz, R. B. & Sevush, S. (1989). Positional dyslexia. *Brain and Language*, *37*, 266–289.

Kinsbourne, M. & Warrington, E. K. (1962). A disorder of simultaneous form perception. *Brain*, *85*, 461–486.

Kučera, H. & Francis, W. N. (1967). *Computational analysis of present-day American English*. Providence, Rhode Island: Brown University Press.

McClelland, J. L. (1985). Putting knowledge in its place: A scheme for programming parallel processing structures on the fly. *Cognitive Science*, *9*, 113–146.

McClelland, J. L. (1986). The programmable blackboard model of reading. In J. L. McClelland & D. E. Rumelhart (Eds.), *Parallel distributed processing, Vol. 2*. Cambridge, Mass.: M.I.T. Press.

McClelland, J. L. & Rumelhart, D. E. (1981). An interactive activation model of context effects in letter perception: Part 1. An account of basic findings. *Psychological Review*, *88*, 375–407.

Patterson, K. & Kay, J. (1982). Letter-by-letter reading: Psychological descriptions of a neurological syndrome. *Quarterly Journal of Experimental Psychology*, *34A*, 411–441.

Patterson, K. & Morton, J. (1985). From orthography to phonology: An attempt at an old interpretation. In K. Patterson, J. C. Marshall, & M. Coltheart (Eds.), *Surface dyslexia: Neuropsychological and cognitive studies of phonological reading*. London: Lawrence Erlbaum Associates Ltd.

Patterson, K., Purell, C., & Morton, J. (1983). Facilitation of word retrieval in aphasia. In C. Code & D. J. Müller (Eds.), *Aphasia therapy*. London: Edward Arnold.

Riddoch, M. J., Humphreys, G. W., Cleton, P., & Fery, P. (1990). Interaction of attentional and lexical processes in neglect dyslexia. *Cognitive Neuropsychology*, *7*, 479–517.

---

[2]This paper was originally considered for publication in *Cognitive Neuropsychology*, and then, while undergoing revision, it was "recruited" for this special issue.

Seidenberg, M. S. & McClelland, J. L. (1989). A distributed, developmental model of visual word recognition and naming. *Psychological Review*, *96*, 523–568.

Siéroff, E., Pollatsek, A., & Posner, M. J. (1988). Recognition of visual letter strings following injury to the posterior visual spatial attention system. *Cognitive Neuropsychology*, *5*, 427–449.

Shallice, T. (1988). *From neuropsychology to mental structure*. Cambridge: Cambridge University Press.

Shallice, T. & Warrington, E. K. (1977). The possible role of selective attention in acquired dyslexia. *Neuropsychologia*, *15*, 31–41.

Stanovich, K. E. (1980). Toward an interactive-compensatory model of individual differences in the development of reading fluency. *Reading Research Quarterly*, *16*, 32–71.

Stanovich, K. E. (1984). The interactive-compensatory model of reading: A confluence of developmental, experimental, and educational psychology. *Remedial and Special Education*, *5*, 11–19.

Stanovich, K. E., West, R. F., & Feeman, D. J. (1981). A longitudinal study of sentence context effects in second-grade children: Tests of an interactive-compensatory model. *Journal of Experimental Child Psychology*, *32*, 185–199.

Treiman, R. (1986). The division between onsets and rimes in English syllables. *Journal of Memory and Language*, *25*, 476–491.

Treiman, R. & Chafetz, J. (1987). Are there onset- and rime-like units in printed words? In M. Coltheart (Ed.), *Attention & performance XII: The psychology of reading*. London: Lawrence Erlbaum Associates Ltd.

Wilson, B., Cockburn, J., & Halligan, P. (1987). *Behavioural Inattention Test*. Titchfield, Hants.: Thames Valley Test Company.

Young, A. W. & Ellis, A. W. (1985). Different methods of lexical access for words presented in the left and right visual hemifields. *Brain and Language*, *24*, 326–358.

COGNITIVE NEUROPSYCHOLOGY, 1990, 7 (5/6) 479–517

Interaction of Attentional and Lexical Processes in Neglect Dyslexia

Jane Riddoch

Cognitive Science Research Centre, University of Birmingham, Birmingham, U.K.

Glyn Humphreys

Cognitive Science Research Centre, University of Birmingham, Birmingham, U.K.

Ping Cleton

University of Leiden, Leiden, The Netherlands

Patrick Fery

St-Danes-Avelines, Belgium

Two cases of "left" neglect dyslexia are examined. The two patients show qualitatively similar problems of reading behaviour, although they differ quantitatively in terms of the exposure durations under which neglect dyslexia is manifest. Like other neglect patients documented in the literature, the two patients made mainly substitution errors to the left-hand letter in words, tending to misname the word as a neighbour of similar length. Unlike some patients, the two patients here showed lexical effects (i.e. they performed better with words than with nonwords, and they found words with many orthographic neighbours more difficult to identify than those with few orthographic neighbours). In addition, the patients were susceptible to attempts to manipulate the locus of attention, they were induced into producing addition errors by placing a hash at the left-hand end of letter strings, and their neglect reflected the position of the letter in the string rather than in the visual field. The argument is made that neglect dyslexia may result from a failure in the interplay between lexical and attentional processes in word recognition.

Requests for reprints should be addressed to Jane Riddoch, School of Psychology, University of Birmingham, Birmingham B15 2TT, U.K.

This work was supported by a grant from the M.R.C. to the first and second authors. We thank JB and MO for all their patience and good humour. In addition, we should like to thank Alfonzo Caramazza, Argye Hillis, Eric Siéroff, and Brenda Rapp for their helpful comments on earlier drafts of this paper.

INTRODUCTION

Unilateral neglect of the side of space contralateral to the side of a lesion can frequently be observed in its more florid manifestation following right cerebral damage (De Renzi, 1982); it may also be observed following damage to the left hemisphere, although usually not in such an exaggerated way; often it is only detectable following sensitive clinical testing (Ogden, 1987).

Recent work has indicated that neglect is not a unitary phenomenon. For instance, double dissociations have been demonstrated in visual scanning tasks (requiring orientation to spatial locations in visual space) and in tactile tasks (requiring orientation to spatial locations within the framework of the patient's body) (see Bisiach, Perani, Vallar, & Berti, 1986; Laplane & Degos, 1983). Furthermore, some patients may be selectively impaired at attending to a particular *spatial location* (see Humphreys & Riddoch, 1990; Posner, Cohen, & Rafal, 1982; Posner, Walker, Friedrich, & Rafal, 1984; Riddoch & Humphreys, 1983; 1987) whereas others may be selectively impaired at disengaging attention from a particular *object* (see Humphreys, Riddoch, Davies, Quinlan, & Price, 1989; Kinsbourne & Warrington, 1962a; Luria, 1959). Such dissociations are consistent with the multiplicity of lesion sites within both cerebral hemispheres that may give rise to neglect (see Mesulam, 1981; Posner & Peterson, 1990). Humphreys, Riddoch, and Müller (Note 1) have developed a sensory-motor framework which may be applied to the different forms of unilateral neglect. Within this framework, it is argued that there are multiple procedures for coding spatial information within the visual system, with the nature of coding depending on the kind of visual information involved and on the type of action that is required. In particular they have argued that the processes concerned with coding variable spatial relations between separate objects (e.g. the different objects on a plate, or words on a page) are independent of those concerned with coding the spatial relations between the parts of a single object (e.g. the letters within a word, or the parts of an object). The coupling of action to these different types of spatial coding is relatively limited, presumably due to constraints on the number of actions that can be performed to different objects at any one time (e.g. see Allport, 1987). Thus coupling stimulus representations to action is attentionally limited. *Visual* neglect may result from an impairment of the between- and/or the within-object coding systems (manifested in, for example, the contrast between selection between spatially separated objects and selection between a set of overlapping objects; cf. Gainotti, D'Erme, Monteleone, & Silveri, 1986). Also, impairments within each of these systems could be due to poor unilateral representation of stimulus information, or to problems linking visually coded representations to action. *Visuo-motor* neglect may result from the impaired coupling of spatially coded representations to a system concerned with innervating a particular action, or from an impairment within one or more action systems.

Within this broad framework which characterises the many types of neglect disorder, neglect in reading may be considered an example of *visual* neglect. A crucial question in understanding this type of neglect, however, is whether it reflects a deficit specific to the reading process. In the earlier documented cases of neglect dyslexia for the left-hand ends of words, patients were reported as suffering from a general neglect syndrome, of which the reading problem was one manifestation (Ellis, Flude, & Young, 1987; Kinsbourne & Warrington, 1962b). Thus the patients were reported as showing neglect in a variety of tasks in addition to reading. Also, Ellis et al.'s patient (VB) was affected by the spatial position of the letters from the patient's viewpoint, rather than their position within the word. For instance, when asked to read words written upside-down she continued to misidentify the leftmost letter in the field, even though this was now the rightmost letter in the word. This suggests that, in this patient, there was a relatively early problem in encoding information from the left side of visual stimuli, irrespective of the nature of the stimulus involved. Indeed, VB showed no advantage of reading words over nonwords. Interestingly, although VB made errors of omission (PAN → AN), substitution (PAN → MAN), and addition (PAN → SPAN), substitution errors occurred most frequently. It appears that the encoding deficit affected the identification of the left sides of words, but it did not affect relatively accurate coding of word length.

However, other cases suggest that neglect can be specific to reading. For instance, Costello and Warrington (1987) report a patient who made left-sided neglect errors in reading but right-sided neglect errors in standard clinical tests of spatial neglect (e.g. line bisection and copying tasks). That is, different problems seem to be implicated in the reading and the spatial tasks. Patterson and Wilson (this volume) further report a patient whose problem seems specific to alphanumeric stimuli.

There are also suggestions that the type of neglect is different in the different cases of neglect dyslexia. Costello and Warrington's (1987) patient made an equal number of substitution and addition errors, unlike VB (Ellis et al., 1987). Thus in this case, word length seems to have been coded more crudely. Siéroff, Pollatsek, and Posner (1988) investigated "neglect" errors in patients with left and right parietal lesions (who showed no clinical manifestation of neglect), elicited by short stimulus presentations (of 100msecs.). They found general advantages for the report of words over nonwords. Such an effect was not apparent in the clinical testing of VB. Siéroff et al.'s data may be conceptualised in at least two ways. Possibly, there may be some form of top-down influence on letter perception in words relative to letter strings (e.g. McClelland & Rumelhart, 1981). This top-down influence helps overcome poor encoding of left side letters in words. Alternatively, words may be said to "escape" neglect because they are encoded as single objects, with neglect reflecting a high-level deficit in mapping multiple visual objects to action (e.g. in mapping multiple letters to their names; this affects nonwords more strongly than words because nonwords cannot be represented as a single lexical unit; see Humphreys et al., Note 1). Either way, neglect in these cases cannot be understood without recourse to some kind of lexical involvement; this would not appear to hold for at least some neglect dyslexics (e.g. VB, Ellis et al., 1987).

In the present paper we attempt to take the proposal of reading-specific neglect further, by considering (1) the level of representation affected in neglect dyslexia, and (2) whether neglect dyslexia can be affected by manipulations of attention. Interest in the first issue arises because pre-lexical stages in word recognition may normally involve several processing stages, which can be characterised by the formation of different types of derived visual representation (e.g. Caramazza & Hillis, this issue; Monk, 1985). For instance, an initial coding of words in terms of letter features in specific retinal positions may be transformed into representations that are abstracted from their particular case and typefont (e.g. Besner, Davelaar, Alcott, & Parry, 1984; Evett & Humphreys, 1981; Humphreys, Evett, & Quinlan, 1990), and from their specific position in the visual field (Humphreys et al., 1990; Mozer, 1987). Identification may be based on these more abstract representations. To the extent that neglect dyslexia is a heterogeneous syndrome, we may expect patterns of disturbance at the different levels of representation (Caramazza & Hillis, this issue). Our interest in the second issue is with whether there are attentional processes specifically tied to word recognition in general and specific types of word representation in particular (e.g. Humphreys & Bruce, 1989; LaBerge, 1983). Our arguments are based on data from two subjects. One patient, JB, showed neglect in a range of tasks other than reading. The other, MO, only showed a "neglect-type" impairment in reading when performance conditions were limited (i.e. with limited tachistoscopic presentation). Despite the quantitative differences in the conditions under which the patients manifest neglect, we suggest that there are qualitatively similar deficits underlying their performance.

CASE ONE: JB

JB (born in 1939) was a businessman before he suffered a road traffic accident in July 1988 when he was hit by a motorcyclist while crossing the road. The accident resulted in a head injury which showed on a C.T.-scan as contusion of the right temporo-parietal region. The E.E.G. report indicated a slowing over the temporo-frontal region and a depression of waves posteriorly. Perimetric examination of his visual fields revealed a left upper quadrantanopia. JB suffered some motor impairment as a result of his accident. This was particularly pronounced in his left arm, where distal movements were impaired. Spoken language was normal. Digit span was normal, but there was a degree of both retrograde and anterograde amnesia. JB's particular complaint was that he was no longer able to read, a pastime which had given him great pleasure premorbidly. Initial investigations suggested that this deficit may have been part of "a neglect syndrome" since on single word reading his errors involved the initial letters of the word so that BAND was read as LAND (alteration of the initial letter) or AND (omission of the initial letter). Detailed investigation was therefore made of his reading deficit. Investigations were carried out over a period of 8 months (November 1988–June 1989). Over this time, JB's reading performance did improve (consistent with previous observations in the literature, see Gainotti, 1968; although also see Seron, DeLoche, & Coyette, 1989). In order to accommodate an improving baseline of performance, all critical comparisons were based on within-session testing. Additionally, in May and June 1989, exposure durations were reduced from 10,000 to 400msecs. in order to obtain similar error rates in performance to those obtained in the earlier sessions.

Initial Investigations

General Neglect

Some observations of general neglect were made by the nursing and rehabilitation personnel. For instance, on occasion JB was observed failing to eat the food on the *left* side of his plate. The classic omission of detail from the left side of drawings was not observed in this case, although his performance on the Rivermead Star Cancellation Test did show clear evidence of neglect. Initial administration of this test indicated that JB explored 48% of the total area and that exploration was restricted to the right-hand side.

Although JB made many errors in reading both text and single words, he did not manifest neglect in written spelling to aural dictation. Given a set of 78 words and nonwords varying in their number of orthographic "neighbours" (see Experiment 4), JB made 35/38 correct spellings to words and 9/40 correct spellings to dictated nonwords. Although there was a clear effect of lexical status on spelling to dictation, none of the errors could be classified as "neglect" errors, and all were phonologically related to the target item (e.g. GNAW → NOUGH, MONTH → MUGS, SALN → SOWN, WOLN → WONE, BLID → BLED).

Reading Impairment

A number of different tests were administered to assess the effects of imageability, orthographic and phonological regularity, the number of orthographic neighbours, and word frequency.

Experiment 1: Imageability Effects

Stimulus materials consisted of 40 words (20 highly imageable and 20 low in imageability). Word length was also manipulated with equal numbers of 4- and 6-letter words. A clear length effect was observed with 90% (18/20) of 4-letter words as opposed to 65% (13/20) of 6-letter words being read correctly. There was no marked effect of imageability. With 4-letter words performance was at the same level for both high and low imageable words; with 6-letter words, 6/10 of low imageable and 7/10 of high imageable words were read correctly. The errors were all of a "neglect" type in that they involved changes to the first letter(s). Of the 9 errors, 5 were substitutions and 4 were omissions; there were no addition errors.

Experiment 2: Effects of Orthographic and Phonological Regularity

The effects of orthographic and phonological regularity were manipulated using a set of low-frequency words (frequencies under 50 per million in Kuçera & Francis, 1967). The stimulus set consisted of 24 orthographically and phonologically regular words (e.g. SPARK), 24 orthographically and phonologically irregular words (e.g. YACHT), and 24 orthographically regular and phonologically irregular words (e.g. STEAK). Word length was manipulated across these stimulus sets, 4-, 5-, 6-, and 7-letter words being used. The number of items in the stimulus sets was unequal with 9 4-letter words, 33 4-letter words, 18 5-letter words, and 12 7-letter words.

Results. Performance was poor. JB scored a total of 36/72 (50%) correct. Because of the small cell numbers in some instances, scores were collapsed over word length. The results are displayed in Table 1. Performance in all 3 conditions was very similar. The majority of errors could be classed as "neglect errors", since the terminal portion of the response was equivalent to the terminal portion of the stimulus word (88% of errors). The initial letter was either omitted (DEARTH → EARTH, 14/36), substituted (GROSS → CROSS, 13/36), or letters were added (BOUGH

→ SLOUGH, 5/36). Of these neglect errors, 60.7% were real words, 39.3% were nonwords. The remaining 22% of errors showed some visual similarities to the target item, but were not of the neglect type (e.g. LATHE → FATHER).

TABLE 1
The Effects of Orthographic and Phonological Regularity (JB: Experiment 2)

OiPi	*OrPi*	*OrPr*
13/24 (54.2%)	12/24 (50%)	11/24 (45.8%)

O = orthographic, P = phonological, r = regular, i = irregular.

Experiment 3. Word Frequency Effects

The stimulus set comprised of 80 items (40 high- and 40 low-frequency words) with frequencies divided at 50 occurrences per million in the Kuçera and Francis (1967) word count. At each frequency level, there were 10 3-, 4-, 5-, and 6-letter words. Performance tended to be better with high-frequency words (37/40, 92.5% correct) as compared with 75% (30/40) of low-frequency words, though this difference was not statistically significant (Chi-square$_{(1)}$ = 3.31, $P > 0.05$). The errors were equally distributed across the different word lengths and were all of the neglect type (9 substitution errors, 3 omission errors, and 1 addition error).

Experiments 1–3 confirm that JB manifests neglect dyslexia. His reading of high-frequency words tends to be better than that of low-frequency words, but there are no effects of imageability or either orthographic or phonological regularity. We next explore the effects of lexical variables by examining the effects of lexical status (words vs. nonwords) and of the number of orthographic neighbours.

Experiment 4. Word Neighbourhood Effects: Lexical Decision and Naming

Method. The stimulus lists were derived from Coltheart, Davelaar, Jonasson, and Besner (1976). They consisted of 4- and 5-letter words and nonwords. The words were further subdivided into high neighbourhood (HiN) and low neighbourhood (LoN) words. The neighbourhood effect with these particular words was defined according to the number of other words created by substituting one letter at any position in the word. HiN and LoN nonwords were created by substituting one letter in a matching word. All nonwords were pronounceable. There were 20 items in each condition except for the HiN 5-letter word and nonword lists where only 19 items were presented. Stimulus presentation was via an Apple II+ Euro-computer. Prior to presentation, a fixation cross appeared for 200msecs. The fixation cross was immediately *above* letter position 3 in both 4- and 5-letter words. There was an I.S.I. (inter-stimulus interval) of 200msecs. between the offset of the fixation cross and target onset. The target remained present for 10,000msecs. Viewed from a distance of 30cm., 4- and 5-letter strings subtended a visual angle of 1.2° and 1.6° respectively. At shorter exposure durations, JB claimed he could not read anything. JB was asked to read the name of the item aloud. Four lists in total were presented, 2 lists containing 4-letter items and 2 containing 5-letter items. Words and nonwords were presented in random order. The lists were presented twice (ABBA then BAAB, where A represents 4-letter lists and B represents 5-letter lists).

The procedure was repeated 3 days later, with the stimuli repeated twice (BAAB then ABBA). JB was asked to make lexical decisions to the items.

Results. The results for stimulus naming are presented in Table 2a. There was a significant effect of orthographic neighbourhood. Chi-square$_{(1)}$ for Hi vs. Lo neighbourhoods was 4.61, $P < 0.05$ (summing over string length and words vs. nonwords). Performance was significantly better for words relative to nonwords (Chi-square$_{(1)}$ = 43.03, $P < 0.001$, summing over string length and orthographic neighbourhood). There was also an effect of word length, with 5-letter words being read better than 4-letter words (Chi-square$_{(1)}$ = 6.18, $P < 0.02$); but not for nonwords (Chi-square$_{(1)}$ = 2.07, $P > 0.05$).

The results for the lexical decision are presented in Table 2b, collapsed

TABLE 2
The Effects of Word Neighbourhood (JB: Experiment 4)

	% Correct Responses (No. in Parentheses)			
	Words		*Nonwords*	
	HiN	*LoN*	*HiN*	*LoN*
(a) Naming Data				
4-letter items	67.5 (27/40)	77.5 (31/40)	27.5 (11/40)	47.5 (19/40)
5-letter items	86.8 (33/38)	92.1 (35/38)	45.0 (18/40)	57.5 (24/40)
(b) Lexical Decision	94.9 (37/39)	92.3 (36/39)	52.5 (21/40)	55.0 (22/40)

Note: Correct responses to four- or five-letter words or nonwords according to whether they are classed as high- or low-neighbourhood words.

over word length. JB made very few errors with words (whether HiN or LoN), although he performed poorly with nonwords. Nonwords that JB named correctly tended to be classified as nonwords, nonwords that he named incorrectly (usually as words, see Table 3), tended to be classified as words. This suggests that his misnaming reflected an initial mis-identification (see also Ellis et al., 1987).

Error Analysis. The total number of errors was 118. They were classified into 3 main categories: neglect errors, visual errors, and other errors. These categories were subdivided according to whether the response could be classed as a word or a nonword. Neglect errors were said to occur when the response differed from the target word either by the omission of the first letter(s) (CLOCK → LOCK, 5.9%), addition of a letter to the beginning of the word (WORD → SWORD, 9.3%), or changes in the first 1 or 2 letters which resulted in a response the same length as the target (PITCH → WITCH, BULLY → FOLLY, 62.7%). An error was classed as visual if the response differed from the target in that middle or end letters were changed (STABE → SPARE, RONCH →

TABLE 3
Error Analysis with High- and Low-neighbourhood Words (JB: Experiment 4)

Type of Stimulus:	*Words*				*Nonwords*			
	HiN		*LoN*		*HiN*		*LoN*	
Type of Response:	*W*	*NW*	*W*	*NW*	*W*	*NW*	*W*	*NW*
(a) 4-letter Items								
Neg: maintain length	7	1	2	1	19	0	9	2
Neg: inc. length	2	0	0	0	6	0	2	0
Neg: dec. length	0	0	1	0	0	0	1	0
Vis: maintain length	2	0	0	1	3	0	4	3
Vis: inc. length	0	0	0	0	0	0	0	0
Vis: dec. length	0	0	1	0	0	0	0	0
Other	1	0	1	2	1	0	0	0
(b) 5-letter-Items								
Neg: maintain length	5	0	1	1	15	4	5	2
Neg: inc. length	0	0	0	0	0	0	0	1
Neg: dec. length	0	0	0	1	0	0	3	0
Vis: maintain length	0	0	0	0	2	1	0	0
Vis: inc. length	0	0	0	0	0	0	3	1
Vis: dec. length	0	0	0	0	0	0	0	0
Other	0	0	0	0	0	0	1	0

Note: Illustrates an analysis of error type according to the category of the target items and the nature of the response.
inc. = increase, dec. = decrease, neg. = neglect error, vis. = visual error.

ONCE). Again, such errors were also classified according to the length of the response relative to the target item (13.6% of visual errors maintained the length of the target item, 0.8% decreased the length, and 3.4% increased the length). The data are presented in Table 3.

Of all the errors, the largest category is the neglect error which maintains the length of the target item (62.7%). This suggests that JB has relatively preserved length information but impaired identity information for the initial letter(s) in the string (see also Ellis et al., 1987; Behrmann, Moscovitch, Black, & Mozer, in press).

Given JB's pattern of errors, we looked more closely at the accuracy of report of letters according to their position in the string in the corpus of words and nonwords. Table 4 indicates the number of letters correct according to their position. There was a significant effect of the position of the letters in the strings both for 4- and 5-letter items (Chi-square$_{(3)}$ = 55.80, $P < 0.001$ and Chi-square$_{(4)}$ = 55.99, $P < 0.001$, respectively). Inspection of Table 4 suggests that this effect is due to reduced accuracy for the first item in the string relative to the other items.

Discussion. JB is sensitive to certain aspects of written material. For instance, performance deteriorated with nonwords relative to words; there was also an effect of the orthographic neighbourhood, with performance being poorer for letter strings with a large number of orthographic neighbours relative to those with fewer neighbours. Both these factors suggest some form of lexical constraint on performance. This is also suggested by

TABLE 4
Neighbourhood Effects: Accuracy of Report According to the Position in the Letter String (JB: Experiment 4)

	Addition of Letters		*Letter Position*				
	+2	*+1*	*1*	*2*	*3*	*4*	*5*
(a) 4-letter Items							
HiN words	—	1	14	20	19	19	—
LoN words	—	—	16	18	19	19	—
HiN nonwords	—	4	8	20	19	20	—
LoN nonwords	—	1	12	19	19	17	—
Total	—	6	50	77	76	75	—
(b) 5-letter Items							
HiN words	—	—	17	19	19	19	19
LoN words	—	—	18	18	19	19	19
HiN nonwords	—	—	10	17	20	19	20
LoN nonwords	—	1	14	19	20	20	20
Total	—	1	59	73	78	77	78

JB's performance on the lexical decision task. He is likely to classify a nonword as a word nearly 50% of the time. Also, when naming nonwords, 84.1% of his errors were due to the production of a real word. The tendency to lexicalise nonwords is most pronounced for those items with many orthographic neighbours relative to LoN items (46/51 real word errors produced as compared with 28/37). The analysis of errors further indicated that they were predominantly of the "neglect" type, in that errors tended to be confined to the beginning of the words. In particular, the initial letter in both 4- and 5-letter or word strings was selectively impaired relative to other letters in the string (see also Patterson & Wilson, this volume).

Perhaps the simplest account of JB's neglect dyslexia is that he has a selective visual field defect. In Experiment 4 the first letter in both 4- and 5-letter words fell in the same retinal position (since fixation was on the third letter in strings of both lengths). JB has difficulty reading the first letter in words of both lengths because only that letter falls in his impaired visual field. Note though that a visual deficit per se is unlikely to produce neglect dyslexia, since patients can be hemianopic and still be able to read. The problem can only be one of an uncompensated field defect. However, even this idea has difficulty in accounting for all of the data. In particular, the error analysis indicates that JB has encoded word length correctly since he primarily makes substitution errors (see Table 4). This suggests that word length information is coded, using information from even apparently neglected letters. We return to discuss the field defect account after Experiment 6.

The effects of the number of orthographic neighbours ("N"), and the word advantage over nonwords can be conceptualised in terms of lexical activation in an interactive processing system (cf. McClelland & Rumelhart, 1981). Let us suppose that JB has impoverished visual information concerning the first letter in words. In an interactive system, there will be a higher likelihood that impoverished visual information accesses a correct lexical entry (for word report), relative to appropriate letter and letter-cluster representations being activated by nonwords. The N effect with words occurs because, on occasions, lexical activation remains insufficient to distinguish between competitor words. The N effect with nonwords would then indicate that nonword reading is based on partially activated lexical representations. The predominance of substitution errors indicates that lexical information is constrained by information about word length.

However, despite the success of the interactive processing account, it remains possible that both the word advantage and the effect of N reflect guessing from the letters JB can identify explicitly. Words will have a higher chance of being guessed correctly than nonwords, as will letter strings having few relative to many orthographic neighbours. N effects will occur with nonwords as well as words because high N nonwords, sharing spelling patterns with many words, are more likely to be guessed as words than are low N nonwords. The predominance of substitution errors is accounted for by guessing being constrained by word length. The guessing account cannot be ruled out here because the majority of JB's errors on nonwords were word responses, and this was more evident for high relative to low N nonwords (see Table 3).

Experiment 5. The Reading of Compound and Noncompound Words

In order to examine whether JB does show influences of guessing in his reading, Experiment 5 contrasted his ability to read compound and non-compound words (matched for length and frequency). If JB identifies the letters at the right-hand end of letter strings and then guesses the identity of the whole string, then he should perform better with noncompound than compound words, given that the first word in the compound may not be predicted from the second. On the other hand, if there is only top-down lexical feedback without guessing, and if feedback is equally strong for words irrespective of the predictability of the word from its constituent letters, there should be no benefit for noncompound over compound words (see Johnson, 1978, for a similar argument concerning sophisticated guessing and the word superiority effect in normals). Siéroff, Pollatsek, and Posner (1988) also examined guessing using compound words. However, they contrasted performance with compound words to that with pairs of unrelated words (matched in length to the compounds). They proposed that pairs of unrelated words were *less* predictable than compound words, and hence that guessing should favour compounds. In the event, they found no difference between compounds and noncompounds, and hence argued that guessing was not a major factor. Our study contrasted single and compound words, where the guessing should favour the non-compounds.

Method. Stimuli consisted of 45 compound (e.g. HEADLINE) and 45 noncompound (e.g. PECULIAR) low-frequency words. All words were 8 letters long. In order to simulate the guessing effects that might be present in left-end neglect dyslexia, a group of 5 normal subjects were given the compound and noncompound words with 1 to 4 left-side letters missing (the number of letters missing was randomly determined for each word). The control subjects were asked to complete each word. Over the 5 subjects there were 177/225 correct completions for noncompound words and 126/225 correct completions for compound words. Completions were significantly more accurate for the noncompound words ($\text{Chi-square}_{(1)}$ = 25.3, $P < 0.001$). For JB, items were presented via an Apple II+ Euro-computer. Prior to presentation, a fixation cross was presented for 200 msec. The fixation cross was immediately *above* letter position 3 in both 4- and 5-letter words. There was an I.S.I. of 200msec. between the offset of the fixation cross and target onset. The target remained present for 10,000msec. Viewed from a distance of 30cm., the letter strings subtended a visual angle of 2.4°. JB was asked to read the words aloud. Testing took place on 2 occasions separated by 3 days. Items were presented in different random orders in the 2 test sessions.

Results. JB scored 72/90 correct on the compound words and 74/90 on the noncompound words. There were 22 neglect errors and 12 visual errors. Of the neglect errors, 5 were omissions, 9 were additions, and 8 substitutions. Some of the errors took the form expected if JB were identifying the right-side word and guessing the identity of the left-side word (e.g. OVERCOME → WELCOME); nevertheless, there was no overall advantage for the noncompound words where this strategy was less applicable. The data give no indication that JB consistently uses a guessing strategy based on the identification of the right-side letters in words.

One other point is that substitution errors did not dominate here. Mean word length was 8 letters. It is possible that JB is only able to code word length relatively crudely for longer words, so that omission and addition errors can also occur. Even so, all errors were within one item length of the target word.

Experiment 6: The Effects of Contrast Reduction

Taking Experiments 4 and 5 together, it appears that, in reading words, JB benefits from top-down lexical processing (benefiting words over non-words), and that he does not employ an explicit guessing strategy. However, it is relevant to assess the kind of stimulus information that influences his reading. For instance, is his reading affected by contrast reduction? To the extent that contrast reduction influences early stages of visual word recognition (e.g. Julesz & White, 1969; Wilson & Anstis, 1969), an interaction between contrast reduction and JB's reading performance would suggest that his reading deficit is at a relatively early stage (e.g. affecting the encoding of letter information).

Method. Experiment 4 was repeated but the intensity of the presented items was reduced by ½. The stimulu were presented on 2 occasions, each test period being separated by 3 days. As before, stimuli were preceded by a fixation cross (200msec. duration) and an I.S.I. of 200msec. The stimuli were presented for 10,000msec. JB was required to read aloud the presented items.

Results and Discussion. As with Experiment 4, the data were scored according to position of letters either in a word or in a letter string. The results are presented in Table 5.

JB's performance did not significantly deteriorate under degradation conditions. The difference in first letter report for 4- and 5-letter words (comparing Experiments 4 and 6) is nonsignificant (Chi-square$_{(1)}$ = 0.14, $P < 0.05$). However, there was a difference in the nature of the errors observed. For instance, there was an increase in the number of *addition* errors (where the response given contains more letters than the target item; e.g. WORD read as SWORD, GARK read as CLARK; see Table 5). This suggests that contrast reduction did affect JB's ability to encode string length. That contrast reduction *increased* addition errors argues further against the explanation of JB's neglect dyslexia in terms of a visual field defect. It is feasible that length information could be computed from partial information in a hemianopic field. It is less feasible that the computed length would increase when the information in that field is degraded. Also, contrast reduction should have *increased* JB's neglect dyslexia given a partial field loss; this argument follows from an application of additive factors logic (Sternberg, 1969). The partial field loss should disrupt the uptake of visual information, as should contrast reduction. The

TABLE 5
The Effects of Stimulus Degradation (JB: Experiment 6)

	Addition of Letters		*Letter Position*				
	+2	*+1*	*1*	*2*	*3*	*4*	*5*
(a) 4-letter Items[a]							
HiN words	—	1	15	19	20	20	—
LoN words	1	1	18	18	19	19	—
HiN nonwords	—	3	8	19	18	18	—
LoN nonwords	—	1	13	20	20	18	—
Total	1	6	54	76	77	75	—
(b) 5-letter Items[a]							
HiN words	—	1	17	18	19	19	19
LoN words	—	—	17	18	19	19	19
HiN nonwords	—	—	12	20	20	18	20
LoN nonwords	2	5	13	18	19	19	20
Total	2	6	59	74	77	75	78

[a]The accuracy of report of letters according to their position in a string under degraded conditions of stimulus presentation.

two effects should therefore interact, with there being a proportionally greater effect of contrast reduction in the neglect field. Against this, contrast reduction had no effect on the absolute level of neglect dyslexia. What other accounts of JB's neglect dyslexia are viable?

Possible Accounts of JB's Neglect Dyslexia. JB's neglect dyslexia cannot be explained simply in terms of a loss of information for letters in particular retinal positions because of the apparent preservation of word length, the variation in word length coding as letter contrast varies, and the failure to increase neglect dyslexia by contrast reduction. One alternative account is that JB's deficit is not one of visual encoding into a retinal representation of words, but that there is an impairment at a higher level of visual representation. For instance, JB's impairment could be at a level of representation where letter strings are coded non-retinotopically, with letters being coded in terms of their spatial positions within letter strings, and not their absolute positions within retinotopic space. A possible representation is one in which letters are coded in terms of their spatial positions to the left or right of the central letter in the strings. We term this a string-level representation. JB may have an impairment affecting the left ends of such a string-level representation. Note that it follows naturally from this account that the first letter in both four- and five-letter words is neglected, since this letter occupies the same string position in the string level representations in these words.

This account is comfortable with the results that are problematic for the visual field/retinal representation account. For instance, word length could be computed correctly for an early (retinal) representation despite the loss at the higher string level. Also, since the string level representation may be abstracted from visual encoding procedures (affected by contrast reduction), contrast reduction may have little effect on neglect.

A rather different proposal is that JB's deficit resides in the attentional processes which normally modulate word recognition (see Siéroff et al., 1988, for a similar argument). In JB's case there is reduced attentional enhancement to the left-hand end of letter strings, leading to the neglect of the first letter in words and nonwords. In effect, this attentional impairment produces an impoverished representation of letter strings. Work with normal subjects indicates that words are read most quickly, and with fewest refixations, if the eye (and, presumably, attention) falls at a "convenient viewing position" (C.V.P.) near the centre of the word (O'Regan & Levy-Schoen, 1987). As words increase in length, so the location of the C.V.P. moves to the left of word centre (O'Regan, Levy-Schoen, Pynte, & Brugaillere, 1984). One reason for this may be that skilled readers of English use an asymmetric "attentional window", wider to the right than the left (see Humphreys & Bruce, 1989). Thus for reading longer words, attention is optimally positioned left of word centre. JB may fail to allocate attention normally to the left-end of letter strings because his attention is chronically oriented to the right of the C.V.P. This may be because patients with unilateral lesions can have a permanent gaze and attentional deviation to the side ipsilateral to the lesion (Jeannerod, 1985). Nevertheless, his attentional orienting may be affected by computation of the C.V.P. Now, since five-letter words will have a C.V.P. more to the left than four-letter words, any deviation of attention to the right of the C.V.P. may have similar effects on the two string lengths. Given an "attentional" window of a limited size, the left-hand letter may be neglected in both four- and five-letter words (see Fig. 1). Note that, in order for this account to work, it is necessary that word length information is computed, since it is word length that determines the C.V.P., and thus the optimal position for attention. Hence, it is a necessary prediction of the account that, if patients have an attentional problem of this sort, they will make a preponderance of substitution rather than omission or addition neglect errors. Note also that the string representation needs to be computed within a retinal co-ordinate system, since we presume that it determines the location for eye movements in reading.

This attentional account accommodates JB's ability to compute word length. It is less comfortable with the null effect of contrast reduction on neglect. If attention modulates letter encoding, unattended (neglected)

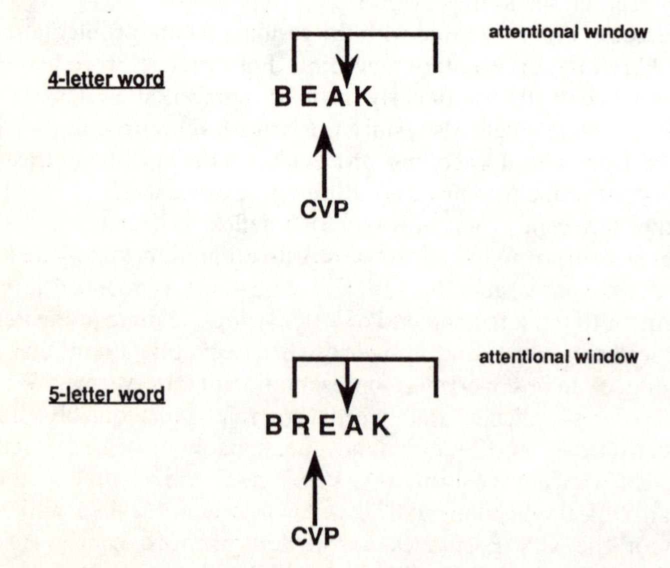

FIG. 1 Example of a "fixed attentional window" being applied to the right of the convenient viewing position (C.V.P.).

ends of the strings should be particularly affected by degradation. However, absolute comparison of performance levels in Experiments 4 (undegraded) and 6 (degraded) is difficult since Experiment 6 took place after Experiment 4 and there may have been both item learning and recovery between the tests. Also, contrast reduction may have two effects. One is to reduce the efficiency of letter coding, impairing letter recognition, particularly for the letters at the end of the string. The other is to produce inappropriate (overextended) coding of string length (cf. the addition errors). This may produce a stronger orienting response to the left (given that the C.V.P. is to the left of centre for long words; see O'Regan & Levy-Schoen, 1987), which may in turn facilitate letter encoding at the left end of the strings. Thus orienting could counteract the effects of degradation on letter encoding.

Other representational and attentional accounts encounter problems with the data. For instance, one possible representational account is that JB has lost first position information in stored lexical representations. Against this, however, JB makes errors with nonwords as well as words. A possible attentional account is that JB has greater problems in reading nonwords than words because he has difficulty *disengaging* attention from previously attended stimuli, rather than having problems engaging or allocating attention appropriately (cf. Posner et al., 1984). Words suffer little because they can be coded as a single lexical object and do not require attention to be shifted and re-engaged. Nonwords may only be coded using sub-string segments (letters and letter clusters), each of which must be attended in sequence. Thus problems with attentional disengagement will have most serious consequences for nonwords (see Siéroff et al., 1988, for an example of this argument). However, this account cannot explain why JB shows left-side neglect, given that nonwords tend to be read sequentially from left to right (indeed, JB often spelled out the letters of nonwords beginning from the second letter on the left of the string). If attention remains engaged on the letters first attended, right-sided neglect should be apparent.

In sum, JB's reading deficit can be accommodated in either of two ways. He could have an impaired representation at a level at which letters are encoded in terms of their position within a letter string rather than in the visual field, or he could have a problem allocating attention to the left end of letter strings, with such attentional allocation being necessary to enhance the encoding of letter information. The attentional account does not need to be committed to the idea of a string-level representation being the locus of JB's processing deficit. This representational or attentional deficit could interact with top-down lexical processes to produce both N effects and an advantage for words over nonwords.

Experiment 7: Left-end Flanking and Degradation

Accounts of JB's impairment in terms of loss to a string-level representation in word recognition, or in terms of chronic orienting to the right of a C.V.P., are consistent with the data from Experiments 1–6. In order to examine the relations between length coding, degradation, and letter report in more detail, Experiment 7 was conducted in which the effects of contrast reduction were combined with effects due to placing a hash sign (#) at the left end of the strings. The idea of this was threefold. First, the hash might be encoded as a member of the letter string, so producing incorrect length information and (possibly) stronger left-orienting. Second, JB was told that the hash sign was present at the beginning of the words and that it would serve as a cue as to where the words began. Thus it might facilitate orienting for this reason too. Third, the #, when present, fell at the position formally occupied by the first letters in four-letter strings. This meant that the first letters in four-letter strings now fell at the same retinal positions as the second letter in four-letter strings in Experiment 4. On a simple retinal account, JB should not neglect under these conditions. Stimuli were either presented under high or dim contrast conditions (as in Experiments 4 and 6 respectively), to assess whether the effects of the hash on length encoding and/or orienting interact with those of stimulus degradation.

Method. The stimuli were the same as in Experiment 4, except that a hash sign (#) was also placed immediately adjacent to the initial letter in each string. JB was told that the # was to act as a cue to help him find the beginning of the word. He understood that the cue was to be present for all the stimulus items. All other stimulus conditions were the same as in Experiment 4. An additional effect of the #, however, was to shift the position of fixation within four- but not five-letter words. With four-letter words, fixation now fell above the *second* letter in the word. With five-letter words, fixation remained above the third letter. As in Experiment 5, stimuli were also presented under "dim conditions". An ABBA design was used to counterbalance the ordering of bright and dim conditions and the order of presentation of the different lists.

Results and Discussion. The results are given in Table 6.

Report of the initial letter in words and nonwords in the # condition here was better than in Experiment 4 (e.g. JB made 62/80 correct letter reports to left-end letters in both 4- and 5-letter strings, relative to 50/78 and 59/80 correct reports in Experiment 4). However, we cannot tell whether this is because the hash improved orienting to the left-end of the strings, or because of JB's improvement over time and/or learning of the lists.

TABLE 6
The Effect of a Cue (#) on Initial Letter Report (JB: Experiment 7)[a]

	Addition of Letters		*Letter Position*				
	+2	*+1*	*1*	*2*	*3*	*4*	*5*
(a) 4-letter Items							
Bright Condition							
HiN words	—	2	17	18	20	20	—
LoN words	1	3	18	19	19	19	—
HiN nonwords	—	9	15	20	20	20	—
LoN nonwords	—	5	12	17	18	16	—
Total	1	19	62	74	77	75	—
(b) 4-letter Items							
Dim Condition							
HiN words	1	6	15	20	20	20	—
LoN words	1	4	16	19	20	20	—
HiN nonwords	—	6	10	20	19	20	—
LoN nonwords	—	8	8	18	18	16	—
Total	2	24	49	77	77	76	—
(c) 5-letter Items							
Bright Condition							
HiN words	—	—	16	19	18	18	19
LoN words	—	1	17	17	18	19	19
HiN nonwords	—	2	13	20	20	19	20
LoN nonwords	—	5	16	19	19	19	20
Total	—	8	62	75	75	75	78
(d) 5-letter Items							
Dim Condition							
HiN words	—	1	15	17	19	19	19
LoN words	—	1	17	19	18	19	19
HiN nonwords	—	1	11	20	20	19	20
LoN nonwords	—	5	16	17	20	20	20
Total	—	8	59	73	77	77	78

[a]The effects of report of adding a # adjacent to the initial letter position under both normal conditions and conditions of stimulus degradation.

More interestingly, JB made considerably more addition errors here, and this was particularly true for 4-letter words (see Table 6). This suggests that the # was coded along with the other letters in the string, and so produced incorrect information about word or nonword length.

There was also a small tendency for addition errors to increase again with dim relative to bright strings (e.g. there were 34 addition errors to dim strings, summing across word length; there were 28 addition errors to bright strings). More importantly, the presence of the # interacted with the effects of contrast reduction, in that neglect was now increased when the words were degraded (report of the first letter in 4-letter words being worse in dim relative to bright conditions; Chi-square$_{(1)}$ = 4.24, $P < 0.05$; there was no effect of contrast reduction on report of the other letters in the string). The effect of degradation may have emerged here rather than in Experiment 6 because the # masked the end-letter in the strings, in effect producing a stronger manipulation of degradation than was otherwise the case. This effect is consistent with the proposal that attention acts to enhance letter processing, producing a differential effect of degradation on the perception of letters at unattended locations in words.

In all conditions, JB neglected the first letter in the strings. This is despite the fact that in 4-letter words, the first letter occurred at the position of the second letter in 4- and 5-letter words in Experiment 4 and of 5-letter words here. Comparisons of the initial letter in a 4-letter string and the second letter in a 5-letter string (occupying the same retinal position) showed a significant advantage for the second letter of a 5-letter string (Chi-square$_{(1)}$ = 10.56, $P < 0.01$ and 21.68, $P < 0.001$ for the bright and dim conditions respectively).

Taken together, Experiments 6 and 7 show that JB's coding of word length is affected by reducing the contrast of words and by flanking the left-end of words with a # symbol, since addition errors are produced when the contrast is reduced and/or a # sign is added. Thus length information appears to be relatively coarsely coded. In addition, *neglect* is increased when there is both contrast reduction and a # sign at the left-end of the string. Neglect interacts with the visual encoding conditions. Also, JB continued to neglect the first letter in letter strings, even though the first letter was presented at different retinal positions in Experiment 7.

The finding that JB neglects the first letter across the conditions in Experiment 7 argues further against a visual field/retinal level representation account of his dyslexia. Although it might be argued that the long exposure durations used with JB means that we cannot ensure that he maintains fixation, a field account must argue that JB fixates in different positions in 4- and 5-letter words and according to whether a # precedes the 4-letter words. There seems no reason for this unless fixation is determined by factors such as the C.V.P. computed using word length information. Even then, JB's ability to encode word length remains problematic (see earlier).

The finding that the visual encoding conditions in Experiment 7 affected neglect also suggests that JB's neglect influences the visual coding of letters. This may be more easily reconciled with an attentional account rather than an account stressing a deficit to a string-level representation abstracted from visual encoding.

Experiment 8: Reading Reversed Words

In Experiment 8, JB was asked to read aloud words presented upside-down (ꓘVƎꓤB). This manipulation has been used in previous studies with neglect dyslexics to assess whether the impaired representation involves visually based (even if not retinotopically based) co-ordinates, or whether it involves a co-ordinate system based on the word (e.g. Caramazza & Hillis, this issue; Ellis et al., 1987; cf. Monk, 1985). In a word-centred co-ordinate system, letters may be represented with respect to particular positions in the word (e.g. B(1),R(2),E(3),A(4),K(5)). Thus a letter would occupy the same position within word-centred space when the word is presented in its usual orientation and when it is presented upside-down. Patients who neglect this type of representation may make errors to the leftmost (or rightmost) letter when the word is presented in its usual orientation, and to the rightmost (or leftmost) letter when the word is inverted, since the critical letter occupies the same position *in the word* in the two cases (e.g. Caramazza & Hillis, this issue). Patients who neglect a visually based representation should make neglect errors to the leftmost (or rightmost) letter irrespective of whether the letter is inverted (Ellis et al., 1987).

Method. JB was given 158 HiN and LoN words and nonwords from Experiment 4 on cards. The cards were inverted and presented to JB one at a time. He was asked to read each letter string aloud.

Results. The number and percentage of strings JB read aloud is given in Table 7.

JB performed *better* with the inverted strings in Experiment 8 than with the same upright strings in Experiments 4–6. However, this reflects the fact that the strings in Experiment 8 were presented on cards for unlimited durations, whilst those in Experiments 4–6 were computer presented for limited durations. JB benefits from the improved visual presentation

TABLE 7
The Effects of Inverting Words and Nonwords (JB: Experiment 8)

	% Correct Responses (Total Correct in Brackets)			
	Words		*Nonwords*	
	HiN	*LoN*	*HiN*	*LoN*
4-letter Items	95.0 (19/20)	100.0 (20/20)	65.0 (13/20)	95.0 (19/20)
5-letter Items	89.5 (17/19)	79.0 (15/19)	85.0 (17/20)	90.0 (18/20)

conditions. His improvement should not be taken to imply a positive effect of string inversion.

JB named 71/78 (91%) of the words correctly, and 67/80 of the nonwords correctly, showing a similar overall trend for a word advantage as found in his naming of computer presented upright strings. More critically, of the 20 errors JB made, 15 were to the leftmost letter in the field (and the rightmost letter in the word, e.g. NՈ˥d → PLUM). Of the remaining errors, 3 were made to letters in the central positions and only 2 to the rightmost letter in the field (and leftmost in the word).

This result suggests that letter position-in-word is less critical than letter position-in-field, in determining JB's performance. This is quite consistent with the attentional-orienting account, which maintains that attention is oriented to letters coded in retinotopic space (see earlier). According to this account, JB's deficit is caused by chronic orienting to the right visual field, which leads to poor encoding of left-side letters. This will be true irrespective of whether the letter string is normally oriented or inverted.

According to a representational account, Experiment 8 indicates that the impaired representation remains encoded in visual (rather than word-centred) co-ordinates. For instance, the representation of a word such as BREAK may take the form: B, position 2 left of centre; R, position 1 left of centre; E, centre; A, position 1 right of centre; K, position 2 right of centre. Impaired encoding of such a representation may still be termed string-based because letter positions are defined relative to the central letter in the string, and not relative to the visual field.

Experiment 9: The Effects of Letter Position-in-field for Words, Pronounceable Nonwords, and Unpronounceable Nonwords

Experiment 7 indicated that letter position-in-field alone does not determine JB's reading performance. Either the effects of position-in-field are modulated by the effects of word length (affecting attentional orienting), or the determining factor is something like spatial position relative to the central letter in the string.

Experiment 9 examined performance when longer letter strings are used, and when the strings are unpronounceable nonwords as well as words and pronounceable nonwords (as used in the earlier experiments).

Method. Twenty 5- and 7-letter word lists were devised. Pronounceable nonwords were created by altering one letter in the above words. Nonpronounceable nonword lists were created by randomising the letters in the words. All items were presented on an Apple II+ microcomputer, and were centred below a fixation cross of 1000msec. duration which signalled stimulus onset. Following an I.S.I. of 200msec., words were exposed for 500msec. JB was asked to name all items. This experiment was performed one month after Experiments 1–8, and JB had recovered to some degree. This was indicated by his 100% correct performance given an exposure duration of 10,000msec. Reducing the exposure duration reduced the accuracy of JB's performance to a level comparable to that in Experiment 4.

Results and Discussion. The results are presented in Table 8.

The data with words largely conform to those found in Experiments 4, 6, and 7. Summing across word lengths, report was worse for the letter in the left-end position relative to the next-to-end position (Chi-square$_{(1)}$ = 5.63, $P < 0.025$). It should be noted, though, that the end-letter neglect was more marked with five- than with seven-letter words. Report of the letters in seven-letter words showed a gradual decline from right to left.

Performance with pronounceable nonwords was worse than with words, but showed a similar pattern. With five-letter strings there was a marked drop in correct report of the first letter (relative to the second letter, Chi-square$_{(1)}$ = 5.03, $P < 0.025$). With seven-letter strings, there was a more gradual decline in performance across letter positions left-of-centre.

Performance was worse again with unpronounceable nonwords. More strikingly, a different pattern of performance emerged. For both five- and seven-letter strings, performance was worse for the letter *next* to the end letter on the left (summing across string length, there was an advantage for the left-end letter relative to its right-side neighbour; Chi-square$_{(1)}$ = 8.47, $P < 0.01$). This pattern of data is particularly noteworthy in view of the consistently worse report of left-end relative to other letters, that we have observed previously with words and pronounceable nonwords.

This relative left-end benefit with unpronounceable nonwords is reminiscent of the improved end-letter report found when normal subjects identify alphanumeric strings under masking conditions (e.g. Merikle, Coltheart, & Lowe, 1971). With normal subjects, this pattern of report as a function of item position in string does not occur with other stimuli, such as geometric shapes (Hammond & Green, 1982). This suggests that it is produced by some material-specific constraint on allocating attention (see Humphreys & Bruce, 1989).

Why might JB manifest this result in his reading of unpronounceable nonwords, but not with words and pronounceable nonwords? Also, why do longer (seven-letter) words and nonwords show a more gradual right-to-left decline in report accuracy than five-letter strings? According to the representational account, the gradual decline of letter report in longer strings may reflect a gradient of degradation with letter information becoming increasingly degenerate as the letters are presented more to the

TABLE 8
The Effects of Letter Position-in-field with Words, Pronounceable Nonwords, and Unpronounceable Nonwords (JB: Experiment 9)[a]

	Addition of Letters		*Letter Position in Word*						
	+2	*+1*	*1*	*2*	*3*	*4*	*5*	*6*	*7*
(a) Words									
5-letter	—	1	—	70 (28)	98 (39)	93 (37)	90 (36)	93 (37)	—
7-letter	—	3	63 (25)	70 (28)	75 (30)	83 (33)	99 (35)	90 (36)	90 (36)
(b) Pronounceable Nonwords									
5-letter	1	5	—	33 (13)	60 (24)	80 (32)	75 (30)	80 (32)	—
7-letter	2	2	45 (18)	45 (18)	70 (21)	75 (30)	80 (32)	85 (34)	83 (33)
(c) Unpronounceable Nonwords									
5-letter	—	1	—	45 (18)	25 (10)	43 (17)	70 (30)	80 (32)	—
7-letter	—	1	25 (10)	10 (4)	43 (17)	45 (18)	28 (11)	53 (21)	75 (30)

[a]Percentage (number) of correct responses (N = 40 for each cell).

left of centre. This of course is little more than a description of the data. The relative end-letter benefit with unpronounceable nonwords could be due to normal attentional processes, which are typically allocated first to the ends of such strings. Performance remains worse with left-side than with right-side letters, however, because left-side letter information is impaired.

There are some problems with this account. One is why this (normal) allocation of attention to the left-end of the strings only occurred with unpronounceable nonwords. In the normal literature, left-end letter benefits remain present with pronounceable letter strings and, in particular, with words (Carr, Lehkuhle, Kottas, & Astor-Stetson, 1976). A second problem is why the report of letters in the second-to-left position is then so impaired in nonwords.

The attentional account we have proposed can only accommodate the data through some modification. According to this account, JB chronically orients to the right of the C.V.P. in letter strings. This alone fails to explain either the gradual right-to-left decline with longer strings, or the relative end-letter benefit with unpronounceable nonwords. A further modification is needed to explain the end-letter benefit with unpronounceable nonwords. We suggest that this benefit indicates a second re-orienting of attention, following JB's initial orienting to the right of the C.V.P. With words and pronounceable nonwords, attention may be held at the initial orienting position because there is relatively strong lexical activation, with the strength of lexical activation determining whether attention is re-oriented or not. With unpronounceable nonwords, there is minimal lexical activation. Under this circumstance, JB may (strategically?) re-orient attention to the left (see Kartsounis & Warrington, 1989; Seron, Coyette, & Bruyer, 1989). However, once this occurs, his attention may again be drawn chronically to the right, producing particularly poor identification for the letter second to the left-end of the string. The more gradual letter identification gradient in longer words may be linked to JB's problems in then coding word length. If the coded length of long words varies across trials, JB may make varying neglect errors, sometimes orienting to the left end of the string, sometimes not. Shallow gradients are associated with variable length coding.

Summary of JB

The results have shown that JB neglects the left-ends of words and pronounceable nonwords in reading. For words and nonwords four- and five-letters long, JB produces a preponderance of substitution over addition and omission errors, and he shows neglect of the first letter even though the retinal position of this letter can vary according to string length

(Experiment 7). In addition, when reading inverted words, his errors remain to letters on the left of the string (in this case, the final letters in words; Experiment 8). There are lexical effects on reading. JB is worse at identifying items with many relative to few orthographic neighbours, and worse at identifying nonwords to words (Experiment 4). JB's neglect dyslexia also interacts with the visual presentation conditions. When words are degraded by contrast reduction, or when a flanking hash sign is added at the end of the string, the number of addition errors increases. When stimuli are both degraded and have a left-end flanker, neglect of the first letter is increased (Experiments 6 and 7). With longer (seven-letter) words there is a tendency for a gradient of neglect, with letter identification gradually decreasing as a function of letter position in the left visual field. There is also a relative enhancement of identification for the first (relative to the second) letter in unpronounceable nonwords (Experiment 9).

We have accounted for this complex pattern of results in two ways. One account maintains that JB has an impaired string-level representation, in which letters are encoded in spatial positions relative to the centre letter in letter strings. The second account maintains that JB's neglect dyslexia is caused by chronic orienting to the right of the C.V.P. for words. We return to details of these accounts following the case report on a second neglect dyslexic, MO.

CASE TWO: MO

MO, born 10.12.47, was a wood machinist by trade. He suffered a sub-arachnoid haemorrhage in November 1988 as a result of an arterio-venous malformation. C.T.-scan demonstrated a right temporo-parietal lesion. He had a left homonymous hemianopia. MO suffered a mild hemiplegia as a result of his lesion (he was able to walk independently, but was unable to use his left hand). His speech was normal and he scored perfectly on the Rivermead Cancellation Test. In contrast to JB, he showed no neglect in drawing or in line bisection, or other everyday life tasks. He showed no impairments in the reading of text. However, when performance was forced (due to limited exposure of words) he showed a deficit similar to that of JB.

Experiment 10: The Effects of N and Lexical Identity

The effects of lexical identity and of orthographic neighbours was investigated in the same way as has been described for JB (Experiment 4). MO's impairment was less severe than that of JB, and in order to obtain errors the exposure duration was reduced to 400msec. (though this is still in excess of that required by non-brain-damaged subjects). In all other respects, the experimental procedure parallels that described for Experiment 4.

Results. The results are displayed in Table 9 (a and b).

1. *Effects of lexical identity and N*

Words were identified more accurately than nonwords (Chi-square$_{(1)}$ = 28.36, $P < 0.001$). Considering full report, there were 31/39 HiN words and 36/39 LoN words correctly reported; for HiN and LoN nonwords the equivalent scores were 13/40 and 21/40 respectively. Performance was better with LoN relative to HiN strings (Chi-square$_{(1)}$ = 3.95, $P < 0.05$).

2. *Position-in-string effect*

As with JB, accuracy or report of the letters in words and nonwords was significantly affected by the position of a letter within a string (Chi-square$_{(3)}$ = 38.56, $P < 0.001$ and Chi-square$_{(4)}$ = 54.11, $P < 0.001$ for 4- and 5-letter words respectively).

3. *Error analysis*

Errors were classified using the same procedure as for JB. There were too few errors to provide a meaningful breakdown across words, nonwords and the 2 string lengths. Overall, there were 52 neglect errors (e.g. COAST → OAST, GLOWN → CLOWN), 4 visual errors (e.g., CAVE → AYE), and one "other" error (WROLK → FOLD). Of the neglect errors, 17 were substitutions, 8 were additions, and 27 were omissions.

Discussion. Although MO does not present as a neglect dyslexic in standard clinical tests, neglect reading errors can be produced using brief exposures of single words. This matches previous findings of neglect in parietal patients using short exposure durations, even though the patients

TABLE 9
Neighbourhood Effects[a] (MO: Experiment 10)

	Additions		*Letter Position*				
	+2	*+1*	*1*	*2*	*3*	*4*	*5*
(a) 4-letter Items							
HiN words	1	1	18	20	19	20	—
LoN words	1	1	18	18	20	20	—
HiN nonwords	—	3	9	18	18	19	—
LoN nonwords	—	—	11	18	19	19	—
Total	2	5	56	74	76	78	—
(b) 5-letter Items							
HiN words	—	—	14	18	19	19	19
LoN words	—	—	18	18	19	19	19
HiN nonwords	—	1	13	16	20	19	20
LoN nonwords	—	2	13	16	20	20	20
Total	—	3	58	68	78	77	78

[a]Illustrates the accuracy of report of letters exposed for 400msec. according to their position in a string.

do not present with clinical neglect (see Siéroff et al., 1988). Under brief exposure conditions, MO's qualitative pattern of performance is similar to that of JB. He makes predominantly neglect errors restricted to the first letter in letter strings, he identifies words better than nonwords, and he tends to identify LoN strings better than HiN strings.

The one difference between error patterns in the two patients is that, unlike JB, MO does not predominately make substitution errors; if anything, MO makes more omission than substitution errors. This result has some consequences for the attentional account of neglect dyslexia. According to this account, the effect of position-in-string found with 4- and 5-letter strings reflects the computation of the C.V.P. for the strings, which in turn is based on relatively preserved coding of string length. However, MO seems to code string length less accurately than JB, since MO makes a proportionally high number of omission errors. This suggests that MO tends to underestimate string length. According to the attentional account, MO should thus tend to compute the C.V.P. further to the right than it really is, and therefore to neglect the second left as well as the left-end position in letter strings. Interestingly, there was some tendency for this to occur with 5-letter strings (e.g. there was correct report for 68/80 letters in the second-left position, relative to 78/80 in the third-left position). Note that such a trend is not consistent with MO's problem being solely due to his visual defect, though this may lead to his underestimations of word length (see Young, Newcombe, & Ellis, this issue (Part 2, 1991)). MO's underestimation of string length on some occasions, particularly with 5-letter strings, seems to lead to increased right-side orienting and poor report of more than one letter on the left side of the string.

The last possibility was investigated in more detail in Experiment 11, which used a reduced (250msec.) duration relative to that used with MO in Experiment 10. By reducing the exposure duration further, the encoding of string length may be affected. Under this circumstance, the attentional account predicts that neglect should be increased, and in particular that there should be a shift in neglect from the left-end position to include other positions in the string ("shrinkage"). The representational account makes less clear predictions. The data in Experiment 10 suggest that MO has impaired representation of letters in position 1 in letter strings. This may reflect a problem in any of the representations mediating word recognition (e.g. from retinal to string or word-centred representations). However, whichever representation(s) are impaired, a reasonable prediction is that there should be a general decrease in identification across the letter string when letter identification time is decreased, which may be exaggerated for left-end items which are most poorly encoded. Left-to-right "shrinkage" of the letters reported across the field is not predicted.

Experiment 11: The Effects of Reduced Exposure

Experiment 10 was repeated under reduced exposure conditions. All other aspects of the experiment were kept constant but stimulus exposure was reduced from 400msec. to 250msec.

Results. The results are displayed in Table 10.

1. *Effects of N and lexical identity*
In terms of the number of correct whole reports, performance was worse here than in Experiment 10. There were correct reports of 19/39 and 26/39 HiN and LoN words, and of 7/40 and 9/40 HiN and LoN nonwords. MO was significantly better with words than with nonwords ($\text{Chi-square}_{(1)} = 22.11, P < 0.001$); however, the effect of orthographic neighbourhood was not significant ($\text{Chi-square}_{(1)} = 1.71, P > 0.05$).
2. *Position in string effect*
Relative to Experiment 10, there was a shrinkage of correct letter identification across the string. For instance, in 4-letter strings there was a significant reduction in report for the first 2 letters in the string ($\text{Chi-square}_{(1)} = 5.86, P < 0.02$ and $\text{Chi-square}_{(1)} = 8.73$, d.f. = 1, $P < 0.01$, respectively) although there is no difference in the report of the third and fourth letters (both $P > 0.05$). The same effect is apparent with 5-letter words. There is a significant reduction in report for the first 3 letters in the

TABLE 10
Effects of Reducing Stimulus Exposure to 250msec.
(MO: Experiment 11)

	Addition of Letters		*Letter Position*				
	+2	*+1*	*1*	*2*	*3*	*4*	*5*
(a) 4-letter Items							
HiN words	—	—	11	16	18	18	—
LoN words	—	—	15	17	20	20	—
HiN nonwords	—	1	5	12	17	18	—
LoN nonwords	—	—	9	14	16	20	—
Total	—	1	40	59	71	78	—
(b) 5-letter Items							
HiN words	—	—	10	11	15	18	19
LoN words	—	—	11	14	18	19	19
HiN nonwords	—	—	5	8	16	18	18
LoN nonwords	—	—	4	7	15	20	19
Total	—	—	30	40	64	75	75

string ($\text{Chi-square}_{(1)}$ = 19.00, 210.94, 13.26, all $P < 0.001$ for the letter positions 1, 2, and 3 respectively). There is no difference in the report for the final 2 letters (both $P > 0.05$). Comparison of performance on the first 2 letters of 4-letter strings with the first 2 letters of 5-letter strings revealed significantly better performance for 4-letter strings ($\text{Chi-square}_{(1)} = 8.20$, $P < 0.01$). There appears to be a dramatic "shrinkage" of the information available for report as a result of reducing the exposure duration.

3. *Error analysis*

MO made 88 "neglect" errors, 3 visual errors, and 6 "other" errors. Of the neglect errors, there were 17 substitutions, 3 additions, and 68 omissions.

Discussion. Reducing the exposure duration of the strings did not impair MO's letter report "across the board", nor did it simply lead to decreased report of the previously neglected first letter position, as would be expected from an account in terms of a simple visual field or representation defect. Rather, there was a shrinkage in correct letter report from left to right in the string. This shrinkage in correct letter report was paralleled by a proportional increase in the number of omission errors (e.g. from 52% of the neglect errors in Experiment 10 to 77% in Experiment 11). This pattern of performance meets the predictions of the attentional account. Given underestimation of word length, the convenient viewing position will be computed as being more to the right. There will then be increased orienting to the right, and consequent shrinkage of correct report for left-side letters. Representation accounts can also accommodate these findings, but they must assume that there is generally impaired encoding of left-side (and not just left-end) letters, which becomes more marked under brief exposure conditions. Note, however, that letters in positions 1 and 2 in 4- and 5-letter words are at the same retinal positions, yet performance is *worse* with 5-letter words. This can be explained by arguing that length underestimations are greater with 5- than with 4-letter words. This produces more rightwards orienting with 5-letter words. In contrast, the result is difficult for a retinal representational account to explain.

Experiment 12: Manipulation of Fixation

The attentional and representational accounts differ in a number of ways. For instance, the attentional account alone stresses the operation of an orienting mechanism which may normally be needed to modulate letter encoding. The attentional account is also comfortable with the idea that letters are encoded retinotopically, so long as orienting is based on the computation of word length. Representational accounts differ according to the level of representation thought to be impaired. For instance, one primary difference between a string-level and a retinotopic representation concerns the defining co-ordinates of the representations. A retinotopic representation will have as its origin the point of fixation. A string-level representation will have, as its origin, the centre of the string. With a string-level representation, moving the point of fixation should not be critical. It would be critical to the formation of a retinal representation. In particular, if MO has an impaired retinal representation, moving the point of fixation to the left-end of a string may improve his performance. The same improvement might also be predicted from the attentional account. If patients start with attention oriented at the point of fixation, neglect of the left-end of letter strings may be reduced by having the patient fixate the left position. Experiment 12 tested these ideas by manipulating the fixation point.

Method. A new list of 4-letter HiN words was created. Words were selected that shared a common ending with at least 3 other words (e.g. TENT, SENT, LENT, RENT). Twenty quartets were assembled and randomly ordered. The resulting stimuli were divided into 2 lists of equal length, the only constraint being that 2 members of each quartet should appear in each list. There were 2 main conditions. In the first, the fixation cross which preceded the word appeared in the same location as it had done previously (i.e. above the third letter). In the second condition, the fixation cross appeared in the character position immediately to the left of that in which the subsequent initial letter would appear. In both conditions, the fixation cross was exposed for 200msec., there was a 200msec. I.S.I., and the target words were presented for 400msec. All words were tested under both conditions, the 2 stimulus lists being presented in an ABBA order.

Results and Discussion. The results are displayed in Table 11. Moving the fixation point has a significant effect on MO's ability to identify the initial letter in a word (Chi-square$_{(1)}$ = 12.86, $P < 0.001$).

TABLE 11
Manipulation of Fixation (MO: Experiment 12)

	Additions		*Letter Position*			
Fixation	*+2*	*+1*	*1*	*2*	*3*	*4*
Above 3rd letter	—	+4	62	80	80	80
Adjacent to 1st letter	—	+1	78	80	80	80

Illustrates the effects of manipulating the position of the fixation cross (a) above the third letter in a four-letter word and (b) adjacent to the first letter in a four-letter word.

Given that a string-level representation, centred on the middle letter in letter strings, should be the same irrespective of fixation, the data counter the argument that MO's neglect is due to an impaired string-level representation. The data are consistent with MO's neglect being affected by the orienting of attention to letter strings. Performance is improved by ensuring that attention is initially oriented to the left end of the string. The data could also be accommodated by arguing that MO's neglect is resolved when letter strings are presented within his intact visual field. However, a visual field/retinal representation account alone cannot explain the full range of data, and in particular why there is a "shrinkage" of the letters MO reports under brief presentation conditions (Experiment 11). To accommodate such data, the visual field/retinal representation account must assume that fixation veers to the right under short exposure conditions and with longer words. We have earlier proposed a computational account of why this may be so; namely, that attentional orienting is based on the coding of word length, which MO underestimates with brief exposures. The visual field/retinal representation account must be allied to attentional orienting mechanisms to explain the data.

GENERAL DISCUSSION

A number of different points may be made as regards neglect dyslexia on the basis of the data collected from JB and MO.

Evidence for Top-down Processes in Neglect

Both JB and MO showed evidence for top-down processes in that both were affected by the lexicality of the stimulus item (see Experiments 4 and 10). Performance was better with words than with nonwords and for JB there was a greater tendency to produce real word errors than nonword errors (Table 3). In addition, both patients demonstrated "neighbourhood effects"; that is, performance was worse for items with a number of neighbours (e.g. BANK) than for items of an equivalent length with few neighbours (e.g. AXLE). The neighbourhood effect tended to be greater for nonwords than for words.

These findings may be explained either in terms of sophisticated guessing, following correct identification of right-side letters, or top-down lexical influences on processing. Experiment 5 showed that JB was no more impaired at reading compound than matched noncompound words. To the extent that the right-side word in compounds does not constrain the identity of the left-side word, we would expect compound words to suffer when sophisticated guessing is applied. We take the equality of report for compound and noncompound words as supporting the interactive lexical processing account.

Evidence for Preserved Knowledge of String Length

Presented with strings containing four or five letters, JB made a majority of substitution errors, suggesting that he is able to code word length (Experiment 4). However, with longer words, this did not hold, and JB made roughly equal proportions of substitution, addition, and omission errors (Experiment 5). Also, when words were degraded or when they were preceded by a hash sign, JB made an increased number of addition errors. These last results indicate that word length is coded quite coarsely. Nevertheless, the data support the idea that word length can be computed independently of letter identification (e.g. Ellis et al., 1987). This is difficult to explain on a simple visual field/retinal representational account which assumes that letter identification and word length coding should both be impaired by visual field/retinal representational loss.

Like JB, MO made a substantial number of substitution errors. Unlike JB, these errors were matched by omission errors; also, the proportion of omission errors increased under brief exposure conditions (Experiment 11). The increase in omission errors was matched by a "shrinkage" in the number of correctly reported letters.

We have suggested that word length information may contribute to the reading of neglect dyslexics in either of two ways. One possibility is that word length information constrains lexical activation. Only words of the appropriate length are activated. Substitution errors arise when the patient incorrectly accepts a word competitor over the target. This could arise even if length information is itself derived from relatively coarsely coded visual information (see earlier). Also, the independent coding of word length information may be preserved in some neglect dyslexics (e.g. JB, here; also, VB, Ellis et al., 1987), but by no means all (e.g. MO, here; also JOH, Costello & Warrington, 1987). Hence substitution errors predominate in some but not all cases.

Although this account of length-constrained lexical activation fits reasonably well with the reported evidence from neglect dyslexia, it does not fit so easily with evidence from the normal literature. For instance, Humphreys, Evett, and Quinlan (1990) examined early visual processes in normal visual word recognition using "orthographic priming" (e.g. where brief presentation of a letter string such as "lasd" facilitates identification of the target word "LAND"). Such priming effects can be understood in terms of the target word's stored representation being activated by the prime. Interestingly, Humphreys et al. also found priming to be of equal magnitude whether primes or targets were the same or different lengths. They therefore proposed that word length information did not directly constrain lexical activation.

An alternative proposal is that length information is used to constrain attentional orienting to words. In particular, word length information is used to compute the C.V.P. in words, with the C.V.P. being computed left of centre in longer words. Left-side neglect dyslexia may be caused by chronic orienting to the right of the C.V.P. However, providing word length information is computed accurately, patients' performance may be determined by the letters' position-in-string, and not their position-in-field, and substitution errors will predominate. In contrast, if there are conditions where word length is not accurately coded (e.g. under brief exposure conditions with MO, when a # prefix is added or with longer words with JB), various effects should result. First, substitution errors should not dominate. Second, if word length is underestimated, left-end letters should be detrimentally affected (due to increased orienting to the right, because the C.V.P. is falsely computed). Third, if word length is overestimated, left-end letters may benefit (for the same reason as underestimation produces increased neglect). Fourth, when length is inaccurately coded, position-in-string may be less important than position-in-field. For instance, in cases where patients sometimes under- and sometimes overestimate word length (e.g. JB, Experiment 5), there will tend to be a gradual decrease in report moving from right-to-left in the string. This is because the attentional focus will shift across trials, but will on average be overly oriented to the right. Data consistent with each of these propositions can be found in Experiments 6, 7, 8, and 9 with JB (Tables 5, 6, 7, and 8), and Experiment 11 with MO (Table 10).

Attentional and Representational Accounts of Neglect Dyslexia

We have distinguished between an attentional account of neglect and an account of neglect based on impaired representations in word processing. With JB, an account based on an impaired word-centred representation was ruled out by the finding that he continued to neglect the left side of words even when they were inverted (Experiment 8). A retinal deficit was ruled out because he showed a tendency to make substitution errors rather than errors of omission or addition (Experiment 4), and he was affected by the position of the letter in the string rather than in the field (Experiment 7). If JB has an impaired representation of letter strings, the representation must be something like that we have termed a string-level representation. However, problems still remain. For instance, in Experiment 7 we showed that neglect lessened when words were preceded by a hash sign. Correlated with this, there was an increase in addition errors. These two results fit more easily with an attentional account of JB's neglect. According to this account, JB chronically orients to the right of the C.V.P. computed from gross word length information. Since the C.V.P.

differs in strings of different lengths, JB shows effects of letter position-in-string rather than position-in-field. Also, when word length is overestimated (e.g. when a hash sign is added to the string), orienting may be further to the left. Overestimations can produce errors of addition, plus also a reduction in neglect (according to how far JB orients to the left on each trial).

With MO, an account in terms of an impaired string-level representation seems unviable, since the position of fixation makes a marked difference to his neglect (Experiment 12). However, it also seems unlikely that his neglect is simply due to a field defect or a problem within a retinal representation of a letter string. For instance, presenting words for increasingly briefer durations produces a left-to-right "shrinkage" in the number of letters correctly reported (Experiment 11). It also produces an increasing number of omission errors. These results only fit with a field defect/retinal representation account which assumes that MO fixates further to the right as stimuli are presented more briefly. There seems little reason to propose that this should be so unless there is increased rightwards orienting under reduced exposure conditions. We propose that this is what occurred, and that the increased rightwards orienting was a function of MO tending to underestimate the length of briefly presented words. MO is facilitated by fixating the first letter in letter strings because attention to the left-end letters is assured.

To accommodate all the data, though, the attentional account needs to be equipped with at least one further proviso. This is that the switching of attention within letter strings is determined by lexical factors. Attention is less likely to be switched as the magnitude of lexical activation increases. With words and pronounceable nonwords, which strongly activate the lexicon, the patients' performance seems to be determined mainly by the initial position where attention is oriented. With unpronounceable nonwords, which activate the lexicon weakly, we suggest that patients sometimes reorient attention to the left-end of the string following the initial orienting response (to the right of the convenient viewing position). Following this, attention is chronically reoriented to the right side. This produces a relative left-end benefit for unpronounceable nonwords (Experiment 9, JB). Thus word identification is determined by an interaction between attentional and lexical factors.

Within- vs. Between-object Coding and Relations to Other Patients

In terms of a framework of attention proposed by Humphreys et al. (Note 1), the deficits in single word and nonword recognition we have described may be conceptualised as deficits in aspects of within-object coding (e.g. the orienting of attention to facilitate within-string letter coding). Humphreys et al. propose that such processes may be functionally (and anatomically) separated from the processes involved in coding the relations between separate objects (such as words on a page). We may therefore expect neglect dyslexia for single words and for text reading to occur selectively in different patients. JB here presented with problems both with single words and with text. In contrast, MO presented with problems only with single words, and then only under limited presentation conditions. MO may either have generally milder problems than JB, or he may have an impairment to within-word but not between-word encoding. The case for a dissociation between these two factors is given further support by Young et al. (this issue (Part 2, 1991)).

Our argument for an attentional disturbance in at least some neglect dyslexics fits other recent data from Siéroff et al. (1988). As mentioned in the Introduction, Siéroff et al. examined neglect dyslexia in parietal patients using short (100msec.) stimulus exposures. A key finding was that words were subject to less neglect than nonwords. Nevertheless, when *two* words were presented, one either side of fixation, patients displayed neglect for the word contralateral to the lesion site. It is difficult to account for the contrasting findings with one and two words in terms of an impairment to a particular level of representation mediating reading (cf. Caramazza & Hillis, this issue). However, it can be understood in terms of a bias in orienting (to the ipsilateral side) coupled with top-down feedback which benefits the identification of single words.

In other cases, though, neglect dyslexia may only be understood with regards to its effect at a particular level of processing. For instance, Caramazza and Hillis (this issue) discuss the case of a left-hemisphere lesioned neglect dyslexic patient who was impaired at identifying the *right end* of upright words but the *left end* (i.e. the same end letters in terms of *word space*) of inverted words. This is unlike JB here and other patients in the literature (VB; Ellis et al., 1987). Caramazza and Hillis propose that their patient (NG) has an impaired word level representation, and so is poor at identifying end letters irrespective of their (left or right) spatial positions. This may reflect an impaired representation per se, or impaired attentional processes which specifically operate on such representations. NG was also impaired at spelling, consistent with there being a common word-level representation mediating both spelling and reading (Caramazza & Hillis, this issue). In contrast, JB showed no neglect in spelling. We propose that the presumed attentional deficit we have diagnosed is specific to visually based processes (as may be expected if it is tied to a retinal co-ordinate system). Indeed, since MO here showed no signs of neglect in other visual tests, the diagnosed attentional processes may also be specific to reading. On a further speculative note, it may even be that specific representation problems tend to be found in cases of left-hemisphere neglect dyslexia, whereas problems in orienting visual attention are more commonly found in cases of neglect dyslexia following right-hemisphere lesions. Further work is needed to assess these proposals.

Manuscript received 28 February 1990
Revised manuscript received 27 July 1990

REFERENCES

Allport, A. (1987). Selection for action: Some behavioural and neurophysiological considerations of attention and action. In H. Heuer & A. F. Sanders (Eds.), *Perspectives on perception and action*. Hillsdale, N.J.: Lawrence Erlbaum Associates Inc.

Behrmann, M., Moscovitch, M., Black, S. E., & Mozer, M. (in press). Perceptual and conceptual mechanisms in neglect dyslexia: Two contrasting case studies. *Brain*.

Besner, D., Davelaar, E., Alcott, D., & Parry, P. (1984). Wholistic reading of alphabetic print: Evidence from the F.D.M. and the F.B.I. In L. Henderson (Ed.), *Orthographies and reading*. London: Lawrence Erlbaum Associates Ltd.

Bisiach, E., Perani, D., Vallar, G., & Berti, A. (1986). Unilateral neglect: Personal and extrapersonal. *Neuropsychologia*, *24*, 759–767.

Caramazza, A. & Hillis, A. E. (1990). Levels of representation, co-ordinate frames, and unilateral neglect. *Cognitive Neuropsychology*, this issue.

Carr, T. H., Lehkuhle, S. W., Kottas, B., & Astor-Stetson, E. C. (1976). Target position and practice in the identification of letters in varying contexts: A word superiority effect. *Perception and Psychophysics*, *19*, 412–416.

Coltheart, M., Davelaar, E., Jonasson, J. T., & Besner, D. (1976). Access to the internal lexicon. In S. Dornic & P. M. A. Rabbitt (Eds.), *Attention and performance VI*. Hillsdale, N.J.: Lawrence Erlbaum Associates Inc.

Costello, A. de L. & Warrington, E. (1987). Word comprehension and word retrieval in patients with localised cerebral lesions. *Brain*, *101*, 163–185.

De Renzi, E. (1982). *Disorders of space exploration and cognition*. Chichester: Wiley.

Ellis, A. W., Flude, B. M., & Young, A. W. (1987). "Neglect dyslexia" and the early visual processing of letters in words and nonwords. *Cognitive Neuropsychology*, *4*, 439–464.

Evett, L. J. & Humphreys, G. W. (1981). The use of abstract graphemic information in lexical access. *Quarterly Journal of Experimental Psychology*, *33A*, 325–350.

Gainotti, G. (1968). Les manifestations de négligence et d'attention pour l'hémispace. *Cortex*, *IV*, 64–91.

Gainotti, G., D'Erme, P., Monteleone, D., & Silveri, M. C. (1986). Mechanisms of unilateral neglect in relation to cerebral lesions. *Brain*, *109*, 599–612.

Hammond, E. J. & Green, G. W. (1982). Detecting targets in letter and nonletter arrays. *Canadian Journal of Psychology*, *36*, 67–82.

Humphreys, G. W. & Bruce, V. (1989). *Visual cognition: Computational, experimental, and neuropsychological perspectives*. London: Lawrence Erlbaum Associates Ltd.

Humphreys, G. W., Evett, L. J., & Quinlan, P. T. (1990). Orthographic processing in visual word recognition. *Cognitive Psychology*.

Humphreys, G. W. & Riddoch, M. J. (1990). Interactions between object and space systems revealed through neuropsychology. In D. E. Meyer & S. Kornblum (Eds.), *Attention and performance XIV*. Hillsdale, N.J.: Lawrence Erlbaum Associates Inc.

Humphreys, G. W., Riddoch, M. J., Davis, A., Quinlan, P. T., & Price, C. J. (1989). "On the distinction between object and space based theories of selection: Neuropsychological evidence". *Experimental Psychology Society*, Cambridge, June 1989.

Jeannerod, M. (1985). The posterior parietal area as a spatial generator. In D. J. Ingle, M. Jeannerod & D. N. Lee (Eds.), *Brain mechanisms and spatial vision*. N.A.T.O. A.S.I. Series. Dordrecht: Martinus Nyhoff.

Johnson, J. C. (1978). A test of sophisticated guessing: A theory of word perception. *Cognitive Psychology*, *10*, 123–153.

Julesz, B. & White, B. (1969). Short-term visual memory and the Pulfrich phenomenon. *Nature*, *222*, 639–641.

Kartsounis, L. D. & Warrington, E. K. (1989). Unilateral neglect overcome by cues implicit in stimulus displays. *Journal of Neurology, Neurosurgery, and Psychiatry*, *52*, 1253–1259.

Kinsbourne, M. & Warrington, E. K. (1962a). A disorder of simultaneous form perception. *Brain*, *85*, 461–486.

Kinsbourne, M. & Warrington, E. K. (1962b). A variety of reading disability associated with right-hemisphere lesions. *Journal of Neurology, Neurosurgery, and Psychiatry*, *25*, 339–344.

Kuçera, H. & Francis, W. N. (1967). *Computational analysis of present-day American English*. Providence, R.I.: Brown University Press.

LaBerge, D. (1983). The spatial extent of attention to letters and words. *Journal of Experimental Psychology: Human Perception and Performance*, *9*, 371–379.

Laplane, D. & Degos, J. D. (1983). Motor neglect. *Journal of Neurology, Neurosurgery, and Psychiatry*, *46*, 152–158.

Luria, A. R. (1959). Disorders of simultaneous perception in a case of bilateral occipito-parietal brain injury. *Brain*, *83*, 437–439.

McClelland, J. L. & Rumelhart, D. E. (1981). An interactive activation model of context effects in letter perception: Part 1. An account of basic findings. *Psychological Review*, *88*, 375–407.

Merikle, P. M., Coltheart, M., & Lowe, D. G. (1971). On the selective effects of a pattern masking stimulus. *Canadian Journal of Psychology*, *25*, 264–279.

Mesulam, M. M. (1981). A cortical network for directed attention and unilateral neglect. *Annals of Neurology*, *10*, 310–325.

Monk, A. F. (1985). Co-ordinate systems in visual word recognition. *Quarterly Journal of Experimental Psychology*, *37(A)*, 613–625.

Mozer, M. C. (1987). Early parallel processes in reading: A connectionist approach. In M. Coltheart (Ed.), *Attention and performance XII*. Hillsdale, N.J.: Lawrence Erlbaum Associates Inc.

Ogden, J. A. (1987). The "neglected" left hemisphere and its contribution to visuospatial neglect. In M. A. Jeanerrod, (Ed.), *Neurophysiological and neuropsychological aspects of spatial neglect*. Amsterdam: North Holland.

O'Regan, J. K. & Levy-Schoen, A. (1987). Eye-movement strategy and tactics in word recognition and reading. In Coltheart, M. (Ed.), *Attention and performance XII*. Hillsdale, N.J.: Lawrence Erlbaum Associates Inc.

O'Regan, J. K., Levy-Schoen, A., Pynte, J., & Brugaillere, B. (1984). Convenient fixation location within isolated words of different lengths and different structures. *Journal of Experimental Psychology: Human Perception and Performance*, *10*, 250–257.

Patterson, K. E. & Wilson, B. (1990). A ROSE is a ROSE or a NOSE. *Cognitive Neuropsychology*, this issue.

Posner, M. I. & Peterson, S. E. (1990). The attention system of the human brain. *Annual Review of the Neurosciences*, *13*, 25–42.

Posner, M. I., Cohen, Y., & Rafal, R. D. (1982). Neural systems control of spatial orienting. *Philosophical Transactions of the Royal Society, London*, *B298*, 60–70.

Posner, M. I., Walker, J. A., Friedrich, F. J., & Rafal, R. D. (1984). Effects of parietal injury on the covert orienting of attention. *Journal of Neuroscience*, *4*, 1863–1874.

Riddoch, M. J. & Humphreys, G. W. (1983). The effect of cueing on unilateral neglect. *Neuropsychologia*, *21*, 589–599.

Riddoch, M. J. & Humphreys, G. W. (1987). Perceptual and action systems in unilateral neglect. In M. Jeanerrod (Ed.), *Neurophysiological and neuropsychological aspects of visual neglect*. North Holland: Elsevier Science Publishers.

Siéroff, E., Pollatsek, A., & Posner, M. I. (1988). Recognition of visual letter strings following injury to the posterior visual spatial attention system. *Cognitive Neuropsychology*, *5*, 427–449.

Seron, X., Coyette, F., & Bruyer, R. (1989). Ipsilateral influences on contralateral processing in neglect patients. *Cognitive Neuropsychology*, *6*, 475–498.

Seron, X., DeLoche, G., & Coyette, F. (1989). A retrospective analysis of a single case neglect therapy: A point of theory. In X. Seron & G. DeLoche (Eds.), *Cognitive approaches to neuropsychological rehabilitation*. Hillsdale, N.J.: Lawrence Erlbaum Associates Inc.

Sternberg, S. (1969). The discovery of processing stages: Extension of Donder's method. In W. G. Koster (Ed.), *Attention and performance II*. Amsterdam: North Holland.

Wilson, J. A. & Anstis, S. (1969). Visual latency as a function of luminance. *American Journal of Psychology*, *82*, 350–358.

Young, A. W., Newcombe, F., & Ellis, A. W. (1991). Different impairments contribute to neglect dyslexia. *Cognitive Neuropsychology*, this issue (Part 2).

REFERENCE NOTE

1. Humphreys, G. W., Riddoch, M. J., & Müller, H. (under review). Where, what, and why: On the interaction between ventral object vision and dorsal space vision in humans. *Psychological Review*.

COGNITIVE NEUROPSYCHOLOGY, 1990, 7 (5/6) 519–554

Focusing on/in Visual-verbal Stimuli in Patients with Parietal Lesions

Eric Siéroff

INSERM 280, Lyon, France

Patients with parietal lesions have been shown to exhibit the phenomenon of visual-verbal extinction between letter strings (when presented with pairs of verbal stimuli) and within a letter string (when presented with multiple, unrelated letters, as in nonwords). A group study is reported with patients suffering from right or left parietal lesions. It is shown that although patients with right lesions show reasonably consistent left extinction with bilateral presentation of nonwords (centred or pairs), patients with left parietal lesions show quite puzzling results: they may present more extinction with pairs of short nonwords than with long centred nonwords; also, the side of extinction is not systematically on the side contralateral to the lesions. A case study is presented of a patient suffering from a left parietal lesion, who shows extinction with pairs of short nonwords but not with centred nonwords. It is argued that he may show a specific deficit in focusing on (selecting) one visual-verbal stimulus, when it is presented with other visual-verbal stimuli. Some hypotheses are developed concerning the different visuo-spatial processes occurring in reading.

INTRODUCTION

Patients with left or right parietal lesions may have difficulties processing simultaneously presented information: the phenomenon of extinction, which can appear with visual-verbal stimuli (i.e. visually presented words and nonwords) in addition to auditory, tactile, or other visual stimuli. Visual-verbal extinction can take several forms. It can occur inside letter strings (e.g. inside a nonword letter string). It can also occur when several letter strings are presented, separated by blank spaces: there can be

Requests for reprints should be addressed to Eric Siéroff, INSERM 280, 151 Cours Albert-Thomas, 69003 Lyon, France.

Patient PF (case study) was seen in Service de Neuropsychologie (Dr. J. Pellat), Hôpital de la Tronche, Grenoble. Other patients (group study) were seen in Laboratoire de Rééducation du Langage (Dr. F. Michel), Hôpital Neurologique, Lyon. I thank for much help B. Naegele, D. David, D. Labourel, M-A. Hénaff, M-H. Giard. I also thank Jane Riddoch and Glyn Humphreys for special help in English corrections.

extinction of one string relative to the other(s). What could be the link between these two phenomena? Also, are extinction phenomena the same following right and left parietal lesions? We will first look at the available data in the literature on reading (one or several letter strings) in right parietal patients, then in left parietal patients.

Several kinds of extinction phenomena for letter strings have been reported, the most documented being neglect dyslexia. We know that hemineglect is much more frequent and more severe in right lesions than in left lesions (Friedland & Weinstein, 1977). Kinsbourne and Warrington (1962) have reported the cases of six patients with left hemineglect (after right parietal lesions), who made frequent errors when reading, confined to the beginnings of words. Most errors were substitutions (like "novel" for "level").

More recently, Ellis, Flude, and Young (1987) have reported a case of left-neglect reading, VB. They showed that errors were not influenced by factors other than visual ones: an incorrect response could be of a different grammatical class from the stimulus; also, a substitution error on the beginning of the word could change the phonology of the segment of the word she correctly perceived. By inverting the word string laterally, they further showed that left neglect was not object centred: their patient still neglected the actual left side of the word, not its first letters, now on the right side (see also Riddoch, Humphreys, Cleyton, & Fery, this issue). Finally, VB had good apprehension of the length of the word, since substitution errors were more frequent than deletions even if deletion of a letter could still make a word (as in "peach"). Ellis et al. (1987) concluded that VB's neglect affected the encoding of letter identity more than the encoding of letter position.

In other studies, lexical status of the letter string has been shown to influence extinction within letter strings. Usually, extinction is significantly smaller within words than within pseudowords (Behrmann, Moscovitch, Black, & Mozer, in press; Brunn & Farah, in press; Siéroff, Pollatsek, & Posner, 1988), and this occurs in free reading as well as with tachistoscopic presentation. The morphological status of the word does not seem to play an important role in this phenomenon: compound words like "somebody" do not usually produce more extinction than noncompound monomorphemic words (Behrmann et al., in press; Siéroff & Michel, 1987; Siéroff et al., 1988). Nevertheless, for some patients, there remains considerable extinction even inside word strings (Ellis et al., 1987; Kinsbourne & Warrington, 1962; Siéroff & Michel, 1987; Siéroff, Note 3), and in some cases this appears to be as strong for words as for nonwords (Bisiach, Meregalli, & Berti, Note 1). Note though that Bisiach et al. used very large stimuli (words 30cm. large, printed on cards), and it is possible that enlargement of the visual display disrupted performance for all types of strings. It has also been shown that relative angle between letters may have an effect. In a case study of a patient with left hemineglect, Siéroff found that abnormal spacing between the letters of a four-letter word (disrupting the form of the word) produced much more left extinction than when long normally spaced eight-letter words (subtending approximately the same visual angle) were presented (Siéroff, Note 3). This was not an effect of the shape itself of the word, since aLtErNaTiNg the letter case in words did not produce such a dramatic effect.

Neglect or extinction inside letter strings has not only been documented in tasks requiring reading aloud. Friedrich, Walker, and Posner (1985) have shown that patients with parietal lesions frequently miss (or at least are slow at processing) letters on the side contralateral to their lesions, when they have to search for a mismatching letter between two letter strings (for words and for nonwords) located one above the other. If we consider neglect and extinction phenomenon as a deficit of spatial orienting of attention, or even as a deficit of disengagement from the side ipsilateral to the lesion when attention has to be oriented toward the opposite side (Posner, Walker, Friedrich, & Rafal, 1984), it is not surprising that neglect is elicited in search tasks such as this (indeed, see Riddoch & Humphreys, 1987).

Left neglect patients not only show extinction inside letter strings, they frequently have difficulty with several words together, as in text reading. For instance, patients can omit words at the beginning of the line, and such omissions can increase as they go down the page. Some patients can read 14 of the 15 words on the first line and only the 5 rightmost words on the last line of the page. Although such a severe deficit is relatively rare, omission of at least some words is frequent in these patients (see Caplan, 1987).

Extinction can also occur when patients are presented with *pairs* of visual-verbal stimuli. Volpe, Ledoux, and Gazzaniga (1979) showed that right parietal patients had extinction of left-sided words when presented with two words, one in each hemifield. Moreover, extinction did not involve a complete loss of information: patients who showed complete left extinction for words could still decide if the extinguished word was identical to the word presented to the right side. Siéroff and Michel (1987) came to a similar conclusion on the basis of a contrast between extinction to one of a pair of words and nonextinction to a single word covering the same angle as the word pairs. Absence of extinction was found even with compound words (like "garde-chasse" = gamekeeper), showing that the result was unlikely to be due to a guessing strategy or lexicalisation responses: responding to only one of the morphemes could result in a lexical response; also, each of the morphemes could be part of several compound words.

In summary, visual-verbal extinction in right parietal patients can occur with single letter strings or with multiple letter strings (e.g. with pairs of words) In addition, extinction is usually on the side of space contralateral to the lesion.

Visuo-spatial deficits in patients with left parietal lesion present a more complex picture. In 1977, Shallice and Warrington studied two patients with a rather intriguing deficit. Although they could read words well, they were unable to name the letters inside the word they had just succeeded in reading. This was interpreted as a difficulty in processing letters when they were surrounded by other letters. Interference was less strong when the letter was surrounded by digits. Also, Shallice and Warrington demonstrated that the deficit was not at the level of programming the response (e.g. naming a number defined by several dots, within a string of digits, was correct). They concluded that their patients had a deficit in some selective attentional mechanism, in that they were unable to filter out the information they were not actually processing. This was clear not only between letters within a letter string, but also between letter strings (words). The patients made frequent migration errors between words, reading "SAND LANE" as "land sane". Also, it has to be noted that errors in reading were not systematically on the (right) side opposite to the lesion.

Patients with right hemineglect after left hemispheric lesion are rare. However, Costello and Warrington (1987) observed the case of a patient with a left occipito-parietal lesion (extending deep inside the right parietal lobe), who showed a right-sided hemineglect in some situations (copying simple shapes, line bisection) along with a left neglect dyslexia: he usually substituted or added letters on the left side of words, and this was stronger with shorter words. Katz and Sevush (1989) have described the case of two patients whose deficit was also quite unexpected. Both patients had a pure left hemisphere lesion and showed a clear right-sided extinction (with pairs of letters and with pairs of words). However, when reading single visual-verbal stimuli, they frequently missed the beginning letters, ipsilateral to the left lesion. Katz and Sevush interpreted this as a deficit in the normal activation of nodes for letters in initial positions.

Also, other studies with left parietal patients have found right-sided extinction in reading single letter strings, for nonwords more than for words (Siéroff & Michel, 1987; Siéroff et al., 1988). Friedrich et al. (1985) found right-sided extinctions in their search task.

Chedru, Leblanc, and Lhermitte (1973) found that omission of words on the side opposite to the lesion was as frequent in cases of left lesions as in cases of right lesions. However, they supposed that the significance of this deficit may be different for these two kinds of lesions. Chedru et al. believed that although left omission of words could be due to severe left hemineglect, right omission of words could be attributed in some cases to some degree of right hemi-inattention plus an additional deficit specific to reading. Indeed, most of their patients with left lesions did not show neglect on other tests.

Siéroff and Michel (1987) found that extinction for pairs of words was common after both right and left posterior lesions, although it was not clear if right extinction (after a left hemisphere lesion) had the same cause as left extinction (after a right hemisphere lesion). Moreover, visual-verbal extinction for pairs of words was sometimes found in the hemifield ipsilateral to the dominant (left) hemisphere. This was termed paradoxical extinction, after the cases of auditory ipsilateral extinction for words (Michel & Péronnet, 1975; Sparks, Goodglass, & Nickel, 1970).

In summary, visual-verbal extinction in left parietal patients can occur with presentation of single letter strings and with presentation of several letter strings. However, extinction can occur on either side, contralateral or ipsilateral to the lesion, across patients and even across conditions of presentation (single or multiple letter strings).

Thus, the relations between extinction *between* letter strings and extinction *within* letter strings remain unclear. Also, there seem to be different underlying causes for extinction after right parietal lesions and extinction after left parietal lesions. The present paper deals with visuo-spatial difficulties in reading after parietal lesions. Both right and left parietally damaged patients were studied. The relationship between deficits in reading one letter string and deficits in reading several letter strings in controlled conditions (i.e., the relationship between processing a single visual-verbal stimulus and visuo-spatial processing of several stimuli) will be considered first. The differential consequence of left and right parietal lesions on visuo-spatial processing in reading letter strings is then considered, and a case study of a patient with a left parietal lesion is presented, in which the nature of the underlying deficit is examined in more detail.

GROUP STUDY: EXPERIMENT 1

This experiment was conducted to study extinction for visual-verbal stimuli after parietal lesions. We report the performance of some patients with parietal lesions in a task of reading aloud stimuli which were presented tachistoscopically. Extinction within single stimuli and extinction between pairs of stimuli will be compared.

Method

Subjects

Patients were selected on the basis of the presence of a unilateral parietal lesion (C.T.-scan). There were four patients with right parietal lesions and five patients with left parietal lesions. Patients were included even if they had some mild difficulties in speech, but they were never

TABLE 1
Clinical Features of Patients Included in the Group Study (for PF See Text)

Lesion (Site; Nature)	*Language*	*Dichotic*[a]	*Sensory/ motor*	*Visuo-spatial*	*Reading*	*Writing*	*Others*
Patient MB, male, aged 33 Right posterior occipito-parietal vascular	Good	Normal	—	Difficulties with left visual field and with depth perception; some simultagnosia	Some discomfort; omission of some short words and some left words; places page at distance	Good	—
Patient PR, male, aged 24 Right temporo-parietal; traumatism	Good	Left extinction	—	Left hemianopia sparing 30 degrees of angle	Slow	Good	—
Patient BO, male, aged 50 Right parietal; vascular	Good	Normal	—	Small field cut on the left (periphery); left extinction	—	—	—
Patient RM, male, aged 72 Right occipito parietal; vascular	Good	Left extinction	Left hypo-esthesia and paresia	Severe left hemi-neglect (all tests); small left field cut (periphery)	Many difficulties with left side of words and of text	Impaired, spatial errors (addition, perseveration)	Globally slow

TABLE 1
(Continued)

Lesion (Site; Nature)	*Language*	*Dichotic*[a]	*Sensory/ motor*	*Visuo-spatial*	*Reading*	*Writing*	*Others*
Patient JPB, male, aged 36 Left posterior, superior parietal, vascular	Difficulties with word segmentation tests	Small left extinction	Right hypo-esthesia	Some autopo-agnosia; right extinction	Slow, and omission of short words	Impaired in spelling and writing	Dyscalculia
Patient AVU, female, aged 30 (Deep) left parietal, vascular	Good	Small left extinction	Right hypo-esthesia	Right hemianopia sparing 30 degrees of angle	Slow, omission of short words, small difficulty of comprehension	Apraxic and spatial agraphia	—
Patient MF, male, aged 41 Left (inferior) parietal and posterior temporal, vascular	Some difficulties with complex syntax; problems with repetition (digit span at 4/5); denomination perfect	Right extinction	—	—	Difficulties with complex text, even in silent reading; difficulties of recognition of long words spelled to him	Good	—
Patient HV, male, aged 33 Small left supra-marginal gyrus; traumatism	Some paraphasia on long words; good repetition and denomination	Left extinction	—	—	Slow	Some difficulties with nonwords	—

[a]Verbal dichotic listening task.

major, and comprehension was always perfect. Most patients had some trouble in reading or at least some discomfort. A more detailed description of each patient is provided in Table 1. All patients were right-handed. All patients were tested at least one month after the onset.

Stimuli

Stimuli were words and nonwords three or eight letters long. The stimuli were randomly allocated to one of three lists.

Words were all high frequency: frequency means were 1625, 1500, and 1540 for short words, and 2116, 2357, and 2086 for long words in lists A, B, and C respectively (Imbs, 1971). Thus, short words were slightly more common than long words. Most of the words were monomorphemic.

Nonwords were constructed from the words, sharing a large number of letters with them. In lists A and B, the pronounceability of the nonwords was not exactly equivalent for short and long nonwords. Some (less than one third) short stimuli were somewhat less pronounceable (like "ksi" or "iln"). This was originally done to reduce the advantage produced by the number of letters in pairs of nonwords (six letters) compared to the number of letters in long centred nonwords (eight letters). Indeed it was difficult to equate the perceptual difficulty in reading these stimuli. Most patients were run with lists A and B. In addition, some patients were run with list C, which was slightly different from lists A and B although using mostly the same stimuli. However, the number of stimuli was smaller (see Procedure), and the short nonwords which were difficult to pronounce were removed. One patient, PF, was run with list C only.

Stimuli were written with upper-case letters. Thus, no accent was present. They were presented on a video screen controlled by an Apple IIe microcomputer. Each letter was 1cm. large. The patients were approximately 50cm. from the screen, so that the maximal visual angle of stimuli (in bilateral presentation) was around 8 degrees, 4 degrees in each hemifield.

Procedure

On each trial, the first item of the screen was a fixation arrow (pointing up), which appeared in the middle of the screen for 1000msec. before disappearing. The stimuli occurred immediately after the offset of the arrow, and were located above the arrow. The fixation arrow indicated the centre of a stimulus string, 8 letters long. Stimuli were presented in 3 conditions, with the trials for all conditions randomised in one block. The 3 conditions were as follows:

1. Unilateral Presentation of Letter String. In this condition, only one short 3-letter stimulus was presented. Each 3-letter stimulus was presented one space to the right or to the left of the location of the arrow (corresponding to the width of one letter). There were 80 unilateral presentations in lists A and B, 40 in list C. Equal numbers of words and nonwords were presented to the right and left of fixation. This was a control condition to evaluate the perceptual ability of the patient in each hemifield without provoking the phenomenon of extinction. However, it is possible that there was some competition between the letters of the nonwords, although they were very short.

2. Bilateral Presentation of Pairs of Letter Strings. In this condition, pairs of short 3-letter stimuli were presented. Each letter string was presented either side of a blank space between the 2 stimuli of a pair. This blank space was centred around the location of the fixation arrow, and was as large as the space of 2 letters. Stimuli appeared randomly in a pair. In each of the lists A and B, there were 40 short nonwords presented in 20 randomly selected pairs and 40 short words presented in 20 randomly selected pairs. There was no mixed pair consisting of one word and one nonword. In list C, there were only 12 pairs of random words and 12 pairs of random nonwords. This bilateral condition was included to produce extinction *between* letter strings.

3. Bilateral Centred Presentation of Letter Strings. In this condition, single strings of 8 letters were presented. The stimuli were centred around the location of the arrow, so that they subtended the same visual angle as the pairs of stimuli. In lists A and B, 20 long nonwords and 20 long words were presented. In list C, only 16 nonwords and 16 words were presented. This condition was done to evaluate extinction *inside* letter strings.

Total number of trials was 160 with lists A and B, and 96 with list C.

Exposure time for the stimuli varied across subjects, ranging from 160msec. to 300msec. to minimise individual differences in global performance. The time of presentation was the same for all conditions. This time of presentation (mostly 160msec.) is indicated for each patient. Stimuli were followed by a patterned mask, made of asterisks, which stayed on the screen until the next trial. Eye movements were not recorded.

Task

Each patient was asked to fixate the top of the arrow and to report the stimuli by reading them aloud: they could name a word, name a nonword, or name constituent letters. They were encouraged to make a response to all stimuli in the test, and to all stimuli on a trial (when there were two stimuli) or to the whole stimulus (when there was a long centred stimulus).

Results

Scoring Methods

There are certain basic findings we want to specify for each patient. One is the phenomenon of extinction (see Siéroff & Michel, 1987): performance in a bilateral condition (pairs of stimuli, or centred stimuli) will be compared to performance in the unilateral conditions. When extinction is present, we further specify if this extinction is dependent on the nature of stimuli (is extinction for nonwords stronger than extinction for words?) and if this extinction is dependent on the type of bilateral presentation (pairs of stimuli or centred stimuli).

Accuracy of report was scored using clusters of three letters, left and right of fixation. This was straightforward for bilateral three-letter stimuli. For centred stimuli, this meant that the two central letters were not counted. The scoring methods corresponded to the scoring methods of Experiment 2 in Siéroff et al. (1988). There were two different scoring methods. The first evaluated the number of letters reported in each cluster. Of course, it was difficult to decide if letters were reported when the response of the patient was a pronounced nonword. A conservative scoring procedure was therefore used: when a phoneme corresponding to a letter of the stimulus was produced, it was counted as correct even if not in the correct place. The second method evaluated the number of letters correctly reported, in the order corresponding to the actual display. This scored the accuracy of registration of relative position between recognised letters.

However, only the first scoring method will be reported since differences between both scoring methods were not dramatic.

As in Siéroff et al. (1988), a laterality index (L.I.) was calculated by the formula $(R - L) \times 100/(R + L)$, where R was the score for the right cluster and L was the score for the left cluster. This was to evaluate the tendency to asymmetrical performance. A positive L.I. indicates a right hemifield advantage, a negative L.I. indicates a left hemifield advantage. Asymmetry in performance was also detected by the actual number of trials which showed an extinction in a bilateral condition; that is on the number of occurrences of superiority of L over R or of R over L. This last score is indicated only when the laterality index is not strikingly asymmetrical, and when asymmetry is compared between bilateral conditions.

Finally, the overall number of letters which were recognised in both left and right letter clusters was compared between different bilateral conditions, that is between pairs of stimuli and long centred stimuli. This was to evaluate the global performance on pairs of letter strings compared to global performance on long centred stimuli, not taking into account the lateral bias.

General results are first presented. Then some more detailed analyses will be provided for each patient. Accuracy of report of left and right

TABLE 2
Results for Experiment 1: Percentage of Letters Correctly Reported (Irrespective of Position) in Left Cluster (L), Right Cluster (R), and Laterality Index (LI)

	Words									*Nonwords*								
	Single			*Pairs*			*Centred*			*Single*			*Pairs*			*Centred*		
Patients	*L*	*R*	*LI*	*L*	*R*	*LI*	*L*	*R*	*LI*	*L*	*R*	*LI*	*L*	*R*	*LI*	*L*	*R*	*LI*
Right Parietal																		
MB	63	82	+13	31	66	+36	71	83	+8	58	73	+11	28	60	+36	39	67	+26
PR	67	97	+18	52	80	+21	68	92	+15	63	88	+17	32	60	+30	32	72	+38
BO	73	90	+10	53	93	+27	97	100	+2	68	90	+14	47	78	+25	52	85	+24
RM	63	90	+18	9	89	+82	49	83	+26	41	80	+32	13	75	+70	22	83	+58
Left Parietal																		
JPB	97	93	−2	86	19	−63	94	94	0	83	84	+1	53	24	−38	71	38	−30
AVU	85	92	+4	73	77	+2	88	92	+2	77	87	+6	40	68	+26	53	92	+26
MF	85	93	+5	62	78	+12	95	97	+1	80	85	+3	45	47	+1	55	77	+16
HV	82	90	+5	57	52	−5	87	95	+5	78	70	−6	53	37	−19	43	68	+22
PF	100	100	0	56	64	+7	90	92	+1	95	98	+2	54	15	−56	58	68	+7

TABLE 3
Percentage Loss of Performance Between Centred Nonwords and Pairs of Nonwords (Experiment 1)

Right Parietal Patients		*Left Parietal Patients*	
MB	17	JPB	29
PR	12	AVU	26
BO	9	MF	30
RM	16	HV	19
		PF	45

clusters and the laterality index in each condition are presented with the first scoring method, for each patient, in Table 2. Differences of overall scores between pairs of nonwords and centred nonwords are shown in Table 3.

General Results

We calculated how many letters were correctly identified for each trial, in each cluster (left or right), with the first scoring method. A four-way ANOVA was computed with one between-subjects factor, lesion (right or left), and three within-subject factors: string type (words or nonwords), condition (unilateral, pairs, or centred), and clusters (contralateral to the lesion or ipsilateral to the lesion).

A main effect for string type emerged: $F(1,7) = 318.9$; $P < 0.001$, showing that words were better identified than nonwords. There was an interaction of string type × condition: $F(2,14) = 15.0$; $P < 0.001$. The superiority of words over nonwords seemed more apparent in the centred condition.

The effect of condition was also significant: $F(2,14) = 61.1$; $P < 0.001$, as well as the interactions of lesion × condition: $F(2,14) = 4.4$; $P < 0.05$; clusters × conditions: $F(2,14) = 6.7$; $P < 0.01$; and cluster × lesion: $F(1,7) = 12.5$; $P < 0.01$. We will see further that extinction was not the same for all bilateral conditions (pairs and centred), and this differed with the side of the lesion. We will look specifically at performance with pairs of nonwords and with centred nonwords, because a difference between these conditions cannot be explained by the number of higher-level units, as might be the case with words.

Right Parietal Lesions

Case 1: MB. Results were obtained for list A and for list B. Time of presentation was 160msec.

There was some asymmetry in favour of right hemifield for each condition, even for unilateral stimuli (L.I. = +13 for words and +11 for nonwords), although the asymmetry was small in this case. This could be due to some sensory deficit mentioned in Table 1, such as hemianopia. However, asymmetry was much stronger for bilateral presentation. This was true for pairs of stimuli (L.I. = +36 for pairs of words as well as for pairs of nonwords) as well as for single centred nonwords (L.I. = +26). Although the L.I. was different in both conditions, the difference becomes minimal if we consider the number of trials showing a right bias (trials where more letters were recognised on the right than on the left): 24 out of 40 trials in both the pairs of nonwords and the centred nonwords. Also, global performance in pairs of nonwords was not significantly different from global performance in centred nonwords ($\chi^2 = 2.67$; $P =$ n.s.). Finally, MB showed a strong word superiority effect on nonwords, and there was no strong asymmetry with centred words (L.I. = +8).

Case 2: PR. Results were obtained for list B only. Time of presentation was 160msec.

There was an asymmetry in favour of the right hemifield in each condition. The asymmetry for unilateral presentation may be caused by the sensory deficit in the left hemifield (cf. Case 1). Compared to this asymmetry for unilateral presentation, asymmetry for centred nonwords and pairs of nonwords was much stronger (respectively L.I. of +38 and +30, 13 and 12 trials out of 20 with right bias), so that we may consider that there was an extinction, and thus an attentional deficit for nonwords. As in Case 1, the asymmetry was similar in pairs of nonwords and in centred nonwords. Also, global performance in pairs of nonwords was not significantly different from global performance in centred nonwords ($\chi^2 = 0.53$; $P =$ n.s.).

As expected, the asymmetry for centred words was small (L.I. = +15) but the asymmetry for pairs of words (L.I. = +21) was not stronger than the asymmetry for unilateral words (L.I. = +18). However, the number of centred words which show right bias was only 8, and the number of pairs of words which show a right bias was equivalent to what had been found for pairs of nonwords (12 trials out of 20). Unfortunately we have no way of considering, with this method, the bias for unilateral words.

Case 3: BO. Results were obtained with list A. Stimuli were presented for 160msec.

He showed a clear left extinction in the bilateral conditions and the centred non-word condition. There was no extinction with centred words. The asymmetry with pairs of nonwords (L.I. = +25) was similar to that with centred nonwords (L.I. = +24). Also, global performance in pairs of nonwords was not significantly different from global performance in centred nonwords ($\chi^2 = 0.58$; P = n.s.).

Case 4: RM. Results were obtained with list A and list B. Time of presentation of stimuli was 300msec.

The disadvantage for report of letters in the left hemifield was pronounced for each condition. This strong asymmetry could be related to a sensory deficit, but also to the strong left hemineglect (in line bisection and in cancellation tasks) which was not present in other patients. It is known that strong left hemineglect can lead to difficulty in processing information in the left hemifield even without any apparent competition from the stimuli in the right hemifield (Posner, Walker, et al., 1987).

Again, there were three conditions showing a much stronger asymmetry than other conditions: presentation of pairs of stimuli (words as well as nonwords) and presentation of centred nonwords. The laterality index was larger for pairs of nonwords (+70) than for the centred nonwords (+58); however, the number of trials with right bias was about the same (34 and 36 respectively, out of 40). Also, global performance in pairs of nonwords was not significantly different from global performance on centred nonwords ($\chi^2 = 2.67$; P = n.s.). Finally, results with centred words were asymmetrical but to the same degree as with unilateral presentation.

Left Parietal Lesions

Case 5: JPB. Results were obtained with list A and list B. Time of presentation was 160msec. JPB was also run with list C of stimuli and showed similar results which are not described here.

JPB showed a right-sided extinction of a "classical" type: strong for pairs of stimuli (L.I. = −63 for words and −38 for nonwords) and for centred nonwords (L.I. = −30). The number of left bias trials was identical for pairs of nonwords and centred nonwords (25 out of 40). Surprisingly, this number was bigger for pairs of words (34). However, Table 2 shows that performance on right hemifield stimuli was identical for pairs of words and nonwords. The bigger bias to the left with pairs of words may be due to the fact that, for example, with 2 letters perceived it remains possible to find the identity of the word, and this occurred more frequently for left words (which JPB responded to first). Finally, JPB had significantly more difficulty with pairs of nonwords compared to centred nonwords ($\chi^2 = 9.5$; $P < 0.01$). This was not found to be the case with patients with right parietal lesions.

Case 6: AVU. Results were obtained with list B. Time of presentation was 160msec.

The results for words showed no strong asymmetry for any of the conditions. The results for nonwords showed a clear *left-sided* extinction in both bilateral conditions, with pairs of nonwords (L.I. = +26, 12 right bias trials out of 20) and with centred nonwords (L.I. = +26, 16 right bias trials). This is a paradoxical extinction, ipsilateral to the lesion, similar to that reported by Siéroff and Michel (1987), although in the previous instance it was demonstrated in pairs of words. There is no left extinction for pairs of words here. Left extinction may result from a right hemispheric lesion. However, in the case of AVU, there is no right hemispheric lesion on C.T.-scan and the left lesion is due to an arterio-veinous malformation. AVU has a lesion deep inside the left parietal lobe, and the possibility of right hemisphere involvement is unlikely. Another point is that AVU, like JPB, showed worse performance with pairs of nonwords than with centred nonwords ($\chi^2 = 6.2$; $P < 0.05$).

Case 7: MF. Results were obtained with list A. Time of presentation was 160msec.

Performance was asymmetrical in some conditions but this asymmetry was never large (L.I. = +12 for pairs of words and +16 for centred nonwords) and did not reach significance. MF was an English teacher, and he was also run with English stimuli (those of the case study on WK, in Siéroff et al., 1988). The level of overall performance was similar to that in French: also, a small right advantage was found with pairs of words (63% correct for the left word and 83% correct for the right one); however, a small left advantage was found with pairs of nonwords (47% correct for the left nonword and 32% for the right one). This suggests that the small asymmetry in MF was not strongly related to one side and may not be a crucial point in this patient. However, MF appeared to have special difficulties with pairs of nonwords compared to centred nonwords ($\chi^2 = 6.9$; $P < 0.01$). In fact, MF found it difficult to respond to both stimuli. Usually, he responded to only one nonword of a pair of nonwords and it could be either the left or the right one.

Case 8: HV. Results were obtained with list A. Time of presentation was 300msec. Tachistoscopic reading was difficult so a longer presentation time was used.

Here, the three crucial conditions (pairs of words, pairs of nonwords, and centred nonwords) led to special identification difficulties compared with other conditions. Asymmetry occurred only for nonwords: there was a significant right advantage for centred nonwords ($\chi^2 = 7.6$; $P < 0.01$) and a small, nonsignificant left advantage for pairs of nonwords ($\chi^2 = 3.4$; P = n.s.)! However, global performances on pairs of nonwords and on centred nonwords were not significantly different ($\chi^2 = 2.2$; P = n.s.). The left extinction for centred nonwords could not be explained by a right hemisphere lesion: HV had a small trauma confined to the left supramarginal gyrus (as a result of being stabbed by a car key!).

It is informative to look at the strategy of response with this patient. He frequently spelled individual letters in unilateral and bilateral short stimuli (words as well as nonwords). A slightly different strategy was used for centred nonwords. In 9 trials (out of 20) he actually spelled aloud the first (leftmost) letters (up to 3) and he then pronounced the rest of the stimulus, or, more precisely, what he perceived from the stimulus. In this case, he did not try to make a unique, integrated response for the centred nonword. It was as if he had two different strategies in reading: one for the rightmost two thirds of centred nonwords, and one for the left part of centred nonwords and for short stimuli (single or pairs). This last strategy does not seem to be efficient since he was worse on the beginning of nonwords. For centred words, only 2 of the 6 erroneous responses used the same strategy. There was no strong asymmetry in reading centred words, although he seemed rather hesitant on the beginning of these words.

Case 9: PF. Results were obtained with list C. He was tested twice, with a six-months interval between both sessions. Time of presentation was 160msec.

As with some of the other left parietal patients, PF showed special difficulties with pairs of stimuli, words as well as nonwords. Performance for pairs of stimuli was about 50% worse than the performance for centred stimuli (for words as well as for nonwords). The difference between pairs of nonwords and centred nonwords was significant ($\chi^2 = 7.0$; $P < 0.01$). The difference between pairs of words and centred words was also significant, but, as we said before, this was less interesting because pairs of words are different from centred words in the number of associated responses. Asymmetry (extinction) existed only for pairs of nonwords ($\chi^2 = 25.5$; $P < 0.01$). The difficulty in processing pairs of stimuli may be stronger for nonwords, although short nonwords in list C were all easily pronounceable letter strings, so this difference between performance in pairs of nonwords and performance in pairs of words cannot be explained solely by a difficulty in making up a laboriously uttered response, or in processing unfamiliar spelling patterns. Maybe, in the case of pairs of words, the difficulty (which remains to be defined) could be attenuated by automatic lexical access for words. It is clear that performance on pairs of stimuli (words as well as nonwords) was dramatically worse than performance on centred stimuli. As was the case with MF, PF most frequently responded to only one word of a pair, but it was not systematically the left one, and the asymmetry with words was not lateralised systematically.

Discussion

It is difficult to have a clear picture of the different kinds of deficits which can be encountered in reading after parietal lesions. However, it is possible, in the light of these data, to make some general points.

First, all patients have a clear word superiority effect, at least when single words and nonwords are presented. The presentation of a single centred nonword always leads to more extinction than the presentation of a single centred word. This confirms the results of previous studies. Centred words may benefit from some automatic processing of letters. This also implies that every patient studied has no (or little) problem in access to the lexicon. Their main deficit appears to be elsewhere. Nonetheless, patients claim some difficulty in reading text, which is more pronounced in some cases. The main difficulties in reading text were a reduced reading speed and a tendency for error (omissions or substitutions of words).

Even when they have little problem with reading single words, right parietal patients show consistent left-sided extinction in some of the conditions presented here, in particular with bilateral presentation of words or nonwords, and with centred nonwords. This result suggests an attentional bias toward the side ipsilateral to the lesion. Left extinction consists of fewer letters being recognised in the left hemifield than in the right hemifield. The number of simultaneously presented stimuli is not important here: performance on pairs of nonwords is similar to performance on centred nonwords.

Extinction (or asymmetry in reading) by right parietal patients is also sometimes found in the other conditions (e.g. with unilateral presentation of words or nonwords, or with centred words), but the effects are smaller in these instances. This may be due to different causes. Of course, an attentional bias which exists even with centred word presentations may be due to nonpathological causes. Some people are poor readers and may not have developed strong automatic processing for words (or at least for some words). We did not check for this but it remains a theoretical possibility. Pathological causes are hemianopia and strong hemineglect. A visual sensory deficit may sometimes lead to less good but not null performance in the affected hemifield, in every condition. Although none of the patients had a complete left hemianopia, all of them were considered to be mildly hemianopic at the beginning of their illness. Some still had a peripheral scotoma (MB, PR, and RM).

A further possibility is that parietal lesions can give rise to deficits in the disengagement of spatial attention from the hemifield ipsilateral to the lesion when attention has to be moved toward the contralateral hemifield (Posner, Walker, Friedrich, & Rafal, 1984; Morrow & Ratcliff, 1988).

However, it has also been argued by some authors (Posner, Inhoff, Friedrich, & Cohen, 1987; Riddoch & Humphreys, 1983; Siéroff, 1990) that a disengagement deficit may not account for all aspects of the neglect syndrome. Other visuo-spatial processing deficits may contribute to the clinical syndrome of visual hemineglect, e.g. deficits in alertness or arousal, in some early (nontransformed) processing of information, or in the ability of contralesional events to attract the attention of the patient. It could theoretically also be a deficit in the global processing of the visual information although this remains to be proven (Posner & Petersen, 1990; Siéroff, 1990). One hypothesis would be that all these deficits are more frequent following right hemisphere lesions: for instance, alertness (Heilman, Watson, & Valenstein, 1985), topological processing (Bellugi, Poizner, & Klima, 1989; Gazzaniga, 1988), and global processing (studies with hierarchical stimuli: Delis, Kiefner, & Fridlund, 1988; Robertson, Lamb, & Knight, 1988) have all been related to right hemispheric functioning.

It is possible that abnormal focused attention can explain severe extinction or neglect. Patients may have a tendency to hyperfocus (ignore global aspects of information). This could even be accentuated by the presence of a fixation item in our conditions, (although the duration of the fixation item was long, possibly allowing easier disengagement). The result is a misorienting of attention which could occur in all presentation conditions, even those which normally do not require reorienting of attention (e.g. with unilateral short stimuli, centred words). Such an explanation could account for RM's data. He showed a strong left hemineglect and poor reading performance on the left side in every condition.

However, a two-fold conclusion can be made concerning patients with right parietal lesions: extinction is always contralateral to the lesion, and extinction is the same for centred nonwords and for pairs of nonwords.

For left parietal patients, the story seems rather more difficult to understand. The only patient who could be a mirror-image of the right parietal patients is JPB. JPB showed right-sided extinction with bilateral presentations of words or nonwords and with centred nonwords. JPB had no asymmetry for other presentation conditions, and he showed the purest classical visuo-verbal extinction. Indeed, he showed no visual field defect and no clinical signs of hemineglect.

The results for the four other patients with left parietal lesions, the results are particularly diverse and require some clarification. In the "non-attention demanding conditions" (with unilateral stimuli, and with centred words), performance was symmetric and good. In the three other conditions, there were large variations. Extinction could either be on the left or on the right, even in the same patient.

The first striking result is that overall performance on conditions with pairs of stimuli is very low. For most patients (even for JPB), performance is much better when reading one eight-letter nonword than two short three-letter nonwords. This is particularly interesting, since right parietal patients showed similar performance with pairs of nonwords and with centred nonwords (see Table 3). This result suggests that left parietal patients may have difficulties in processing and responding to two simultaneous stimuli. Extinction for pairs of stimuli (and specifically nonwords) was observed on the right for PF and maybe for HV, on the left for AVU (paradoxical extinction), and could be not systematically lateralised for MF. Actually, the side of the extinction may not be totally relevant here. The point may be that patients are poor at processing and/or responding to two stimuli in tachistoscopic presentation.

The second striking result is a tendency, in some patients, towards left extinction for long centred nonwords. The case of HV is particularly interesting because he showed an inconsistent strategy in reading. On most trials with pairs of nonwords, he spelled the letters alone, as he did for the beginning of centred nonwords; in contrast, he pronounced (directly assembling phonemes) the second part of the centred nonwords. One question here concerns the similarity between HV and the cases presented by Katz and Sevush (1989), or even that presented by Costello and Warrington (1987). HV's deficit is much less severe and clear cut, and does not exist for words. Nonetheless, HV has difficulties with the *beginnings* of long centred nonwords, although he shows *right-sided* extinction in conditions of paired stimuli. This may be explained in various ways. One possibility is that HV is slow at transcoding information from a visual code to a phonological code. He may begin to spell letters whilst waiting for the transcoding to be achieved. A second possibility is that HV could be particularly slow at focusing attention at the beginning of a long stimulus. In the case of long unique nonwords, we could consider "at least" two strategies in "reading" the stimulus: one would be a fast processing of the global letter string, and the second one would be some slow processing consisting of focusing and orienting to each letter. Maybe normal reading is a combination of both processes. Normal subjects often show superior identification of the first letter in letter strings. This superiority is not only due to minimal lateral interference, since the first letter is usually better recognised than the last (see for example, Eriksen & Eriksen, 1974). A possibility is that the superiority of the first letter identification reflects the operation of a sequential attentional process, and is due to initial focusing of attention on the left. HV has no particular difficulty with words, but he may be slow at reading the beginning of nonwords by this mechanism of focusing attention, although processing of the rest of the stimulus is relatively intact. A similar explanation could be valid for some other patients with left parietal lesions, although they do not necessarily show the kind of response strategy HV used.

HV may not show a pure deficit: he has difficulty with pairs of nonwords and also with centred nonwords. Another patient, PF, clearly has worse performance with pairs of nonwords than with centred nonwords. He may show a pure deficit in focusing attention on one visual-verbal stimulus among others. When presented with several stimuli, he may have difficulty focusing attention on each item. With two visual-verbal stimuli presented tachistoscopically, he could be slow in focusing on the first left stimulus. There may then be little time left to process the second stimulus, producing right side extinction. Before going further with the discussion, we will describe the case of PF in some more detail.

CASE STUDY: PF

Observation

PF is a 43-year-old man, strictly right-handed (according to a number of different questionnaires), working as a technician. He had a previous history of cardio-vascular disease, myocardic infarctus in 1981, and high blood pressure. In December 1987, he suffered from headaches and acute acalculia and difficulty in apprehending the size of objects. The beginning of illness was rapidly progressive in a few days, without real ictus. While hunting, he did not shoot a particular rabbit because he thought it was a young one, although in fact the rabbit was an adult, as a friend told him. Several days later, while working, he discovered he was unable to perform simple arithmetic operations (e.g. subtraction).

Initial neurological examination found some epicritic hypoesthesia and astereognosia of the right hand, without any sign of hemiplegia. He had also some apraxia with the right hand. There was a right visual extinction to simple stimuli, without any field cut. A number of neuropsychological disturbances were present. He had a digital agnosia, a problem in right/left discrimination without autotopoagnosia, dyscalculia of a spatial kind (he had special difficulties with subtractions: he did not know which digit to subtract from which), and dysgraphia (omission, inversion, and substitution of letters; sometimes he rotated the letters in writing; oral spelling was correct). Thus he showed a clear Gerstmann syndrome.

Although he never had any aphasic signs, he had some deficits associated with the Gerstmann syndrome. He had a deficit in reading nonwords and short words in text. He also had a visuo-spatial deficit; he had no problem with topographical notions, but he had strong difficulties with the Reversal Test (Edfeldt, 1955), and found the perception of volumes difficult.

Finally, he had no auditory verbal extinction in a dichotic listening task. His short-term memory was good, with a digit span of seven (forwards) and five (backwards). Similar spans were obtained with words.

Two years later, in summer 1989, he still complained of the same difficulties; in calculating, in writing, in reading, and in some tasks requiring visuo-spatial capacity (for example, in the perception of volume in a picture), also in using his right hand. His visual extinction with simple stimuli had disappeared (see Naegele, David, Pellat, & Siéroff, Note 2).

We will focus here only on his reading difficulties. PF complained that, although he gained much pleasure in reading before his illness, he now could not read for more than 10 minutes. The effort to read was so great that he fatigued quickly and could not remember what he was reading. Consequently, he claimed that he was unable to read even the most simple book.

The C.T.-scan shows an infarct in the left hemisphere. The posterior part of inferior lobule (angular gyrus) and the middle part of the superior lobule were damaged.

Experiment 1

Experiment 1 (in the group study) showed that PF had difficulties with nonwords, at least when they were presented bilaterally (Table 2). He also had some difficulties with bilateral presentation of words. The most striking result was the difference between reading two short three-letter nonwords and reading one long centred eight-letter nonword (Table 3). There was a strong right extinction only with the presentation of two nonwords. There are two points to make about this. The first is that it is not a true right-sided extinction. For instance, when PF was asked to read the right nonword first and the left nonword second, he showed a clear opposite left extinction (this was tried with a small version of Experiment 1). The second is that the deficit was particularly strong, since global results on both nonwords of a pair were inferior to results on a left unilateral nonword presented alone: in a pair of nonwords he identified 1.6 letters out of the 3 letters of the left nonword and 2.1 letters overall out of the 6 letters of both nonwords, although he identified 2.9 letters out of the 3 letters of a unilateral left nonword. Performances on the left short nonword in the unilateral condition and in the bilateral condition are significantly different ($\chi^2 = 31.9$; $P < 0.01$). Not only does PF have difficulty accessing the second right nonword of a pair, but he does not identify the first left nonword as well as when it is presented alone (unilateral presentation).

It is important to note that PF had no problem with short-term memory. Also, after listening to a list of 7 words, he could easily recall which word was before or after a specific word the examiner uttered, even if he was not asked to repeat all the words themselves. Furthermore, if the deficit in reading 2 nonwords presented tachistoscopically was the expression of a short-term memory deficit, there would be a strong difference between spelling individual letters (like saying "M.I.N.U" after the nonwords "min ope") and pronouncing his response (i.e. after assembling phonemes, like saying "mine" or "mone"). These two strategies were used slightly less than 50% of the time each (some trials led to no response). PF identified more letters when pronouncing his response (2.9) than when spelling letters (2.0). However, this difference cannot explain the extinction, which existed for both response strategies. Clearly, even when he was pronouncing his response, PF still did not have enough capacity to read both nonwords. These results rule out an explanation of his deficit by a short-term memory loss or by a deficit in transcoding visual information into phonology.

Another possibility is that PF has specific difficulties in focusing attention on one particular stimulus when pairs of stimuli are presented. This is examined in a further series of experiments. Experiments 2–4 investigate the effect of manipulating lexical status on performance. Experiment 5 investigates the influence of an attentional bias on PF's reading. We finally give some observations on PF's reading of text.

Lexical Status of the Stimuli

Experiment 2: Pairs of Words/Compound Words

Clearly, PF was better at reading words than nonwords (Table 2). However, he usually showed an extinction in reading pairs of words. This extinction was not systematically lateralised: he usually responded only to one word of a pair, which may not be always the left one. We may ask how much processing is performed on an extinguished stimulus. For instance, was PF able to read both words better when they form a unique compound word?

Method. We presented a list of 44 pairs of words twice (with a period of one month between presentations). The list consisted of 22 pairs of unrelated words like "LUNE PAIX" (= moon, peace), and 22 pairs of words like "CHEF LIEU" (= chief, place, chief town), which is a compound word made of two root morphemes. Frequency of means (Imbs, 1971) are grossly equivalent for unrelated words (1323) and for each morpheme of the compound words (999 for the left one, 1059 for the right one); however, the global compound words had a lower mean name frequency (2828). Half the stimuli consisted of 4-letter and half of 5-letter words. All stimuli were written in upper case. There was a blank space between both words, equivalent to the width of one letter. The procedure was similar to Experiment 1. Stimuli were presented tachistoscopically. Each stimulus was preceded by a fixation arrow and followed by a mask (a similar procedure was used in Experiments 3 and 4). Time of presentation of stimuli (one word in each hemifield) was 200msec.

Results. The number of words correct was scored (that is, the words for which he was correct on all letters), since only words were used in the experiment. The results were combined for the 2 sessions, so there were 44 pairs of unrelated words and 44 pairs of compound pairs. There was a strong right extinction for unrelated pairs: 39 left words were correctly identified, compared with only 4 right words (in this experiment, extinction was on the right side possibly because only pairs of stimuli were presented). However, results with compound pairs were much better: 39 left words and 25 right words were correctly recognised. Overall 24 compound word pairs were correctly recognised, compared with only 4 pairs of unrelated words. This difference is significant ($\chi^2 = 20.8$; $P < 0.01$). There is strong facilitation due to the lexical status of the stimuli. This result is similar to that found with other patients with parietal lesions (see Table 4, in which results from some other patients studied in Experiment 1 are also reported).

It is important to note that guessing cannot explain these results. PF gave only two responses which were a compound word made of the left word of the unrelated pairs and of an incorrect second word, saying for example "abat-jour" (= lamp shade) for "abat noir" (= slaughter, black),

TABLE 4
Comparison of Performance with Unrelated and Compound Word Pairs (Experiment 2): Results in Absolute Number Correct of Words Recognised on the Left (L) and on the Right (R), and Number of Pairs of Words Recognised Together (Pairs), for Different Types of Pairs of Words, in PF and Some Other Patients

	Unrelated Pairs			*Compound Pairs*		
Patients	*L*	*R*	*Pairs*	*L*	*R*	*Pairs*
PF	39	4	4	39	25	24
RM	0	33	0	11	35	10
AVU	17	18	5	27	28	23
JPB	34	0	0	37	10	9
MF	18	17	9	34	33	28
HV	31	14	6	35	29	25

although it was possible to build such compound words with about two thirds of the left words of unrelated pairs.

In a similar experiment, three months later, PF was asked to read the same list of words presented tachistoscopically (44 pairs of words overall). The presentation time was 160ms. However, on this occasion, PF had to read the right word first, then the left word. A sophisticated response-guessing strategy predicts a smaller advantage for compound words in this situation. For unrelated pairs (22), correct responses were 2 for the left and 17 for the right. For related pairs (22), correct responses were 12 for the left and 18 for the right. This is an almost perfect mirror-image of his performance in the normal experiment. This does not accord with a guessing strategy.

The difficulties PF has in processing pairs of visual-verbal stimuli do not appear to exist in every situation. Rather, difficulties seem to occur when PF has to focus attention on each stimulus of a pair, as in the case of pairs of unrelated words (or in the case of pairs of nonwords). When two words of a pair form a compound word, PF performs much better. With compound words, it is possible that higher-level units can facilitate the processing of several simultaneously presented stimuli.

Experiment 3: Spacing the Letters of Words

Spacing the letters of words has been shown to disrupt the word form (Holender, 1985; Paap, Newsome, & Noel, 1984). It has also been shown to have a dramatic effect on word reading in the case of a left hemineglect patient, WC (Siéroff, Note 3). One possibility is that the global form is disrupted through spacing the letters, and reading must be based on sequential letter analysis. Neglect may then be worsened if neglect patients have problems orienting attention. Will such a manipulation of the word form have an effect on PF, who had a left parietal lesion?

Method. In a first experiment (a), 20 words (mean frequency 1858) and 20 nonwords of 5 letters with a blank space between letters (width equivalent to one letter) were presented for 60msec. Nonwords were constructed from the words. In a second experiment (b), 80 short 3-letter or 4-letter words (mean frequency 1673) with a blank space between letters (width equivalent to 2 letters) and 80 long words (mean frequency 2351) of 7, 8, 9, or 10 normally spaced letters were presented for 60msec. The angle subtended by spaced letter stimuli and nonspaced letter stimuli was globally similar. Stimuli were centred across fixation.

Results. Accuracy of report was scored using clusters of one letter for 3-letter words, 2 letters in 4- and 5-letter words, 3 letters in other words, left and right of fixation.

Results of Experiment (a) and of Experiment (b) show that PF had no difficulty with spaced letter words (with the two different widths) and he performed well even when reading spaced letter nonwords (see Table 5). PF's deficit does not preclude his ability to read words under conditions where the activation of letter codes is likely to be accelerated relative to word codes. Results for nonwords were particularly surprising in comparison with performance with pairs of nonwords (Experiment 1). Maybe regularly spaced 5-letter nonwords still make some globally apparent unit PF was able to apprehend. This was not the case when letters clearly form 2 distinct letter strings, as in pairs of nonwords. Thus, the behaviour of PF in reading spaced stimuli is opposite that of case WC (Siéroff, Note 3), who had a right parietal lesion. For PF, reading was better in words where letters were separated with blank spaces rather than in long centred words with normal letter spacing. However, results for such long words were good, and no difference was found between 7-letter words and 10-letter words. In conclusion, PF does not show extinction when there are blank spaces between letters or letter strings, as long as they can form some global unit.

TABLE 5
The Effects of Regular Spacing (PF Experiment 3): Percentage of Letters Correctly Reported (Irrespective of Position) in Left Cluster (L) and in Right Cluster (R)

Stimuli	*L*	*R*
Experiment a		
Spaced letter words	100	100
Spaced letter nonwords	83	68
Experiment b		
Spaced letter words	100	99
Normal long words	90	92

Experiment 4: Illegal Nonwords

In Experiment 1, PF's deficit was more pronounced with pairs of nonwords than with centred nonwords. Possibly, this is because the centred nonwords used in Experiment 1 resemble long words. We now examine whether performance with centred illegal nonwords, which are very different from words, resembles that with pairs of nonwords or with reading centred psuedowords.

We can outline two further possibilities. Firstly, PF's specific deficit in reading pairs of nonwords could be attributed to a difficulty in orienting attention along the letters within the stimulus. In this case he should show more difficulty with illegal nonwords, in which the process of orienting attention through the string of letters would appear to be even more necessary than with pseudowords. Reading illegal nonwords has been shown to be more sensitive to spatial attentional bias (produced by a spatial cue) than are pseudowords in normals (Siéroff & Posner, 1988). Secondly, the specific deficit in reading pairs of nonwords could be due to a difficulty to individualise, to select, to focus on and/or to process one letter string among others. If this is so, PF should have no especial difficulty with illegal nonwords. Performance would be expected to be only slightly lower than for pseudowords (similar to normals).

Method. Forty words 7, 8, or 9 letters long and 40 illegal nonwords 7, 8, or 9 letters long were presented for 160msec. Illegal nonwords were constructed from the words, so as to produce strings that are hard to pronounce (like "IASNEATFI" or "ADFRLEE"). Stimuli were presented centred at fixation.

Results. PF had no specific difficulty with illegal nonwords, and performed no worse with them than with pseudowords in other experiments (see Table 6). Apparently, PF is able to orient attention through a letter string and this may be contrasted with his poor ability to focus deliberately on one letter string among others. The question arises as to the nature of the processes necessary to perform the two tasks.

TABLE 6
Performance with Words and Illegal Nonwords for PF (Experiment 4): Percentage of Letters Correctly Reported (Irrespective of Position) in Left Cluster (L) and in Right Cluster (R)

	L	*R*
Words	88	93
Illegal nonwords	71	62

PF made lexical errors 25% of the time when reading illegal nonwords. The percentage of lexical errors with illegal nonwords is not so great as with pseudowords (35%: in Experiment 1), but it represents some tendency to lexicalise. However, he was more confident in accepting a pseudoword than an illegal nonword as a word. Because of the large number of lexicalised responses, the results are inconclusive. The superiority of centred nonword report relative to pairs of nonwords may be due to some lexical-like type of processing. However, a possibility remains that PF was using an available process of a global spatial approach to the letter string, independently of its word resemblance. Whatever strategy PF used, he is able to read out information from an illegal nonword.

Manipulation of Attention

We now address the question of whether biasing PF's attention to one location influences his performance. In particular, we ask whether it is possible to enhance PF's performance by cueing spatial attention. We will use the method of spatial cueing, which has been shown to orient attention "automatically". Cue location and the nature of the task demands will be manipulated systematically.

Experiment 5: Spatial Cueing

Method. Words and nonwords from lists A and B were used, with unilateral (see Experiment 1), bilateral, and centred presentations. The number of stimuli was identical to Experiment 1 for these lists. A digit was used as a spatial cue, and this digit appeared before the stimuli, immediately below the first or the last letter of each stimulus (two possibilities in unilateral and centred presentations, four possibilities in pairs of stimuli). Thus, the order of events on the screen was: fixation item, cue, stimuli, mask. The presentation time was 80msec. for the cue (digit) and 160msec. for the stimuli (words or nonwords).

This manipulation was employed in each of three task conditions. Each condition was run as a separate block.

In condition (a), PF had to read the stimuli and to ignore the digit. List A was used.

In condition (b), PF had to read the digit and the stimuli. List B was used. In this case, more stimuli than in condition (a) had to be identified.

In condition (c), PF had to read the stimulus on the same side as the digit (without reporting the digit) and ignore the other stimulus. Thus, for pairs of stimuli, he had to read only one stimulus of the pair. In unilateral and centred presentations, he had to read the whole stimulus. This tests the ability of PF to select one stimulus for processing on the ground of the side of the cue. List A was used.

Results. Results are given and discussed only for bilateral presentation of nonwords (pairs and centred), using the same scoring method as in Experiment 1. In Table 7, these results are compared to results without the digit cue (Experiment 1, list C). For pairs of nonwords, results are compiled as "cue in the left hemifield" or in "cue in the right hemifield".

TABLE 7
Pairs of Nonwords and Long Centred Nonwords with Spatial Cue, a Digit (Experiment 5, with Three Different Tasks), for PF: Percentage of Letters Reported Correctly (Irrespective of Position) in Left Cluster (L), Right Cluster (R), and Laterality Index

	Expt. 1 No Cue			*Expt. 6a Ignore Cue*			*Expt. 6b Name Cue*			*Expt. 6c Choose Side*		
Nonwords	*L*	*R*	*Side of the Cue*	*L*	*R*	*LI*	*L*	*R*	*LI*	*L*	*R*	*LI*
Pairs	54	15	Left	64	27	−41	47	13	−57	10	—	
			Right	40	34	−8	34	39	+7	—	7	
Centred	58	68	Left	68	60	−6	63	23	−47	50	15	−54
			Right	55	48	−7	37	20	−30	38	18	−36

Thus, cue in the left hemifield comprises the two cases in which the cue is in the left hemifield: when the cue is on the left of the left stimulus, and when the cue is on the right of the left stimulus (but still inside the left hemifield). Results were collapsed in this way because the number of cases in each condition was too low (5).

First, as was expected, the cue seemed to have an effect of orienting spatial attention irrespective of whether the digit had to be named (see results for conditions [a] and [b]). However, a right cue did not enhance global performance on both nonwords of the pair: it just lessened the left advantage. The cue did seem to have an effect on centred nonwords, but only when the digit was named. However, this effect was both small and difficult to interpret, and it might reflect the small number of trials. Alternatively, it is possible that the ability to disengage attention from the cue in order to process the stimulus (or the part of the stimulus) on the opposite side is much better with unique global stimuli like centred nonwords than with pairs of nonwords (even when leftwards orientation is required, which is the opposite of normal left–right scanning of text). For pairs of nonwords, more than for centred nonwords, it may be difficult to reorient and "refocus" attention. Furthermore, if PF is taking advantage of global processing for centred nonwords, it is possible that the cue has less of an effect.

Second, in pairs of nonwords with condition (b), the stronger memory load had no dramatic effect on PF's performance. There was a discrepancy in performance between conditions (a) and (b), though it is not large. Moreover, in this case, the cue (digit) was identified 85% of the time.

The most interesting results are in condition (c). This particular task (where only the stimulus on the same side as the digit had to be read) had a dramatic effect on performance with pairs of nonwords. Instead of facilitating the processing of only one letter string of the pair, the task disrupted

PF. Performance was poor for both members of the pair. He could identify only a few letters, and, most of the time, could not give a response. If we consider only his responses for the left stimulus of a pair of nonwords with a left cue, correct performance was significantly lower in condition (c) compared to condition (b) ($\chi^2 = 9.94$; $P < 0.01$), although performance on this same stimulus was not significantly different between condition (a) and condition (b) ($\chi^2 = 1.68$; P = n.s.). Reading aloud the digit (condition [b]) did not have a dramatic effect, although when required to orient but not respond to the cue (condition [c]) performance deteriorated. In contrast, results on centred nonwords (he had to recall the whole string in this case) were similar to other conditions, (a) and (b).

After the experiment, PF admitted that he could not actually decide which one of the two letter strings he had to respond to in condition (c). By the time he had made his decision (frequently at random), he was not able to recall the letter string anymore.

This may show that the deficit is not in the processing of the letter string itself (transforming the visual input in a phonological code), but in selecting which stimulus to process when there are several stimuli. We have seen that when PF was told in advance which stimulus to respond to first (Experiment 2), his performance was not impaired. In condition (c) of the present experiment, PF has to respond quickly to one of two stimuli in response to a cue, and this he finds difficult. It thus appears that it takes him time to select the stimulus he has to process.

Reading Text

In January 1990, PF had already improved in reading text. He read aloud at the rate of 120 words per min. from a text of 265 words. However, reading was not fluent: PF made 9 hesitations (mainly omissions of short words, not only functional, then corrections) and 4 errors. We may parallel these omissions with the special difficulty he had in reading several short words in tachistoscopy. He made also some errors on words with visual orthographic similarities; for instance, he read "poisson" (= fish) for "poison", "étrille" (= [he] curries) for "trille" (= [he] trills), etc. The kind of errors PF made between orthographically close words (poison/poisson) was found under tachistoscopic conditions as well. He had difficulties with words that shared many letters in common with other words; maybe more specifically with words having the same letters in a different order (inverted digrams), such as "tri" (= sorting) and "tir" (= shooting). Difficulties with long words may have been less apparent because of the decreased effects of the number of orthographic neighbours.

In a test of silent reading (text 800 words long, on gardening) for 3.45min., he showed good comprehension of the text and easily answered different questions (though he did not remember any of the first and last names of the story). However, he claimed that he usually has difficulties in understanding what he is reading.

Discussion

PF has some problems in reading text. He omits some short words and he finds reading particularly effortful. The question is whether or not we can relate this impairment in text reading to his bad performance on some tachistoscopic presentations of letter strings. PF has severe difficulties in reading pairs of two verbal stimuli.

When the pairs are words, the deficit is less striking than when they are two nonwords. Nonetheless, PF shows difficulties with two words. This deficit can be lessened when the two words make a compound word (Experiment 2), showing that some processing on the second rightmost word is possible. In this case, the two letter strings can be conceived as a lexical unit and can possibly benefit from some parallel processing. This is unlikely to result from guessing, and the advantage of compound words does not appear to occur at the level of response programming, since, when PF is asked to begin his response with the rightmost word, he shows similar difficulty with nonrelated words, while not being disadvantaged with compound words. PF has no short-term memory deficit, neither does he have difficulty in transcoding visual information into phonology (see Experiment 4 with illegal nonwords and Experiment 5[b] with cue). Difficulties with pairs of verbal stimuli may be the expression of an attentional deficit in processing one visual-verbal stimulus from amongst others. The deficit may be elicited specifically when spacing the letters makes two (or more) distinct letter strings. However, spacing the letters of words apart in a regular fashion produces no particular difficulty for PF in reading words, possibly because they can still be treated as a regular global unit (Experiment 3). In this case, PF could consider the display as only one letter string, and this was also true of regularly spaced letter nonwords.

PF's deficit may be in selecting one stimulus from among others for further processing, that is to focus on one particular stimulus. This selection can be biased with spatial cueing (the cue being a digit), whether the cue is reported or not (condition [a] and [b] of Experiment 5). A cue may have a passive attentional effect utilisable by PF. However, PF has difficulty in responding to the stimulus on the same side of the cue (Experiment 5, condition [c]). Active selection remains difficult, even in this simple task.

PF may be particularly slow at selecting and processing one particular visual-verbal stimulus among others, so that no information from the second visual-verbal stimulus is available, when attention is required for processing. Thus, PF's deficit will be elicited when and only when focused selection is rendered necessary. The more focusing necessary, the stronger his deficit: his performance was poor when there were two stimuli in the display (with pairs of unrelated words, or pairs of nonwords), it was even worse when he had to quickly select one particular stimulus of the pair on the side of a cue.

Another question concerns the relation between a deficit in reading multiple letter strings and performance in reading single letter strings. Compared with HV, PF has little difficulties with long nonwords. However, he has some impairment in distinguishing between words sharing letters. For example, he was at chance in deciding if a word presented tachistoscopically was the word "tri" or the word "tir". Even if words can benefit from some parallel processing, focusing of attention on only one part of the word may be necessary when words differ in a small degree (like with "poison" and "poisson"). With PF, such errors also occurred with longer words, but much less frequently, maybe because disambiguation was less necessary as words become more dissimilar. It was difficult to ascertain whether it was the same deficit affecting reading of multiple letter strings and of single letter strings. However, we may argue for a similar underlying problem in the two tasks if we consider the problem to be in focusing, that is in changing the actual window of processing, in the sense of LaBerge and Brown (1989). This change in the size of the window may be dependent on different factors (task, complexity of the text, orthographic neighbourhood, etc.). Apparently, there is no obstacle to see it as a general mechanism used in reading. The only difference between the two situations (focusing on one word among others, and focusing on one part of a word) would be the actual "window" size, and the circumstances of focusing, and we have no response yet to the question of whether there can be different focusing deficits.

GENERAL DISCUSSION

We have tried to show that the deficit of PF may be at the level of focusing on one letter string when presented with others. It seems that it is the operation of active selection which is disturbed, rather than the processing of the letter string itself. When presented with a pair of letter strings under time-limited conditions, selection would be so slow in PF that processing could occur only on one letter string, and the second letter string may have been forgotten. There are two further points to make about this deficit. First, it does not occur every time there are blank spaces between letters in the display. Reading pairs of words is easier when some parallel processing can develop, as in the case of compound words (due to some benefit from top-down feedback?). Similarly, PF's deficit is not worse every time there is a spatial cue to process, but rather when he has to select the order of processing. Performance depends on higher-level constraints (the absence of a higher-level unit, or task demands), when these constraints ask for some focusing of attention. Second, it has to be understood that the deficit in selective focusing is quite different from a deficit in orienting, and the extinction which results may not be lateralised consistently on the side opposite to the lesion as when there is a deficit in the orienting of spatial attention.

A deficit of focusing attention could explain the results of some other patients with left parietal lesions described in the group study, who read a long centred nonword better than two short nonwords under tachistoscopic presentation conditions, and who omit words (usually short ones) in reading text. It is not clear, however, to what extent PF's deficit can resemble the cases described by Shallice and Warrington (1977). Their patients might have special difficulties in filtering information outside of the focus of attention (as evidenced by their migration errors). PF rarely showed this kind of error. However, stimuli were not constructed in order to elicit this phenomenon in our experiments, so the data are inconclusive. Finally, Rayner, Murphy, Henderson, and Pollatsek (1989) have reported the case of a patient with a developmental dyslexia, and for whom they hypothesised that the deficit was in selecting one letter string for further processing (parsing the unit into subunits) or in filtering information outside of this letter string (excluding letters outside the focus of attention).

So, selective focusing is important in reading, in different situations. Focusing is needed to select one particular word in a text (which is a novel arrangement of words), or on one stimulus of a pair of visual-verbal stimuli, as in the present tachistoscopic presentations. According to LaBerge and Brown (1989), a system called the position analyser, determines the window of processing, that is the information which is filtered in order to be presented to another system, the shape identifier. When reading text, identification of a word could be possible only when the window of processing corresponds to the limits of this word. The second situation of focusing could be the narrowing of attentional window of processing on units smaller than words (letters, letter clusters), in some conditions.

A question is whether or not the deficit we have described in processing several letter strings can also explain the difficulties some patients have in processing only one letter string. PF was only mildly impaired in reading long nonwords and showed a small effect of orthographic neighbours for words. However, he also showed a slight right-sided advantage for centred stimuli, which is surprising when we consider his strong left advantage when presented with pairs of stimuli. Other patients we have described in the group study (HV), showed special difficulty in reading single letter strings, e.g. as in processing the beginning letters, a deficit which has been found in other patients of the literature, following lesions of the left parietal lobe (Costello & Warrington, 1987; Katz & Sevush, 1989). The deficit in focusing on the beginning of the string of letters and the deficit in focusing on one particular part of a word (to disambiguate, for example, a word from his close orthographic neighbours) may be different but closely related. Also, it may be that these deficits and the deficit in focusing on one particular visual-verbal stimulus amongst others are different but closely related. For instance, these processes may all involve narrowing an attentional window, but to different sizes. Another question would be the link between such deficits and deficits in processing local aspects of hierarchical stimuli (Robertson et al., 1988).

In contrast to this (these?) deficit(s?), some patients with parietal lesions may show only, or at least principally, a deficit in orienting attention. Such patients would show extinction on one side which is consistently opposite to their lesion in all conditions requiring sequential operations. This may be the case for the four patients with right parietal lesion and with JPB who has a left parietal lesion (although only right parietal patients have an extinction which is similar for pairs of nonwords and for centred nonwords). For the fourth patient with a right parietal lesion, RM, the story may be yet more complicated. He has a strong clinical left neglect and demonstrates an asymmetry that is stronger than those of other patients in almost all conditions. Even though he shows a clear centred word superiority effect on centred nonwords, his results for centred words are quite asymmetric. One possibility is that he has some difficulty apprehending the whole stimulus or the whole display, perhaps due to some difficulty with global processing. This may be true with any kind of stimulus presentation (unilateral, pairs, centred). It has been shown that patients with right hemispheric lesions have difficulties with global aspects of hierarchical stimuli (a large letter made of small ones), whereas patients with left hemispheric lesions have difficulty with local aspects of hierarchical stimuli (Delis et al., 1988; Robertson et al., 1988). It is theoretically possible that hemineglect is the expression of a double deficit (at least): one of orienting spatial attention, and one of global processing (Siéroff, 1990). Patients could show severe hemineglect because they have an abnormal tendency to hyperfocus attention, before misorienting attention toward the side ipsilateral to their lesion.

In conclusion, the final identification of letter strings requires more than an identification of the letter strings themselves: it requires some position analysis of the letter string. This may be accomplished by positioning an attentional window, and this could be affected by higher order processes, in accordance with task demands and instructions. The mechanisms of positioning could presumably be divided into operations of orienting (like lateral orienting) and operations of focusing. Normal reading involves a complex interaction between these processes. For example, focus operations could depend on a balance betweeen a tendency to enlarge the window of processing and a tendency to narrow the size of this filter, and this could exist at different levels (text, groups of words, single letter strings). There could be the need for some global apprehension of the limits of the text or of the limits of the letter strings (between blank spaces): this could represent some low-level operation in the filter (like the apprehension of gross physical differences). Another component operation could be a narrowing of the window of processing, the selection of the size of the channel for final identification: this would represent some higher-order type of processing, and it could be closely related to the word identification system, as well as to higher-level constraints (task demands). A possibility is that there could be a differential implication of each hemisphere in these processes. Parietal lesions could disrupt one or the other of these operations, and we have described the case of a patient with a left parietal lesion who shows a deficit in focusing on one visual-verbal stimulus among others.

Manuscript received 7 March 1990
Revised manuscript received 15 June 1990

REFERENCES

Behrmann, M., Moscovitch, M., Black, S. E., & Mozer, M. (in press). Perceptual and conceptual mechanisms in neglect dyslexia: Two contrasting case studies. *Brain*.

Bellugi, U., Poizner, H., & Klima, E. S. (1989). Language, modality, and the brain. *Trends in Neuroscience*, *12*, 380–388.

Brunn, J. L. & Farah, M. J. (in press). Spatial attention in word reading: Further evidence from neglect patients. *Cognitive Neuropsychology*.

Caplan, B. (1987). Assessment of unilateral neglect: A new reading test. *Journal of Clinical & Experimental Neuropsychology*, 9, 359–364.

Chedru, F., Leblanc, M., & Lhermitte, F. (1973). Visual searching in normal and brain-damaged subjects (contribution to the study of unilateral inattention). *Cortex*, 9, 94–111.

Costello, A. D. L. & Warrington, E. K. (1987). The dissociation of visuospatial neglect and neglect dyslexia. *Journal of Neurology, Neurosurgery, and Psychiatry*, *50*, 1110–1116.

Delis, D. C., Kiefner, M. G., & Fridlund, A. J. (1988). Visuospatial dysfunction following unilateral brain damage: Dissociations in hierarchical and hemispatial analysis. *Journal of Clinical and Experimental Neuropsychology*, *10*, 421–431.

Edfeldt, A. W. (1955). Reading reversal and its relation to reading readiness. *Research Bulletins from the Institute of Education*, University of Stockholm, *1*.

Ellis, A. W., Flude, B. M., & Young, A. W. (1987). "Neglect dyslexia" and the early visual processing of letters in words and nonwords. *Cognitive Neuropsychology*, *4*, 439–464.

Eriksen, B. A. & Eriksen, C. W. (1974). The importance of being first: A tachistoscopic study of the contribution of each letter to the recognition of four-letter words. *Perception and Psychophysics*, *15*, 66–72.

Friedland, R. P. & Weinstein, E. A. (1977). Hemi-inattention and hemisphere specialisation: Introduction and historical review. In E. A. Weinstein & R. P. Friedland (Eds.), *Advance in Neurology, Vol. 18*. New York: Raven Press, 1–31.

Friedrich F. J., Walker, J. A., & Posner, M. I. (1985). Effects of parietal lesions on visual matching: Implications for reading errors. *Cognitive Neuropsychology*, *2*, 253–264.

Gazzaniga, M. S. (1988). The dynamics of cerebral specialisation and modular interactions. In L. Weiskrantz (Ed.), *Thought without language*. Oxford: Oxford University Press, 218–238.

Heilman K. M., Watson, R. T., & Valenstein, E. (1985). Neglect and related disorders. In K. M. Heilman & E. Valenstein (Eds.), *Clinical neuropsychology*. Oxford: Oxford University Press, 243–293.

Holender D. (1985). Disruptive effect of precueing on the identification of letters in masked words: An attentional interpretation. In M. I. Posner & O. S. Marin (Eds.), *Attention & performance XI*. Hillsdale, NJ: Lawrence Erlbaum Associates Inc., 613–629.

Imbs, P. (Ed.) (1971). *Trésor de la Langue Française*. Paris: Editions du C.N.R.S.

Katz, R. B. & Sevush, S. (1989). Positional dyslexia. *Brain and Language*, *37*, 266–289.

Kinsbourne, M. & Warrington, E. K. (1962). A variety of reading disability associated with right hemisphere lesion. *Journal of Neurology, Neurosurgery, and Psychiatry*, *25*, 339–344.

LaBerge, D. & Brown, V. (1989). Theory of attentional operations in shape identification. *Psychological Review*, *96*, 101–124.

Michel, F. & Peronnet, F. (1975). Extinction gauche au test dichotique: Lésion hémisphérique ou lésion commissurale? (Apport de l'étude des potentiels évoqués acoustiques). In F. Michel & B. Schott (Eds.), *Les syndromes de disconnexion calleuse chez l'homme*. Actes du Colloque International de Lyon, 1974, 85–117.

Morrow, L. A. & Ratcliff, G. (1988). The desengagement of covert attention and the neglect syndrome. *Psychobiology*, *16*, 261–269.

Paap, K. R., Newsome, S. L., & Noel, R. W. (1984). Word shape's in poor shape for the race to the lexicon. *Journal of Experimental Psychology: Human Perception and Performance*, *10*, 413–428.

Posner, M. I., Inhoff, A. W., Friedrich, F. J., & Cohen, A. (1987). Isolating attentional systems: A cognitive-anatomical analysis. *Psychobiology*, *15*, 107–121.

Posner, M. I. & Petersen, S. E. (1990). The attention system of the human brain. *Annual Review of Neuroscience*, *13*, 25–42.

Posner, M. I., Walker, J. A., Friedrich, F. J., & Rafal, R. D. (1984). Effects of parietal injury on covert orienting of attention. *The Journal of Neuroscience*, *4*, 1863–1874.

Posner, M. I., Walker, J. A., Friedrich, F. J., & Rafal, R. D. (1987). How do the parietal lobes direct covert attention. *Neuropsychologia*, *25*, 135–146.

Rayner, K., Murphy, L. A., Henderson, J. M., & Pollatsek, A. (1989). Selective attentional dyslexia. *Cognitive Neuropsychology*, *6*, 357–378.

Riddoch, M. J. & Humphreys, G. W. (1983). The effect of cueing on unilateral neglect. *Neuropsychologia*, *21*, 589–599.

Riddoch, M. J. & Humphreys, G. W. (1987). Perceptual and action systems in unilateral visual neglect. In M. Jeannerod (Ed.), *Neurophysiological and neuropsychological aspects of spatial neglect*. North Holland: Elsevier, 151–181.

Robertson, L. C., Lamb, M. R., & Knight, R. T. (1988). Effects of lesions of temporal-parietal junction on perceptual and attentional processing in humans. *The Journal of Neuroscience*, *8*, 3757–3769.

Shallice, T. & Warrington, E. K. (1977). The possible role of selective attention in acquired dyslexia. *Neuropsychologia*, *15*, 31–41.

Siéroff, E. (1990). Héminégligence, langage et asymétrie cérébrale: Données récentes. *L'année Psychologique*, *90*, 67–91.

Siéroff, E. & Michel, F. (1987). Verbal visual extinction in right/left hemisphere lesion patients and the problem of lexical access. *Neuropsychologia*, *25*, 907–918.

Siéroff, E., Pollatsek, A., & Posner, M. I. (1988). Recognition of visual letter strings following injury to the posterior visual spatial attention system. *Cognitive Neuropsychology*, *5*, 427–449.

Siéroff, E. & Posner, M. I. (1988). Cueing spatial attention during processing of words and letter strings in normals. *Cognitive Neuropsychology*, *5*, 451–472.

Sparks, R., Goodglass, H., & Nickel, B. (1970). Ipsilateral versus controlateral extinction in dichotic listening resulting from hemisphere lesions. *Cortex*, *6*, 249–260.

Volpe, B. T., Ledoux, J. E., & Gazzaniga, M. S. (1979). Information processing of visual stimuli in an "extinguished" field. *Nature*, *282*, 722–724.

REFERENCE NOTES

1. Bisiach, E., Meregalli, S., & Berti, A. (1985). *Mechanisms of production-control and belief-fixation in human visuospatial processing: Clinical evidence from hemispatial neglect.* Oral communication: Eighth Symposium on Quantitative Analyses of Behavior, at Harvard University: "Pattern recognition and concepts in animals, people, and machines".
2. Naegele, B., David, D., Pellat, J., & Siéroff, E. *A case of Gerstmann syndrome.* Manuscript in preparation.
3. Siéroff, E. *Perception of visual letter strings in a case of left neglect: Manipulation of the word form.* Submitted for publication.

Neglect and the Peripheral Dyslexias Part 2

GUEST EDITOR
M.J. Riddoch

(Part 1 appeared in Volume 7, issue 5/6, 1990)

COGNITIVE NEUROPSYCHOLOGY, 1991, *8* (3/4) 177–191

Different Impairments Contribute to Neglect Dyslexia

Andrew W. Young
University of Durham, Durham, U.K.
Freda Newcombe
M.R.C. Neuropsychology Unit, Radcliffe Infirmary, Oxford, U.K.
Andrew W. Ellis
University of York, York, U.K.

We report investigations of the reading abilities of SP, a right-handed woman who had suffered a sub-arachnoid haemorrhage from a right middle cerebral artery aneurysm. When reading text SP showed "neglect dyslexia". She omitted words from the left side of the page and often misread the beginnings of words, either by deleting (e.g. WANT read as "ant") or substituting (BAND read as "sand") their initial letters. SP's tendency to *omit* words was markedly affected by their position along the left–right axis, yet the same variable did not affect her tendency to make initial-letter *misreadings* in the same way. When words were presented so that their beginnings fell in the hemianopic region of her visual field she showed a marked tendency to make misreadings involving the deletion of initial letters. In contrast, when words were presented so that they had fallen entirely in the intact part of her field of vision, SP made errors that were mostly initial-letter substitutions. We thus suggest that neglect dyslexia involves different underlying impairments, which are often (but not inevitably) present in combination with each other. Words are omitted from the left side of the page because of defective location of line beginnings. Initial-letter deletions occur primarily when the patient fails to make adequate compensatory eye movements to words that have been fixated with their beginnings falling in the hemianopic area of the visual field. Initial-letter substitutions, however, reflect damage to mechanisms involved in letter and word recognition.

Requests for reprints should be addressed to Prof. Andy Young, Department of Psychology, University of Durham, Science Laboratories, South Road, Durham DH1 3LE, U.K.

This work was supported by M.R.C. Programme Grant PG7301443 to Freda Newcombe and John Marshall, and by M.R.C. Project Grant G8519533 to Andy Young. We are indebted to SP and her husband for their co-operation at all stages. We thank Marlene Behrmann, Alfonso Caramazza, Glyn Humphreys, Jane Riddoch, and Eric Siéroff for helpful comments on a previous draft.

INTRODUCTION

"Neglect dyslexia" is the name often used for a form of reading impairment that can follow right cerebral hemisphere brain injury, in which patients may omit words positioned on the left-hand side of a page of text and misread the beginnings of words (Ellis, Flude, & Young, 1987a; Kinsbourne & Warrington, 1962). In this paper, our interest is focussed on the causes of these types of error.

Although there is obviously a parallel between the omissions and misreadings found in cases of neglect dyslexia, in that they both involve the left side, either of the page (for omissions) or of individual words (initial-letter misreadings), there are reasons for thinking that the two types of error may not be different manifestations of the same underlying deficit. Ellis et al. (1987a, p. 460) suggested this on two grounds. First, their patient, VB, typically omitted words from approximately half of each line of text, whereas her misreadings usually only involved the first letter or two of a word, regardless of its length. Second, VB tended to *substitute* the "neglected" letters when misreading words (wig misread as "big", brief as "grief", etc.) but did not substitute other words for those omitted from the left side of the page.

Other evidence also points to a dissociation between omissions and misreadings. Costello and Warrington (1987) reported the reading abilities of a patient, JOH, who had lesions affecting both the left and right parietal lobes. JOH made errors at the beginnings (left) of words when reading single words. When reading text, however, JOH did not fail to read to the end of a line or return to the beginning of the next line. He did make word omission errors, but these could be to words from the left, centre, or right of the page. This was in marked contrast to his *right-sided* visuospatial neglect in line bisection or copying tasks. JOH thus presented a complex picture of left-sided misreadings of single words, no lateral bias in word omissions, and right-sided visuospatial neglect. Costello and Warrington (1987) emphasise that different neuropsychological mechanisms may underlie the different manifestations of unilateral neglect, and suggest that the errors affecting word beginnings found in cases of neglect dyslexia may be due to an abnormal distribution of attention in the visual word-form system. A further case of dissociation between word misreadings and visuospatial neglect is mentioned by Bisiach, Vallar, Perani, Papagno, and Berti (1986, pp. 479–480). Their patient, MT, showed no neglect in an item-cancellation task, and yet would read only the last 2 letters of 10-letter words.

Ellis et al. (1987a) proposed that neglect dyslexia is simply a manifestation of a more general visual neglect which happens to compromise the reading process. The findings already detailed show that this proposal is incorrect, but they tend to support Ellis et al.'s (1987a) more specific suggestion that omissions and initial-letter misreadings arise in different ways. The errors made in neglect dyslexia are worthy of further detailed investigation.

In the present paper we report on the reading abilities of another patient with neglect dyslexia, SP, and investigate the way in which omission and initial-letter misreading errors are affected by a word's *position*. This is examined both in terms of position on the page and, for initial-letter misreadings, in terms of position in SP's field of vision. The importance of investigating the influence of position within SP's field of vision lies in its potential for assessing the influence of visual field defects which have been thought to contribute to visuospatial neglect and to neglect dyslexia (Gianutsos & Matheson, 1987; Ishiai, Furukawa, & Tsukagoshi, 1987).

CASE REPORT

SP was a right-handed woman, born in 1933. She passed School Certificate, and had worked as a secretary in Government offices and business prior to marriage. She had also been a gifted amateur artist and pianist. For a few years she had complained of right-sided headaches which occurred several times a month. In late May 1985 she had a sudden onset of severe headache and vomiting, which lasted over 24 hours but then subsided. In June 1985 she developed the same symptoms, remained comatose and underwent surgical treatment for a sub-arachnoid haemorrhage from a right middle cerebral artery aneurysm. The aneurysm was clipped, and a surrounding intracerebral haematoma evacuated. C.T.-scan 8 days postoperatively showed only minimal hydrocephalus and minimal right to left shift. SP sustained a profound left hemiparesis and a left homonymous hemianopia. She was referred to the M.R.C. Neuropsychology Unit at the Radcliffe Infirmary, Oxford, in June 1986 for remedial advice because of the slow course of her recovery.

Neuropsychological investigation in June and September 1986 showed severe impairments of memory and face processing. SP was unable to remember any items from stories presented an hour earlier (Wechsler Memory Scale stories, I: immediate recall scores 3.5, 5: delayed recall 0, 0), and could not draw from memory any parts of the Rey-Osterrieth figure (A), which had been copied 45 minutes previously (copying score 27.5/36: delayed recall score 0/36). For face processing, there was very poor recognition of familiar faces (3/20) and poor performance of the Benton Test of unfamiliar face matching (32/54). These memory and face processing impairments were unchanged at long-term follow-up in February 1988 (Wechsler Memory Scale stories, II: immediate recall scores 2, 5: delayed recall 0, 0; Rey-Osterrieth figure B: copying score 18.5/36: delayed recall score 0/36; Recognition of familar faces: 4/20; Benton Test of unfamiliar face matching: 34/54). A more detailed investigation of the problems with faces is given by Young, de Haan, and Newcombe (in press).

W.A.I.S. verbal I.Q. was 89 in June 1986, and was essentially unchanged at 93 in February 1988. Language comprehension and spontaneous speech were normal, and oral spelling was unimpaired.

When first seen (June 1986), SP showed left-sided neglect in reading, writing, copying drawings, item-cancellation tasks, and picture description. Some details concerning her writing were reported by Ellis, Young, and Flude (1987b). On follow-up in June 1987, there were no longer any errors in item cancellation or in writing, and no errors in reading a passage of complex text (Bazin, 1966, p. 30). There were, though, still some errors involving initial letters of single words. In reading a list of 57 words which can have the initial letter deleted or substituted by another letter to produce a different word (e.g. blight, which could be misread as light or slight), SP made 4 errors in June 1987 (jaunt read as "taunt", jangle as "tangle", marrow as "arrow", jowl as "towel"). Thus SP continued to make initial-letter misreadings (4/57) when she no longer made word omission errors, but only in reading individual words, and only at an overall rate well below that previously found.

INVESTIGATION OF SP's NEGLECT DYSLEXIA

SP's neglect errors in reading were investigated in September and October 1986. At this time she showed marked left-sided neglect in item cancellation tasks. Figure 1 shows an example.

FIG. 1 Neglect of left side of page by SP in an item-cancellation task in which she was asked to mark all the circles.

Comparison with VB

We begin our analysis of SP's reading by reporting her performance on tasks that demonstrate her neglect dyslexia and allow some comparison to the previous case we investigated in detail, VB (Ellis et al., 1987a).

SP's reading of a short passage of text is shown in Fig. 2. Both word omissions and initial letter misreadings are evident. When asked to read aloud 18 4-letter words (printed in block capitals) with "substitutable" initial letters (i.e. words, such as FOOT, in which the initial letter can be changed to make other words; BOOT, LOOT, MOOT, etc.) she made 8 mistakes, all involving initial letters. In 4 of these, initial letters were deleted (MEND read as "end", WANT as "ant", CASH as "ash", BEND as "end"), and in the other 4 errors, initial letters were replaced by other letters (MALT read as "salt", BAND as "sand", BEST as "nest", FEAR as "dear"). These errors are all "neglect errors" according to the criteria used by Ellis et al. (1987a), who defined neglect errors operationally as errors in which the target and error words are identical to the right of an identifiable "neglect point" in each word, but have no letters in common to the left of the neglect point. In all cases, SP gave an explanation of the meaning of the substituted word when her comprehension was tested.

In a further test of single word reading, SP was shown 40 4-letter words in block capitals printed in normal (horizontal) orientation, and the same words in vertical orientation. Again, these were all words with substitutable initial letters. The words were shown one by one, with unlimited presentation time. An ABBA design was used, in which 20 words were shown in normal orientation, 20 in vertical orientation, a further 20 in

```
__ _    #    #    #    #
As I went to the shops

_    iced #  #     #
I noticed a man with

_    #      #       #
a large yellow suitcase

 landing on   #    #   #
standing in front of the

        #       #    #   #
railway station. He asked

__  #   #   #   #    #
me the way to the bank.
```

FIG. 2 SP's reading of a passage of text. Following the convention adopted by Ellis, Flude, and Young (1987a), # indicates the words that were correctly read, dashes indicate words that were omitted, and misreadings are written above the target word.

vertical orientation, and 20 in normal orientation. SP made 10 errors to words in normal orientation, but no errors to vertical words.

The absence of errors to vertical words demonstrates directly that SP's reading problems involve left–right spatial co-ordinates. The finding is the same as that arising from our investigation of VB (Ellis et al., 1987a), and it forms a marked contrast to cases (such as those described by Caramazza & Hillis 1990, *Cognitive Neuropsychology*, 7, 391–445; Katz & Sevush, 1989), in which word beginnings are misread regardless of orientation.

Of SP's 10 errors to normally oriented words, one fell into the "other real-word errors" category on Ellis et al.'s stringent criteria (BEAD read as "seed"). The remainder were all neglect errors, 3 deletions (RINK read as "ink", MEND as "end", RICE as "ice"), and 6 substitutions (HAIL read as "mail", GAIT as "wait", YARD as "ward", TOUR as "four", YOLK as "folk", RANK as "bank").

On these tests, then, SP shows similarities to VB in that she makes both word omission and initial-letter errors in reading text, and errors in single word reading for words in the conventional "horizontal" format, in which initial letters may be substituted or deleted. Like VB, her neglect point lies close to the beginnings of the words, and like VB her reading of the same words presented in vertical orientation is accurate. There are, however, some apparent differences of detail. In the small corpus of errors arising from these single word reading tasks given to SP, she seemed to make neglect errors to a higher proportion of single words presented with unlimited exposure than did VB (29% for SP, around 8% for VB), and a smaller proportion of her errors fell into the categories not considered to be purely neglect errors (6% for SP, 34% for VB). Both points could be accommodated within the view that SP's neglect dyslexia for single word reading was the more severe.

Reading of Words in Different Positions on the Page

Sets of words for which the first letter can be deleted or substituted by another letter to produce another word (e.g. FLAP, which can be deleted to LAP, or have its initial letter substituted to make CLAP or SLAP) were matched on word frequency. Each set contained 9 words, 3 each of 4 letters, 5 letters, and 6 letters. There were 5 matched sets in all, listed in Appendix 1.

Each set of words was positioned in random order in one of 5 equally spaced vertical columns from the leftmost to the rightmost side of a page of A4 paper. The words were printed in block capital letters, and there was only one word on each horizontal line, as in Fig. 3.

Different sheets were prepared, so that each set of words appeared once in each of the vertical columns on one of the sheets. SP was given each of

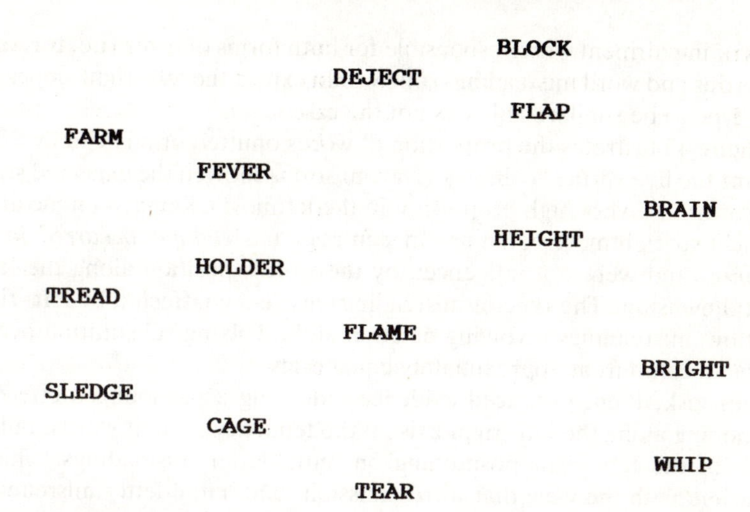

FIG. 3 Example of arrangement of words used in testing SP's reading of single words in different spatial positions.

these sheets, and asked to read aloud all the words on them. Her responses were noted. Later, to increase the amount of data, she was given some of the sheets to read for a second time. Thus, in total, she had eventually been asked to read 315 words, with 63 in each of the 5 vertical columns.

In performing this task, SP made a total of 77 omissions in which she did not attempt to read the word at all. Of the 238 words she did tackle, 190 were correctly read. Her 48 errors consisted of 47 neglect errors by Ellis et al.'s (1987a) criteria, and one nonword response (JOWL read as "towl"; she spelt this for us, and then asked "What's that?"). For the neglect errors, 24 involved substitution of initial letters (HANGER read as "danger", etc.), 21 were deletions (CHAT read as "hat", etc.), and there were 2 additions (LEASE read as "please", ELATE as "relate"). Of the 24 neglect errors involving substitution of initial letters, 18 were the same length as the target (GLOWER read as "blower", etc.) and 3 were one letter shorter (WRACK read as "jack", BRIGHT as "eight", ACORN as "horn").

These data confirm that SP made neglect errors at a rather higher rate than VB (in this task, SP made neglect errors to 20% of words she attempted to read), and that the proportion of errors that were not neglect errors was very low for the words SP did try to read (2% in this task), in contrast to VB (34%; Ellis et al., 1987a; p. 447) and to Baxter and Warrington's (1983) patient JAF (31%; see Ellis et al., 1987a; p. 447).

It is also possible to use these data to examine the occurrence of word omissions and misreadings (effectively, all misreadings are neglect errors, since even the single nonword response "towl" involved substituting the initial letter of JOWL) in each of the five vertical columns. If a common locus of impairment were responsible for both forms of error (i.e. for word omissions and word misreadings) one would expect the left–right slopes for each type to be similar. This was not the case.

Figure 4 illustrates the proportion of words omitted or misread by SP in each of the five vertical columns. The omissions showed the expected steep decline from a very high proportion in the leftmost column, to none at all in the two rightmost columns. In contrast, *misreadings occurred in all columns*, and were not influenced by the word's position along the left–right dimension. The type of misreading was also unaffected by left–right position; misreadings involving deletion and involving substitution occurred in all columns at approximately equal rates.

This task, then, produced evidence indicating a pronounced effect of positioning along the left–right axis on the tendency to omit words, but no effect of the left–right positioning on initial-letter misreadings. This is consistent with the view that word omissions and initial-letter misreadings arise in different ways.

An alternative way of thinking about the data represented in Fig. 4 would be to consider that the omissions and misreadings *do* reflect the same underlying problem, but at two different spatial scales. From this standpoint, omissions occur when the *whole page* is the target of attention, and the left side of the page is neglected, whereas misreadings occur when an *individual word* is the target of attention, and its left side is neglected.

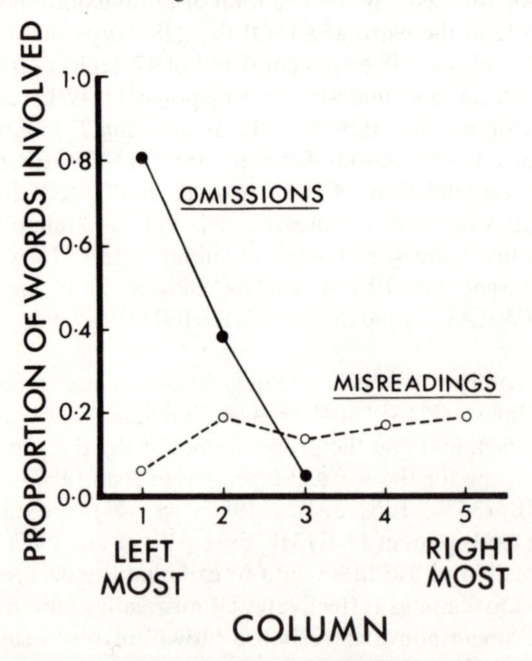

FIG. 4 Proportion of words omitted or misread by SP from each of five vertical columns.

This is certainly a possible interpretation for the present data, since the difference between the functions relating omissions and misreadings to left–right spatial position is much less dramatic if the proportions of misreadings are conditionalised on the probability of making an omission at each location on the left–right axis.

Although we accept this as a possibility for the present data, we pointed out in the Introduction to this paper that such a conception will not account for all aspects of the findings on omissions and misreadings in neglect dyslexia.

Reading of Words in Different Positions in SP's Field of Vision

As well as investigating the influence of left–right position on a page, we considered it important to understand the effects of position in SP's visual field. Normal reading involves a complex pattern of eye movements to fixate words of interest (Rayner, 1978; 1983). When a word is fixated it falls across the fovea, so that its beginning lies in the left visual field and its end in the right visual field (McConkie, Kerr, Reddix, & Zola, 1988; Rayner, Well, & Pollatsek, 1980). Since SP had a left homonymous hemianopia, as do most neglect dyslexia patients (though not all; see Kinsbourne & Warrington, 1962), a word fixated in this way would have its beginning in the blind area of her visual field. Investigations were carried out to determine what effect this might have. These were directed toward two questions. First, what would happen if words were presented to SP with their beginnings in her hemianopic visual field? Would she make eye movements to compensate for the hemianopia? Second, would SP make neglect errors to words presented in her intact right visual field?

To determine the effect of presenting words with their beginnings in the hemianopic visual field, SP was asked to fixate a central point, and then a word was presented (back-projected using a slide projector controlled by a Compur shutter) across the fixation point (with the centre of the word lying at the point of fixation) for 3 seconds, which gave SP plenty of time to read it. This procedure was repeated for 40 trials, using each of the matched sets of 10 imageable nouns of 3, 4, 5, or 6 letters in length from Young and Ellis (1985; Experiment 1). The words were printed in upper-case lettering, and subtended horizontal visual angles of 1°10″ per letter.

SP made 11 errors in these 40 word-reading trials. Eight were deletions (CAT read as "at", FOX as "ox", NAIL as "ail", CHAIR as "hair", PIANO as "no", TABLE as "able", MOTHER as "other", VALLEY as "alley"), one was a substitution (FLOWER read as "gower"; we accepted this as a word because it is a proper name and a place name in English), and two were nonword responses that also involved substitution of initial letters (BARREL read as "sarrel", FOREST as "drest").

These results demonstrate that SP does make initial-letter misreading errors when word beginnings initially fall in the hemianopic area of her visual field. It is noticeable, too, that 10 of her 11 errors were *shorter than* the target word. She seemed to be willing to change fixation to read letters positioned left of fixation, but only to the minimum extent necessary to come up with a plausible response. The other obvious feature of the data is that there were no errors involving omission of the target word; when some of a word's letters fell in her area of intact vision, SP would always try to read it.

Because SP made initial-letter misreadings when word beginnings fell in the hemianopic area of her visual field, it was important to determine whether or not this could provide a complete account of her misreadings. Two studies were therefore carried out to investigate whether or not she would misread the initial letters of words when these had appeared in her intact right visual field.

The first study made use of a technique taken from Ellis et al. (1987a; pp. 449–450). This involved presenting a red digit 1cm. to the left of a word printed in black upper-case letters. SP was asked to report the digit and then identify the word. Accurate report of the digits would ensure that each of the words had fallen in her right visual field whilst its accompanying digit was identified. Of course, this technique does not accurately control SP's fixation while she actually reads the word; it only ensures that the word had fallen in her intact right visual field whilst the digit was being identified.

Sixty-four words were used in this task, 16 each of 3, 4, 5, and 6 letters. The same words had been used in this task with VB (Ellis et al., 1987a), who had made an average of 7 neglect errors each time the set of words was presented.

SP was only shown the set of words once. She reported 63 of the 64 digits correctly (misidentifying 8 as "6" on one trial). On the 63 trials with a correctly reported digit she made 14 misreadings. One of these fell into Ellis et al.'s "other real-word errors" category (GLOWER read as "clover"), but the other 13 were *all* neglect errors by Ellis et al.'s criteria. Twelve involved initial-letter substitutions (BAT read as "eat", GONG as "long", MINK as "wink", NOON as "moon", CLOVE as "glove", FABLE as "table", FROWN as "brown", GORSE as "horse", WORRY as "lorry", BELIEF as "relief", DEJECT as "reject", RUMBLE as "jumble"), and one was an addition (EAR read as "fear"). There were no errors involving the deletion of initial letters.

These results show that SP did make initial-letter misreadings to words that had fallen entirely in her intact visual field. Interestingly, however, these misreadings involved *substitution* of initial letters, in contrast to her tendency to produce initial-letter *deletions* when the beginning of a word fell in her hemianopic field.

The second method used to investigate whether or not SP would misread the initial letters of words when these had appeared in her intact right visual field involved tachistoscopic presentation. Unlike the previous method, this does establish with certainty that the word was entirely in the RVF *at the time it was read*. Four-letter words were presented (unmasked) in the RVF for 150msec. each. This presentation time is sufficiently short to prevent SP's being able to change her fixation position (Young, 1982). The words were presented in upper-case lettering, subtending a horizontal visual angle of 4°40′, and with the centre of each word offset by 4°40′ from the fixation point. After a brief practice session, 40 trials involving reading tachistoscopically presented words were given to SP. Interspersed randomly with these word-reading trials were 20 fixation control trials, in which no word was presented but a digit appeared at 1°10′ to the right of the point of fixation. SP was asked to report the digit when this happened. Note that the fixation control digits were presented closer to the fixation point than any of the letters in the words; hence accurate report of these digits would guarantee that the initial letters of the words had fallen in SP's right visual field.

Eighteen of the 20 fixation digits were correctly reported by SP. On the word-reading trials, however, she made 19 errors involving the beginnings or ends of the words. For 15 of these errors the beginning of the word was misread (KILL read as "hall", SLOW as "blow", etc.), and in the other 4 cases the end of the word was misread (TRAY read as "trap", COAT as "cope", etc.). Even though the word beginnings fell in an area of higher acuity than the word endings, more errors were thus made to the initial than to the final letters (sign test, n = 19, x = 4, 2-tailed $P < 0.05$). As before, most misreadings of the initial letters of RVF words involved substitutions (13/15), with only 2 cases of initial-letter deletions.

DISCUSSION

Our investigation of SP's reading abilities lends further support to the view that different underlying impairments contribute to neglect dyslexia, which is best considered as involving different underlying impairments which are often (but not inevitably) present in combination with each other. In this respect, we see neglect dyslexia as no different to many other neuropsychological problems which, when carefully analysed with appropriate experimental techniques, can be shown to involve different and dissociable causes of "symptoms" which may initially seem to form a syndrome cluster in many patients (see Ellis & Young, 1988, for several further examples). We also accept entirely that what can seem at first sight to be the same symptom may have different underlying causes in different patients, and that the factors we have demonstrated to underly SP's reading impairments may not necessarily hold in all cases of neglect dyslexia.

For SP, we have found evidence pointing toward differences between the causes of word *omissions* and initial-letter *misreadings*, and differences between misreadings involving the *deletion* or the *substitution* of initial letters. We will discuss each difference in turn, and then explain their implications for understanding the nature of neglect dyslexia.

Word Omissions and Initial-letter Misreadings

SP only omitted words when they were positioned toward the left side of the page, whereas her initial-letter misreadings were largely unaffected by the word's position along the left–right axis. Hence a factor which affected one type of error dramatically (left–right position on the page) had no effect on the other type of error.

This finding is consistent with Ellis et al.'s (1987a) suggestion that the two types of error reflect different underlying deficits. We have noted, though, that the finding is also consistent with a single type of deficit operating at two different spatial scales (in this case, whole page or individual word). However, this single deficit conception cannot deal easily with observations already made in other patients, such as VB's tendency to misread only the initial letters of words regardless of their lengths, and her tendency to substitute initial letters of words but omit words on the left of the page (Ellis et al., 1987a).

Because SP omitted items from the left side of the page both in reading and in cancellation tasks (see Fig. 1), it is tempting to conclude that her tendency to omit words from the left side of the page in reading arises in the same way as her cancellation task omissions. Costello and Warrington's (1987) findings, however, caution against reaching this conclusion too readily. As we noted, their patient JOH showed right-sided neglect in item-cancellation tasks, yet his word omission errors could occur to words on the left, centre, or right of the page.

It is thus possible that the disruption underlying word omission errors is more directly related to reading than might at first appear. This would be consistent with other reports of domain-specific forms of unilateral neglect (e.g. Young, de Haan, Newcombe, & Hay, 1990). One possibility for further investigation is that word omissions reflect an impairment of the systematic pattern of saccadic eye movements needed in order to read along each line of text and then move to the beginning of the next line, in which the line beginnings are not found correctly.

Deletion and Substitution of Initial Letters

Although initial-letter misreadings were found at all positions on the page, the nature of SP's initial-letter misreadings was affected by the word's initial positioning in her visual field. When the beginning of a word fell into the hemianopic part of her visual field SP tended to delete initial letters, whereas when the word fell entirely in her intact right visual field she tended to produce misreadings which involved initial-letter substitutions.

Perhaps the most important aspect of these findings is that they confirm Kinsbourne and Warrington's (1962) and Ellis et al.'s (1987a) demonstrations that *initial-letter misreadings can occur even when a word has fallen in the intact part of the visual field.* This result was obtained for SP both by using Ellis et al.'s (1987a) technique of requesting report of a digit positioned to the left of the word to be read and by using brief tachistoscopic presentation with digits as fixation control stimuli.

The fact that initial-letter misreadings could occur to words which had fallen in the intact area of SP's visual field shows that the left hemianopia so frequently found in cases of neglect dyslexia does *not* in itself account for the misreadings. For the same reason, Gianutsos and Matheson's (1987; p. 204) suggestion that initial-letter substitutions are produced by reduced sensitivity of the left central field cannot apply to SP.

The general point, that there is not an exact relation between the presence of left visual field defect and neglect dyslexia is, of course, consistent with the observation that many patients have left hemianopias *without* neglect dyslexia; they simply compensate for their hemianopia by making appropriate eye or head movements. Similarly, Kinsbourne and Warrington (1962) noted that not all neglect dyslexia patients have left hemianopias, which implies that failure to compensate for hemianopia cannot be the whole story for reading errors in neglect dyslexia.

Recently, however, Ishiai et al. (1987) have demonstrated that at least some neglect patients do fail to make the eye movements needed to compensate for their visual field defects, and have suggested that this may contribute to the observed patterns of performance. Again, though, it is clear that since SP made initial-letter misreadings of RVF words, failure to compensate for her left hemianopia cannot provide a complete account of her problems.

We think, however, that failure to compensate for her hemianopia may have some role to play in SP's misreadings. Our evidence suggests that it contributes to initial-letter deletions, rather than the substitutions observed following RVF presentation. Initial-letter deletions formed SP's predominant responses to words presented across the fixation point, with their beginnings in her hemianopic field. Her strategy in reading these words seemed to be to move her eyes leftwards only to the minimum extent necessary to produce a plausible candidate word, which could in consequence be shorter than the word actually shown to her. This tendency to shorten the target word was not evident if the beginning of the target had fallen in SP's right visual field, when initial-letter substitutions became the predominant form of error.

We do not, of course, intend to imply that failure to compensate properly for hemianopia is uninteresting. Many patients with hemianopias have no obvious problem in moving their eyes to achieve adequate compensation. SP's failure to compensate fully when words fell across the fixation point is thus of interest, and requires explanation. Here, we draw attention only to the fact that it is associated with a characteristic type of error, in the form of initial-letter deletions.

The Nature of Neglect Dyslexia

Our view of neglect dyslexia, then, is that it usually involves a *combination of impairments. Words are omitted* from the left side of the page because of defective location of line beginnings. *Initial letters are deleted* from words when these are fixated with their beginnings in the hemianopic area of the visual field and the patient fails to make adequate compensatory eye movements. *Initial-letter substitutions*, however, can occur even when the word has fallen entirely within an intact part of the visual field, and must thus reflect damage to mechanisms involved in letter and word recognition.

This conception implies that neglect can affect reading in different ways, depending on the functional loss of impairment. In addition, although many patients with neglect dyslexia would be expected to show all of the three forms of impairment we have identified, there should also be cases in which these types of impairment can dissociate from each other. Bisiach et al.'s (1986; pp. 479–480) patient, MT, whose errors were apparently mostly initial-letter deletions, would be an example of this. Further investigation of these cases in which one type of neglect dyslexic reading error predominates should allow for more exact specification of the way in which each type of error arises.

Manuscript received 7 March 1990
Revised manuscript received 15 June 1990

REFERENCES

Baxter, D. M. & Warrington, E. K. (1983). Neglect dysgraphia. *Journal of Neurology, Neurosurgery, and Psychiatry*, *46*, 1073–1078.

Bazin, G. (1966). *The Louvre*. London: Thames & Hudson.

Bisiach, E., Vallar, G., Perani, D., Papagno, C., & Berti, A. (1986). Unawareness of disease following lesions of the right hemisphere: Anosognosia for hemiplegia and anosognosia for hemianopia. *Neuropsychologia*, *24*, 471–482.

Costello, A. de L. & Warrington, E. K. (1987). The dissociation of visuospatial neglect and neglect dyslexia. *Journal of Neurology, Neurosurgery, and Psychiatry*, *50*, 1110–1116.

Ellis. A. W., Flude, B. M., & Young, A. W. (1987a). "Neglect dyslexia" and the early visual processing of letters in words and nonwords. *Cognitive Neuropsychology*, *4*, 439–464.

Ellis. A. W., Young, A. W., & Flude, B. M. (1987b). "Afferent dysgraphia" in a patient and in normal subjects. *Cognitive Neuropsychology*, *4*, 465–486.

Ellis, A. W. & Young, A. W. (1988). *Human cognitive neuropsychology*. London: Lawrence Erlbaum Associates Ltd.

Gianutsos, R. & Matheson, P. (1987). The rehabilitation of visual perceptual disorders attributable to brain injury. In M. J. Meier, A. L. Benton, & L. Diller (Eds.), *Neuropsychological rehabilitation*. Edinburgh: Churchill Livingstone, 202–241.

Ishiai, S., Furukawa, T., & Tsukagoshi, H. (1987). Eye-fixation patterns in homonymous hemianopia and unilateral spatial neglect. *Neuropsychologia*, *25*, 675–679.

Katz, R. B. & Sevush, S. (1989). Positional dyslexia. *Brain and Language*, *37*, 266–289.

Kinsbourne, M. & Warrington, E. K. (1962). A variety of reading disability associated with right hemisphere lesions. *Journal of Neurology, Neurosurgery, and Psychiatry*, *25*, 339–344.

McConkie, G. W., Kerr, P. W., Reddix, M. D., & Zola, D. (1988). Eye movement control during reading, 1: The location of initial eye fixations on words. *Vision Research*, *28*, 1107–1118.

Rayner, K. (1978). Eye movements in reading and information processing. *Psychological Bulletin*, *85*, 618–660.

Rayner, K. (Ed.) (1983). Eye movements in reading: Perceptual and language processes. In H. A. Whitaker (Ed.), *Perspectives in neurolinguistics, neuropsychology, and psycholinguistics*. New York: Academic Press.

Rayner, K., Well, A. D., & Pollatsek, A. (1980). Asymmetry of the effective visual field in reading. *Perception and Psychophysics*, *27*, 537–544.

Young, A. W. (1982). Methological and theoretical bases of visual hemifield studies. In J. G. Beaumont (Ed.), *Divided visual field studies of cerebral organisation*. London: Academic Press, 11–27.

Young, A. W., de Haan, E. H. F., & Newcombe, F. (in press). Unawareness of impaired face recognition. *Brain and Cognition*.

Young, A. W., de Haan, E. H. F., Newcombe, F., & Hay, D. C. (1990). Facial neglect. *Neuropsychologia*, *28*, 391–415.

Young, A. W. & Ellis, A. W. (1985). Different methods of lexical access for words presented in the left and right visual hemifields. *Brain and Language*, *24*, 326–358.

APPENDIX 1

Matched sets of words for which the first letter can be deleted or substituted by another letter to produce another word.

Set A	*Set B*	*Set C*	*Set D*	*Set E*
BILL	BROW	CAPE	CHAT	GALL
FARM	CAGE	PEEL	FLAP	WHIP
TRAY	JOWL	TEAR	WINK	ZONE
ACORN	FEVER	CLOVE	BLOCK	BRAIN
JAUNT	LARCH	FLAME	ELATE	LEASE
TREAD	SABLE	GRAIN	SHORN	WRACK
HALTER	BLIGHT	DEJECT	GLOWER	BRIGHT
SLEDGE	JANGLE	MARROW	HEIGHT	HANGER
VOWING	HOLDER	PLAYER	LEAVES	PREACH

COGNITIVE NEUROPSYCHOLOGY, 1991, *8* (3/4) 193–212

Right Neglect Dyslexia: A Single Case Study

Elizabeth K. Warrington
The National Hospital for Neurology & Neurosurgery, London, U.K.

A single case study of a right neglect dyslexic is reported. The patient's (RYT) single word reading difficulty was characterised by paralexic errors that affected word endings. An analysis of the error corpus demonstrates the maintenance of word length in his error responses and a gradient of accuracy across individual words irrespective of their length. The actual neglect point was found to be a function of word length. It is concluded that right neglect dyslexia is a reading-specific deficit in which there is activation of an inappropriate visual word form.

INTRODUCTION

Right neglect dyslexia is an uncommon syndrome as compared with left neglect dyslexia. Since the first brief clinical description of this syndrome was reported in 1957 (Warrington & Zangwill), no further examples of this type of reading deficit have been documented until 1989 (Hillis & Caramazza, 1989; 1990). Neglect dyslexia is characterised by the occurrence of paralexic errors that have a spatial bias. The left neglect dyslexic misreads the beginnings of words. The errors are not simply omissions, but typically consist of the production of an alternative *real* word. Several corpora of left neglect dyslexic responses are available (e.g. Baxter & Warrington, 1983; Ellis, Flude, & Young, 1987). The maintenance of word length appears to be a core characteristic of this syndrome and, perhaps paradoxically, long words are no more vulnerable than short words. In fact, in one case an inverse word length effect was observed (Costello & Warrington, 1987). Semantic and derivational errors rarely occur. The one well-documented

---

Requests for reprints should be addressed to Prof. Elizabeth K. Warrington, The National Hospital for Neurology and Neurosurgery, Queen Square, London WC1N 3BG, U.K.

I wish to thank Dr. L. J. Findley for permission to investigate RYT and to report the findings. I am grateful to Ms. Helen Oxley for her assistance in the analysis of the data and to Dr. L. D. Kartsounis for his helpful comments on the manuscript. In particular I wish to thank Dr. R. A. McCarthy for directing my attention to this case and for her assistance in assessing his dyslexia.

right neglect dyslexic on record made paralexic errors with a spatial bias to the right (Hillis & Caramazza, 1990).

Ellis et al. (1987) introduced a stringent criterion (possibly overstrict) for the identification of a "neglect" error. Only those errors in which the response was identical to the target to one side of a "neglect point" having *no* letters in common on the other side were accepted as neglect errors. Ellis et al. found that 2/3 of their patients' responses were left neglect errors and a majority of the remaining responses were alternative real words having an overall visual similarity.

This single case report describes a patient with features of a right neglect dyslexia. The aim is twofold: first to establish the similarity of right neglect dyslexia with left neglect dyslexia, and second to consider the implications of this syndrome both for models of the reading process and for theories of neglect.

CASE REPORT

RYT, a 40-year-old (d.o.b. 4.5.44) right-handed bus driver, was first investigated at Oldchurch Hospital in 1972 after he had developed sudden weakness of the arm and leg following a flu-like illness. On examination there was a spastic hemiparesis in the right arm and leg. The original diagnosis of a slow-growing left parietal astrocytoma was not confirmed by subsequent serial scans, which were negative. He was referred again in 1985 for investigation of recent difficulties in reading and writing. On examination, apart from a mild right-sided hemiparesis, there were no neurological signs of note. Visual-evoked potentials were normal. A C.T.-scan showed a well-defined small area of calcification seen above and lateral to the body of the left lateral ventricle and there was moderate widening of the lateral ventricle. The appearances were considered to be consistent with calcification in a previous cerebral infarct. He was presumed to have had a further small infarct that was not visible on the scan.

NEUROPSYCHOLOGICAL ASSESSMENT

RYT was referred as an out-patient by Dr. L. Findley to the Psychology department of the National Hospital on 26.3.85. He attended at irregular intervals on an out-patient basis during the next three months. During this time his reading appeared to improve slightly. RYT was assessed on a shortened form of the W.A.I.S. and obtained a verbal I.Q. of 81 and a performance I.Q. of 91. Whereas his age-scaled scores on the Vocabulary and Similarities subtests were within the average range (SS 8 and 10 respectively) his Digit Span and Arithmetic scores were borderline/defective (SS 6 and 4 respectively). His recognition memory for visual

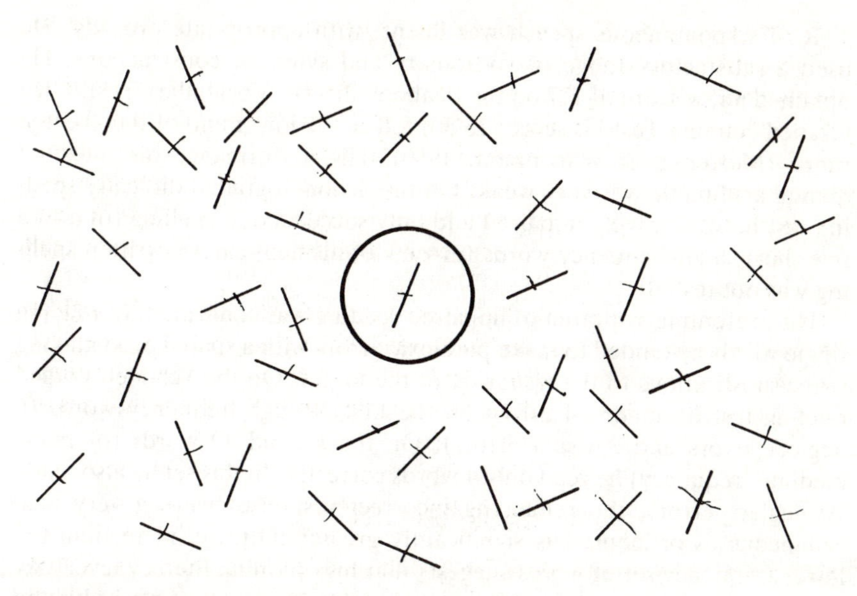

FIG. 1 RYT's performance on Albert's cancellation test.

material (faces) was within the lower limits of the normal range; he scored close to the 25th percentile. On a comparable test of recognition memory for verbal material (words) he scored below the 5th percentile (Warrington, 1984).

There was no evidence of any perceptual impairment or spatial neglect. RYT correctly identified 19/20 "unusual" view photographs. He completed Albert's (1973) cancellation test accurately in 90secs. using his nonpreferred left hand (see Fig. 1). On an adaptation of Willison's (Note 1) Digit Copying Test there was no neglect of the items on the right side of the page. There was no suggestion of any spatial or neglect errors in his copy of the Ogden (1985) drawing (see Fig. 2).

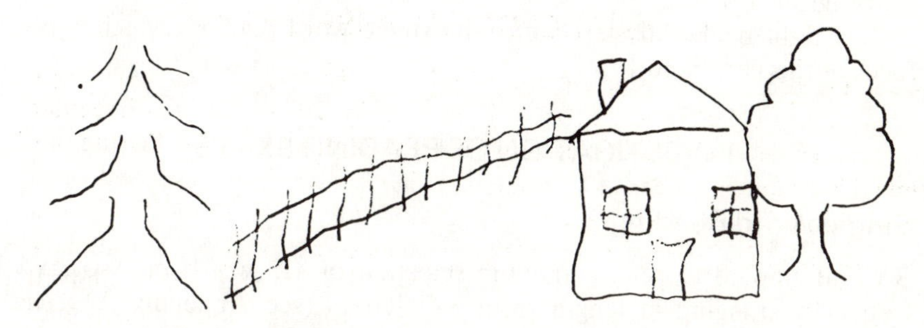

FIG. 2 RYT's copy of the Ogden drawing.

RYT's spontaneous speech was fluent, with appropriate prosody. He used a satisfactory range of vocabulary and syntactic constructions. He obtained a raw score of 127 on the Peabody Picture Vocabulary Test. On a Graded Naming Test his score (13/30) fell at the lower end of the average range (McKenna & Warrington, 1980). His performance on a test of mental arithmetic was very weak. On the Schonell graded difficulty spelling test he was gravely impaired and only succeeded in spelling (orally) a few short, high-frequency words (in view of his hemiparesis written spelling was not tested).

His presenting symptom of impaired reading was confirmed. In reading single words he tended to make paralexic errors with a spatial bias; making letter substitutions to the *right* side of the target. On the Schonell graded reading test he made 14 errors on the first 40 high-frequency words (6 neglect errors and 3 visual errors). On the second 40 words (of intermediate frequency) he read only 4 words correctly. In this set he also made 10 neglect errors; the remaining incorrect responses were a very miscellaneous assortment. His significantly greater difficulty in reading the lower-frequency set of words suggests that his optimum literacy level may not have been good and that his premorbid reading vocabulary was limited to high-frequency words. He made numerous errors in attempting to read c.v.c. nonsense syllables.

In reading text he complained that all the words became "jumbled" and his reading of one simple short passage was disorganised. No further attempt to assess his text reading was made. Although he was able to name single letters accurately he made errors attempting to name letters in a matrix of letters and when a target letter was flanked by other letters. It was considered that his dyslexia had two elements:

1. an "attentional dyslexia" which resulted in a decrement in his ability to read words and letters that were presented in the context of other words and letters. Thus his ability to read words and letters in an *array* was less good than when he attempted to read them in isolation (Shallice & Warrington, 1977).
2. a right neglect dyslexia affecting single word reading, which is the focus of this case report.

INVESTIGATION OF READING SKILLS

Single Word Reading

RYT attempted to read a random selection of 425 words of A or AA frequency, ranging in length from 3–7 letters (see Appendix A). The percent correct for each word length is given in Table 1. It is clear that his

TABLE 1
Reading Responses and Word Length

Word Length	*N*	*Correct*	*Neglect*	*Visual*	*Misc.*	*Omissions*
3	56	70%	76%	12%	12%	0%
4	139	50%	45%	30%	7%	17%
5	100	43%	49%	33%	5%	12%
6	79	51%	23%	28%	15%	33%
7	50	22%	33%	26%	20%	20%
Total	425	48%	43%	28%	11%	18%

general reading competence is not good. Nevertheless his residual reading skills are sufficiently preserved to warrant a more detailed analysis of his dyslexic syndrome. There was a significant effect of word length ($\chi^2 = 25.58$, d.o.f. = 4, $P < 0.001$), which can be attributed to his relatively good score on the 3-letter words and poor score on the 7-letter words.

His error responses were classified as follows:

1. Neglect errors: real word responses in which the target and error words are identical to the left of an identifiable neglect point, but in which there are no letters in common to the right of the neglect point (call–calf, truth–truck, season–seaside). As an aside it should be noted that in the case of right neglect dyslexia, by definition, neglect errors would include derivational error responses (i.e. responses that have the same root morpheme but an incorrect derivational ending; dance–dancing).
2. Visual errors: real word error responses which do not meet the criterion for a neglect error, but nevertheless have a visual similarity, such that at least half the letters in the target word were present in the response (e.g. took–talk; agree–argue; prince–price).
3. Omissions: this category of "no response" was in fact encouraged in this patient whose optimum literacy skills were judged not to be of a high order.
4. Miscellaneous: all other responses.

The percentage of the total number of each type of error for each word length is given in Table 1. Nearly one half of all his error responses were classified as neglect errors. The proportion of neglect errors decreased somewhat with increasing word lengths. The proportion of visual errors was fairly constant across the 5-word lengths (apart from 3-letter words). Of the total number of neglect errors only *10* could be given the alternative classification of a "derivational" error. The proportion of neglect errors is very likely to be an underestimate. Using this very strict criterion for identifying neglect errors, in which *all* the letters to the right in the response must differ from those in the target, it is possible that a number of visual errors were misclassified. It thus seemed appropriate to undertake a more detailed analysis of the position of letter errors within the word.

The number of letters correct for each position in the neglect error responses for each word length are given in Fig. 3. A variable scale on the abscissa has been used in order to superimpose the "beginning", "middle", and "end" letters for the pool of 3, 5, and 7 (see Fig. 4). For each of these 3

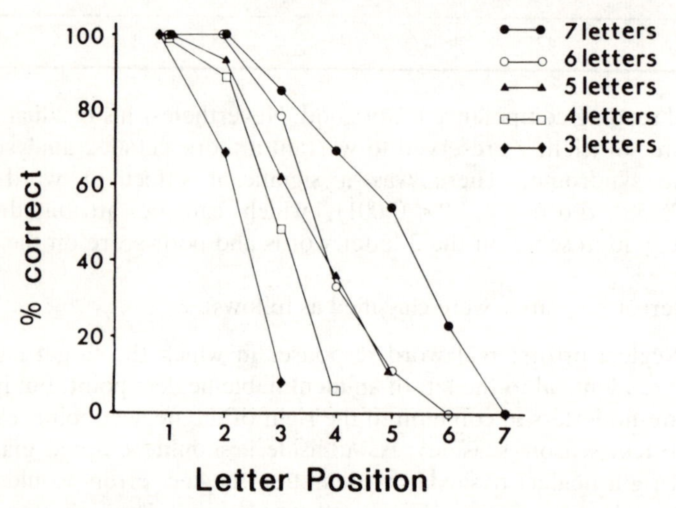

FIG. 3 Letter position errors (neglect errors only) for each word length.

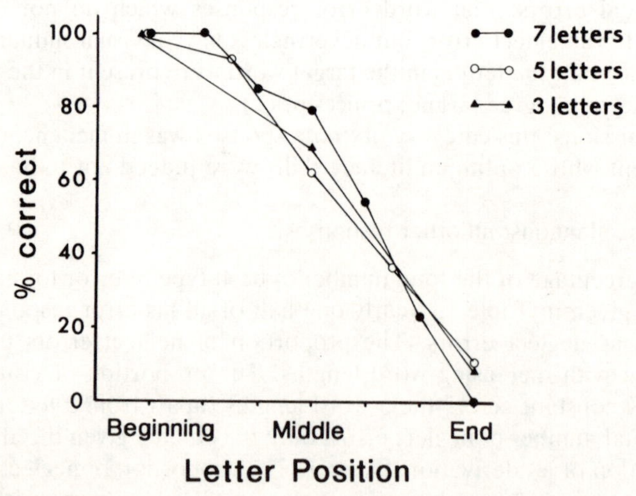

FIG. 4 Letter position errors (neglect errors only) for 3, 5, and 7 letter words.

word lengths a very similar gradient of decrement in letter accuracy from the beginning to the end of the word has been obtained. These gradients are virtually unchanged if one includes RYT's visual error responses in this analysis (see Fig. 5). The mean number of letters to the left of the neglect point increases as a function of word length (see Fig. 6). This is further evidence of a gradient of neglect that "shifts" to the right.

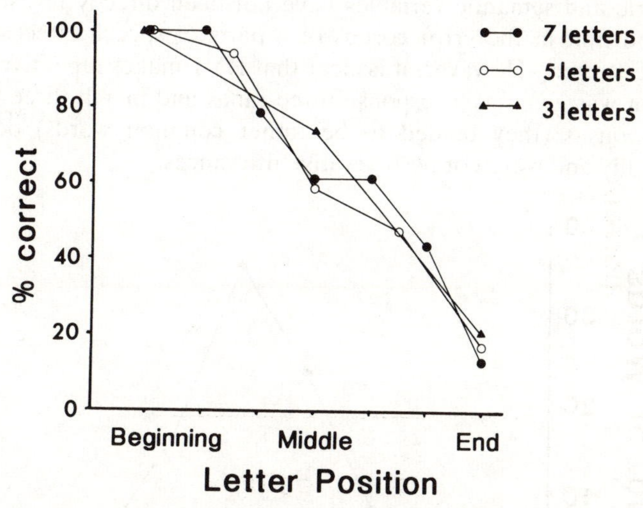

FIG. 5 Letter position errors (summing neglect and visual errors).

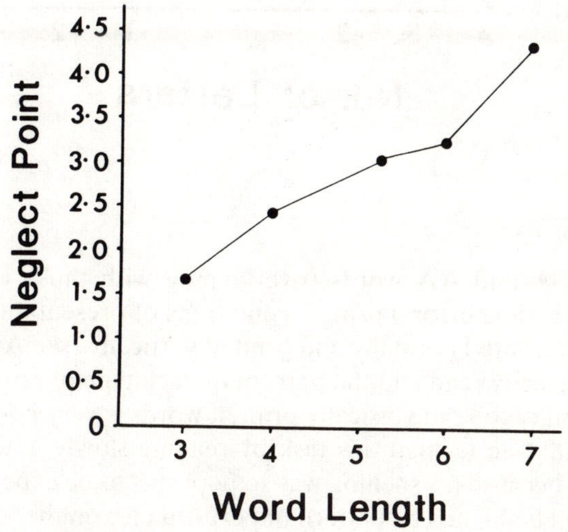

FIG. 6 Position of neglect point.

The word length of a neglect error response can be longer, shorter, or the same as the target (e.g. mark–march; lose–low; rush–rust). The distribution of RYT's neglect error responses classified in terms of their length with respect to the target word is shown in Fig. 7. Seventy-four percent of these error responses were within the range ±1 letter of the target word. Clearly, then, there is a close and symmetrical correspondence between the word length of the target and the neglect error response.

Linguistic and semantic variables have not been directly investigated. There is no hint in the error corpus of a parts of speech effect or of a concreteness effect. However, it is clear that RYT makes repetitive errors (e.g. spoon was given as a response three times and march three times). These responses (they tended to be rather common words) occurred spasmodically and were not perseverative utterances.

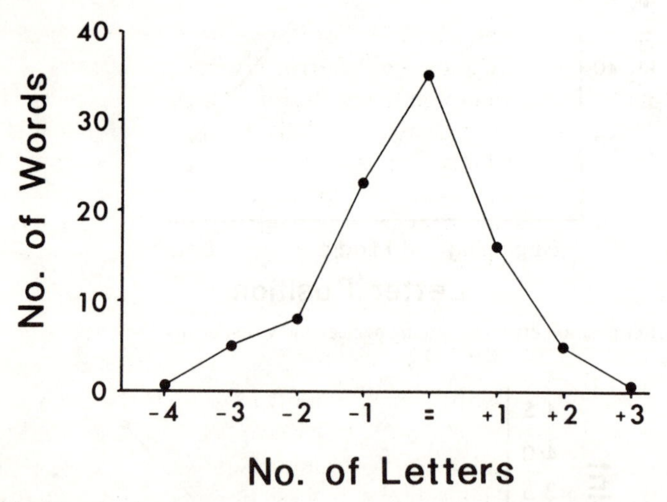

FIG. 7 Word length of response.

Vertical Reading

RYT read 328 A and AA words (overlapping with those used for the analysis of his reading errors) using 2 conditions of presentation (using an ABBA design): printed normally and printed vertically (see Appendix B). The percent correctly read and the percent of each type of error is given in Table 2. His ability to read vertically printed words is very poor indeed. It was observed that he tackled this task by reading slowly down letter-by-letter. Perhaps because his spelling was so poor it is to be expected that his error rate would be high. The pattern of performance on the words read in the horizontal condition was very similar to that documented in the main

TABLE 2
Horizontal vs. Vertical Reading

	Correct	*Neglect*	*Visual*	*Misc.*	*Omissions*
Vertical (N = 328)	13%	25%	35%	7%	33%
Horizontal (N = 328)					
4 Letters	58%	70%	17%	3%	10%
5 Letters	49%	50%	41%	4%	4%
6 Letters	57%	32%	47%	2%	17%
Total (Horizontal)	55%	53%	33%	3%	10%

error corpus (see Tables 1 and 2), both in terms of level of performance and in the proportion of each type of error response.

RYT had already attempted to read a subset of *134* of these words in the original documentation of his reading skills. Of these words that had been attempted twice, 77 of his responses were either both correct or both wrong and 57 of his responses were correct on one occasion and incorrect on the other. The contingency coefficient was 0.17 ($P > 0.05$), which indicates a rather low degree of consistency between his responses on 2 occasions.

Compound Word Reading (23.4.85)

Forty-five compound words, each comprising 2 constituent words (e.g. horseshoe, snowflake, armchair, etc.) were selected (see Appendix C). RYT attempted to read these compound words and their "split" components. He was tested alternating "blocks" of 5 words (compound) and 10 words (split). In spite of the fact that the majority of the split words were of A or AA frequency and that only a minority of the compound words were of this frequency, his ability to read the compound words was quite creditable (*58%* correct as compared with 84% correct for the first and 64% correct for the second components of the compound words). The average word length of this set of compound words was between 8 and 9. It is of note that his overall level of reading this set of words is considerably better than the original set of high-frequency 7-letter words (see Table 1).

Tachistoscopic Reading

A pool of 72 words was presented tachistoscopically for an exposure duration of 150secs. This pool of words was counter-balanced for word length (4, 6, 8 letters), concreteness (low and high) rating and frequency (high and low). RYT read correctly 33% of these words and there was no significant effect of either word frequency (14/36 vs. 10/36), word length (9/24 vs. 8/24 vs. 7/24), or word concreteness (12/36 vs. 13/36). Although his overall performance is weak the fact that his tachistoscopic reading is only slightly below the level of his reading in free vision establishes that RYT is reading words as whole units and at the very least establishes that he is not attempting to read using a letter-by-letter strategy (e.g. Warrington & Shallice, 1980). Similar results have been reported for left neglect dyslexics (Kinsbourne & Warrington, 1962).

DISCUSSION

This case report describes a patient, RYT, whose acquired dyslexia was characterised by paralexic errors with spatial bias that affected the right side of words and by the occurrence of visual errors. He appeared to have a right neglect dyslexia that was comparable in all respects (other than direction) to that of left neglect dyslexia.

Error responses of left and right neglect dyslexia frequently have the following characteristics in common:

1. For the individual patient word length is not an important variable for competence in single word reading; except in those instances where a paradoxical inverse word length effect has been recorded (e.g. Costello & Warrington, 1987; Patterson & Wilson, 1990).
2. There is a maintenance of target word length in the neglect error response.
3. When this exact maintenance of word length does not apply, additional letters are as common as omissions in the neglect error responses.
4. There is (with one notable exception, viz. Patterson and Wilson) a gradient of accuracy across words irrespective of word length.
5. A strictly defined neglect point is a function of word length.
6. Qualitatively similar responses have been reported with tachistoscopic presentation and in free vision.
7. Semantic similarity is infrequent and neologisms are uncommon responses.

This is a remarkable symmetry: all the more remarkable considering there are other quite distinct "left–right" properties of English orthography that are not symmetrical. English text is read from left to right, individual words are read from left to right and perhaps most relevant for the neglect dyslexic, for the individual word there is greater specification to the left (the first few letters are more predictive of the whole than the last few). In the "*right*" syndrome, reading habits are in the same direction as the neglect deficit but in the left syndrome they are opposed. It would appear that their common core is a spatially biased attentional deficit, sufficient to overcome normal reading habits.

Most contemporary models of reading incorporate or at least acknowledge that there are two very distinct classes of dyslexic syndromes: the "peripheral" dyslexias and the "central" dyslexias (for review, see Shallice, 1988). There is general agreement that the neglect dyslexias are one of the subtypes of the peripheral dyslexias: the procedures that achieve access to a stored orthographic representation of the printed word, a visual word-form unit, are impaired. However, there is still controversy as to whether this type of reading difficulty reflects a more pervasive neglect syndrome or whether it is a reading-specific neglect and can thus be accepted as one subtype of dyslexia. Furthermore accounts differ as to the precise stage in the transcoding between a string of letters and a specific lexical item in the visual word-form system that is damaged.

Considering first the selectivity of neglect; there is reasonably good evidence that neglect dyslexia and spatial neglect are dissociable syndromes. For the left neglect syndromes the double dissociation has been documented. Particularly striking in this regard was the patient with a gross spatial neglect of the left such that in reading text, only the rightmost words on a page were read. This same patient was not a neglect dyslexic in so far as single words, including compound words, were read competently and the incidence of paralexic errors was minimal (Kartsounis & Warrington, 1989). In the present case there was no evidence of right-sided neglect other than the predominance of right neglect errors in reading individual words. The more frequent occurrence of left neglect than right neglect would appear to mirror the more frequent occurrence of left spatial neglect than right spatial neglect. It is argued that both right and left neglect dyslexia can occur as highly selective deficits and that evidence other than neglect phenomenon are to be viewed as additional associated deficits.

Turning to the problem of the locus of impairment, there are a number of properties of this syndrome that suggest that neglect dyslexia reflects an impairment in the procedures for accessing a visual word form unit rather than in the early stages of visual analysis of graphemic units. Within this framework the deficit is "central", operating at the level of the whole word. The absence of weak word length effects (short words are as vulnerable as long words and in at least one case more so) and the maintenance of word length in the paralexic error responses are particularly pertinent in this regard. These two characteristics taken together provide strong grounds for the central representation account of neglect dyslexia. That these characteristics be so identical in the right and the left neglect dyslexia suggests that they have a common cause.

To be more specific about the "central" locus of spatially biased paralexic errors in reading, it is helpful to consider the present case in terms of the Caramazza and Hillis (1990) model of the different levels of representation. Specifically, in parallel with Marr's (1982) theory of object recognition, they differentiate between representation in a spatially defined co-ordinate system and a word-centred co-ordinate system. They argue, mainly from the evidence of a "word-centred" effect—their patient NG's reading accuracy was good to the left of the word centre and poor to the right, irrespective of word length—that the "impairment is at a stage of processing where word-centred graphemic representations are computed". In the present case also, it is suggested that the deficit implicates a word-centred representation.

The amount of graphemic information that can be processed is not necessarily the limiting factor in neglect dyslexia. In the present case the neglect point shifts to the right with increasing word length. There is a gradient such that number of correct graphemes in the error response is directly related to the whole word length. The compound word data is quite telling in this regard. In the present case (and more dramatically in a case of left neglect dyslexia, Costello & Warrington, 1987) compound words were read as well if not better than shorter words of higher frequency. In the case of compound words, given that the neglect point is a function of whole-word length and that word length is accurately encoded, the relatively low error rate can be accounted for by constraints imposed by the number of words in the lexicon that "map" onto the stimulus configuration (e.g. pen . . . , wind . . .). If such constraints are important in determining spatially biased paralexic errors then it is plausible to suggest that it is the accessing of a stored representation of the visual word form that is faulty. Consequently an inappropriate target within the visual word-form system is activated.

The spatial bias of the errors suggests that wrong target *selection* follows from an abnormal distribution of attention in the access procedures. Here we have evidence that the attentional mechanisms operating on the stored representations of written words, as well as operating in extra-personal space, are characterised by a left–right gradient (De Renzi, Gentilini, Faglioni, & Barbieri, 1989). It appears that this balance can be disturbed in highly specific tasks.

Our conclusion for right neglect dyslexia is the same as for left neglect dyslexia. There is an abnormal distribution of attention, such that an inappropriate word-form unit is activated. It seems that these units have spatial properties and that the "left" side appears to determine an incorrect real-word response to the target.

Manuscript received 7 March 1990
Revised manuscript received 15 June 1990

REFERENCES

Albert, M. L. (1973). A simple test of visual neglect. *Neurology*, *23*, 658–664.

Baxter, D. M. & Warrington, E. K. (1983). Neglect dysgraphia. *Journal of Neurology, Neurosurgery, and Psychiatry*, *46*, 1073–1078.

Caramazza, A. & Hillis, A. E. (1990). Levels of representation, co-ordinate frames, and unilateral neglect. *Cognitive Neuropsychology*, *7*, 391–445.

Costello, A. De Lacy & Warrington, E. K. (1987). Dissociation of visuo-spatial neglect and neglect dyslexia. *Journal of Neurology, Neurosurgery, and Psychiatry*, *50*, 1110–1116.

De Renzi, E., Gentilini, M., Faglioni, P., & Barbieri, C. (1989). Attentional shift towards the rightmost stimuli in patients with left visual neglect. *Cortex*, *25*, 231–237.

Ellis, A. W., Flude, B. M., & Young, A. W. (1987). "Neglect dyslexia" and the early visual processing of letters in words and nonwords. *Cognitive Neuropsychology*, *4*, 439–464.

Hillis, A. E. & Caramazza, A. (1989). The graphemic buffer and attentional mechanisms. *Brain and Language*, *36*, 208–235.

Hillis, A. E. & Caramazza, A. (1990). The effects of attentional deficits on reading and spelling. In A. Caramazza (Ed.), *Cognitive neuropsychology and neurolinguistics: Advances in models of language processing and impairment.* Hillsdale, N.J.: Lawrence Erlbaum Associates Inc.

Kartsounis, L. D. & Warrington, E. K. (1989). Unilateral visual neglect overcome by cues implicit in stimulus arrays. *Journal of Neurology, Neurosurgery, and Psychiatry*, *52*, 1253–1259.

Kinsbourne, M. & Warrington, E. K. (1962). A variety of reading disability associated with right hemisphere lesions. *Journal of Neurology, Neurosurgery, and Psychiatry*, *25*, 339–344.

Marr, D. (1982). *Vision*. San Francisco: W. H. Freeman & Company.

McKenna, P. & Warrington, E. K. (1980). Testing for nominal dysphasia. *Journal of Neurology, Neurosurgery, and Psychiatry*, *43*, 781–788.

Ogden, J. A. (1985). Antero-posterior interhemispheric differences in the loci of lesions producing visual hemineglect. *Brain and Cognition*, *4*, 59–75.

Patterson, K. & Wilson, B. (1990). A rose is a rose or a nose: A deficit in initial letter identification. *Cognitive Neuropsychology*, *7*, 447–477.

Shallice, T. (1988). *From neuropsychology to mental structure*. Cambridge University Press: Cambridge.

Shallice, T. & Warrington, E. K. (1977). The possible role of selective attention in acquired dyslexia. *Neuropsychologia*, *15*, 31–41.

Warrington, E. K. (1984). *Recognition memory test.* Windsor, Berks.: N.F.E.R.-Nelson Publishing Co. Ltd.

Warrington, E. K. & Shallice, T. (1980). Word form dyslexia. *Brain*, *103*, 99–112.

Warrington, E. K. & Zangwill, O. L. (1957). A study of dyslexia. *Journal of Neurology, Neurosurgery, and Psychiatry*, *20*, 208–215.

REFERENCE NOTE

1. Willison, J. R. (1988). *Neuropsychological investigations of a set of mental speed tests.* Unpublished Ph.D. Thesis, University of London.

APPENDIX A

Corpus 1: Words Correctly Read

and
art
ask
box
boy
but
buy
car
dog
dry
due
ear
eat
egg
fly
for
get
god
got
his
how
ice
led
leg
let
lie
Mrs
nor
not
pay
put
red
she
six
sky
try
two
use
you
ball
bear
blow
blue

each
farm
felt
fire
fish
four
give
gold
good
hall
hand
have
high
hire
inch
into
iron
kill
kiss
land
late
lead
left
live
long
look
meat
post
rest
ride
room
rose
seat
seek
seem
sell
sign
sold
some
song
soon
stop
then

wear
week
well
wide
wife
wild
will
along
black
break
catch
daily
early
earth
floor
going
happy
hurry
issue
judge
lower
march
mouth
music
other
paper
plain
point
queen
raise
right
sleep
south
spoke
stock
stool
store
sweet
table
taken
teach
trust
voice

arthur
battle
beauty
beside
beyond
cannot
circle
colour
coming
common
dollar
double
escape
europe
favour
finger
french
gentle
george
german
honour
indeed
letter
listen
master
method
mother
myself
narrow
object
public
regard
settle
spring
strong
travel
window
winter
yellow
america
article
between
british

body	till	watch	himself
came	time	white	husband
camp	told	whole	instead
coat	type	whose	meeting
come	upon	wrong	morning
cook	very	wrote	outside
deep	vote	young	support
duty	wave	always	

Corpus 2: Reading Errors

Target	*Response*	*Target*	*Response*	*Target*	*Response*	*Target*	*Response*
are	'any'	mark	'march'	ought	'enough'	pretty	—
arm	'arch'	mary	'march'	paint	'plan'	prince	'price'
can	'come'	mean	'meal'	plant	'plan'	proper	—
hot	'honey'	miss	'mist'	pound	'poor'	refuse	'referee'
ill	'if'	more	—	quite	'quick'	remain	'rump'
lay	'lee'	most	'mostly'	reach	'result'	season	'seaside'
lip	'lit'	move	—	scene	'sky'	second	'spoon'
met	'men'	real	'rest'	sense	—	should	'shovel'
new	'news'	rich	'rip'	serve	'source'	spirit	—
now	'most'	ring	—	seven	'sewage'	spread	'spoon'
own	'owe'	rule	'rub'	shade	'shady'	strike	'straw'
ran	'rare'	rush	'rust'	short	'shore'	sudden	'wrong'
run	'rub'	safe	—	shout	'shoe'	suffer	—
sir	'stir'	seen	—	sight	—	toward	'tow'
sit	'lie'	shot	'soldier'	since	'splice'	weight	—
top	'ten'	show	'sure'	space	'spoon'		
war	'wear'	sick	—	speak	'spoon'	against	'gold'
		side	'guide'	spend	'spoon'	another	'any'
army	'any'	soil	'solid'	stone	'stop'	brother	'body'
back	'body'	step	—	stood	'soon'	brought	'nuy'
bank	'boss'	such	'suck'	taste	'tease'	chicago	—
base	'bee'	suit	'guild'	these	'the'	clothes	'clothing'
beat	'bee'	sure	'tough'	thing	'then'	college	'colleague'
call	'calf'	than	'that'	think	'thing'	command	—
care	'cath'	that	'the'	third	'thought'	country	'court'
cold	'coat'	them	'then'	train	'trial'	declare	'decay'
dead	'deep'	took	'talk'	tried	—	destiny	—
deal	—	view	'viva'	truth	'truck'	example	'exam'
dear	'duty'	wash	'waste'	uncle	—	explain	'exam'
does	'door'	whom	'hoe'	visit	'visa'	express	'exam'
drop	'door'	agree	'argue'	woman	'wing'	finally	'finance'
east	'each'	allow	'although'			general	'generate'
easy	'eye'	alone	'along'	afraid	—	germany	'german'
fact	'fight'	blood	'black'	amount	—	herself	'himself'

Target	*Response*	*Target*	*Response*	*Target*	*Response*	*Target*	*Response*
fail	—	board	'body'	arrive	'rest'	include	—
fair	'fairy'	cause	'came'	belong	'table'	journal	'journey'
fall	—	chest	'cheese'	better	'between'	mention	'mother'
fill	'filth'	clear	'claim'	butter	'but'	million	'milk'
find	'far'	close	'clome'	caught	'engage'	nothing	'noting'
form	'form'	cloud	'cloudy'	decide	—	officer	'office'
free	'fire'	dance	'dancing'	degree	—	opinion	'option'
from	'fire'	death	'duty'	demand	—	present	—
full	'gulf'	eight	'eye'	desire	—	problem	'probably'
glad	—	enemy	'engulf'	except	'exploit'	produce	—
gone	'get'	fight	'fighting'	figure	—	quickly	'quick'
hang	'hand'	first	'fire'	forget	'forge'	realise	—
hard	'head'	force	'forgive'	former	'forever'	require	—
help	'him'	given	'give'	golden	'gold'	soldier	'spoon'
hill	'hall'	glass	'glue'	height	'higher'	special	'spoon'
hold	'health'	grant	—	leader	'label'	station	'stalk'
idea	—	guess	—	length	'lend'	suppose	'skull'
kind	'knight'	heard	'head'	matter	'meeting'	teacher	'teach'
king	'kitchen'	human	'humane'	member	—	through	'tough'
knee	'knife'	leave	'leaving'	nation	'nappy'	various	'value'
last	'list'	light	—	number	'march'	village	'vigil'
lose	'low'	never	'nerve'	obtain	'oblige'		
many	'man'						

APPENDIX B

Words Read Correctly

away	*lose	*first	famous
baby	lost	fresh	farmer
*back	luck	*going	*favour
*ball	moor	*grant	*figure
*base	next	green	flower
bill	nose	guide	*former
bird	page	*happy	friend
burn	play	henry	future
*came	poor	horse	garden
city	post	house	*gentle
club	pull	*hurry	*golden
*come	race	*issue	ground
*cook	*rich	*light	heaven
dark	*ride	*lower	*height
date	*rule	*march	indeed
*deep	*seen	marry	itself

down
*duty
fell
*felt
*fill
find
*fire
*fish
food
foot
*four
*full
gain
game
gate
*glad
*gold
*gone
*good
half
*hall
*hand
head
heat
home
into
john
join
just
lift

shop
*side
*sign
snow
soft
*some
*song
stay
*suit
tell
*that
they
thus
*till
town
turn
*view
west
what
when
*wife

*alone
brown
build
child
class
drink
every

money
*mouth
*music
night
offer
peace
price
prove
raise
*reach
round
*serve
shore
sleep
table
touch
*uncle
waste
water
*woman
would

*always
*battle
behind
*belong
*cannot
danger
*desire
enough

knight
*leader
*letter
little
london
manner
middle
*mother
*nation
notice
*number
*object
*pretty
*prince
reason
*refuse
*regard
*second
sister
*spread
*spring
street
*suffer
summer
system
travel
twelve
valley
wonder
*yellow

*Word used in consistency data

Reading Errors

*army	arm
*bear	—
*beat	bet
best	beside
*blow	blue
*body	boom
both	bottle
*care	care
*coat	coach
*deal	dean
*does	doze
*stop	steam
*such	—
tear	team
than	that
thee	they
tire	tired
true	train
*very	every
warm	warn
*wear	that
study	sturdy
*taste	tammy
their	the
*thing	that
*truth	true
under	unduly
until	untidy
*voice	boiling
affair	affect
around	arouse

door	down	above	about	broken	brown
*east	ease	admit	—	direct	—
even	every	allow	although	except	exceed
face	fast	began	begave	family	farmer
*fact	favour	begin	bean	fellow	fever
*fail	—	being	beside	finish	—
feel	kneel	built	but	follow	—
flow	flour	claim	clinch	forest	forgive
*free	fresh	cover	clover	*forget	forgive
girl	grit	cross	crow	*george	geography
gray	gate	dress	dresser	*german	germany
grew	grey	front	frost	happen	happy
grow	gray	guard	garden	health	heaven
*hang	—	*heard	heel	*honour	honeymoon
*hard	hen	known	knock	island	isolate
*have	—	learn	leaf	labour	label
hear	horse	*never	nerve	market	month
held	hell	order	ordeal	*method	meth
*high	height	*ought	orgy	minute	—
hope	hall	*paint	painter	modern	modest
*king	kite	*paper	page	native	nature
knew	knee	piece	peace	nearly	neatly
know	known	place	plague	period	post
lady	lap	*plant	plague	person	posse
*late	later	*pound	poor	*proper	—
less	lead	power	powder	*public	pupil
life	lift	reply	rusty	really	—
lord	lock	*shade	shady	record	redeem
loss	lose	share	shoe	*remain	—
*mary	march	*short	shoe	report	poet
meet	meeting	*since	stir	return	resting
mile	mild	*south	soup	*season	seaside
must	music	*speak	spree	*should	shed
none	nose	*spend	spread	square	squash
paid	patch	stand	stamp	stream	street
pair	pear	state	scratch	*sudden	study
*seem	seen	*stone	—	*toward	torch
*sell	self	*stood	spooler	unless	unclean
*sick	—				

*Word used in consistency data

APPENDIX C

Compound Word	*Response*	*Single Word*	*Response*	*Single Word*	*Response*
armchair	√	arm	ache	chair	√
bagpipe	√	bag	beg	pipe	√
bedroom	√	bed	√	room	√
blacksmith	blackened	black	√	smith	√
bullfrog	√	bull	√	frog	√
cartwheel	√	cart	cat	wheel	√
cloudburst	clampage	cloud	clown	burst	bush
crybaby	√	cry	√	baby	ball
daybreak	daydream	day	√	break	√
daylight	√	day	√	light	√
doorstep	doorway	door	√	step	stir
dustbin	√	dust	√	bin	blade
eyebrow	eyebrows	eye	√	brow	bod
farmhouse	farmyard	farm	√	house	√
fireplace	airy something	fire	√	place	√
footwear	footage	foot	√	wear	wave
greenhouse	√	green	√	house	√
hairpin	√	hair	√	pin	√
headscarf	headache	head	hair	scarf	scared
hillside	hijack	hill	√	side	√
horsehair	horseshoe	horse	√	hair	√
horseshoe	√	horse	√	shoe	√
lighthouse	√	light	√	house	√
loophole	loop phone	loop	toe	hole	hedge
moonshine	√	moon	√	shine	shoe
nightfall	nightface	night	√	fall	fair
penknife	√	pen	pin	knife	√
pinball	√	pin	√	ball	√
raincoat	√	rain	√	coat	√
seagull	sky glass	sea	√	gull	√
shoelace	√	shoe	√	lace	√
skylight	ski lift	sky	√	light	√
snowflake	√	snow	√	flake	√
sundial	sunshade	sun	√	dial	dish
sunshine	√	sun	√	shine	√
swimsuit	swimwear	swim	√	suit	√
teapot	√	tea	√	pot	√
tightrope	√	tight	√	rope	rose
tombstone	√	tomb	√	stone	sure
toothache	√	tooth	√	ache	√
toothbrush	√	tooth	√	brush	bush
toothpaste	√	tooth	√	paste	√

Compound Word	*Response*	*Single Word*	*Response*	*Single Word*	*Response*
whitewash	whistle	white	√	wash	√
wigwam	wigan	wig	√	wam	worn
windmill	√	wind	√	mill	milk

COGNITIVE NEUROPSYCHOLOGY, 1991, *8* (3/4) 213–248

Directing Attention to Words and Nonwords in Normal Subjects and in a Computational Model: Implications for Neglect Dyslexia

M. Behrmann and M. Moscovitch
University of Toronto, Ontario, Canada

M. C. Mozer
University of Colorado, Boulder, Colorado, U.S.A.

In a previous paper, we proposed that patients with neglect dyslexia process information appearing on the unattended side. This information, if encoded sufficiently, may be used to trigger top-down knowledge, leading to the interaction of spatial attention and lexicality. The current studies examine this question in normal people. Subjects' attention was biased to the end of a letter string by a cue (underline bar) and lexical decisions were made to the underlined section of the letter string (for example, east and garm). These studies showed that reaction times were slower when distracting information appeared on the left than when no distractors were present (for example, arm). Furthermore, when the distractors played a lexical role and formed a word with the underlined string (for example, farm), lexical decisions were even slower. These results showed that distractors are processed at least to the level of lexical access and influence reading performance of the attended underlined string. We have also considered these findings in the light of an existing connectionist network of spatial attention and word recognition and have accounted for the data in a series of simulations. The convergence of findings from the neuropsychological, cognitive, and computational work supports the interaction between attention and higher-order lexical knowledge.

Requests for reprints should be addressed to M. Behrmann, Rotman Research Institute of Baycrest Centre, 3560 Bathurst Street, North York, Ontario, Canada M6A 2E1.

The first author is a fellow of the Ontario Ministry of Health Research Personnel Development Program. This work was supported by grants from the Natural Sciences and Engineering Research Council and the James S. McDonnell Foundation to Morris Moscovitch and Michael Mozer respectively. The authors thank the reviewers and David Plaut for the valuable comments and suggestions.

INTRODUCTION

Unilateral spatial neglect is a neurobehavioural disorder that leads to deficits in orientation to stimuli that appear in the hemispace contralateral to the side of brain damage. Reading impairments have long been associated with hemispatial neglect, especially in patients with right parietal lesions (Kinsbourne & Warrington, 1962; Leicester, Sidman, Stoddard, & Mohr, 1969). Patients with such impairments ignore the left side of an open book, the beginning words of a line of text or the beginning letters of single words, producing errors such as "HOOK" → "book", "GLOVE" → "love", and "SUNDAY" → "Monday". This reading disorder, which has been termed "neglect dyslexia", cannot be attributed to a primary motor or sensory deficit nor to a primary language impairment. Instead, the neglect of contralesional information is thought to arise from a disruption in the allocation of attention to the contralateral hemispace. Although neglect dyslexia has long been recognised as a clinical entity, fine-grained analysis of the disorder has only recently been undertaken in a series of single case studies (Baxter & Warrington, 1983; Ellis, Flude, & Young, 1987; Kartsounis & Warrington, 1989; Siéroff, Note 1; single case studies 1990) and group studies (Brunn & Farah, in press; Siéroff, 1990; Siéroff, Pollatsek, & Posner, 1988).

In our own study on neglect dyslexia (Behrmann, Moscovitch, Black, & Mozer, 1990), we argued that the disorder is determined by the interaction between degraded perceptual input caused by an attentional deficit and later top-down processes. In the case of patients with right-hemisphere lesions, the primary impairment takes the form of a left-right gradient of attention with maximal activation in the extreme ipsilesional hemispace and least activation in the contralesional hemispace. The information appearing on the right-hand side is processed accurately. Provided the attentional gradient is not too steep, the information appearing on the left is also registered but to a lesser degree. According to this view, the attenuated or degraded contralesional information may be fully recovered through the assistance of top-down processes. The top-down assistance, however, is only helpful in those instances where previous lexical representations exist. If there are no existing representations, as in the case of nonwords, the benefit from higher-order knowledge is not obtained (and is even less obvious for unpronounceable nonwords) (see Siéroff et al., 1988, for a similar argument). Therefore, the two critical factors that determine the amount of interaction with top-down knowledge are the slope of the gradient and the prior existence of lexical representations.

Support for this account was obtained in several reading experiments administered to two subjects with neglect dyslexia following a single right-hemisphere lesion (Behrmann et al., 1990). The extent of the attentional disruption was measured on two different tasks: a feature detection task in which a single oddball letter must be detected in a uniform horizontal array of letters, and a conjoined feature detection task in which individual heterogeneous letters in the horizontal array must be reported. Plotting accuracy of detection as a function of serial position in both tasks revealed a steeper slope or attentional gradient for subject AH than for subject HR. AH was impaired at picking up elementary stimulus features on the left of the display in both the simple and conjoined feature task. On the experimental reading tasks, AH's neglect of the left-sided information was only minimally affected by conceptual features of the stimulus such as lexical status and morphemic composition. HR, on the other hand, was able to detect the oddball relatively well in the simple task but was impaired on the conjoined feature task for stimuli appearing on the left. On the reading tasks, HR's ability to pick up left-sided information was significantly influenced by manipulations of the high-level abstract features of the stimulus. Thus, HR read words significantly better than nonwords and he also tended to preserve morphemic boundaries by reporting right-embedded morphemes where possible; for example, as in FARM → "arm". In addition, he reported the left-sided word of a pair of simultaneously presented words more often when the two words could be combined to form a compound word; for example COW BOY, than when they could not; for example, SUN FLY.

Taking the results of the attentional tests together with the results of the reading experiments, we concluded that the interaction between degraded perceptual information caused by an early attentional deficit and higher-order knowledge, then, is primarily a function of the slope of the attentional gradient. When the slope is precipitous, as in the case of AH, information from the left of the display is too poorly registered to trigger existing lexical codes that can then feed back on the incoming perceptual input. When the slope is more gradual, as in the case of HR, information on the contralateral side, although attenuated, is sufficient to engage higher-order knowledge.

The primary assumption underlying this view is that information appearing in regions of low attentional activation is still processed rather than abolished. Support for the existence of a more or less continuous gradient favouring rightward direction of attention comes from a variety of neuropsychological and anatomical sources. Several studies have shown, for example, that the performance of subjects with neglect is superior when the stimulus appears ipsilaterally and that there is a gradual fall-off as information is presented further into contralateral hemispace. Friedrich, Walker, and Posner (1985), for example, presented two strings of letters one above the other to normal and right or left parietal lesion subjects.

The subjects were required to judge whether the two strings were identical. On those trials in which there was a mismatch, the different letter appeared either at the beginning, middle, or end of the string. The patients with right parietal lesions, in contrast to those with left lesions and with control subjects, detected mismatches significantly more slowly and less accurately when the mismatch appeared on the extreme left, even though they did not show obvious neglect on clinical testing. Performance improved steadily for mismatches at the middle and end of strings. It is unlikely that this pattern resulted from a fundamental sensory (visual field) deficit since all patients, except one, were able to detect visual information across the field. The relative superiority of right- over left-sided information, with a gradual and steady decrease towards the left, is consistent with the notion of a continuous gradient across (and within) the visual fields. Similar findings were obtained by De Renzi, Gentilini, Faglioni, and Barbieri (1989) in a letter search task in which normal and brain-damaged subjects with and without neglect had to detect the presence of "A" or "a" amongst a horizontal array of four letters. Only right-hemisphere brain-damaged subjects with visual neglect showed a monotonic decrease in reaction time, with the slowest time in the leftmost position of the array and fastest time in the rightmost position, again suggesting that a gradient of attention underlies neglect. The presence of a gradient is also supported by anatomical evidence. Rizzolatti and colleagues (Rizzolatti, Gentilucci, & Matelli, 1985; Rizzolatti, Scandolara, Matelli, & Gentilucci, 1981) have shown that 29% of the neurons in the postarcuate cortex of the monkey have exclusively contralateral fields while 3% have exclusively ipsilateral and 68% have bilateral fields. At the lateral periphery, therefore, space representation relies on the contralateral cortex whereas each hemisphere tends toward equal value as one approaches the midline: "in the case of a lesion of one hemisphere, the whole visual field will be affected (i.e. neglected) but with a gradient of severity going from a maximum in the extreme contralateral hemifield to a minimum in the extreme ipsilateral hemifield" (Rizzolatti et al. 1985, p. 262.).

Recently, we obtained support for the "interactive-gradient" from a series of computational simulations using a distributed connectionist model of two-dimensional object recognition and selective attention, called MORSEL (Mozer, 1987; 1988; 1990). MORSEL was originally designed to account for a broad spectrum of psychological data, including perceptual errors which arise when two objects appear simultaneously in the visual field. Because MORSEL contains both a word-recognition system and an attentional mechanism, it appeared to be a particularly appropriate framework within which to consider neglect dyslexia. We hypothesised that damage to MORSEL's attentional mechanism (hereafter, A.M.) results in a probabilistic failure to process visual information along a left–right retinotopic gradient. Conducting simulation studies of the "damaged" model, we observed reading impairments remarkably similar to those found in neglect dyslexic patients. We found, for example, that retinal presentation position affected the A.M.'s ability to select an item; consequently, responses to words presented further over to the right were more accurate than responses to words presented on the left. The contribution of higher-order knowledge was also observed in MORSEL. The effect of lexical status was seen with words preserved relative to nonwords. In addition, the left-hand word of a simultaneously presented pair of words was less often neglected when it formed a component part of a real compound word, as in COW BOY than when it did not, as in SUN FLY. Higher-order knowledge in MORSEL takes the form of "semlex" units (semantic/lexical) which feed down and assist in the synthesis of a plausible interpretation of the activated perceptual data. Existing lexical representations may thereby enhance the recovery of the attenuated left side of words but not of nonwords, producing the word superiority effect frequently shown by neglect dyslexic patients (Behrmann et al., 1990; Caramazza & Hillis, 1990; Riddoch, Humphreys, Cleton, & Fery, 1990; Patterson & Wilson, 1990; Siéroff et al., 1988). The results of the computational simulations, therefore, support the general finding that information in unattended regions is still encoded and can produce interactions with higher-order knowledge. Thus, a lesion to the early or peripheral connections which draw attention to objects in the field has remote effects which are manifest on higher-order variables such as lexical and morphemic status.

The purpose of the present paper is to examine the interaction of attention and top-down knowledge in normal subjects by directing the subjects' attention to one part of the stimulus and assessing the effect of the unattended or distracting information on performance. Although we did not expect normal subjects to restrict their attentional focus as narrowly as neglect subjects, we did predict that biasing attention to the right should produce the same pattern, but not degree, of reading impairment in normal people as in neglect patients. In keeping with our previous results, we expected that even when attention is drawn to the right side, information on the left still plays a significant role in reading performance.

The design and rationale of our experiments are as follows: attention is cued to the right of a stimulus by underlining a part of a letter string on the right-hand side. The underline bar serves to direct attention but also forms an integral part of the task as subjects are required to perform a lexical decision on the underlined portion of the stimulus. Subjects are explicitly instructed to ignore the rest of the string (which is not underlined). A reaction time (R.T.) clock is stopped when the subject depresses one of two response keys ("Yes" or "No"). We then examine the effect of the distracting left-sided information on performance. If the information which is not underlined is processed, it should influence the subjects even though they are consciously instructed to pay attention to one part of the string. To determine the depth to which the distracting information is processed when attention is cued to the right, we compared performance across the following conditions: no left-sided information is present (e.g. cat and cat); left-sided information is present but bears no relationship to the stimulus (e.g. @arm); left-sided information is graphemic and makes up an orthographically legal string (e.g. garm); left-sided information is graphemic and, combined with the underlined section, produces another real word (e.g. farm). We predicted that these conditions would lead to increasingly longer R.T.s in lexical decision to the underlined part. If the mere presence of left-sided information influences performance, R.T.s to "@arm" should be slower than to "arm" or "arm" (Eriksen & Eriksen, 1974). If the left-sided information is processed deeply and there is an effect of graphemic information and an even more specific lexical effect, R.T.s to "farm" should be longer than latencies to "garm", which should, in turn, be significantly longer than responses to "@arm".

The final experiment is a simulation study to examine lexicality (farm versus garm) in the context of MORSEL. Based on the performance of neglect patients and on previous simulations (Behrmann et al., in press; Mozer & Behrmann, in press), we predicted that even when attention is directed to the right side of the string, top-down influences will play a role in reading behaviour. Therefore, there should be a significant difference in the model's response to target items such as farm compared to items in which the surrounding context, e.g. garm, did not constitute a real word.

EXPERIMENT 1: LEXICAL DECISION TO ATTENDED RIGHT SIDE OF STIMULUS WITH DISTRACTING INFORMATION ON THE LEFT

The first experiment was designed to show that the content of the left-sided distracting information affects R.T. to the attended right-sided target in normal subjects. Thus, even when subjects are explicitly instructed to attend to and make a lexical decision on the underlined section on the right, we predicted that the lexical status of the whole string would affect R.T. differently if it formed a real word when coupled with the underlined segment compared to when it did not form a real word. Thus, R.T.s to items like farm would be longer than to items like garm and R.T.s to letter strings like east would be longer than to bast, producing a main effect of the context or whole stimulus. In keeping with the existing lexical decision literature, we also predicted a main effect of status of the underlined part with R.T.s to underlined words being shorter than R.T.s to underlined nonwords.

Methods

Stimuli

The stimuli were 384 letter strings, ranging in length from 4 to 10 letters (see Appendix 1). Half of the strings were real words whereas the other half were orthographically legal nonwords derived from the real word counterpart. In each string, some subset of letters on the right-hand side, ranging in length from 3–6 letters, was underlined. On half the trials, the underlined target was a real English word while on the other half it was an orthographically legal nonword. The design was a 2-by-2 orthogonal design with lexical status of the whole stimulus or context (word or nonword) crossed with lexical status of the underlined target (word or nonword). Ninety-six stimuli were drawn from each of the following conditions:

1. Word-in-word: WIW, for example, f<u>arm</u>;
2. Word-in-nonword: WIN, for example, g<u>arm</u>;
3. Nonword-in-word: NIW, for example, e<u>ast</u>; and
4. Nonword-in-nonword: NIN, for example, b<u>ast</u>.

On half the WIW trials, the frequency of occurrence of the target was greater than that of the context while on the second half, the reverse was true. Mean frequency of the target words was 23 per million (s.d. 34) and mean frequency of the context words was 12 per million (s.d. 78) (Francis & Kuçera, 1982).

Subjects

Sixteen right-handed undergraduate college students, 10 of whom were female, participated for course credit in an introductory psychology course. Mean age was 21.5 (s.d. 3.4). The subjects who participated in the following experiments were all drawn from the same pool as those in this experiment, with the result that they were similar in age, educational characteristics, and handedness. No single subject participated in more than one experiment.

Procedure

Stimuli were presented in amber writing against a black field on a video screen driven by an I.B.M. microcomputer. Subjects viewed the display binocularly at a distance of approximately 40cm. Each trial began with the presentation of a centrally placed fixation asterisk which appeared for 500msec. followed by a 500msec. delay. The stimulus then appeared for an unlimited duration in one of two locations, either centred over the fixation point ("central") or displaced to the right so that the beginning letter appeared in the character space immediately to the right of the fixation point ("right"). The visual angle subtended by the stimuli ranged from 1.9° to 4.8°. The "right" condition was included because many subjects with neglect dyslexia also have a visual field defect and stimuli are usually presented only in the right visual field in those cases. Half the subjects performed the task with the central display while the other half performed it with the right display.

The subjects were instructed to attend to the underlined portion and to indicate whether it constituted a real word or not by pressing the left or right button with the index and middle finger of their dominant hand. The "Yes" and "No" buttons were counterbalanced across subjects so that half responded "Yes" with the middle finger and half responded "Yes" with the index finger. Speed and accuracy of responding were emphasised. R.T. was measured using a millisecond clock. The interval between trials, measured from response, was 2 seconds. A practice block containing 16 novel items, 4 drawn from each condition, was presented first and feedback was given. The 96 stimuli from the 4 conditions were randomised and presented as 4 blocks of 96 items. All subjects saw all blocks although order of presentation was counterbalanced across subjects.

Results and Discussion

A three-way repeated measures ANOVA using context (word, nonword) and target status (word, nonword) as within-subject factors and mode of presentation (central, right) as a between-subject factor was computed first with R.T. (correct responses only) and then with the error data. There was no significant effect of mode of presentation ($F[1,14] = 0.54$, $P > 0.10$) and thus the data from central and right presentation were collapsed for all further analyses.

Figure 1 shows the difference in reaction time between underlined targets (words and nonwords) as a function of the status of the context, collapsed across mode of presentation. As predicted, a significant main effect of underlined target emerged ($F[1,14] = 65.8$, $P < 0.001$), with responses to words being faster than to nonwords. This is in keeping with the well-established phenomenon of superior lexical decision to words relative to nonwords (Rayner & Pollatsek, 1989). There was also a significant effect of context ($F[1,14] = 20.8$, $P < 0.001$), with responses to whole words being *slower* than responses to whole nonwords. There were no significant interactions. The results of the subject analysis were confirmed on an item analysis in which the mean R.T. to each individual item was obtained by collapsing across the reaction times of all subjects to each item. The two-way analysis with items as the random factor revealed main effects of underlined target and whole context (underlined target: $F[1,190] = 47.5$, $P < 0.001$; context: $F[1,190] = 210.0$, $P < 0.001$) and no interaction, supporting the findings of the subject analysis.

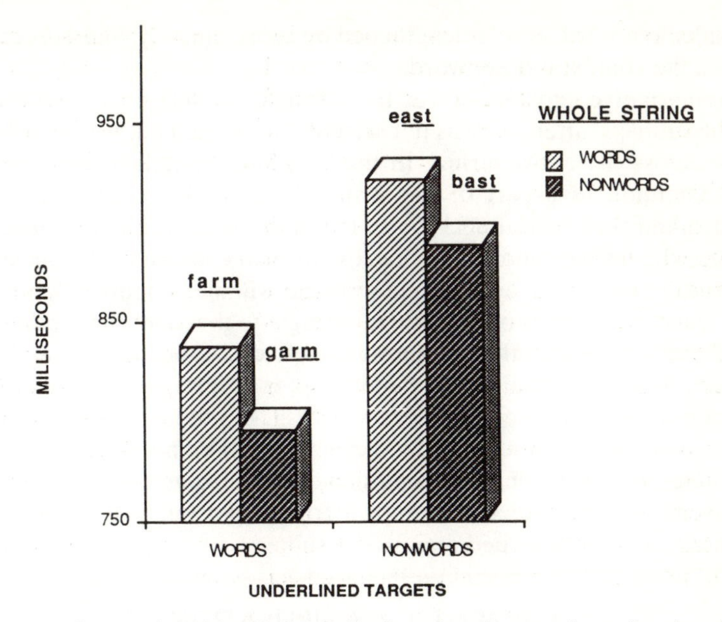

FIG. 1 R.T. (in msec.) to right-sided underlined words and nonwords as a function of status of whole string.

Conducting an ANOVA with length of the underlined item (3, 4, 5, 6 letters), context (word, nonword) and underlined target (word, nonword) revealed no main effect of length ($F[3,45] = 1.13$, $P > 0.10$) nor any interactions between context and underlined target. Mean R.T.s for 3-, 4-, 5-, and 6-letter targets (collapsed across all conditions) were 861.1, 907.5, 809.3, and 821.1msec. respectively. An ANOVA with length of whole context (4–10 letters), lexical status of context (word, nonword), and underlined target (word, nonword) as factors revealed a significant 3-way interaction ($F[6,90] = 3.5$, $P < 0.01$). There was no apparent pattern to this interaction and there was no obvious trend for longer strings to produce longer R.T.s. Mean R.T.s for 4-, 5-, 6-, 7-, 8-, 9-, and 10-letter whole context (collapsed across all conditions) were 807.4, 895.3, 883.2, 883.4, 856.7, 844.4, and 872.1msec. respectively.

The error analysis revealed a main effect of underlined string ($F[1,14] = 10.9$, $P < 0.01$), with significantly more errors being made to words than to nonwords. The mean number of errors (N = 96) was 6.2 to WIW, 5.1 to WIN, 2.8 to NIW, and 3.2 to NIN. No other effects were significant.

These results suggest that even when attention is biased to one side, the information appearing on the opposite side influences performance. Also, as predicted, the lexical status of the distracting information appears to play a meaningful role. When the context in which the underlined string is embedded is a word, R.T. is lengthened by approximately 40msec. relative to when the context is a nonword.

An alternative explanation for the effect of the left-sided distractor is that the subjects' attention was not selectively engaged but was distributed evenly across the entire string. In this case, the underline cue does not direct attention to a part of the string. Instead, the whole stimulus is attended and then lexical decision to the underlined segment occurs after access to the lexical representations for the whole stimulus. The next two experiments were thus designed to examine whether attention was selectively cued to a part of the letter string by the underline bar. One experiment was designed to maximise the effects of the attentional cue by providing sufficient time for the build-up of attention prior to the appearance of the target for the lexical decision task. In the next experiment, we assessed whether attention is indeed directed to the underlined section by comparing the speed of processing of additional, unrelated information sharing the same location as the underlined portion with information appearing in other non-cued regions.

EXPERIMENT 2: MANIPULATION OF ATTENTIONAL CUE WITH LONGER S.O.A.

Although the results of Experiment 1 are statistically robust and significant, the interpretation is not yet clear. In order to demonstrate that the manipulation is potent and that the subjects' attention is being directed to the underlined portion (and not diffusely to the entire stimulus), we repeated Experiment 1 but this time we provided subjects with sufficient time to build up a tight attentional focus around the underlined region. Various experiments on covert attentional shifts have suggested that in order to ensure the effective allocation of attention, it is desirable to cue attention in advance and with maximum reliability (Yantis & Johnston, 1990). Such studies have shown that time is required to build up and engage attention. For example, in those tasks in which an attentional cue precedes the appearance of the target, the benefit of the cue (or validity effect) is enhanced when the cue precedes the target by stimulus onset asynchrony (S.O.A.) times in the range of 400msec. and longer (Butter, Buchtel, & Santucci, 1989; Morrow & Ratcliff, 1988; Posner, Cohen, & Rafal, 1982). Given that in the experiments reported here, the S.O.A. between the cue which directs attention (i.e. the underline bar) and the item was 0msec., attention might have been distributed more broadly since there was insufficient time to focus attention narrowly. The following experiment, therefore, assesses whether the same pattern of results emerges when the S.O.A. is longer and subjects have the opportunity to build up and shift their attention. In all the experiments, the underline bar was always valid, i.e. the target always appeared in the location cued by the underline bar. This 100% reliability and the increased S.O.A.s in the following experiment, therefore, provide maximum incentive for focusing attention (Yantis & Johnston, 1990). If, under these conditions, the results replicate the previous findings, they would support the claim that attention was being focused narrowly on the underlined target.

Stimuli and Procedure

The same 4 conditions and 384 stimuli used in Experiment 1 were used in this Experiment. Unlike Experiment 1, however, the attentional cue (underline bar) appeared after the fixation point and remained on the screen for 500msec. prior to the appearance of the letter string. As in Experiment 1, the letter string then appeared on the screen with some right-sided subcomponent underlined. The subjects were required to decide the lexical status of the underlined part and to press the appropriate response button. The rest of the string was to be ignored. Subjects were instructed to maintain central fixation at all times. Eye movements were monitored with the use of an overhead mirror and trials in which overt gaze shifts were detected were removed from the analysis.

Results and Discussion

Subjects maintained central fixation well and less than 3% of the trials were removed from the analysis because of overt eye movements. The results of this experiment revealed a significant main effect of underlined target ($F[1,15] = 42.3$, $P < 0.001$) and of whole context ($F[1,15] = 7.9$, $P < 0.01$) with no interaction between them. Underlined words produced faster R.T.s than underlined nonwords and whole nonwords led to faster responses than whole words, as observed in Experiment 1. This pattern was confirmed on an item analysis in which the mean times for each individual item were compared. The 2-way analysis with items as the random factor revealed main effects of underlined target and whole context (underlined target: $F[1,190] = 34.3$, $P < 0.001$; context: $F[1,190] = 76.2$, $P < 0.001$) and no interactions.

The difference in milliseconds between underlined words and nonwords as a function of whole context for the experiments with 0 and 500msec. S.O.A.s is shown in Fig. 2. Conducting an ANOVA with S.O.A. (0 as in Experiment 1 and 500msec. in this case) as a between-subject factor and lexical status of context (word/nonword) and underlined target (word/nonword) as within-subject factors revealed no effect of S.O.A. ($F[1,30] = 0.4$, $P > 0.10$) but main effects for context and underlined targets (context: $F[1,30] = 22.9$, $P < 0.001$; target $F[1,30] = 84.1$, $P < 0.001$).

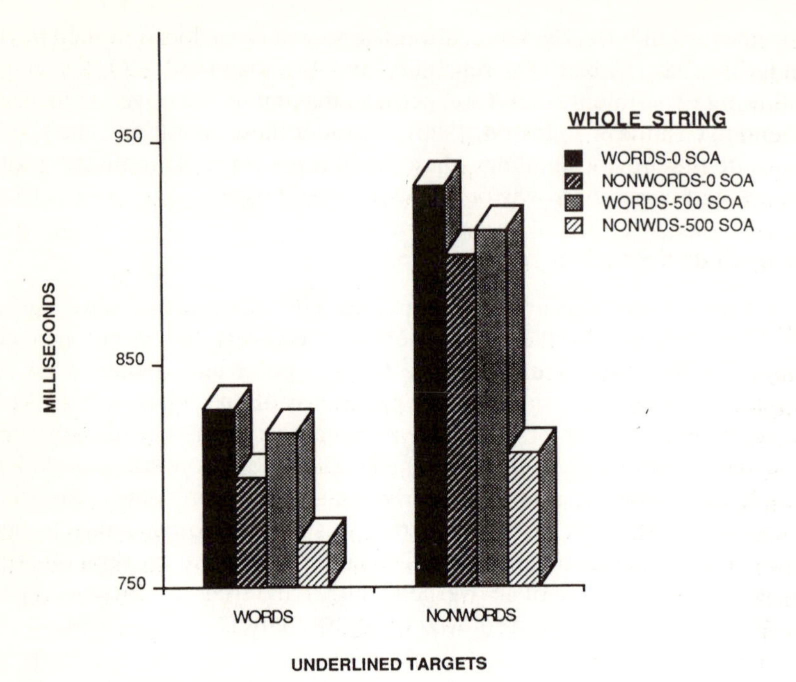

FIG. 2 R.T. (in msec.) to right-sided underlined words and nonwords as a function of status of the whole string for 0 and 500msec. stimulus onset asynchrony.

These findings indicate that the interval between cue and target which allows for build-up and direction of covert attention produces similar results to those observed when the target and underline cue appear simultaneously. These results suggest that even when attention is optimally cued and directed, the left-hand side of the stimulus still has an effect on performance. To confirm further that attention was focused on the underlined region, we conducted an additional experiment to show that information in the attended region was processed preferentially relative to information in the non-underlined region.

EXPERIMENT 3: FACILITATION OF INFORMATION PROCESSING FROM UNDERLINED REGION

Previous work on selective attention has emphasised the facilitation in information processing when attention is oriented to a particular location in visual space (Eriksen & Hoffman, 1973; Posner, Cohen, & Rafal, 1982). We argued that if attention was indeed being cued selectively by the underline bar, information appearing concurrently with the letter string would be processed faster when it fell in the same region as the underline cue than when it fell in the non-underlined portion of the letter string. To test this hypothesis, we included an additional 60 letter strings in which a dot appeared concurrently with the string above one of the letters. Whenever the subjects saw a dot, they were to signal by pressing a response key. When no dot appeared, they were to proceed with the lexical decision task as before. Our prediction was that R.T.s to the dot would be shorter when the dot appeared above the underlined letter string than when it appeared on the opposite side.

Stimuli and Procedure

The same conditions, stimuli, and procedure used in Experiment 1 were employed in this experiment. In addition to the 384 stimuli for lexical decision, however, an additional 60 stimuli were added as part of a concurrent dot detection task. These 60 stimuli appeared simultaneously with a small black dot (approximately 1mm. above the stimulus), which remained on the screen for 67msec. and then disappeared, leaving the letter string exposed for an unlimited duration. On 30 of the 60 stimuli the black dot appeared in the region of the underlined section, whereas on the remaining trials it appeared in the non-underlined region. The exact location of the dot was distributed evenly across all letters of both the underlined and non-underlined portions of the string. The 60 dot trials were equally divided between the 4 conditions and presented randomly in the 4 blocks set up in Experiment 1. The instructions were identical to those of Experiment 1. In addition, however, the subjects were told that if they detected a small black dot, they should respond immediately and not perform the lexical decision task. If the trial did not contain a dot, the subjects should proceed with lexical decision. Thus, in addition to the "yes"/"no" keys pressed with the right hand (counterbalanced side), the subjects pressed a single key with the left hand for the dot detection. Eight subjects (5 female) participated in this experiment.

Results and Discussion

Two analyses were conducted: a two-way ANOVA with lexical status of target and lexical status of whole string as within-subject factors for the lexical decision task, and a *t*-test to compare R.T.s to the dot in the underlined region and R.T.s to the dot on the opposite side. There was a significant interaction between target and whole string ($F[1,7] = 7.8$, $P < 0.05$), with the effect of the whole string being more marked when the target was a word. Thus, the difference between WIW (e.g. "farm"; mean 825.2msec.) and WIN (e.g. "garm"; mean 758.5msec.) was greater than the difference between NIW (e.g. "east"; mean 971.5msec.) and NIN (e.g. "bast"; mean 950.4msec.). The main effects of target ($F[1,7] = 50.7$,

$P < 0.001$) and of whole string ($F[1,7] = 5.9$, $P < 0.05$) were still significant. The item analysis confirmed the main effects (underlined target: $F[1,190] = 9.3$, $P < 0.001$; whole string: $F[1,190] = 6.1$, $P < 0.05$) but not the interaction ($F[1,190] = 2.4$, $P > 0.05$). The error analysis across subject and across items failed to reveal any significant effects for the underlined target or the whole string. These results replicate those of Experiment 1, showing an effect of the non-underlined left-sided information on the lexical decision to the right-sided targets.

On the concurrent dot detection task, subjects failed to detect the dot on less than 6% of the trials. The paired *t*-test comparing R.T.s when the dot appeared in the underlined region (mean 490.8msec.) and when it appeared elsewhere (mean 539.2msec.) revealed a significant difference ($t[1,7] = 3.26$, $P < 0.01$) across subjects. This was confirmed in the item analysis ($t[1,59] = 2.9$, $P < 0.02$).

The replication of Experiment 1, together with the significant difference in detection as a function of location of the dot, suggest that attention is indeed being selectively cued to the right side of the stimulus and that preferential processing is given to information appearing on that side. In addition, information on the left which is not attended is still being processed and affects performance. An alternative explanation for these findings, based on fundamental reading biases in a left-to-right language such as English, may account for these results. Readers normally attend most closely to the beginning or left of a word because it is more informative than the end (Bruner & O'Dowd, 1958), and then they usually scan the word from left to right. It is possible, then, that even when attention is directed to the right, the strong leftward inclination in reading ensures the processing of the left-hand side. Thus, the contribution of the left-hand side derives not from the recovery of the attenuated left side through top-down codes but rather comes about because of the fundamental left-sided reading bias. If this latter explanation held, we would not expect to see information on the right side of a string playing a role in lexical decision when the left-hand side of the string is underlined. If, however, the right-hand side has a similar effect on the underlined component, it would support our hypothesis that distracting information, although attenuated, is still processed to a lexical level. This hypothesis was tested in the next experiment.

EXPERIMENT 4: LEXICAL DECISION TO ATTENDED LEFT SIDE OF STIMULUS WITH DISTRACTING INFORMATION ON THE RIGHT

If the influence of left-sided distractors that was observed in the previous experiments was caused by a left-sided reading bias, then similar effects should not be observed when distracting information is presented on the right. On the other hand, such influences would be apparent if the distracting information gains access to higher-order knowledge, as our hypothesis predicts. To distinguish between these alternative interpretations, subjects were presented with the identical task to that in Experiment 1 except that the underlined portion fell on the left side of the letter string and the distractors appeared on the right.

Stimuli and Procedure

As in Experiment 1, 384 words taken from 4 conditions were presented for lexical decision of the underlined target. The design was also orthogonal, with lexical status of the whole string (word, nonword) crossed with that of the underlined portion (word, nonword). Unlike Experiment 1, however, the embedded portion in this experiment appeared at the beginning rather than at the end of a word. Thus, the 4 conditions were as follows:

1. Word-in-word: WIW for example farm;
2. Word-in-nonword: WIN for example fark;
3. Nonword-in-word: NIW for example sort; and
4. Nonword-in-nonword: NIN for example sorp.

Because increasing string length was found not to be critical in the previous experiment and because words exceeding 8 letters often contained inflections, the range of the length of the whole strings was restricted to between 4 and 8 letters. The length of the underlined target ranged between 3 and 6 letters. Frequency of the target (mean 41, s.d. 76) exceeded the frequency of the context (mean 27, s.d. 93) on half the trials; the reverse held true for the remaining trials.

The procedure was identical to that of Experiment 1 except that all stimuli were centred on the fixation point. Because mode of presentation was not found to be significant in the previous experiment, only central presentation was used.

Results and Discussion

A two-way ANOVA was conducted, first with R.T. and then with the error data with lexical status of the context and underlined target as within-subject factors. Mean R.T. in all four conditions are shown in Fig. 3. As in the previous experiments, there was a significant main effect of underlined portion ($F[1,15] = 34.8$, $P < 0.001$), with underlined words producing faster responses than nonwords, and a significant main effect of context ($F[1,15] = 36.15$, $P < 0.001$), with whole words yielding slower responses than whole nonwords. No other effects were significant. The within-item ANOVA (mean R.T. to each item collapsed across all subjects) also revealed a main effect of underlined target and whole context (target: $F[1,190] = 6.7$, $P < 0.01$; context: $F[1,190] = 57.6$, $P < 0.001$), with no

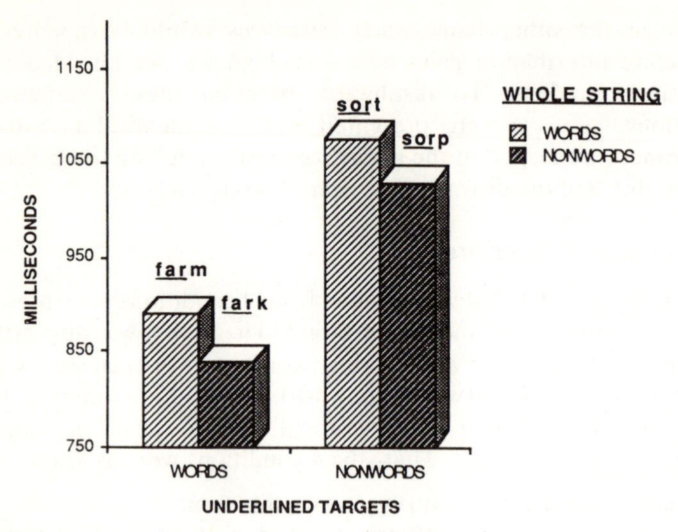

FIG. 3 R.T. (in msec.) to left-sided underlined words and nonwords as a function of status of whole string.

interaction between them, supporting the results of the subject R.T. analysis. The mean number of errors made to WIW, WIN, NIW, and NIN were 13.6, 10.3, 9.2, and 5.6 respectively. Significantly more errors were made to underlined words than to nonwords ($F[1,15] = 17.1$, $P < 0.001$), and significantly more errors were made when the context was a word compared to when it was a nonword $F[1,15] = 35.6$, $P < 0.001$). The interaction between target and context was not significant ($F[1,15] = 0.14$, $P > 0.10$).

The results of Experiment 1 and Experiment 4 were both entered into an ANOVA to assess whether there were any differences between the subjects' performance when attention was biased to the left or the right of strings. A three-way ANOVA with context and underlined target as within-subject factors and attentional bias (left, right) as a between-subject factor was conducted. There was no significant effect of attentional bias ($F[1,30] = 3.37$, $P < 0.1$), but the significant main effects of context ($F[1,30] = 30.52$, $P < 0.001$) and of target ($F[1,30] = 44.9$, $P < 0.001$) still held. No interactions were significant. The mean difference between R.T.s for targets embedded in whole words compared to targets in whole nonwords was 37msec. in Experiment 1 and 43msec. in Experiment 4 (see Figs. 1 and 3).

The findings from Experiment 4, then, are equivalent to those of Experiment 1. Taken together, these findings suggest that there is a significant effect of the distractor on the R.T. to the underlined portion irrespective of direction of attention. Left-sided reading biases cannot account for this effect. Because the effects are similar regardless of whether the attended portion is on the left or the right, we concluded that performance was influenced by the pickup of information from the "unattended" side. In addition, because there is a significant effect of context, we concluded that the lexical status of the distracting information is critical. Lexical decisions to the underlined portion took longer when the distractor was a whole word than when it was a nonword.

EXPERIMENT 5: SPECIFIC EFFECTS OF LEFT-SIDED INFORMATION IN LEXICAL DECISION

Although we have shown a relative difference in performance on items like farm and garm, we do not know the extent of the specificity of the left-sided information. For example, we do not know whether the distracting information has any influence if it is a nonword (e.g. garm) compared to when it does not play a graphemic role (e.g. @arm). This experiment, then, compares performance when the left-sided distracting information is graphemic and when it is nongraphemic (the "at" sign). Furthermore, we compare R.T.s on lexical decisions to the right-sided target when distracting information is present and when it is absent. To assess this, we compared R.T.s to make lexical decision to strings such as "@arm", "garm" and "farm" with those to strings in which no information appeared on the left, for example "arm" and "arm" (Eriksen & Eriksen, 1974). If the distracting information is processed irrespective of its lexical or graphemic status, it would interfere with lexical decisions to the underlined portion and yield longer R.T.s in comparison to those conditions in which no distractors are present. If the graphemic status of the neglected information is relevant, however, then significant differences should also be observed between the condition in which the distractor is not graphemic (i.e. the "at" sign) and that in which the distractor is graphemic but nonlexical.

Method

Stimuli

Subjects made lexical decisions to items appearing in the following five conditions:

1. *Neutral*: letter strings appeared alone and were not accompanied by any extraneous information such as underlining, letters, or other symbols; for example "cat" or "bew". The items consisted of the underlined targets taken from Experiment 1. Half the items were words and half nonwords.

2. *Underlined*: the same items presented in the neutral condition were

presented here but this time they were underlined; for example "cat" and "bew".

3. *"At" sign*: the same items presented in the previous condition were presented here. These stimuli, however, were coupled with nongraphemic information ("at" signs) which appeared on the left-hand side. The number of "at" signs corresponded to the number of letters appearing in the item in Experiment 1. For example, "@arm" consisted of one "at" sign, corresponding to "farm", whereas items like "@@end" and "@@ock" contained two (blend and clock) and "@@@ret" and "@@@vice" (secret and mervice) three symbols respectively.

4. *Graphemic*: this condition consisted of the items taken from WIN and NIN conditions from Experiment 1; i.e. the underlined target was either a word or a nonword and the context was a nonword (e.g. garm or wast). The left-sided distracting information, therefore, was graphemic but did not have lexical status.

5. *Lexical*: the items from conditions WIW and NIW from Experiment 1 were included here. The context or whole string, therefore, always constituted a word although the underlined target was either a word or a nonword (e.g. farm or east). The graphemic and lexical conditions in this experiment were a replication of Experiment 1.

Procedure

The presentation of the items followed the procedure used in the previous experiments. Condition was a within-subject variable so that all subjects completed trials from all conditions. The neutral, underline and "at" conditions were presented in blocked format while the graphemic and lexical were presented together to replicate the procedure used in Experiment 1. Each condition contained 96 trials. To avoid repeated exposure to the same items in all 5 conditions, 2 versions of the stimuli were drawn up and half the subjects saw one version and the remaining half saw the other. Therefore, at most, subjects viewed the same item in 3 of the 5 conditions. The order of conditions was varied across subjects.

Results and Discussion

Figure 4 shows the mean reaction time for target words and nonwords in all five conditions. A two-way repeated measures ANOVA, conducted with condition (neutral, underlined, "at", graphemic, and lexical) and lexical status of target (word, nonword) as within-subject factors, revealed significant main effects for target type ($F[1,2] = 187.1$, $P < 0.001$) and for condition ($F[2,45] = 58.2$, $P < 0.001$) and no interaction. Words yielded faster responses than nonwords and reaction times increased steadily from the neutral condition through the intermediate conditions to the lexical

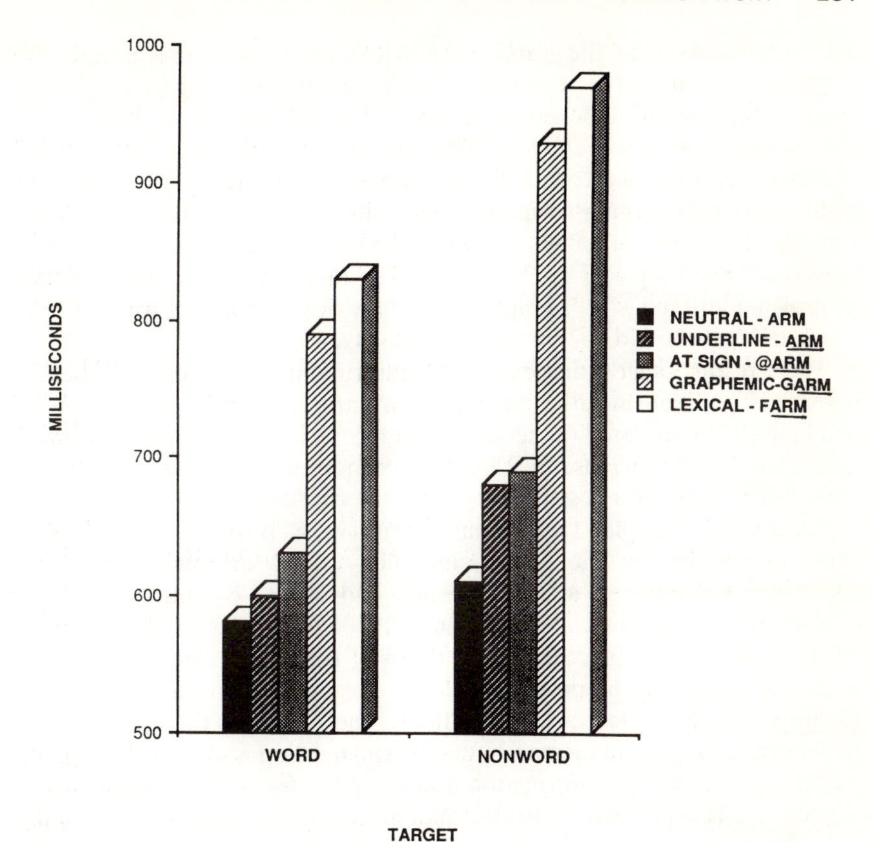

FIG. 4 R.T. (in msec.) to left-sided targets embedded in one of five different strings.

condition. Post-hoc comparisons using Student-Newman-Keuls and the Bonferroni adjustment for multiple comparisons revealed significant differences between all conditions with the exception of the underline and "at" condition when the underlined string is a nonword. The difference of 23msec. between the underline and the "at" condition when the underlined string was a word, however, was statistically significant.

The results of this experiment are relatively straightforward: when no information is present on the left but the stimulus is underlined, there is a significant increase in response time. When information is present on the left-hand side, it leads to longer R.T.s than when there is no information present. When left-sided information is present and is graphemic, it produces considerably slower responses (approximately 150msec. slower) than when the information is non-alphabetic, as in the "at" condition. Finally, as in Experiment 1, when the left-sided information plays a lexical role this increases R.T. even further. The big difference in R.T. between the "at" condition and the graphemic and lexical conditions may be a result of the fact that in the "at" condition, the distractor "@" was repeated in all trials because of the blocked presentation and subjects might have been able to dismiss it to some extent. The same was not true in the graphemic and lexical conditions in which the distractor differed from trial to trial. A within-item analysis comparing the identical item across all five conditions revealed a significant effect of condition (collapsed across words and nonwords; $F[4,188] = 17.1$, $P < 0.001$). The mean R.T.s for items in the neutral, underlined, "at", graphemic, and lexical conditions were 582.4, 626.2, 645.8, 843, and 867.9msec. respectively.

These results suggest that extraneous information in the display is being registered (as seen in difference between "arm", "arm", and "@arm") and highly differentiated (as seen in difference between "@arm", "garm", and "farm"). The increase in R.T. across conditions is consistent with the finding that there is a cost incurred with filtering extraneous information out of the visual display (Kahneman, Treisman, & Burkell, 1983). Moreover, in addition to the lateral inhibition effects in which nontarget adjacent information ("at", graphemic, and lexical conditions) affects perception of a target (Kolers & Rosner, 1960; Wolford & Hollingsworth, 1974), there is also a specific lexical effect of the unattended information with real words (farm) producing slower responses than either the "at" (@arm) or graphemic (garm) conditions. The results of the experiments with normal subjects demonstrate that when attention is selectively cued to a part of the stimulus, information outside of the focus of attention is still processed. This nonattended information affects performance differentially depending on its status, suggesting that the identity and lexical status of the distracting information contributes to performance. These findings support an interaction between attention and high-order knowledge, since nonattended information can still be recovered and processed to a high level.

EXPERIMENT 6: SIMULATION STUDY OF MORSEL

The final experiment was designed to examine the effect of nonattended information on word recognition in a distributed connectionist architecture, MORSEL. The use of computational modelling for examining normal reading and its breakdown, albeit in its infancy, is beginning to infiltrate the literature (Hinton & Shallice, in press; Patterson, Seidenberg, & McClelland, 1989; Seidenberg & McClelland, 1989). The common finding in these studies is that the dynamic framework provided by the networks can account for interactions which would otherwise seem counterintuitive. MORSEL was originally designed to account for perceptual errors made by normal subjects in word reading under performance limiting conditions. Following its successful implementation, we used the existing network to account for the behaviour of neglect dyslexia patients by damaging the attentional mechanism in MORSEL (Mozer & Behrmann, 1990). We showed that the complex interaction between a low-level attentional deficit and more abstract behaviours can be explained within the framework of this computational model. The prediction from these previous findings, then, is that (in addition to the neglect dyslexia behaviours) MORSEL should be able to account for the phenomenon observed in normal subjects, namely that the type of information that appears on the left determines the lexical decision times to attended targets on the right. Holding all parameters and details of MORSEL constant from the previous simulations (minus the lesion to the model that we made in the neuropsychological simulations), we hoped to obtain converging evidence that would suggest a top-down interaction between attention and existing higher-order representations.

Before describing these simulations, we provide a brief overview of MORSEL's key properties. The computational details and dynamics of the network are described in Mozer and Behrmann (1990). The essential components of MORSEL (see Fig. 5) are (1) a connectionist network that constructs location-invariant representations of visually presented letters and words, called BLIRNET; (2) a network that constructs a consistent interpretation of the activated perceptual data provided by BLIRNET, called the pull-out (P.O.) net, and (3) an attentional mechanism (A.M.) that guides the efforts of BLIRNET. When a stimulus word appears on MORSEL's "retina", the features associated with each letter activate primitive detectors. This activation is propagated through successive layers of BLIRNET, which constructs a distributed representation of the word's orthography. Visually similar words receive spurious activation. The role of the P.O. net, then, is to "clean up" the noisy pattern of activity generated by BLIRNET in response to the target and to synthesise a coherent response to the input pattern. The selection and interpretation of the P.O. net is also assisted by higher-order knowledge of English words. These semlex units bias the selection towards previously encountered words over the selection of nonwords. It is here that lexical status is embodied and this information feeds down and affects the P.O. net selection process.

The final component of MORSEL, the A.M., controls the flow and order of information through BLIRNET by constructing a "spotlight" around a selected region of the "retina". The activation of input features within the selected region is thereby enhanced relative to features outside the bounds of attention. The A.M., however, serves to bias processing from selected areas but does not absolutely inhibit activations for unattended regions. Rather, activations from "unattended" regions are transmitted with a lower probability. In the simulations of neglect dyslexia,

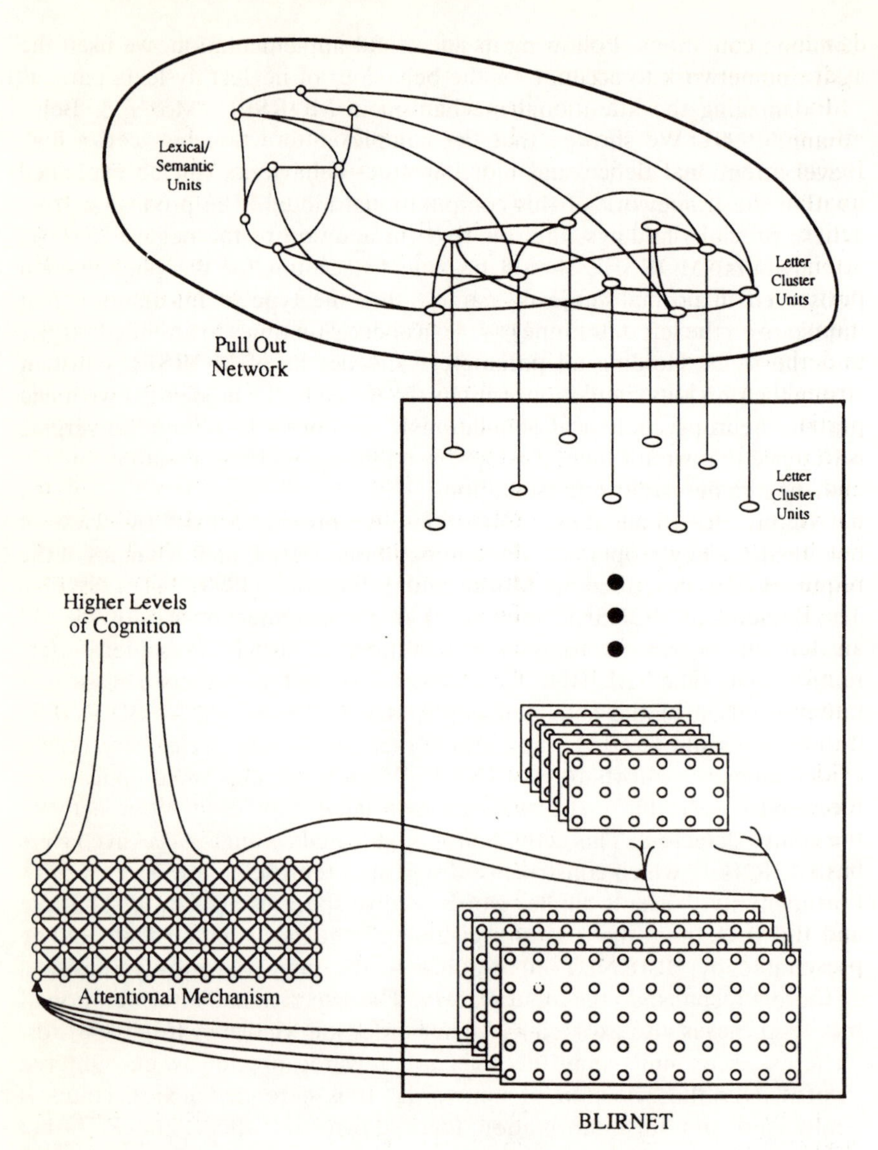

FIG. 5 A sketch of the essential components of MORSEL.

we damaged the connections from the input feature maps to the A.M. These connections serve to attract attention to locations where objects appear in the visual field. The damage was graded monotonically, being most severe at the left extreme of the "retina" and least severe at the right, corresponding to the left hemispatial neglect. The magnitude of the damage was such that inputs at the left extreme were only half as effective at drawing attention as those at the right.

In the simulations of the normal subjects described here, the region of attention was set to correspond to the underlined portion of the stimulus. Because MORSEL does not entirely inhibit information from the unattended region, input outside the focus of attention also becomes partly active. In the current version of MORSEL, the ratio of activity for the attended to unattended region is about 20:1.[1] Consider the consequence of partial activation of the unattended information in the present experiments. When, for example, f<u>arm</u> is presented, we assume that just the underlined portion is attended, causing BLIRNET to activate "arm" strongly and "farm" partially.[2] Additionally, BLIRNET produces spurious partial activations of visually similar words. The task of the P.O. net, then, is to read out the underlined part and to suppress the whole string (context) and other alternatives. To the extent that the context and other alternatives are strongly activated relative to the underlined section, the P.O. net has a more difficult selection task; this is reflected in the P.O. net requiring a larger number of iterations to settle on a stable activity pattern. The P.O. net competition is influenced by the lexical status of the items: if an item has a semlex representation, this top-down knowledge serves to reinforce the item's orthographic representation. This support can facilitate processing if the underlined target is a word, or can impede processing if the distractor is a word. In the former case, the top-down and bottom-up evidence are consistent; in the latter case, the top-down evidence reinforces the distracting word, and thereby makes it more difficult to resolve the competition between the underlined target and the context. This is the basis for our prediction that MORSEL will respond more rapidly to words ("arm" in "f<u>arm</u>" and "g<u>arm</u>") than to nonwords ("ast" in e<u>ast</u> and w<u>ast</u>), and to words presented in a nonword ("arm" in "g<u>arm</u>") than to words presented in a word ("arm" in "f<u>arm</u>").

Conducting a simulation to test these predictions is complicated by the fact that occasionally the P.O. net selects the whole string, "farm", or

[1]If MORSEL attends to some information, why should the nonselected information be analysed at all? We give two reasons why this mode of operation makes sense from a computational perspective. First, if the A.M. has difficulty selecting precisely the relevant region, information from nearby regions should nonetheless be processed in case it is relevant. Second, partial processing of unattended information allows facilitatory priming from one fixation to the next in reading (see Rayner, McConkie, & Zola [1980] and Rayner & Pollatsek [1988] for empirical evidence of such priming).

[2]Words are represented by a distributed pattern of activity over a set of letter-cluster units, but that is irrelevant for the present discussion. When we say that a word is activated, we mean that the pattern of activity produced by the model is consistent with the pattern of activity corresponding to the word.

some other alternative instead of the target—"arm". Human subjects in our experiments experience the same difficulty as well; this is one source of errors, as when subjects respond to the whole string "east" instead of the target "ast". Often, however, subjects become aware that the perceived string does not match the underlined portion of the stimulus string. Some type of *verification process* is required to detect the incongruity between the perceived and target strings. One simple possibility is the use of word length cues. However, because MORSEL does not encode word length explicitly, we propose an alternative means of verification. We assume a process (which we do not model directly) that focuses on the first letter of the underlined portion of the stimulus string and matches it against the first letter of the string read out by the P.O. net. If the two letters disagree, MORSEL is triggered to reprocess the stimulus with the distracting information further suppressed.

We can now describe in greater detail the sequence of processing steps that MORSEL takes to perform the lexical decision task on the underlined portion of a stimulus string. When the stimulus is first presented, the A.M. begins selection of the underlined portion. Simultaneously, BLIRNET begins processing the entire stimulus. Both because the A.M. has not yet had time to suppress the irrelevant portion of the string, and because the unattended portion is partly analysed by BLIRNET, initially BLIRNET activates the whole context as well as the underlined target. Operating on this input, the P.O. net must select one item as the response. We assume that the P.O. net continues to cycle until *equilibrium* is reached; we define this to be the point at which the activity of each unit in the P.O. net changes by less than 1% from one cycle to the next, or until a maximum of 50 cycles is obtained. Next, the verification process is carried out. If verification fails, the P.O. net is allowed to reprocess its input; this time the unattended information is completely filtered. The model responds "yes"—i.e. the underlined portion is a word—if there is a coalition of semlex units with activity close to 1.0, indicating that the selected string has an associated semantic activity pattern and is hence a word. Otherwise, the model responds "no". The model's processing time is the number of cycles the P.O. net requires to reach equilibrium. If verification fails and the P.O. net must reprocess the stimulus, we add the processing times from the first and second settlings of the P.O. net. We can also measure the proportion of trials on which the model makes an error on the lexical decision task.

This is the first time MORSEL has been used to simulate reaction-time performance. To do so, we needed to make several new assumptions about the model; specifically, the nature of the verification process and the P.O. net equilibrium criteria described earlier. However, MORSEL was not at all sensitive to these assumptions, as we elaborate later. The simulations were run using the same parameters as we used for our studies of neglect dyslexia (Mozer & Behrmann, 1990), although to obtain good quantitative fits, it was necessary to increase the strength of the bottom-up input from BLIRNET to the P.O. net relative to the top-down support from the semlex units. This parameter is one we have always supposed is under the control of the subject, and depends on the specific nature of the task (e.g., whether nonwords are expected as well as words). In the simulations, we used 12 words from the WIW condition of Experiment 1, varying both the length of the underlined and whole strings. The stimuli selected were: FARM, CLOCK, ESTATE, TREASON, QUART, CEREAL, TRACTOR, RESOURCE, RABBIT, MANDATE, UNIVERSE, and CARNATION. Rather than generating different stimulus sets for the other WIN, NIW, and NIN conditions, we used exactly the same stimuli but redefined the whole context and/or underlined target as nonwords. To elaborate, a word is distinguished from a nonword in MORSEL because the words are associated with a set of semlex units. Thus, we simply removed the semlex units for the *target* to transform the WIW stimuli into NIW stimuli, and so forth. This ensured that the 4 conditions were identical on all dimensions except for the lexical status of the target and distractor (context).[3]

The details of the simulations are reported in Mozer and Behrmann 1990, Appendix 4). Several aspects of the simulations bear mentioning. Because it was not computationally feasible to simulate the P.O. net with its full complement of orthographic and semlex units, a special P.O. net was constructed for each stimulus item. The P.O. net for a particular item consisted of the orthographic and semlex units necessary to represent the target, the distracting context, and a variety of alternative responses that were visually similar to the presented stimulus (e.g. WARM, FARCE, and BARM for "FARM"). For the WIW condition, there was an average of 347 orthographic units, 336 semlex units, and 7876 connections; for the other conditions, there were slightly fewer semlex units and connections.

Each stimulus item was presented to MORSEL 100 times. MORSEL can yield different responses on different trials due to 2 random factors—noise introduced in BLIRNET and the specific pattern of orthographic-semlex unit connectivity. Figure 6 shows the average number of cycles required for the P.O. net to settle in each condition for correct responses. These data from the pull-out net are in qualitative agreement with the human R.T. data obtained in Experiment 1, in the sense that the rank orderings of the response times are identical; responses to nonword targets are slower than to word targets, and responses to word distractors are slower than to nonword distractors. Conducting an ANOVA with stimulus items as the random factor, the main effects of underlined and whole string are both significant (underline: $F[1,11] = 42.8$, $P < 0.001$; whole:

[3]Too bad we cannot match conditions for human subjects in this manner!

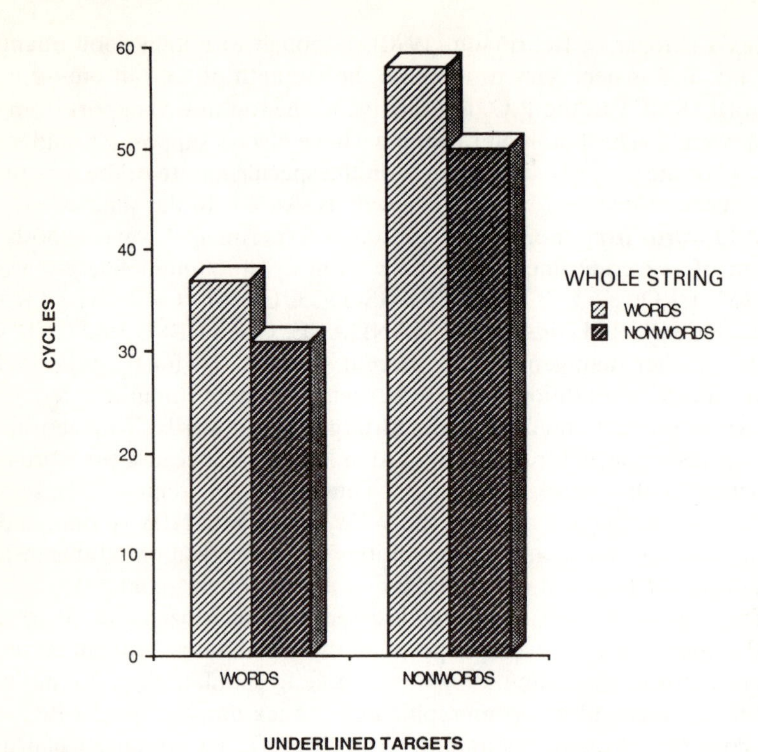

FIG. 6 Mean number of cycles for MORSEL's P.O. net to settle as a function of status of the whole string.

$F[1,11] = 13.5$, $P < 0.01$), whereas the interaction is not ($F[1,11] = 3.3$, $P = 0.098$). Conducting specific comparisons of the WIW versus WIN conditions and the NIW versus NIN conditions, both indicate reliable effects (WIW/WIN: $F[1,11] = 28.7$, $P < 0.001$; NIW/NIN: $F(1,11) = 8.0$, $P < 0.02$). The qualitative pattern of results is quite insensitive to parameters of the model such as the P.O. net equilibrium criteria and the relative strength of bottom-up versus top-down activation. The main effects of underlined and whole string are statistically reliable for a wide range of parameter settings. However, some parameter settings cause the interaction to become significant, with the difference between nonwords in words and in nonwords (NIW and NIN) being smaller than the difference between words in words and in nonwords (WIW and WIN).

Error rates produced by the model were below 6% in each condition. The majority of the errors were lexicalisations. The remainder were cases in which the model got stuck between two responses (e.g. orthographic features of one item but semlex features of a second item). The appearance of lexical errors is compatible with the observation that many subjects with neglect dyslexia produce errors in oral reading that are primarily lexical (Behrmann et al., 1990). Subjects with neglect dyslexia also tend to produce errors that approximate the length of the target string. Although this pattern has been attributed to the fact that neglect subjects encode word length in some rudimentary way (Behrmann et al., 1990; Ellis et al., 1987; Patterson & Wilson, 1990; Riddoch et al., 1990), this is not the case with MORSEL. At present, MORSEL has no representation of word length and the substitution errors which also approximate the length of the target string arise because the alternative possible responses provided for the model are of the same length as the target. It may well be the case, however, that if we were to examine the activity of the letter clusters in the pull-out net, we might find that clusters making up a response of the same length as the target would be most active. Since information on the left of the string does receive partial activation in MORSEL, we would expect features on the left to be activated even if they were not strong enough to drive the correct response. Unlike specific letter content, word length may be computed accurately as it can be derived from fairly crude information.

The results of the simulation studies show a good qualitative match to the findings from the normal subjects. These findings suggest that even when attention is maximally activated in one region (right in this case, but the same applied to the left), the minimal activation provided to the distracting information is sufficient to allow for processing of the target and the distracting context. The time taken to settle on an appropriate and stable output leads to an increased number of cycles when the distracting context forms a word.

Given that the word–nonword difference observed in neglect patients and normal subjects can be accounted for in MORSEL, it is important to consider whether the same convergence of results might be found on other types of stimuli. In our previous paper, we have shown that morphemic status as well as physical contiguity of stimuli affects the behaviour of patients with neglect dyslexia. Thus, two morphemes which are either semantically related or not and presented either contiguously or not, are read more accurately when they are both physically adjacent and when they form a compound word (e.g. COW BOY). These two properties, physical separation and morphemic relatedness, have yet to be tested in greater detail. Experimental work is currently underway in which these two variables are manipulated orthogonally in normal subjects and in MORSEL.

CONCLUSION

Considered together, the results of these experiments indicate that normal subjects continue to process irrelevant or to-be-ignored information (Expts. 1–5), even when attentional cueing is optimal and attention has sufficient time to build up (Expts. 2 and 3). Furthermore, this distracting information plays a specific role, producing differential effects on performance depending on the lexical status of the surrounding context (Expts. 1 and 5). The finding that category or identity information of the distractors is available is supported by previous experiments by Styles and Allport (1986). In these studies, normal subjects were instructed to name selectively just one object among a briefly presented array of other objects differing from the target in category. They found that even at short S.O.A.s, identity information is available and that even when the target differed considerably from the distracting objects, performance was still affected by the distractors.

In our study, the pattern of results obtained in the MORSEL simulations also showed the interaction between attention and lexicality observed in the normal subjects. These findings are remarkably similar to the pattern of performance observed in some patients with neglect dyslexia. Many of these patients tend to make reading errors of the same length as the target (Behrmann et al., 1990; Ellis et al., 1987; Kinsbourne & Warrington, 1962). Thus, the neglected information on the left is often substituted in a form of "backward completion" so that "hair" may be read as "fair" or "pair" rather than omitted as "air". The presence of substitution errors suggests that the neglected information on the left is encoded but that it is not processed sufficiently well to produce the correct response. Furthermore, it has been shown that the pattern of neglect behaviour is affected by the lexical status of the left-sided information, suggesting that the unattended information is processed to a deep level.

The results of the present study are also consistent with previous findings on neglect subjects in domains other than reading. It has been shown, for example, that information appearing on the left may be processed and used in a same/different judgement task (Volpe, Ledoux, & Gazzaniga, 1979) and in making preference judgements about pictures (Marshall & Halligan, 1988), even when the information is not available for explicit report.

Kartsounis and Warrington (1989) have proposed that the extent to which the left-sided information is processed in patients with hemispatial neglect depends on the meaningfulness of the right-hand side. On their account, information appearing on the unattended left-hand side is only processed if the right side cannot be interpreted. This explanation is supported by Seron, Coyette, and Bruyer (1989), who showed that the left side of an object is processed when the attended right side is ambiguous. For example, when the perceived object is meaningless (e.g. a horizontal "handle"), attention is triggered to the left and the additional left-sided information helps disambiguate the meaningless object (into a rake, hair-brush, cannon, etc.). This view, however, cannot account for the fact that even in conditions in which meaningful words were embedded on the right of other words (WIW), we still see an effect of left-sided information in the normal subjects (as in farm versus garm). Similarly, Ellis et al. (1987) found that their neglect subject, VB, still tended to substitute the first letter of the stimulus even when deleting the initial letter still yielded a plausible real-word response. For example, VB still read BLOCK as "clock" even when the right side was a meaningful response, "lock", on its own. In view of these findings, it seems that an explanation based on the meaningfulness of the attended right-hand side is not sufficient to account for the behaviour of all patients with neglect dyslexia.

An alternative explanation advanced by us (Behrmann et al., 1990; Mozer & Behrmann, 1990) and others (Siéroff et al., 1988) is that word reading is not primarily affected by the meaningfulness of the right-hand side. In the studies of the normals and MORSEL described here, we see that even when the right-hand side is meaningful, distracting left-sided information is still processed. Thus, the time to make a lexical decision to the right is critically dependent on the lexical status of the left-sided unattended information. We propose, therefore, that information on the left is also picked up and, depending on its lexical and morphemic status, differentially affects reading performance. This explanation is also consistent with the data from the neglect patients and the computational simulations of neglect dyslexia (Behrmann et al., 1990; Mozer & Behrmann, 1990). In those studies, we showed that two morphemes presented simultaneously were both read more accurately when they made up a compound word (for example, COW BOY) than when they did not (for example, SUN FLY). When the two morphemes did not share a unifying lexical representation as in the case of the compound words, the left-sided morpheme tended to be neglected or extinguished. Based on these findings, we proposed that the left-sided information is registered and can interact with existing lexical representations, producing effects of stimulus lexicality and morphemic status.

These findings have several implications for the role of spatial attention in visual pattern recognition and reading. Rather than supporting theories of early or late attentional selection, the data reported in this paper are most compatible with a more hybrid account of attention (Mozer, in press; Pashler & Badgio, 1987). According to this account, selective attention operates early on, but not in an all-or-none fashion. While the region under focus receives enhanced activation, information in other regions also receives activation but to a lesser extent. This poorly activated information can later be used to feed back and enhance recovery of the leftmost information provided that there are existing representations to guide this top-down feedback process. Clearly, in the case of words which have prior entries in the orthographic lexicon, this higher-order knowledge is available and can be used in this top-down fashion.

Although our account explains the deficit observed in many patients with neglect dyslexia (Behrmann et al., 1990; Ellis et al., 1987), it was not designed to explain neglect disorders that arise at higher levels of representation. Examples of such disorders include those in which the contralesional side of an internally generated representation are neglected, in which the neglect is observed across a range of input and output modalities, or in which neglect is object-based rather than spatiotopic (Barbut & Gazzaniga, 1987; Bisiach, Luzzatti, & Perani, 1979; Caramazza & Hillis, 1990). How can these other deficits be accommodated in MORSEL, in which the attentional mechanism operates at a low level of processing? In order to analyse an item which arises in conceptual space, it might be necessary to map an abstract object- or word-centred representation onto a more concrete spatiotopic representation. This instantiation of the abstract representation produces an activity pattern in BLIRNET which captures the essentials of the stimulus but does not contain the richness of a true perception. Once the abstract representation is mapped, then the patient is operating in an imagined spatiotopic frame and the stimulus is viewed from a particular vantage point, then the attentional system operates on this iconic representation in the same way as for perception. This notion of a concrete mapping onto lower layers of BLIRNET is consistent with the report by Baxter and Warrington's (1983, p. 1075) patient that "attempting to spell (was) like reading off an image in which the letters on the right side were clearer than those on the left". Such a mapping process might then lead to deficits of one side of an internal representation but the same "hardware" is used for imaging stimuli and for processing incoming visual input.

In addition to neglect deficits that arise at different levels of processing, there are also neglect deficits that occur within a particular domain of processing. For example, there are now several reports of patients with neglect dyslexia in the absence of generalised hemispatial neglect (as tested on other visual tasks; Patterson & Wilson, 1990; Riddoch et al., 1990) or with neglect in restricted domains such as in face recognition (Young, de Haan, Newcombe, & Hay, in press). Any account of selective attention must make provision for such dissociations. One way of doing so would be to posulate individual and independent attentional mechanisms, each subserving a particular domain of processing. A more parsimonious view, however, would be to show that a single attentional mechanism serves all domains, as in the case of MORSEL, but that the individual domains might interact differently with attention or become "disconnected" from the unitary attentional mechanism.

A comprehensive account of selective attention will have to account for the specificity of attentional deficits both at different levels of representation and in different processing domains. For the moment, the convergence of findings from the neglect dyslexic patients, the normal subjects, and the connectionist model has shed some light on the interaction between selective attention and orthographic processing. We are encouraged that the extension and elaboration of the theoretical and implemented computational models will allow for a fuller account of selective attention and its impairment. We also recognise, however, that the path ahead is not without its obstacles.

Manuscript received 7 March 1990
Revised manuscript received 15 June 1990

REFERENCES

Barbut, D. & Gazzaniga, M. (1987). Disturbances in conceptual space involving speech and language. *Brain*, *110*, 1487–1496.

Baxter, D. & Warrington, E. K. (1983). Neglect dysgraphia. *Journal of Neurology, Neurosurgery, and Psychiatry*, *46*, 1073–1078.

Behrmann, M., Moscovitch, M., Black, S. E., & Mozer, M. (1990). Perceptual and conceptual mechanisms in neglect: Two contrasting case studies. *Brain*, *113*, 4, 1163–1183.

Bisiach, E., Luzzatti, C., & Perani, D. (1979). Unilateral neglect, representational schema, and consciousness. *Brain*, *102*, 609–618.

Bruner, J. S. & O'Dowd, D. (1958). A note on the informativeness of parts of words. *Language and Speech*, *1*, 98–101.

Brunn, J. & Farah, M. (in press). The relation between spatial attention and reading: Evidence from the neglect syndrome. *Cognitive Neuropsychology*.

Butter, C. M., Buchtel, H., & Santucci, R. (1989). Spatial attentional shifts: Further evidence for the role of polysensory mechanisms using visual and tacile stimuli. *Neuropsychologia*, *27* (10), 1231–1240.

Caramazza, A. & Hillis, A. E. (1990). Levels of representation, co-ordinate frames, and unilateral neglect. *Cognitive Neuropsychology*, *7*, 391–445.

De Renzi, E., Gentilini, M., Faglioni, M., & Barbieri, C. (1989). Attention shifts towards the rightmost stimuli in patients with visual neglect. *Cortex*, *25*, 231–237.

Ellis, A., Flude, B., & Young, A. W. (1987). Neglect dyslexia and the early visual processing of letters in words and nonwords. *Cognitive Neuropsychology*, *4*, 439–464.

Eriksen, B. A. & Eriksen, C. W. (1974). Effects of noise letters upon identification of a target letter in a nonsearch task. *Perception and Psychophysics*, *16*, 143–149.

Eriksen, C. W. & Hoffman, J. E. (1973). The extent of processing of noise elements during selective encoding from visual displays. *Perception and Psychophysics*, *14*, 155–160.

Francis, W. N. & Kuçera, H. (1982). *Frequency analysis of English usage*. Boston: Houghton Mifflin Company.

Friedrich, F. J., Walker, J., & Posner, M. I. (1985). Effects of parietal lesions on visual matching. *Cognitive Neuropsychology*, *2*, 253–264.

Hinton, G. & Shallice, T. (in press). Lesioning a connectionist network: Investigations of acquired dyslexia. *Psychological Review*.

Kahneman, D., Treisman, A., & Burkell, J. (1983). The cost of visual filtering. *Journal of Experimental Psychology: Human Perception and Performance*, *9*, 510–522.

Kartsounis, L. D. & Warrington, E. K. (1989). Unilateral visual neglect overcome by cues implicit in stimulus arrays. *Journal of Neurology, Neurosurgery, and Psychiatry*, *52*, 1253–1258.

Kinsbourne, M. & Warrington, E. K. (1962). A variety of reading disorders associated with right hemisphere lesions. *Journal of Neurology, Neurosurgery, and Psychiatry*, *25*, 339–344.

Kolers, P. & Rosner, B. S. (1960). On visual masking (metacontrast): Dichoptic observation. *American Journal of Psychology*, *70*, 2–21.

Leicester, J., Sidman, M., Stoddart, L. T., & Mohr, J. P. (1969). Some determinants of visual neglect. *Journal of Neurology, Neurosurgery, and Psychiatry*, *32*, 580–587.

Marshall, J. C. & Halligan, P. (1988). Blindsight and insight in visuo-spatial neglect. *Nature*, *336*, 22–29.

Morrow, L. A. & Ratcliff, G. (1988). The disengagement of covert attention and the neglect syndrome. *Psychobiology*, *16*(3), 261–269.

Mozer, M. (1987). Early parallel processes in reading: A connectionist approach. In M. Coltheart (Ed.), *Attention and performance XII: The psychology of reading*. Hillsdale, N.J.: Lawrence Erlbaum Associates Inc.

Mozer, M. (1988). A connectionist model of selective attention in visual perception. In *Proceedings of the Tenth Annual Conference of the Cognitive Science Society*. Hillsdale, N.J.: Lawrence Erlbaum Associates Inc., 195–201.

Mozer, M. C. (in press). *The perception of multiple objects: A connectionist approach*. Cambridge, MA: M.I.T. Press/Bradford Books.

Mozer, M. C. & Behrmann, M. (in press). On the interaction of selective attention and lexical knowledge: A connectionist account for neglect dyslexia. *Journal of Cognitive Neuroscience*.

Pashler, H. & Badgio, P. C. (1987). Attentional issues in the identification of alphanumeric characters. In M. Coltheart (Ed.), *Attention and performance XII: The psychology of reading*. Hillsdale, N.J.: Lawrence Erlbaum Associates Inc.

Patterson, K., Seidenberg, M., & McClelland, J. (1989). Connections and disconnections: Acquired dyslexia in a computational model of reading processes. In R. G. M. Morris (Ed.), *Parallel distributed processing: Implications for psychology and neurobiology*. Oxford: Oxford University Press.

Patterson, K. & Wilson, B. (1990). A rose is a rose or a nose: A deficit in initial letter misidentification. *Cognitive Neuropsychology*, *7*, 447–477.

Posner, M. I., Cohen, A., & Rafal, R. (1982). Neural systems control of spatial orienting. *Philosophical Transaction of Royal Society of London*, *298*, 187–198.

Rayner, K., McConkie, G. W., & Zola, D. (1980). Integrating information across eye movements. *Cognitive Psychology*, *12*, 206–226.

Rayner, K. & Pollatsek, A. (1988). Eye movements in reading. In M. Coltheart (Ed.), *Attention and performance XII: The psychology of reading*. Hillsdale, N.J.: Lawrence Erlbaum Associates Inc.

Rayner, K. & Pollatsek, A. (1989). *The psychology of reading*. Englewood Cliffs, N.J.: Prentice-Hall.

Riddoch, M. J., Humphreys, G., Cleton, P., & Fery, P. (1990). Levels of coding in neglect dyslexia. *Cognitive Neuropsychology*, *7*, 479–517.

Rizzolatti, G., Gentilucci, M., & Matelli, M. (1985). Selective spatial attention: One centre, one circuit, or many circuits? In M. I. Posner & O. S. M. Marin (Eds.), *Attention and performance XI*. Hillsdale, N.J.: Lawrence Erlbaum Associates Inc., 251–265.

Rizzolatti, G., Scandolara, C., Matelli, M., & Gentilucci, M. (1981). Afferent properties of periarcuate neurons in macaque monkeys. II: Visual responses. *Behaviour and Brain Research*, *2*, 147–163.

Seidenberg, M. & McClelland, M. (1989). A distributed, developmental model of word recognition and naming. *Psychological Review*, *96*, 523–568.

Seron, X., Coyette, F., & Bruyer, F. (1989). Ipsilateral influences on contralateral processing in neglect patients. *Cognitive Neuropsychology*, *6*(5), 475–489.

Siéroff, E. (1990). Focusing in/on verbal visual stimuli in patients with parietal lesions. *Cognitive Neuropsychology*, *7*, 519–544.

Siéroff, E., Pollatsek, A., & Posner, M. I. (1988). Recognition of visual letter strings following injury to the posterior visual spatial attention system. *Cognitive Neuropsychology*, *5*, 451–472.

Styles, E. A. & Allport, D. A. (1986). Perceptual integration of identity, location, and colour. *Psychological Research*, *48*, 189–200.

Volpe, B. T., Ledoux, E., & Gazzaniga, M. (1979). Information processing of visual stimuli in an "extinguished" field. *Nature*, *282* (13), 722–724.

Wolford, G. & Hollingsworth, S. (1974). Lateral masking in visual information processing. *Perception and Psychophysics*, *16*, 315–320.

Yantis, S. & Johnston, J. C. (1990). On the locus of visual selection: Evidence from focused attention tasks. *Journal of Experimental Psychology: Human Perception and Performance*, *16* (1), 135–149.

Young, A. W., de Haan, E. H. F., Newcombe, F., & Hay, D. C. (1990). Facial neglect. *Neuropsychologia*, *28*, 5, 391–416.

REFERENCE NOTE

1. Siéroff, E. (1990). *Perception of visual letter strings in a case of left neglect: Manipulation of the word form*. Manuscript submitted for publication.

APPENDIX 1

Stimuli for Experiment 1

Word-in-word	*Nonword-in-word*	*Word-in-nonword*	*Nonword-in-nonword*
3 letters underlined			
farm	east	garm	bast
hair	full	dair	tull
cage	tell	lage	rell
sale	sack	rale	dack
face	limb	hace	simb
rate	veil	nate	weil
quart	group	clart	broup
tulip	water	solip	sater
mouse	money	bouse	soney
voice	crime	maice	trime
space	flesh	prace	blesh
peace	stick	blace	plick

Word-in-word	*Nonword-in-word*	*Word-in-nonword*	*Nonword-in-nonword*
rabbit	letter	cobbit	ditter
target	doctor	larget	bictor
throne	effect	strone	splect
garden	studio	borden	windio
choice	secret	sprice	monret
supply	fabric	fapply	labric
cottage	inquiry	partage	greniry
average	gallery	motrage	sollery
harbour	fatigue	prenour	lotigue
trumpet	concern	drampet	montern
justice	council	jantice	trancil
veteran	payment	soteran	woyment

4 letters underlined

clock	frame	plock	trame
blend	south	flend	pouth
grain	front	prain	dront
place	catch	flace	fatch
black	press	clack	fress
class	truck	plass	druck
cereal	handle	doreal	bandle
forest	figure	burest	bagure
injury	result	anjury	tesult
spring	script	skring	stript
system	legend	hostem	fogend
effort	global	wafort	flobal
mandate	century	pindate	montury
surface	mixture	corface	caxture
measure	horizon	blasure	forizon
husband	harmony	losband	bermony
student	problem	spadent	rinblem
service	control	farvice	santral
platform	industry	pritform	cranstry
pleasure	attitude	steasure	stontude
surprise	chlorine	hontrise	selerine
thousand	disaster	crensand	drinster
incident	mountain	selodent	sountain
accident	progress	bosident	hontress

Word-in-word	*Nonword-in-word*	*Word-in-nonword*	*Nonword-in-nonword*
5 letters underlined			
estate	ribbon	ostate	sibbon
flight	course	clight	lourse
knight	crease	dright	trease
bridge	planet	cridge	blanet
ground	chance	pround	thance
factor	method	mactor	lethod
tractor	defense	practor	refense
example	funeral	stample	luneral
impulse	channel	ampulse	stannel
thought	protein	shought	frotein
history	country	mistory	bruntry
revenue	station	davenue	plation
guidance	survival	flodance	canvival
approach	solution	monroach	bolution
universe	distress	plaverse	bontress
merchant	prisoner	serchant	plasoner
purchase	evidence	blochase	clidence
aircraft	property	lurcraft	fraperty
assistance	principle	planstance	clunciple
generation	committee	deneration	sallittee
tantamount	technique	plonamount	beminique
lionheart	guerillas	stanheart	tatrillas
livestock	democracy	brenstock	floncracy
clapboard	principal	flomboard	stincipal
6 letters underlined			
treason	company	freason	pompany
factual	college	tactual	nollege
faction	society	haction	tociety
bracket	witness	tracket	bitness
theater	gesture	sheater	lesture
platter	barrier	blatter	darrier
resource	business	disource	musiness
mistress	emission	hostress	prission
republic	opponent	lapublic	laponent
district	champion	bistrict	frampion
distance	activity	fistance	lativity
division	question	sevision	clestion
spiritual	magnitude	slaritual	sannitude
confusion	passenger	tanfusion	dinsenger

Word-in-word	*Nonword-in-word*	*Word-in-nonword*	*Nonword-in-nonword*
migration	salvation	logration	fonvation
carnation	structure	wirnation	splucture
narration	existence	merration	honstence
semantics	tradition	splantics	prodition
footbridge	experience	bronbridge	blatrience
atmosphere	university	senosphere	brogersity
themselves	literature	hermselves	salarature
attractive	reputation	applactive	clontation
detonation	commitment	fetonation	smenitment
federation	solidarity	bontration	extodarity

COGNITIVE NEUROPSYCHOLOGY, 1991, *8* (3/4) 249–273

Simultaneous Form Perception and Serial Letter Recognition in a Case of Letter-by-letter Reading

Janice Kay
University of Exeter, Exeter, U.K.
Richard Hanley
University of Liverpool, Liverpool, U.K.

This paper examines the performance of a letter-by-letter reader, PD, on tests which involve the perception of words and letter-strings under tachistoscopic presentation conditions. Unlike the patients recently reported by Bub, Black, and Howell (1989) and Reuter-Lorenz and Brunn (1990), PD shows no evidence of processing the letters of a word in an "ends-in" fashion. Instead, letters appear to be recognised serially from left to right. Furthermore, PD does not show an advantage of words over pseudowords when asked to report the letters from briefly presented letter-strings. In addition, unlike control subjects, he does not show a word superiority effect in same/different judgements about two simultaneously presented letter-strings (Friedrich, Walker, & Posner, 1985). A final experiment reveals that his ability to recognise letters under sequential processing conditions is relatively unimpaired, as is his ability to match letters on the basis of physical features with simultaneous presentation. It is suggested that the precise locus of the deficit which precipitates letter-by-letter reading differs from one case to another, and that PD's primary impairment is caused by an inability to identify more than one letter at the same time.

INTRODUCTION

Letter-by-letter reading is a form of acquired dyslexia in which reading aloud is extremely laboured and reading time increases in line with the number of letters in a word. According to Warrington and Shallice (1980) and Shallice (1988), patients who use a letter-by-letter strategy while reading do so because of an impairment to the visual word-form system. This means that such patients are no longer able to make use of lexical representations to identify written words when attempting to read them

Requests for reprints should be addressed to Janice Kay, Dept. of Psychology, University of Exeter, Washington Singer Labs., Perry Road, Exeter EX4 4QG, U.K.

aloud. In order to compensate, they recognise words by gaining access to a word-form system used in written *spelling* by using letter-name information as if the word had been spelled aloud. The letter-by-letter strategy occurs because the mechanism of auditory or "reverse" spelling is the way in which the spelling system is accessed.

Patterson and Kay (1982), in contrast, argue that the locus of the deficit is not in the visual word-form system itself. Letter-by-letter reading occurs, they suggest, because these patients can no longer recognise letters in parallel. This means that they are unable to access the word-form system in the normal way. Instead the system has to be accessed by means of serial letter identification, a process which is both slow and error-prone. In addition, both Patterson and Kay (1982) and Shallice (1988) accept that some patients have a further impairment which makes it difficult for them to recognise letters even when they are presented in isolation.

Recently, two reports have been published which cast some doubt on the view that letter-by-letter reading is associated with damage to the word-form system. Bub et al. (1989) and Reuter-Lorenz and Brunn (1990) both described cases of letter-by-letter readers who were able to report more letters from tachistoscopically presented letter strings when they comprised real words than when they were random letter strings. In addition, the letter-by-letter reader described by Reuter-Lorenz and Brunn showed a significant recognition advantage for letters in words than letters in pseudowords. Reuter-Lorenz and Brunn also showed that the observed word advantage could not simply be accounted for by a "sophisticated guessing strategy" favouring the consciously driven production of words, since their patient was more likely to produce pseudowords or nonwords than words in response to pseudoword and nonword stimuli.

Word-superiority effects are popularly thought to reflect activation from word-level recognition units to letter-level recognition units (McClelland & Rumelhart, 1981). The results of Bub et al. and Reuter-Lorenz and Brunn, therefore, suggest that letter-by-letter readers *are* able to access higher-level representations in the word-form system during reading, contrary to the views of Shallice (1988).

Furthermore, these studies also present evidence which conflicts with Patterson and Kay's (1982) suggestion that letter-by-letter reading comes about because letters can only be identified serially. Under tachistoscopic conditions, both WL (Reuter-Lorenz & Brunn, 1990) and JV (Bub et al., 1989) reveal evidence of recognising the letters in a word in an "*ends-in*" manner. That is, they reported letters in four-letter strings more accurately from serial positions 1 and 4 than from positions 2 and 3. Such a pattern of performance does not appear to be consistent with Patterson and Kay's view that letter-by-letter readers process letters serially from left to right.

In this study, we have investigated the performance of another letter-by-letter reader on a series of similar tasks. It is obviously important to discover whether the locus of the primary impairment in letter-by-letter reading differs from one patient to another. In the case of access to the word-form system, the situation has not yet been resolved. Warrington and Shallice (1980) report that their patient JDC did *not* show a word superiority effect when he was asked to report letters from tachistoscopically presented words and pseudowords. However, as Reuter-Lorenz and Brunn (1990) point out, the procedure used by Warrington and Shallice differed in several important respects from that typically used in demonstrations of the word-superiority effect in non-brain-damaged subjects. Consequently, it remains an open question whether or not all letter-by-letter readers show a word superiority effect when the standard paradigm is used.

The case of letter-by-letter reading presented in this paper is the patient PD. In an earlier report we examined the nature of the compensatory strategies which PD appears to use in reading (see Hanley & Kay, Note 2). The patient's written spelling to dictation is severely impaired, and the overwhelming majority of the errors that he makes are phonological regularisations (e.g. *photograph* → fotergraf; *circle* → serkel). In contrast, reading aloud is less severely impaired, and the errors that he makes are primarily visual paralexias (e.g. *victor* → visitor; *choir* → cheer). On the basis of this and other aspects of his reading and spelling performance, Hanley and Kay argued that it is unlikely that PD reads using the spelling system "in reverse", contrary to the views of Warrington and Shallice (1980). Rather, it was suggested that letter-by-letter reading demonstrated by this patient involves serial access of the visual word-form system, following the account proposed by Patterson and Kay (1982). Here, we report our attempt to substantiate this claim by examining PD's ability to process individual letters and letter strings under tachistoscopic viewing conditions.

CASE DETAILS

PD is 32 years old, right-handed, and lives in the Northeast of England. In November 1982 he suffered a left thalamic haemorrhage which partly ruptured into the lateral ventricle. It was caused by a very small arterio-venous malformation (A.V.M.) lodged in the posterior thalamus, extending into the brain stem, and fed from the left posterior cerebral artery. The A.V.M. was not excised because of the technical difficulty and extreme risk of the procedure. His clinical notes at that time indicate that he had a right homonymous hemianopia with sparing of the macula and a right hemiparesis with right hemianaesthesia. On follow-up, one year later, these problems had not resolved, and mild expressive dysphasia was also recorded. We began to see PD in November 1987. His visual-field defect and hemiparesis remain, but he has only residual word-finding difficulties, affecting proper names in particular, in spontaneous conversation. Despite the visual field deficit, his contrast sensitivity function is normal (Pelli, Robson, & Wilkins, 1988), as is visual acuity measured with the Snellen chart (6/6).

His performance is also within the normal range on tests of object recognition, memory, and spoken language. His score of 43 on the Warrington (1984) Recognition Memory Test for Faces is normal. On tests devised by Hanley, Pearson, and Young (in press), he was good at recognising the faces and names of celebrities who have become famous since 1985, as well as those who were famous before 1980. He has an auditory forward digit span of 6 items and he shows good overall performance, together with a strong effect of phonological similarity, in serial recall of auditorily presented letters. He made 6 errors out of 80 on the nonword repetition test from the P.A.L.P.A. battery (Kay, Lesser, & Coltheart, in press), which is within the normal range and he made only one error out of 80 on a test of auditory lexical decision. He also scored 30/30 on Bradley's (1980) test of phonological awareness. His score of 15 on McKenna and Warrington's (1983) Graded Naming Test represents "average" performance, and he scored 40/40 on the spoken word-picture matching test from the P.A.L.P.A. battery. He also scored 36/36 on Humphreys and Riddoch's object decision task.[1]

Reading Performance

Letter Identification Skills

PD's letter identification skills are relatively well preserved. He scored 50/52 on tests of naming upper- and lower-case letters, 25/26 on a test of lower-case to upper-case matching, and 25/26 on spoken-letter to written-letter matching. These tests were taken from the P.A.L.P.A. battery. In reading aloud single words he does not generally name letters overtly, but on the occasions when he has done so, we have not observed him to make errors. On the other hand, he sometimes makes errors in naming the word (e.g. *fact* → "fast", f,a,c,t; *session* → "season"; s,e,s,s,i,o,n), a point that we shall take up later. What is clear, though, is that his reading problems go beyond difficulties in recognising single letters.

Single Word Reading

Over the course of testing, we have given PD 279 single words to read aloud in different reading tasks. Of these, 164 (59%) were read correctly.

---

[1]G. Humphreys kindly allowed us to use this test.

Figure 1 illustrates the mean length of time (in seconds) that PD takes to read correctly individual words of different letter lengths from one of the reading tests (one devised by Ellis, Flude, & Young, 1987). The test consists of lists of 18 3-, 4-, 5-, and 6-letter words matched on imageability ratings. There was no pressure on PD to respond quickly and he managed to read successfully 54/72 (75%). The figure shows quite clearly that the longer the letter length of the word, the longer he takes to read it aloud. Letter length, not syllable length, is the principle factor in this relationship, since there is no effect of number of syllables on reading speed (using either mean or median measures) when number of letters is held constant (Hanley & Kay, Note 2). When he was given lists that manipulate word frequency, PD was slower to read lower-frequency than higher-frequency words. There were no differences in accuracy. He showed similar effects with high- and low-imageability words: he took longer to read aloud low-imageability words, but he was just as accurate in reading low- as high-imageability words.

PD made 105 errors on our initial reading tests. Of these, 94, by far the majority, can be categorised as being visually related to the target. Of the remainder, 10 are neologisms (e.g. *tongue* → /tŋgi/) and one can be considered as a semantic error (e.g. *bridge* → path). Twelve of the visual paralexias are straightforward letter misidentifications, 10 of them involving the letter "b" (e.g. *bread* → dread; *bump* → pump). Five of the paralexias were difficult to classify, but may be cases of letter misidentifications leading to visual paralexias (e.g. *body* → baby). The remaining 77 were *visual* errors. Examples include *canal* read as "candle", *feather* read as "further" and *victor* read as "visitor". We looked closely at the characteristics of 63 of these visual errors (since 14 of the 77 errors could have been classified differently, as morphological errors such as *nerve* → nervy, for example, they were excluded from this error analysis). Many of

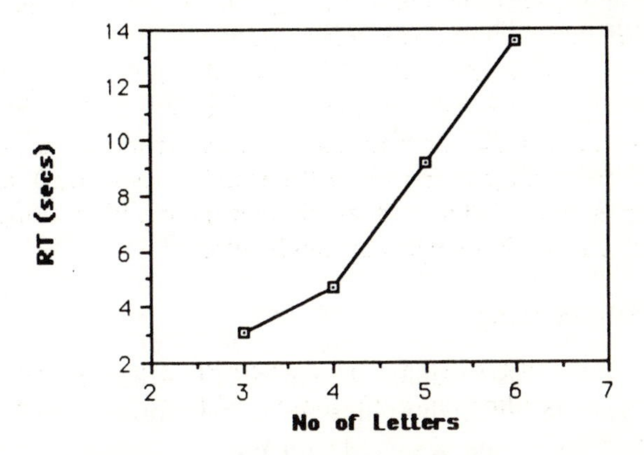

FIG. 1 Single word reading aloud as a function of letter length.

PD's errors seemed to preserve the first few letters of the target string (e.g. *barge* → bark). An analysis of serial position effects, following the procedure of Wing and Baddeley (1980), showed a significant difference between the positions of letters PD was likely to preserve ($\chi^2_4 = 42.07$): the first letter was almost always preserved, but none of the other letter positions differed appreciably from chance estimates. There was also a significant correlation between letter length of target and error ($r = 0.73$): PD's visual errors tended to maintain letter length of target. Target and error responses did not differ in lexical frequency ratings.

EXPERIMENTAL INVESTIGATIONS

Experiment 1: Orthographic Context Effects in Lexical Processing

It is well recognised that under conditions of rapid visual presentation, letters embedded in words or word-like strings (pseudowords) are recognised by normal subjects with greater accuracy than when they constitute random letter strings. Popular theoretical accounts of the superiority of letter recognition in words attribute the effect to feedback from familiar visual letter patterns contained within higher-order representations to facilitate lower-level letter processing. The finding that the letter-by-letter reader, JDC, did *not* show the expected advantage for words led Warrington and Shallice (1980) to formulate their proposal that the deficit in reading is to be found in the visual lexicon or word-form system, so that higher-level information is no longer able to influence letter processing.

Recent work by Reuter-Lorenz and Brunn (1990) casts doubt on the soundness of the failure of Warrington and Shallice to observe a word superiority effect. Reuter-Lorenz and Brunn suggest that lack of pattern-masking of stimuli, lack of control of overall performance level, and lenient scoring criteria may all have contributed to the failure to find the effect. All these factors have been shown to reduce the magnitude of the effect in normal subjects (e.g. Estes & Brunn, 1987; Johnston & McClelland, 1973; McClelland, 1976). When Reuter-Lorenz and Brunn took these methodological considerations into account, their letter-by-letter reader WL *was* significantly more accurate in reporting letters in words than letters in pseudowords and random letter strings, leading these authors to conclude that higher-level visual representations are sufficiently intact at least for the word advantage to appear. We followed the same procedure in examining whether PD would also show a word-superiority effect in letter recognition. This procedure also enabled us to investigate whether PD would show signs of an "ends-in" procedure in letter recognition similar to that which Reuter-Lorenz and Brunn observed with WL.

Method

Subjects. As well as our case study subject, a non-brain-injured control subject took part in this and the other experiments reported here. The control subject was 64 years of age and was selected as a control because of generally slow reaction-time performances. She did not, of course, show effects of letter length on reading speed, or any other sequelae of letter-by-letter reading.

Materials. Ninety-five 4-letter words were selected from the Kuçera and Francis (1967) lists. All were low in frequency (less than 15 per million) and none of the letters in each word was duplicated. Ninety-five pronounceable nonwords (pseudowords) and 95 random, nonpronounceable strings were formed by shuffling the letters of each word (e.g. *nest*, *sten*, *tsne*). Words, pseudowords, and nonwords were then sorted into 6 lists of 25 items (experimental set) and 9 lists of 15 items (practice set). Items derived from the same letter set did not appear in the same list. The practice set was used to determine the threshold for duration of the letter strings (see following).

Design and Procedure. The experiment (along with the others reported in this paper) was run on an Apple Macintosh SE computer, using the PsychLab package written by Gum and Bub (Note 1). Each string comprised 4 upper-case letters and subtended 2° of visual angle, with the final letter of each string 1° to the left of fixation. The fixation point was a full stop which remained on the screen for the duration of the experiment. Each letter string was presented for a predetermined time and was immediately followed by a pattern mask (&&&&) for 100msec.

Each subject was told at the beginning of the experiment that some of the letter strings would be familiar to them, while others would be unfamiliar. They were told that their task was to report each letter of the string in its correct position and guessing was encouraged. The subjects were asked to write down their responses on sheets in which there were rows of 4 boxes for each of the 4-letter items. The experimenter began each trial by pressing the space bar on the keyboard when the subject was ready. Order of trials was randomised, and subjects were *not* told beforehand whether the next trial would contain a word, pseudoword, or random letterstring.

Laboratory studies have shown that the best conditions for a word superiority effect to appear require masked exposure and an accuracy level of around 45–55% correct (e.g. Adams, 1979; McClelland, 1976). The duration at which that level of accuracy could be obtained was determined experimentally at the beginning of the test sessions. During presentation of the practice set stimuli, exposure durations were adjusted so that subjects' level of accuracy reached 65–75% *without* a mask and dropped to 45–55% accuracy *with* a mask.

Results and Discussion

PD required a masked exposure duration of 1750msec. to achieve required levels of accuracy, whereas the control required only 50msec. When items with correct letters in their correct positions were counted, PD was found to have identified successfully 22/50 words, 22/50 pseudowords, and 8/50 random letter strings. Differences between words and random letters and between pseudowords and random letters are both significant ($P < 0.01$), although there is obviously no difference between words and pseudowords in the number correctly identified. The control subject identified significantly more words (41/50) than pseudowords (25/50), and significantly more pseudowords than nonpronounceable nonwords (6/50). These differences were all significant at $P < 0.01$.

An analysis of PD's error responses was carried out by marking correct and incorrect letters according to serial position of the string (excluding trials on which there were no errors). Figure 2 illustrates the percentage of correct reports of individual letters across each of the four letter positions. It shows quite clearly that, *regardless of string type*, letters in the first two positions of the error are generally identified correctly, the third letter position is slightly less well identified, but the final letter is considerably less likely to have been reported. This pattern of response is in accord with what one would expect from a serial processing strategy in which letters are processed in a left-to-right sequence and is different from the pattern shown by the control subject who generally performs at least as well on the final letter as on the second and third letters. In contrast to PD, following the same procedure, patient WL (Reuter-Lorenz & Brunn, 1990) was most accurate in reporting first and *last* letters of letter strings. This pattern was also observed in the control subject tested in the same experiment as WL, and would also be expected in normal subjects under lateralised viewing conditions (Bouma, 1987).

The failure to find an advantage of words over pseudowords in PD's performance is not only different from the control subject, it is also different from the pattern shown by Reuter-Lorenz and Brunn's (1990) patient WL. Some recent accounts propose that the pseudoword superiority effect comes about because pseudowords can make use of the system set up for word recognition whereby activation spreads between lexical members of an orthographic neighbourhood (cf. McClelland & Rumelhart, 1981). On this view, words are additionally advantaged merely because they can activate their whole-word descriptions as well as common segments in visually similar words. Since PD *does* appear to be able to take

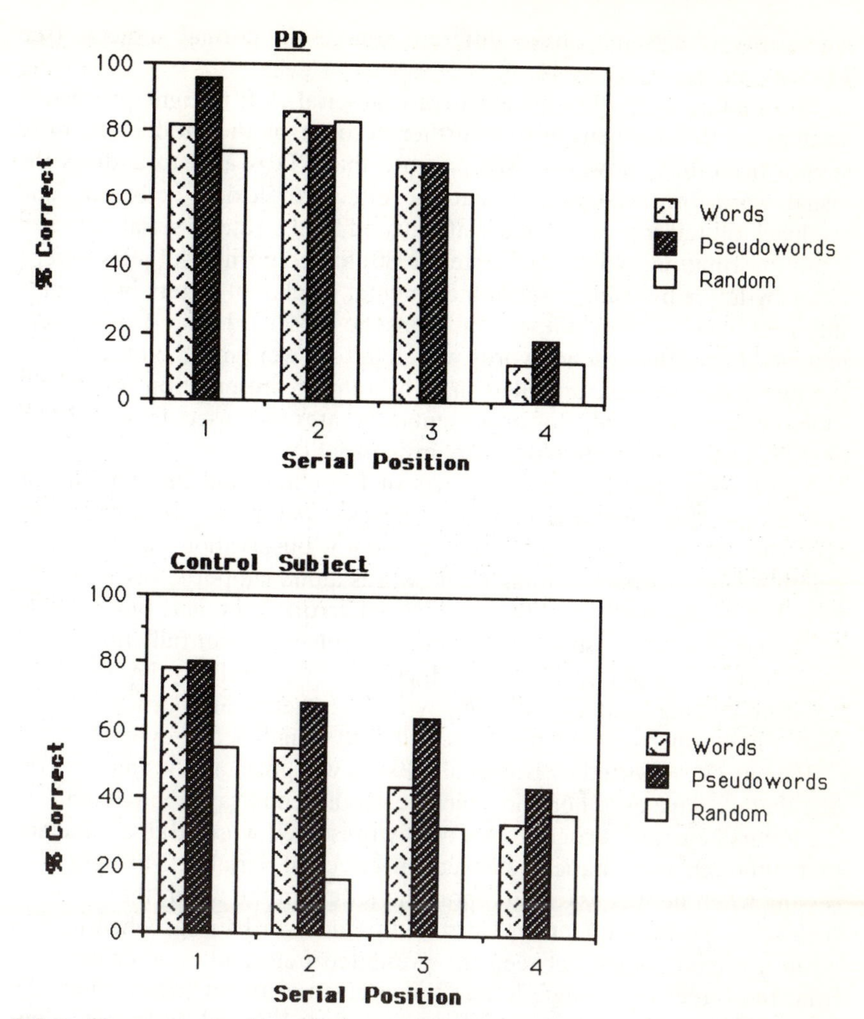

FIG. 2 The percentage of letters correctly reported in each serial position in Experiment 1 on trials in which one or more letters were reported incorrectly.

advantage of higher-order information about commonly occurring letter patterns compared with his ability to report random letter strings, the question is whether this information is specified *lexically*. Note that one need not invoke the suggestion that PD uses higher-order lexical orthographic knowledge. The advantage for words and pseudowords might have come about because there is a level between word and letter descriptions in which sub-lexical information about letter patterns is represented. Alternatively, common letter patterns may be more readily coded in phonological short-term memory than random conjunctions of letters. Both these proposals are consistent with the view that the word and pseudoword superiority effects may have different sources in normal subjects (see Manelis, 1974).

The finding that PD appears to use a serial, left-to-right processing strategy in this task suggests a further account of the moderated word superiority effect, however. We propose that PD *is* able to address the visual word-form system but that the effects of lexical activation and feedback on letter processing are attenuated by the rate of serial access of letter information. Note that Forster (1980) forced normal subjects to read letter-by-letter by using a serial incremental display of letters in a same–different task. Under these conditions he observed that words were matched faster than pseudowords, which in turn were matched faster than random letter strings, provided that the rate of presentation was "fast" (40msec./letter). Under slower presentation rates (400msec./letter), differences between the string types were insignificant.

The finding that PD shows effects of frequency and imageability on reading speed in normal reading also suggests that he may be able to gain access to the visual word-form system and our observation that he makes mainly visual errors in reading single words aloud supports this view. We have not established *why* PD makes visual errors, however, but this may be, in part, because visual word-forms themselves are not fully functional. Note that we cannot easily ascribe these errors entirely to the use of his serial processing strategy, since many other patients and normal subjects do not make such errors when forced to read serially letter-by-letter.

Patient JV, reported by Bub et al. (1989), was given a task similar to the one that we have used here, in which he was asked to say aloud as many of the letters he could recognise in a briefly presented word. Bub et al. claim that although their patient showed an effect of serial left-to-right processing when he was asked to report the letters in the word, there was no such serial position effect for word and pseudoword strings when he was given a forced choice between the presented item and another differing from the target by a single letter. When given a forced choice, then, JV behaved like Reuter-Lorenz and Brunn's patient WL and showed evidence of "ends-in" processing. When asked to name letters, he showed a serial processing effect like PD. It seems that for Bub et al.'s patient, more information about briefly presented letter strings was activated than could actually be retrieved for an *explicit* naming response. In Experiment 2, we examined whether this might also be the case for PD.

Experiment 2: A Second Look at Orthographic Context Effects

We used the procedure described by Friedrich et al. (1985), which was devised to examine the visual processing skills of patients with parietal lobe damage. Subjects were asked to decide whether two simultaneously presented letter strings were the same or different. On "different" trials, Friedrich et al.'s control subjects responded more quickly when the mismatch occurred at the start or at the end of words rather than in the middle, consistent with use of an ends-in procedure in letter recognition. This task, therefore, enabled us to investigate whether PD might show evidence of ends-in processing when the task does not require explicit naming. Furthermore, Friedrich et al.'s control subjects responded more quickly when the stimuli comprised words rather than nonwords. This meant that we were also able to examine whether PD would show a word superiority effect under conditions where memory factors are likely to be negligible.

Friedrich et al. (1985) always presented stimulus pairs in the same case. In our study, we also presented the stimuli in different case. The reason for this was to discover whether PD would experience more difficulties when decisions could not be made on the basis of physical identity and required that the abstract identities of the letters be established.

Method

Materials. Eighteen common words (6 4-letter words, 6 5-letter words and 6 6-letter words) were paired with 18 words of the same letter and syllable length, differing by only a single letter. The different letter was either at the beginning (e.g. *cork-work*), middle (e.g. *firm-farm*), or end (e.g. *plum-plug*), with the same number of word-pairs in each of these conditions. The "middle" of the word for 4-letter words was either the second or third letter (e.g. *wind-wand*, *fate-face*), and either the third or fourth letter for 6-letter words (e.g. *clever-clover*, *hearth-health*). These pairs required a "different" response.

Eighteen "same" pairs were constructed using equal numbers of 4-, 5-, and 6-letter words (e.g. *cork-cork*, *lemon-lemon*, *health-health*). Nonword pairs were devised by jumbling constituent letters of word pairs to form nonpronounceable strings. "Different" nonword pairs maintained the same point of difference found in corresponding word pairs (e.g. *crko-wrko*, *rafm-rifm*, *lpum-lpug*). Eighteen "different" nonword pairs and 18 "same" pairs were constructed.

Design and Procedure. On each trial, two letter strings were presented, one appearing horizontally immediately above the other. Strings with six letters subtended 3° of visual angle, strings with five letters 2.5°, and strings with four letters 2° of visual angle. The final letter in each string appeared 1° to the left of the fixation point. Stimulus pairs remained on the screen until the subject made a response.

Stimulus lists were shown in two modes of presentation in an ABBA design:

(A) *Difference case*: One member of each pair appeared in upper case, the other in lower case (e.g. *cork-WORK*). Upper- and lower-case versions appeared an equal number of times in each position of the pairs.

(B) *Same case*: Both pairs were presented in lower case.

As PD used the index finger of his nonpreferred left hand for making a response, two keys on the bottom row of the left side of the keyboard were designated as "same" and "different" buttons. The keys were separated by a third key and PD returned his index finger to the bar underneath this key before the beginning of every trial. The control subject also used the same configuration of keys with her nonpreferred left hand.

Results

Mean reactions times for both PD and the control subject to produce correct "same" judgements to *same-case* and to *different-case* stimuli are shown in Fig. 3. Figure 4 presents the results from "different" decisions. For the control subject, a two-factor analysis of variance of correct "same" responses to *same-case* items revealed significant effects of string length (4-, 5-, and 6-letters) on reaction times ($F[2,102] = 16.21$; $P < 0.001$) and string type (word or nonword) ($F[1,102] = 53.36$; $P < 0.001$) and a significant interaction between these two factors ($F[2,102] = 10.87$; $P < 0.001$). Further analyses of the interaction using Newman-Keuls tests showed that (1) only reaction times to nonwords slowed with increasing letter length; length of word stimuli had no effect on R.T.s, and (2) mean R.T. differences between word and nonword responses were only significant with 5- and 6-letter stimuli (both at $P < 0.001$), but not with 4-letter items. A similar pattern of results was observed with *different-case* stimulus pairs. Analysis of variance showed significant effects of string length ($F[2,102] = 11.7$; $P < 0.001$), string type ($F[1,102] = 139.56$; $P < 0.001$) and a significant interaction ($F[2,102] = 9.03$; $P < 0.001$). Newman-Keuls tests showed that (1) the length effect (increasing R.T.s with increasing letter length) was present only for nonwords and not for words, and (2) there was an R.T. advantage for words at all letter lengths.

PD's results present a different picture. In making correct "same" decisions to stimulus pairs displayed in the *same case*, he showed a significant main effect of string length ($F[2,102] = 12.96$; $P < 0.001$), but no effect of string type ($F[1,102] = 0.64$) and no significant interaction ($F[2,102] = 1.05$). For PD, then, reaction times increase with letter length of stimulus pairs, but this happens for word as well as nonword pairs. In making correct "same" responses to pairs presented in *different cases*, he again showed a significant effect of string length ($F[2,102] = 18.24$; $P < 0.001$), but no effect of string type ($F[1,102] = 0.84$) or interaction between these factors ($F[2,102] = 0.97$).

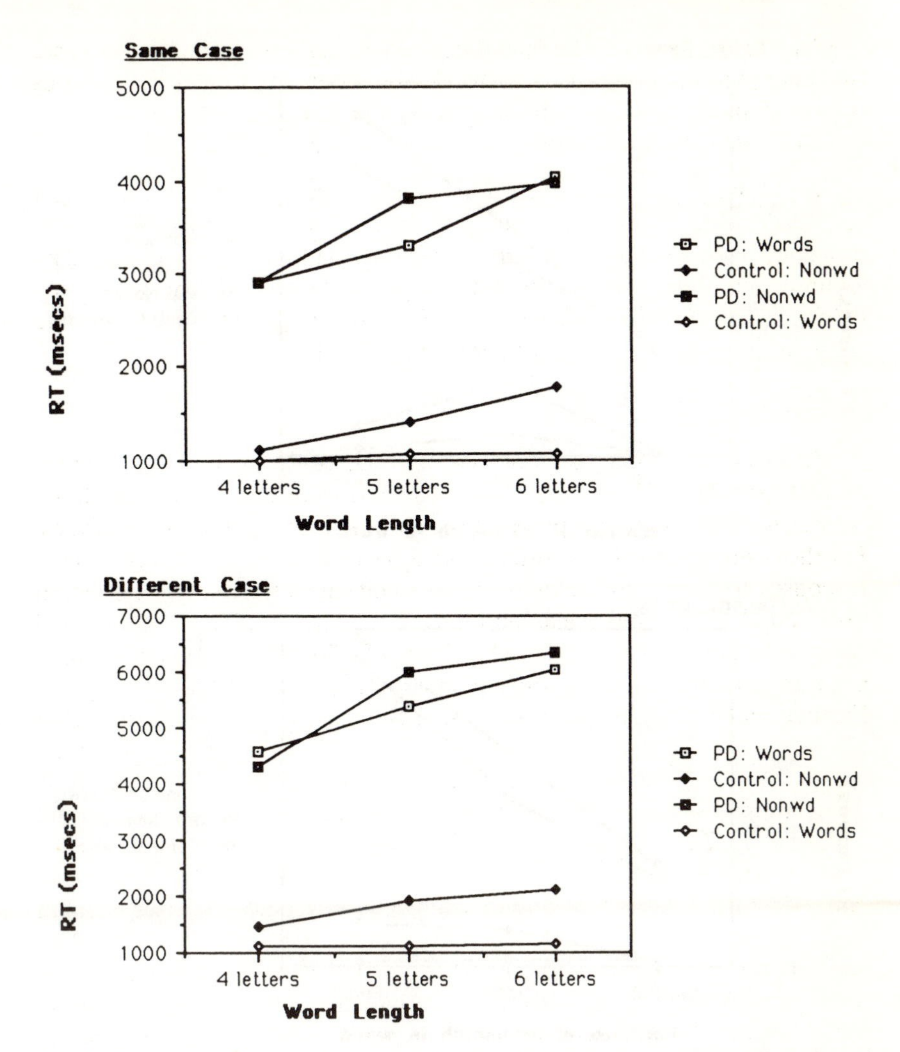

FIG. 3 The time taken to make "same" decisions in Experiment 2 as a function of word length and case.

Analysis of variance of "different" responses to *same-case* material demonstrates that, for the control subject, the position of difference between the stimulus pairs (initial, middle, final letters) had a significant effect on reaction time responses ($F[2,102] = 8.31$; $P < 0.001$), as did string type (word or nonword) ($F[1,102] = 9.19$; $P < 0.005$). The interaction between these factors was not significant ($F[2,102] = 2.58$). Analyses of these simple main effects show that when the difference between the stimulus pairs (whether word or nonword) occurs in the middle of the

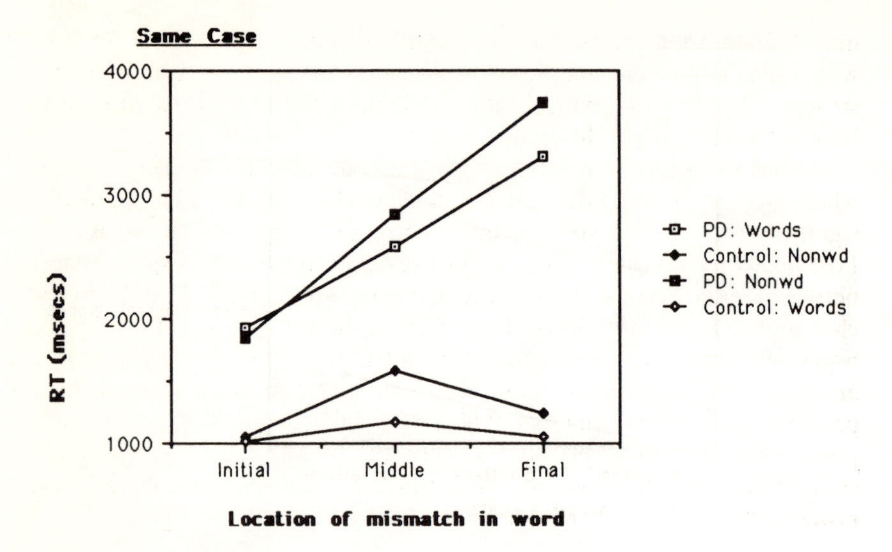

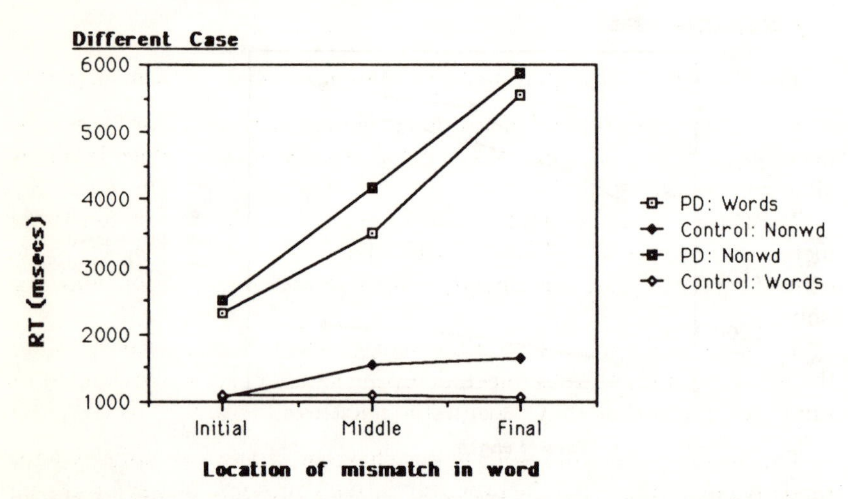

FIG. 4 The time taken to make "different" decisions in Experiment 2 as a function of the location of the difference within the word.

strings (e.g. *beach-bench*), reaction times were slower than when the difference occurs either at the beginning or end of the word (these positions did not differ). When "different" decisions to *different-case* material were analysed, a slightly different pattern of results emerged. The position of difference within the stimulus pairs exerted a significant effect ($F[2,102] = 9.24$; $P < 0.001$), as did string type ($F[1,102] = 37.85$; $P < 0.001$). This time, however, the interaction between position of difference and string type *was* significant ($F[2,102] = 10.85$; $P < 0.001$). Newman-Keuls tests revealed that (1) a word advantage was present for pairs which differed at the middle and ends, but not at the beginning of the strings; (2) for word pairs, there were no significant R.T. differences between each point of difference.

Again, PD showed a different pattern of results. For *same case* pairs, whereas there is no effect of string type ($F[1,102] = 1.67$), there is a significant effect of position of difference ($F[2,102] = 39.16$; $P < 0.001$). Post-hoc tests revealed that, in PD's case, he is fastest to spot changes between initial letters, then those between middle letters, and finally, changes between end letters. This effect is the same with both word and nonword stimuli, and no reaction time advantage for words was observed at any letter position. Pairs presented in *different cases* showed an identical pattern: no effect of string type ($F[1,102] = 2.65$), but a significant effect of position of difference ($F[2,102] = 66.12$; $P < 0.001$). Post-hoc tests again showed that, for both words and nonwords, initial letter changes were fastest, then middle letter changes and finally end letter changes.

Discussion

The findings of this experiment can be summarised in three main points:

1. PD fails to show a word advantage with either "same" or "different" decisions, whereas the control subject shows a word advantage in almost all experimental manipulations;
2. PD takes longer to make correct "same" judgements as letter length increases, regardless of whether stimulus pairs are words or nonwords. The control subject, on the other hand, shows letter length effects on nonwords only;
3. PD takes longer to spot letter changes when they occur at the end of the word. For the control subject, detecting letter changes takes longest for same case pairs when they occur in the middle of the word.

The overall pattern of results that we have shown for our letter-by-letter reader again indicate that he processes visually presented letter strings in a serial, left-to-right, fashion. Bub et al. (1989) suggest that a serial processing strategy may, to some extent, be dependent on the task demands: their letter-by-letter reader showed left-to-right processing of stimulus strings when the task required explicit report, but an "ends-in" pattern typical of normal encoding when the task was to judge which of two items (word, pseudoword, or nonword), which differed in just one letter, had just been displayed. Bub et al. (1989, p. 372) are cautious in their interpretation of these findings, but state that "the complete absence of any serial position effect on probe recognition scores . . . and their high level of accuracy, does indicate that some information is available to JV that is not captured by free report". The same-different task used here did not require explicit identification of stimulus pairs, but PD shows a very definite serial position effect nonetheless.

Our interpretation of the finding that PD fails to show a word superiority effect in this experiment is that for him, unlike normal subjects, activation of letter recognition units does not lead to the rapid activation (and feedback) of lexical representations in the visual word-form system that is a property of normal word recognition. This is due, in part at least, to the serial processing procedure that he uses. We would suggest that PD decides on "same" and "different" judgments *before* lexical representations are fully activated in the visual word-form system, by comparing letter identities across stimulus pairs. This view is supported by the length of time PD takes to read single words aloud in reading tests (e.g. word reading times illustrated in Fig. 1 show that he took 4.7sec. on average to read 4-letter words aloud, 9.2sec. to read 5-letter, and 13.6sec. to read 6-letter words aloud).

The control subject behaved in the same way as the control group reported by Friedrich et al. (1985) in making decisions to same-case stimuli. As Friedrich et al. only presented materials in the same case, it is worth investigating whether different processing mechanisms underpin position-of-difference effects with different-case pairs that we observed for our control subject. This finding notwithstanding, few differences in the effect of case presentation were observed. Perhaps the most obvious, however, was that PD took considerably longer to make decisions to different-case pairs than to same-case pairs (an overall increase of 1947msec. when stimulus pairs were the same and 1287msec. when they were different, compared with 237msec. and 70msec., respectively, for the control subject). This is consistent with the view that PD has particular problems when the decision must be based on more abstract letter processing rather than on physical identity. This distinction is investigated further in Experiment 3.

Experiment 3: Letter Processing Abilities

The results of the previous experiment show that PD found it particularly difficult to decide whether two letter strings were the same when they were presented in different case. This experiment examined his ability to make this decision when the stimuli were simply two letters. The letters were presented either sequentially or simultaneously, in either the same case or in different case. The procedure was based on that used by Posner and Mitchell (1967) and was identical to the one employed by Reuter-Lorenz and Brunn (1990, Experiment 2). Their patient, WL, was significantly slower than their control subjects at making "same" decisions when the letters were presented simultaneously. This occurred regardless of whether the letters were in same case (and could therefore be matched on the basis of either physical identity or some form of abstract letter identity), or were in different case (and could therefore be matched on the basis of abstract letter identity only). This is consistent with a general impairment in simultaneous form perception. WL also performed very slowly when letters were presented in different case under sequential presentation conditions, suggesting that he suffers from an additional deficit in letter analysis.

Method

Materials. Four stimulus letters with very different upper- and lower-case forms were selected (*Aa*, *Rr*, *Gg*, *Hh*). Each letter subtended approximately $0.7 \times 0.5°$ of visual angle. Two lists of 192 trials were comprised of 96 same and 96 different pairs. Of the 96 *same* pairs, 48 were physically identical and were divided equally into upper-case and lower-case pairs (e.g. *AA* or *aa*). Forty-eight had the same identity, but were presented in different cases (e.g. *Aa* or *aA*). The 96 *different* pairs were constructed by pairing each upper- and lower-case letter with the other 3 letters in the set (e.g. *ar*, *ag*, *ah*). "Different" pairs maintained equal numbers of same-case and cross-case stimuli (e.g. *ar*, *aR*, *Ar*, *AR*). Letter pairs were presented in random order in each of the lists.

Procedure. Stimulus items appeared side-by-side 1° to the left of the fixation point. Following the procedure of Reuter-Lorenz and Brunn (1990), two S.O.A.s were used. In the *simultaneous* condition both members of the pair appeared on the screen at the same time. In the *sequential* condition there was a 500msec. interval between the onset of the first and second members of the pair. In both conditions the stimulus pair remained on the screen until the response key was pressed. Subjects were instructed to respond "same" if the letters were either physically identical or had the same name; otherwise they were told to respond "different". The configuration of the decision keys was the same as that used in the previous experiment.

Results

The control subject and, more pertinently, PD, made few errors on this task (98% and 92% correct respectively). Reaction times (msec.) for both same and different decisions to each stimulus type and under each mode of presentation are displayed in Fig. 5.

Reaction-time data produced by PD and the control subject were analysed in separate three-factor ANOVA, with decision type (same, different), match type (physical match, nominal match), and S.O.A. (0, 500msec.) as separate factors. As one can see from Fig. 5, PD was faster to

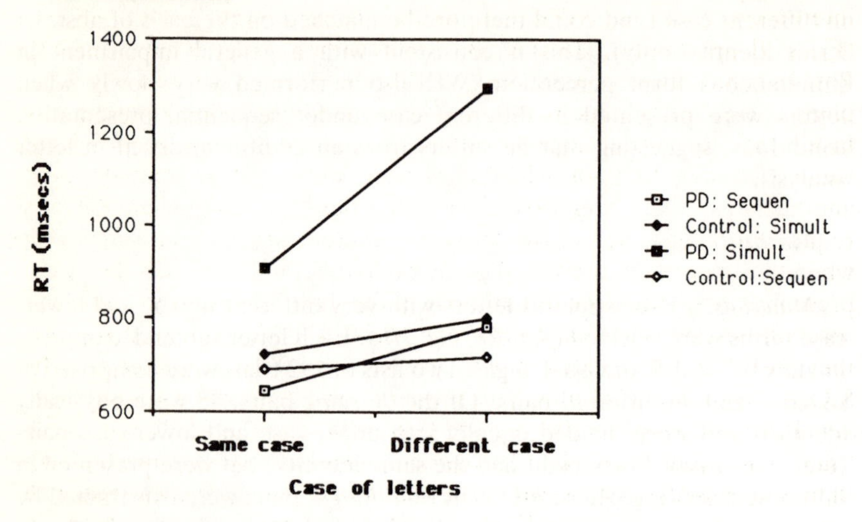

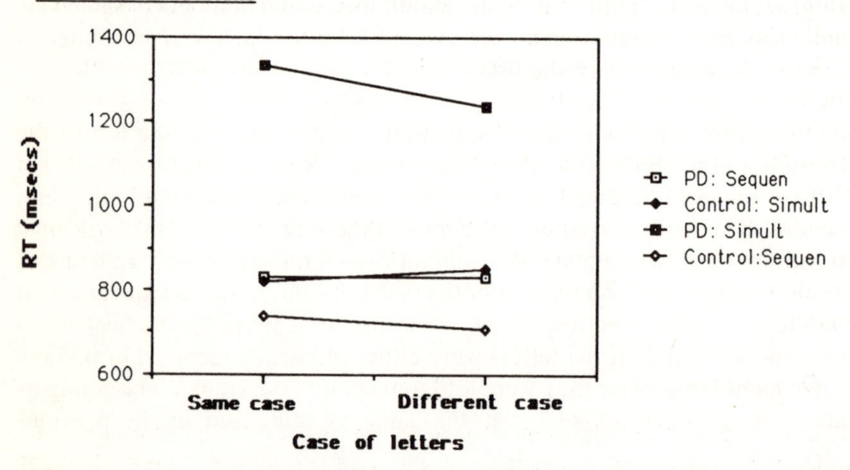

FIG. 5 The time required to make same and different decisions in Experiment 3 under simultaneous and sequential presentation conditions.

judge that letter pairs were the same than that they were different ($F[1,159] = 27.84$; $P < 0.001$). He was also significantly faster to make a decision when letter pairs were displayed sequentially than when they appeared simultaneously ($F[1,159] = 226.8$; $P < 0.001$). Physical matches were carried out significantly faster than name matches ($F[1,159] = 13.93$; $P < 0.001$), although the interaction between match type and decision type ($F[1,159] = 28.5$; $P < 0.001$) indicates that physical matching was only faster when "same" decisions were required. The significant three-way interaction between decision type, match type, and S.O.A. ($F[1,159] = 9.80$; $P < 0.002$) allows us to elaborate these findings further. Post-hoc comparisons using Newman-Keuls reveals that deciding on a physical match when the two letters were the same was only significantly faster than a name match decision when letter pairs were presented *simultaneously*, and not when they were presented sequentially. Put another way, there was a significant reaction-time cost when PD was required to judge whether two letters in different case had the same name when they were both presented at the same time, but not when they were presented one after the other. When the two letters were different, reaction times to same-case and cross-case stimuli were longer than when they were the same letter, but they were not affected differentially by S.O.A. In addition, simultaneous presentation consistently produced longer R.T.s than sequential presentation with different decisions. With "same" decisions, however, simultaneous decisions took very much longer than sequential decisions when they involved name matches, but with physical matches Newman-Keuls revealed that the difference between simultaneous and sequential presentation did not quite reach significance at $P = 0.05$.

In contrast, the only comparisons that reached statistical significance for the control subject were those associated with type of decision (different decisions took longer than same decisions, $P < 0.001$), and the type of presentation (simultaneous presentation was associated with longer R.T.s than sequential presentation, $P < 0.001$). None of the interactions was significant. Figure 5 suggests that PD's response times are particularly long in comparison with the control subject under simultaneous processing conditions when a decision cannot be made on the basis of a physical match.

Discussion

Deciding whether the same two letters presented in the same case are indeed the same can be carried out solely on the basis of their identical physical characteristics. The decision can also be reached, however, by deducing that the letter pairs have a common identity (whether that name code is derived from a common abstract visual form or from an abstract phonological form). Only the latter option is available to make a correct decision when the two letters are presented in different cases. We have shown that, overall, PD finds it more difficult to judge the identity of cross-case matches than physical matches, suggesting that he indeed uses more than one means of deciding whether two letters are the same. Nominal matching was considerably more affected than physical matching by S.O.A., so that reaction times to decide that 2 letters were the same increased by a substantial 511msec. when letter pairs were presented simultaneously compared with sequential presentation. Physical and nominal matching times were significantly different under conditions of simultaneous exposure, but did not differ under sequential exposure conditions. When the letters in a pair were different, simultaneous presentation also delayed reaction-time decisions relative to sequential presentation. Here, though, both cross-case *and* same-case stimuli provoked significant reaction-time increases, suggesting that PD is using information about letter identity rather than relying on straightforward physical differences when two different letters are presented in the same case (e.g. *A R*, *g a*).

Overall, these results suggest that PD's main impairment comes about under simultaneous presentation conditions when he has to make abstract letter-identity decisions. These findings fit quite neatly with Kinsbourne and Warrington's (1962) early claim that a simultaneous processing deficit emerges in letter-by-letter reading particularly when stimulus *identification* is required.[2]

Comparison with Patient WL (Reuter-Lorenz & Brunn, 1990)

Like PD, WL was significantly more impaired in making nominal matches than in matching on the basis of physical features. In judging that two letters were the same, WL also showed a strong effect of S.O.A., with reaction-time increases of approximately 450msec. under simultaneous exposure conditions relative to sequential onset. However, unlike PD, WL showed no interaction between match type and S.O.A.: both nominal *and* physical matching times increased to the same extent with simultaneous presentations. Reuter-Lorenz and Brunn propose that WL therefore shows two separate and possibly independent deficits which affect letter processing. One involves impairment in the encoding of simultaneous visual input and the other involves impairment in the operations that underlie name matches. More specifically, the authors suggest that WL is impaired in a stage in visual word recognition at which abstract letter identities are determined (following theoretical elaboration of this notion by Coltheart, 1981, and Evett & Humphreys, 1981).

---

[2]As PD took longer to judge that physically identical letter pairs were the same when they were presented simultaneously (although not significantly so), and because response times to same case/same decision items in Experiment 2 were also slowed, we conclude that his simultaneous processing deficit also affects physical identity matching to a degree, even though physical identity matching may itself be unaffected.

It is clear that, like WL, PD has a substantial deficit in processing simultaneously presented visual material. Whether the deficit is specific to letters and words, or also includes other forms of written material (e.g. digits, logographs), or visual material in general (simultanagnosia), we have yet to determine experimentally. Certainly, though, PD's ability to distinguish between real and made-up line-drawings of objects (Humphreys' and Riddoch's object decision task) is unimpaired, at least when time pressures are not imposed. What we have established is that the deficit appears particularly when identification of letter stimuli is required and is much less obvious when letter matching need not entail letter identification. In addition, since nominal matching occurred without significant reaction-time penalty under sequential processing conditions, we cannot conclude that PD also has a separate and possibly independent impairment in letter processing.

GENERAL DISCUSSION

Perhaps the most interesting aspect of the findings from the foregoing experiments is the implication that there are several important differences between individual letter-by-letter readers in terms of the point at which the normal reading process has broken down.

Letter Identification

Although PD does make an occasional error in letter identification (Hanley & Kay, Note 2), it is clear that this is a relatively mild impairment. In addition, the speed at which he made decisions about abstract letter identity under sequential presentation conditions in Experiment 3 was very similar to that of the control subject. By contrast, WL (Reuter-Lorenz & Brunn, 1990) was very slow at making this type of decision. Although the task was not directly comparable, JV, the letter-by-letter reader described by Bub et al. (1989), also shows evidence of impaired letter processing on same–different judgements about letter identity under tachistoscopic conditions. Thus PD's letter identification skills appear to be very much less severely impaired than those of WL and JV. Note that in terms of naming latencies in word reading, PD and JV show broadly comparable effects of letter length (3–6 letters) on reading speed, whereas WL is substantially faster at all letter lengths.

Serial Processing of Letters

Despite his superior letter identification skills, PD shows much stronger evidence of left-to-right serial processing of letters than either WL or JV. Regardless of whether the task involves explicit report of letter identities

(Experiment 1), or deciding whether two letter-strings are the same or different (Experiment 2), PD shows no sign of an "ends in" strategy in processing letters. In contrast, there is evidence that WL employs an "ends in" procedure in explicitly reporting letters in words and that JV also processes letter-strings in a similar way, at least when the task requires a forced-choice response.

It would be interesting to know whether WL uses an "ends in" strategy in recognising words in other situations, including reading words under normal conditions. As Ellis, Young, and Anderson (1988) point out, an "ends in" strategy is not necessarily inconsistent with a letter-length effect, since the longer the word the longer it will take to reach the letters in the middle. Investigation of WL's performance using the techniques employed by Friedrich et al. (1985) would provide further information on this question.

Word-superiority Effects

PD also differs from WL in that he shows very limited evidence of a word-superiority effect in processing letters. Unlike WL, PD does not report letters more accurately when they appear in words than in pseudowords (Experiment 1), and he did not show any advantage of words over random letter-strings in same–different decisions in Experiment 2. It would, therefore, appear to be the case that for some letter-by-letter readers, such as PD and perhaps JDC (Warrington & Shallice, 1980), activation of letter recognition units does not lead to rapid activation of lexical representations in the word-form system. This, we suggest, may be a consequence of a serial processing procedure. For others, such as WL, these associations appear to be at least partially operational, although it does not necessarily follow that these links play any role in the way that this patient reads words under normal circumstances. It would be interesting for future studies to determine whether word superiority effects in letter-by-letter readers are dependent upon the availability of an "ends in strategy" in letter processing.

Simultaneous Form Perception

PD was very seriously impaired in making same decisions about simultaneously presented letter-strings when the letters were presented in different case and it was impossible to base a decision on physical identity. In Experiment 3, when letters were visible simultaneously, PD's matching was much less severely impaired when the letters were presented in the same case. WL, by contrast, was every bit as impaired with same-case matching as with different-case matching (Reuter-Lorenz & Brunn, 1990).

The particular difficulty that is shared by both patients in processing *abstract* forms of letters in parallel may be the one that is critical, however, in producing the letter-by-letter reading deficit.

Conclusion

It is clear from the present investigation that letter-by-letter reading is a strategy that is used to compensate for subtly different types of reading impairment in individual cases. PD appears to suffer from an inability to identify letters in parallel (cf. Patterson & Kay, 1982). He also uses a left-to-right processing strategy in the reading tests we have explored with him. Other letter-by-letter readers such as WL (Reuter-Lorenz & Brunn, 1990) seem able to use information from the ends of words which suggests that a serial procedure is not an obligatory feature of letter-by-letter reading (see also Rapp & Caramazza, this issue). Similar gradient effects have been reported with tachistoscopic presentation for some neglect dyslexic patients (e.g. patient MO reported by Riddoch et al., this issue), although these effects are manifested in different ways in the two syndromes. Future work must explore the precise form of these and other impairments in peripheral dyslexias. This in turn may provide rich insights into the nature of the psychological processes involved in the early stages of word recognition.

Manuscript received 23 March 1990
Revised manuscript received 15 June 1990

REFERENCES

Adams, M. J. (1979). Models of word recognition. *Cognitive Psychology*, *11*, 133–176.

Bouma, A. (1987). Serial position curves for the identification of letter strings in visual half-field studies. *Journal of Clinical and Experimental Neuropsychology*, *9*, 22.

Bradley, L. (1980). *Assessing reading difficulties: A diagnostic approach*. London: Macmillan.

Bub, D. N., Black, S., & Howell, J. (1989). Word recognition and orthographic context effects in a letter-by-letter reader. *Brain and Language*, *36*, 357–376.

Coltheart, M. (1981). Disorders of reading and their implications for models of normal reading. *Visible Language*, *15*, 245–286.

Ellis, A. W., Flude, B., & Young, A. W. (1987). 'Neglect dyslexia and the early visual processing of letters in words and nonwords. *Cognitive Neuropsychology*, *4*, 439–464.

Ellis, A. W., Young, A. W., & Anderson, C. (1988). Modes of word recognition in the left and right cerebral hemispheres. *Brain and Language*, *35*, 254–273.

Estes, W. K. & Brunn, J. L. (1987). Discriminability and bias in the word superiority effect. *Perception and Psychophysics*, *42*, 411–422.

Evett, L. & Humphreys, G. W. (1981). The use of abstract graphemic information in lexical access. *Quarterly Journal of Experimental Psychology, 33A*, 325–350.

Forster, K. I. (1980). Absence of lexical and orthographic effects in a same–different task. *Memory and Cognition, 8*, 210–215.

Friedrich, F. J., Walker, J. A., & Posner, M. I. (1985). Effects of parietal lesions on visual matching: Implications for reading errors. *Cognitive Neuropsychology, 2*, 253–264.

Hanley, J. R., Pearson, N. P., & Young, A. (in press). Impaired memory for new visual forms. *Brain*.

Johnston, J. C. & McClelland, J. L. (1973). Visual factors in word perception. *Perception and Psychophysics, 14*, 365–370.

Kay, J., Lesser, R., & Coltheart, M. (in press). *Psycholinguistic assessments of language processing in aphasia (P.A.L.P.A.)*. London: Lawrence Erlbaum Associates Ltd.

Kinsbourne, M. & Warrington, E. K. (1962). A disorder of simultaneous form perception. *Brain, 85*, 461–486.

Kuçera, H. & Francis, W. N. (1967). *Computational analysis of present-day American English*. Providence, Rhode Island: Brown University Press.

McClelland, J. L. (1976). Preliminary letter identification in perception of words and letters. *Journal of Experimental Psychology: Human Perception and Performance, 2*, 80–91.

McClelland, J. L. & Rumelhart, D. E. (1981). An interactive activation model of context effects in letter perception. *Psychological Review, 88*, 375–407.

McKenna, P. & Warrington, E. K. (1983). *The Graded-Naming Test*. Windsor: N.F.E.R.-Nelson.

Manelis, L. (1974). The effect of meaningfulness in tachistoscopic word perception. *Perception and Psychophysics, 16*, 182–192.

Patterson, K. E. & Kay, J. (1982). Letter-by-letter reading: Psychological descriptions of a neurological syndrome. *Quarterly Journal of Experimental Psychology, 34A*, 411–441.

Pelli, D. G., Robson, J. G., & Wilkins, A. J. (1988). The design of a new letter chart for measuring contrast sensitivity. *Clinical Vision Science, 2*, 187–199.

Posner, M. I. & Mitchell, R. F. (1967). Chronometric analysis of classification. *Psychological Review, 74*, 392–409.

Posner, M. I. & Snyder, C. R. R. (1975). Attention and cognitive control. In R. L. Solso (Ed.), *Information processing and cognition: The Loyola Symposium*. Hillsdale, N.J.: Lawrence Erlbaum Associates Inc.

Rapp, B. C. & Caramazza, A. (1990). Spatially determined deficits in letter and word processing. *Cognitive Neuropsychology, 7*, 653–689.

Reuter-Lorenz, P. A. & Brunn, J. L. (1990). A prelexical basis for letter-by-letter reading. *Cognitive Neuropsychology, 7*, 1–20.

Riddoch, M. J., Cleton, P., Fery, P., & Humphreys, G. W. (1990). Interaction of attentional and lexical processes in neglect dyslexia. *Cognitive Neuropsychology*, this volume.

Shallice, T. (1988). *From neuropsychology to cognitive structure*. Cambridge: Cambridge University Press.

Warrington, E. K. (1984). *Recognition Memory Test*. Windsor: N.F.E.R.-Nelson.

Warrington, E. K. & Shallice, T. (1980). Word-form dyslexia. *Brain, 103*, 99–112.

Wing, A. M. & Baddeley, A. D. (1980). Spelling errors in handwriting: A corpus and a distributional analysis. In U. Frith (Ed.), *Cognitive processes in spelling*. London: Academic Press.

REFERENCE NOTES

1. Gum, T. & Bub, D. N. (1988). *PsychLab*. Software for the Apple Macintosh. Montreal Neurological Institute, Quebec, Canada.
2. Hanley, J. R. & Kay, J. (1989). *Letter-by-letter reading does not involve the spelling system*. Paper presented to the Experimental Psychology Society, Oxford.

COGNITIVE NEUROPSYCHOLOGY, 1991, *8* (3/4) 275–311

Spatially Determined Deficits in Letter and Word Processing

Brenda C. Rapp and Alfonso Caramazza
The Johns Hopkins University, Baltimore, U.S.A.

We describe the performance of a brain-damaged subject, HR, whose reading performance can be described as letter-by-letter reading. On a number of experimental tasks she exhibited deficits in letter and bar detection. Her performance in these tasks indicated that her impairment in nonlexical letter detection tasks is spatially determined. We interpret the results within a multi-stage model of prelexical visual/perceptual processing. Within such a model, the impairments can be attributed to deficits at retino-centric and stimulus-centred levels of representation. We explain HR's letter-by-letter reading performance in terms of these deficits. In addition, we attempt to account for the differences in reading performance among patients with spatially determined deficits in terms of the proposed multi-stage model of word recognition.

INTRODUCTION

The recognition of a printed word in reading involves, among other things, the mapping of a spatially arranged set of visual forms onto a stored representation of letter identities and positions. For example, the presentation of the visual information such as *CHAIR* or *chair* allows us to access the knowledge that C+H+A+I+R is a word of the English language. In order to do this, the reading system must solve the problem of extracting and representing, from an array of light intensities, information regarding the identity and order of letters. Considerable research efforts have been dedicated to increasing our understanding of the nature of the represent-

---

Requests for reprints should be addressed to Brenda Rapp, Cognitive Science Centre, The Johns Hopkins University, Baltimore, MD 21218, U.S.A.

This research was supported by N.I.H. grant NS22201 and by grants from the Seaver Institute and the McDonnell/Pew Program in Cognitive Neuroscience. This support is gratefully acknowledged. We would like to thank HR and her husband, GR, for their patience, good humour, and friendship throughout this project. We also would like to thank Marlene Behrmann, Glyn Humphreys, Jane Riddoch, and Eric Siéroff for helpful comments on an earlier version of this paper.

ations and processes required to achieve this mapping from visual to orthographic information.

One potential source of data has been the performance of patients who have suffered neurological damage. Among the patients of interest are those who exhibit symptoms of unilateral spatial neglect—loosely defined as a difficulty in processing information in the part of space that is contralateral to the hemisphere of lesion. The deficits of these patients are not necessarily restricted simply to reading but can extend to other tasks within the visual domain that require the adequate processing of spatially arrayed stimuli. However, the performance of such patients is potentially of interest to those who wish to study the reading process, precisely because in reading a spatially arrayed input must be processed successfully (see Kinsbourne & Warrington, 1962). Thus, data from patients with deficits in spatial processing may provide clues regarding the way in which spatial aspects of the visual array are processed and represented in reading.

In this paper we will describe the performance of a patient who demonstrates a deficit in spatial processing. As has been the case with neglect patients, the spatial aspects of the deficit will allow us to draw certain conclusions regarding the levels of representation and processing involved in reading. The patient we studied, however, differed from patients with unilateral visual neglect in a number of ways. First, she did not exhibit the classical symptoms of neglect in terms of her performance on copying, line cancellation, and line bisection tasks. Second, her reading performance differed from that often reported for neglect patients. That is, she did not produce responses typical of "neglect dyslexia" that consist of substitutions or deletions of the part of a word that lies in the neglected region of space (PEACH → pea or pearl). Instead her reading can be described as "letter-by-letter" reading—the patient claimed that she could not read a word unless she first identified each of the individual letters of the word (PEACH → P,E,A,C,H → peach). However, it is important to emphasise that we will use the terms neglect dyslexia and letter-by-letter reading simply as descriptive of observable behaviours. Applying such a description, therefore, has no implications regarding the homogeneity of the group of patients so described. We take it that there is no reason to suppose, a priori, that any given pattern of behaviour results from only one possible deficit to the underlying processing system or, vice versa, that apparently dissimilar deficits arise from fundamentally distinct forms of impairment.

Data from the patient described in this report will be used to: (1) draw inferences regarding the multiple levels of spatial representation computed in the course of reading, and (2) develop a hypothesis that accounts for certain differences in reading performance that are observed among patients with spatial deficits—specifically we will offer a proposal to account for the fact that this patient's reading can be characterised as letter-by-letter reading while the reading of neglect patients has the characteristics of neglect dyslexia described earlier.

CASE HISTORY

HR, a high-school graduate, homemaker, and avid reader, suffered a left C.V.A. subsequent to coronary bypass surgery in 1985 at the age of 62. C.T.-scan results indicated a low-density region behind the occipital horn of the left lateral ventricle. Perimeter testing revealed a field cut beyond 15° in the right eye and 25° in the left eye. Corrected acuity was 20/20 in the right eye and 20/40 in the left. Though naturally left-handed, as a child she was required to write with her right hand in school.

Testing in our laboratory was carried out between 8/86 and 10/89.[1] Testing results indicated that HR's spontaneous speech was fluent and well formed with evidence of a slight anomia. The latter impairment revealed itself in picture naming, where she was 85% (44/52) correct. Sentence completion was flawless (10/10). Repetition of single words and nonwords was 100% (53/53) correct, as was her auditory comprehension of sentences (26/26). HR demonstrated impaired performance in spelling, where her accuracy in writing to dictation was 63% (205/325) and in oral spelling 62% (26/42). In both tasks errors were primarily phonologically plausible spellings (e.g. fruit → frute, in writing; grief → G,R,E,E,F, in oral spelling).

HR showed no difficulties in line cancellation and bisection tasks or in copying complex drawings (see Fig. 1).

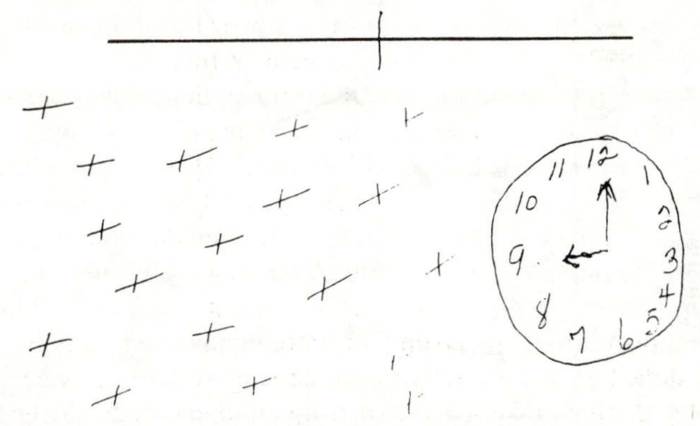

FIG. 1 Examples of HR's performance in copying, line bisection, and line cancellation.

[1]Although some quantitative improvement was noted during this time, performance remained, qualitatively, the same. For example, although letter-by-letter reading was performed more quickly and more words were read apparently without letter-by-letter identification, HR continued to read most words in a letter-by-letter manner at the end of the testing period.

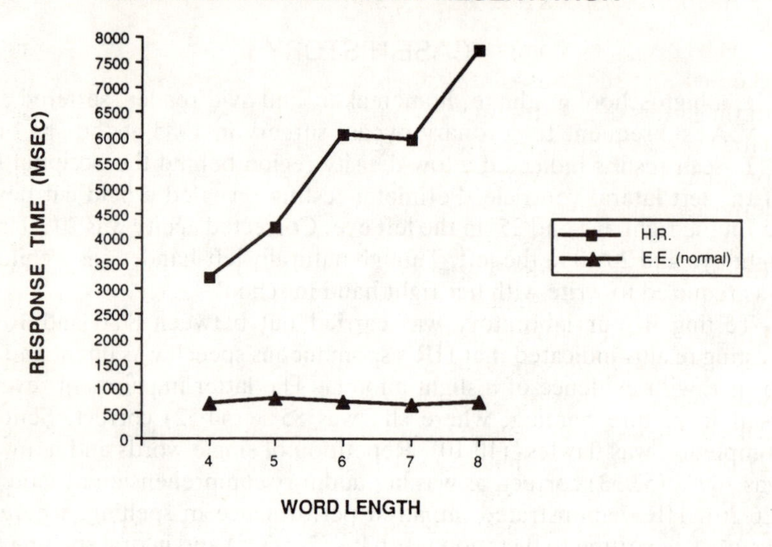

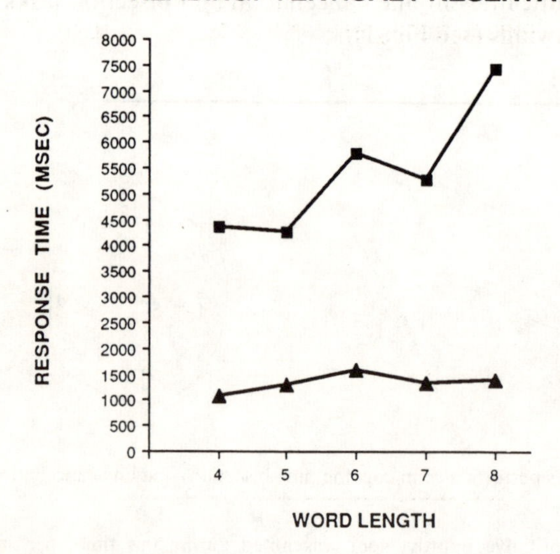

FIG. 2 The relationship between word length and response time in reading for HR and control subject EE.

Reading

Response Times and Word Length

Her principal complaint concerned her difficulties in reading. She claimed that she could not read naturally but instead had to identify most of the letters of a word, one at a time, before she could recognise the word. However, as is often reported for letter-by-letter readers, she reported that on some occasions words were recognised effortlessly, without letter-by-letter identification.

As is typically described for other letter-by-letter readers (see Bub, Black, & Howell, 1989; Farah & Wallace, this issue; Friedman & Alexander, 1984; Kay & Hanley, this issue; Patterson & Kay, 1982; Reuter-Lorenz & Brunn, 1990; Shallice & Saffran, 1986; Warrington & Shallice, 1980), reading response times (the time between the presentation of a word and the onset of a response) increased as a function of word length. This occurred for both horizontally and vertically displayed words (see Fig. 2) presented with unlimited viewing duration. Lexical decision times for words and nonwords showed a similar function (Fig. 3). As would be expected, her reading accuracy as a function of word length varied according to exposure duration (Fig. 4).

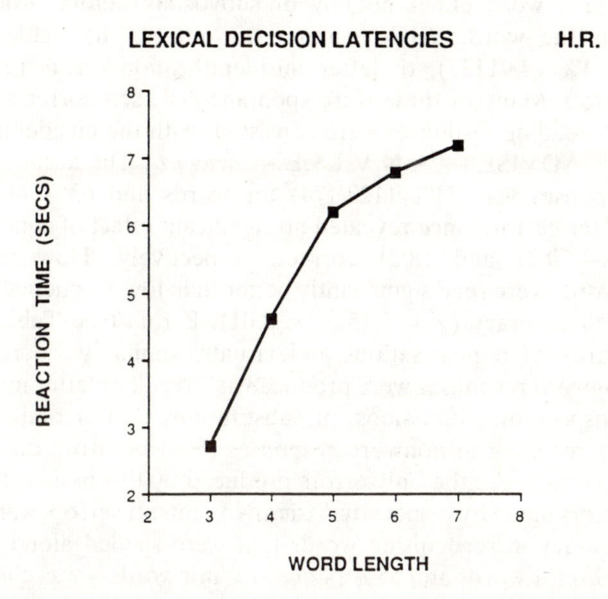

FIG. 3 The relationship between word length and response time in lexical decision for HR.

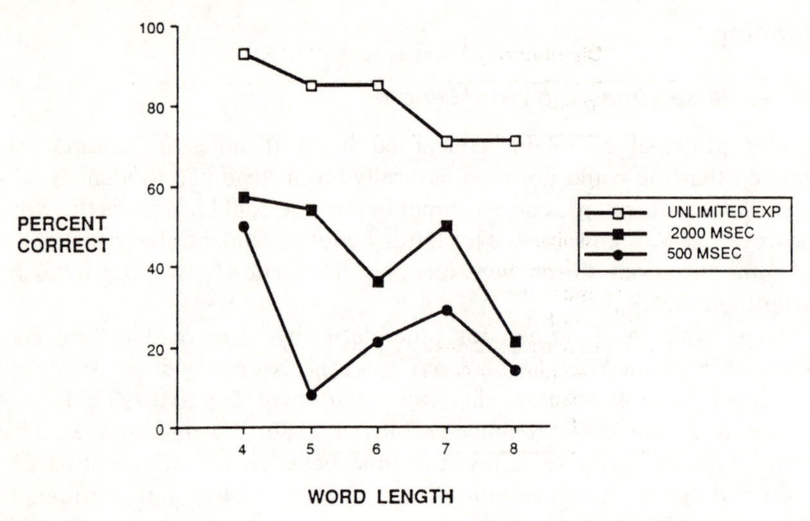

FIG. 4 The relationship between word length and reading accuracy with different exposure durations for HR.

Error Types

Within an unlimited exposure duration HR typically identified most of the letters in a word either audibly or subvocally before producing a response for the word. While naming the letters, she made a small proportion, 4% (43/1127), of letter misidentification errors (e.g. Y/R; N/D, S/T, etc.). Many of these were spontaneously self-corrected. When uncorrected, reading responses were consistent with the misidentification; for example, ADVISE → A,N,V,I,S,E → /ænvɔiz/. The accuracy of her reading responses was 73% (127/174) for words and 63% (43/68) for nonwords. Her performance revealed no significant effect of concreteness/abstractness—20/21 and 18/21 correct, respectively. However, high-frequency words were read significantly better than low-frequency words—85% vs. 65% accuracy ($\chi^2 = 7.15$, $P < 0.01$). Errors (see Table 1) consisted primarily of regularisations and visually similar word responses, although nonword responses were produced as a result of letter misidentifications, transpositions, omissions, or substitutions. Letter omissions and substitutions resulting in nonword responses (5%) occurred on the right side of words and were the only errors produced by this patient that were similar to errors made by neglect dyslexics. No semantic errors were made.

HR's accuracy in recognising words that were spelled aloud to her—77% (151/196) for words and 65% (44/68) for nonwords—was comparable to her performance in reading.

TABLE 1
Distribution of Responses in Oral Reading

Type of Response	*% (no.)*
Correct	73% (127/174)
Regularisations	9% (16/174)
ARGUE → /ɑrdʒu/	
Visually similar word	7% (13/174)
SCIENCE → /sɪns/	
Letter misidentification	5% (8/174)
DENY → B,E,D,Y → /bɛdi/	
Omissions & substitutions	5% (8/174)
RIOT → /raɪou/; ANNOY → /ʌnau/	
Transpositions	1% (2/174)
STARVE → /streɪv/	

Access to Semantic Information

Shallice and Saffran (1986) and Bub and Bruemmer (1988) have claimed that semantic information may be available to letter-by-letter readers under conditions when they are unable to identify a word correctly (but see Patterson & Kay, 1982; Warrington & Shallice, 1980). We attempted to determine if semantic information was available to HR under limited exposure conditions, when she would often report that she had not had time to "see" the word.

Following procedures similar to those described by Shallice and Saffran (1986), stimuli were presented in alternating blocks for either 2-choice categorisation or reading. A total of 8 blocks were presented using an exposure duration of 500msec. for each item. Before each block HR was told the 2 semantic categories (e.g. body parts/animals) that the words to be presented in the block belonged to. On categorisation blocks she was asked only to categorise the items and not to attempt to read them orally. Reading accuracy was 64% (48/75) while categorisation accuracy was 89% (67/75). We can take performance on reading trials as an indication of the number of words read accurately on the categorisation trials (48/75). If we further assume that on the remaining categorisation trials half of the responses (14) were categorised correctly by chance, then we find that, on the basis of her reading ability and guessing, she should have been correct on 62/75 of the categorisation trials. Her actual categorisation accuracy of 67/75 was not significantly different from this ($\chi^2 = 0.88$, n.s.). Thus, we found no evidence that HR accessed the meaning of words she was unable to identify correctly.

The Locus of Impairment

Until recently, most researchers who have attempted to determine the nature of the deficit in patients exhibiting letter-by-letter reading have proposed that the deficit is specific to reading and, therefore, post-perceptual. That is, they have suggested that the impairment is not one affecting the perceptual processes involved in analysing a visual array at a processing stage prior to engagement of the reading system.

Specifically, Warrington and Shallice (1980) located the impairment to the *word form system*, the system that is dedicated to detecting orthographic units of different sizes. This post-perceptual localisation was based on evidence from a number of experiments designed to assess the integrity of certain perceptual functions in nonreading tasks with two patients. One task was designed to assess the angle of attention scan—the degree of visual angle that the patient could attend to. Warrington and Shallice had one of the 2 patients report the identity of 2 digits presented at either end of a string of letters with the number of intervening letters varying from 3–7. The patient was able to report 90% of the letters correctly with a 150msec. exposure duration. The fact that performance did not vary with the number of intervening letters was taken as evidence that a reduction in angle of attention scan was not implicated. However, this might not be surprising given that the same patient was, at least on one occasion, able to read 80% of 4/8-letter words correctly with only a 100msec. exposure duration. In addition, normal performance on this task was not reported, making an interpretation of the patient's absolute level of performance impossible. Another set of experiments was designed to assess visual short-term memory. These experiments consisted of a number of tasks in which 3–5 letters or numbers were briefly presented (50–100msec.) and the patients had to report the stimuli. Warrington and Shallice argued that the performance of the 2 patients was no different from that reported on similar tasks for other left-hemisphere patients who were not letter-by-letter readers. Thus, they concluded poor performance on these tasks could not be the cause of the letter-by-letter reading behaviour. We would point out, however, that the performance of one of the patients on one of these tasks was, in fact, superior to that of the left-hemisphere lesion group. This fact not withstanding, poor performance on these tasks by the left-hemisphere group could have resulted from a different underlying impairment than the poor performance of the letter-by-letter readers. Thus, although Warrington and Shallice examined the possibility of a deficit in perceptual processing, it is not clear that such a deficit was clearly ruled out by these findings.

Patterson and Kay (1982) assumed that the post-perceptual interpretation proposed by Warrington and Shallice was adequate and proposed that the impairment represented a disconnection between a *letter-*

form analysis system and the *word form system* such that the word form system could only be accessed in serial fashion: letter-by-letter. Without further elaboration of the notion of serial vs. parallel access to the lexicon, this seems to be fundamentally a restatement of the observation that the patients read in letter-by-letter fashion.

Shallice and Saffran (1986) suggested, among other possibilities, that letter-by-letter reading reflected the operation of a right-hemisphere reading mechanism whose activity could be appreciated only when the left-hemisphere reading system had been disrupted. However, as Shallice and Saffran (1986, p. 454) themselves point out: "the RH hypothesis is too powerful, since it allows RH reading capacity to be invoked to explain any finding whenever it is needed".

More recently, Bub et al. (1989) reported that their patient exhibited superior letter identification performance with briefly presented words than with briefly displayed random letter strings. On the assumption that effects of orthographic regularity such as these require relatively intact word form representations, they concluded that the deficit in letter-by-letter readers cannot be attributed to an absolute inability to access the word form system. They did not, however, discard the possibility that the deficit might, nonetheless, be post-perceptual. Bub et al. discussed not only the possibility raised by Patterson and Kay (1982) of a deficit in accessing the word form system, but also the hypothesis, proposed by Shallice and Saffran (1986), that letter-by-letter reading might result from the "weak" activation of lexical representations.

In contrast to these reports, Friedman and Alexander (1984) observed that the letter-by-letter patient they studied processed a variety of briefly presented visual stimuli (e.g. letters, words, and pictures) more slowly than normal subjects. As a consequence these researchers attributed letter-by-letter reading to generally "slowed visual processing". These findings, although they do not provide an explanatory account of letter-by-letter reading, are nonetheless consistent with the possibility that a deficit that is not specific to reading might be involved in the performance of at least certain patients who exhibit letter-by-letter reading.

Reuter-Lorenz and Brunn (1990) also argued for a prelexical locus, suggesting that their patient's performance could be accounted for by a deficit in letter identification. They also reported (as did Bub et al., 1989) that their patient showed a word superiority effect, where letters in words were reported more accurately than letters in pseudowords or nonwords. As did Bub et al., they argued that such findings suggest that a deficit to the word form system is not a necessary condition for letter-by-letter reading. However, it should be pointed out that the finding of superior performance with words or orthographically regular strings does not necessarily imply *intact* lexical and post-perceptual processes. Given that the mechanisms underlying word superiority effects are not well understood, it is possible that such effects can be sustained by only relatively intact lexical or sublexical representations and processes.

Farah and Wallace (this issue) and Kay and Hanley (this issue) also provide evidence consistent with a visual/perceptual locus of impairment. Kay and Hanley report results that indicate that their patient, normal in the identification of letters presented sequentially, was specifically impaired in the simultaneous identification of letters.

It is apparent that, currently, there is a convergence of reports suggesting that letter-by-letter reading performance may be the result of a visual/perceptual impairment. Nonetheless, the nature and characteristics of the possible perceptual-attentional-visual deficit/s clearly require further elaboration.

We have argued that, for reading, the task of the visual system involves extracting, from an array of light intensities presented to the retina, the information about letter identity and order that is necessary for addressing the lexicon. Clearly this is a complex task involving numerous processing stages and computations. In the context of object recognition, Marr (1982) claimed that the visual system computes representations of a stimulus at a number of levels at which different types of information are represented within distinct co-ordinate frames. Marr referred to these representational levels as: the primal sketch, the 2½D-sketch, and the 3D-sketch; and the co-ordinate systems as: retinotopic, viewer-centred, and object-centred. In the specific context of reading we will refer to roughly analogous levels of representation using the terms retino-centric feature level, stimulus-centred letter shape level, and word-centred graphemic level (see Caramazza & Hillis, 1990, for a more detailed discussion) (see also Monk, 1985, for a related proposal). These ideas, outlined briefly next, will serve as a framework within which to interpret performance at prelexical stages of processing (see Fig. 5).

At the *retino-centric* level of representation the location of an item is described in terms of its retinotopic co-ordinates—by the location on the retina at which the item is presented. Therefore a word presented to the upper left quadrant of the visual field will be represented in the upper left quadrant at a retino-centric level of representation. The information represented at this level is that of visual *features*: bars, orientation, end points, etc.

At the *stimulus-centred* level of representation the location of an item is described in terms of a stimulus-centred co-ordinate system in which the location of any part of a stimulus is defined, not with reference to the portion of the retina to which it is projected but, instead, with reference to the stimulus itself. Thus, the location of an item, such as one letter in a horizontal array of letters, is not dependent on the absolute spatial location at which the letter is presented but is, instead, determined by the position

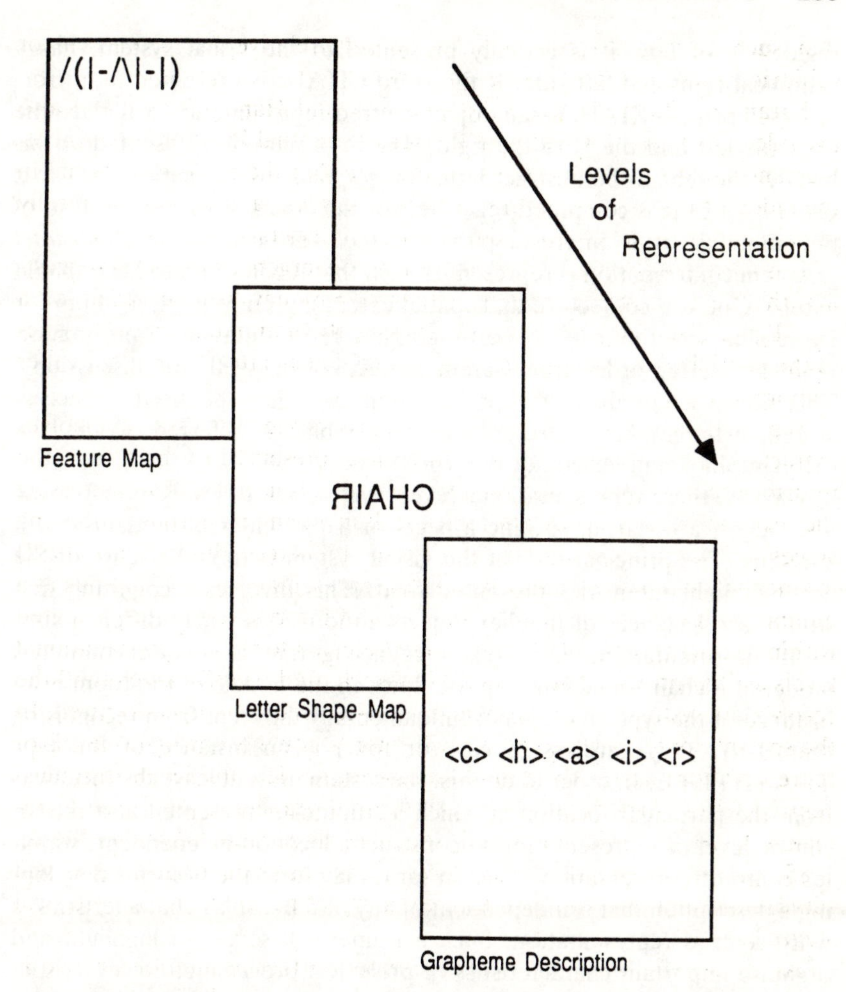

FIG. 5 Schematic illustration of levels of representation in visual word recognition for a mirror-reversed word projected to the upper left quadrant. The first level of analysis is the retino-centric feature map (upper left panel), followed by a stimulus-centred letter shape map (middle panel), and finally the word-centred grapheme description (lower right panel).

of the letter within the horizontal array. If the *rightmost* letter of the letter string is presented to the upper *left* quadrant of the visual field, it will be represented on the *right* side of a stimulus-centred representational space. The information represented at this level is hypothesised to consist of the organisation of feature information into a representation of *shape*; in the specific case of a written word, into letter shapes.

Finally, at the *word-centred* level of representation the co-ordinates of an item are determined by the canonical orientation of the word. A word, regardless of how it is actually presented to the visual system, has a canonical right and left side. If the word CHAIR is presented in mirror-reversed print—ЯIAHƆ—an object-centred representation will place the C to the left and the R to the right. The information represented at this level is thought to be abstract letter or *graphemic* information such that C+H+A+I+R is computed regardless of the actual size, case, or font of the stimulus. It is interesting that at the word-centred level *abstract* graphemic information is represented such that it continues to have *spatial* extent. One can conjecture that spatial extent is a convenient medium for expressing, in the case of orthographic representations, information regarding letter order (see Caramazza & Hillis, 1990, for discussion). This constructed abstract representation can then be used to access stored orthographic representations in what is referred to as the orthographic input lexicon or the word form system.

Clearly, these representational levels correspond to levels of increasing abstraction away from specific aspects of a particular instantiation of a stimulus. The principal task of the visual system is to make sense of the array of light intensities presented to it. This involves recognising that stimuli are instances of familiar objects although they may differ in size, location, orientation, etc. Thus recognising that a never-encountered model of a chair found lying upside down in the middle of the room is an instance of the type chair, is not fundamentally different from recognising that Ǝ⅃ᗺAT (regardless of case or font) is an instance of the type T+A+B+L+E. In order to do this, the system must at least abstract away from the particular location at which a stimulus is presented at a retinocentric level of representation to construct a location-independent, stimulus-centred representation. This, in turn, may form the basis for developing a description that is independent of any of the display characteristics: a word-centred representation. Such a framework serves to highlight and organise important characteristics of prelexical processing; however, specific claims are not being made regarding the exact number of levels (thus, there may be more than three), the discreteness of these representational stages, or the possibility of interactivity among processing levels.

Given such a view of the computations that are involved prior to accessing the lexicon in reading, it is evident that a deficit at any of these prelexical levels of processing should affect the ability of a patient to access the lexicon normally. Thus, we designed a number of tasks to examine in some detail the possibility that a deficit at a prelexical level of processing could result in the letter-by-letter reading performance observed in HR.

We will present data in this report that indicate that HR was impaired in a number of nonreading tasks; an impairment that can be attributed to a deficit to perceptual/attentional processes operating prior to the lexical processing system. As indicated earlier, this patient's performance will allow us to draw certain conclusions regarding aspects of representation and processing in reading. Furthermore, the fact that we will be able to account for the letter-by-letter reading performance of this patient in terms of a prelexical deficit will allow us to argue that, although letter-by-letter reading behaviour may result from different underlying impairments in different patients, the conclusion that letter-by-letter reading (in any particular patient) is the result of a post-perceptual deficit is clearly premature.

Experiment 1: Visual Search

Treisman (1988) has argued that stimuli that differ in terms of their constituent visual features can easily be distinguished from one another. Therefore when an X is presented among Os, subjects have the impression that the X appears to "pop out" because Xs and Os share few features (see also Duncan & Humphreys, 1989). In fact, when subjects are asked to distinguish between highly discriminable items, such as detecting the presence of an X among Os, Egeth, Jonides, and Wall (1972) and others have found that visual processing is relatively unaffected by the number of stimuli in the visual field. Thus, ideally it takes normal subjects no longer to detect the presence of an X among three Os than it does to detect X among six Os. This is referred to as the absence of an effect of display size. The search for an X among Os is a task that does not actually require letter identification, since subjects need only to detect the presence of features such as line segment, diagonal, end points, etc. in order to determine the presence of an X. Thus, it has been argued that subjects need only monitor feature level information to perform such a task. Under such conditions attentional demands are thought to be minimal and the items in the display can be processed relatively simultaneously—in parallel. In the case where stimuli (e.g. T and L) share visual features (e.g. horizontal line, vertical line), a task that requires subjects to search for a T among Ls cannot be accomplished by detecting the presence of a single feature. It has been suggested that in such cases attention must be allocated to each item in the display in order to determine if the conjunction of features at each location constitutes a T or an L. In such cases each display item is examined in a sequential manner—a serial process—and display size effects are observed (though see Duncan & Humphreys, 1989).

Therefore, in order to attempt to assess the integrity of visual processing at the early level of feature representation in HR, we used a visual search task in which she was required to search for an X among Os. We hypothesised that if a visual search task is performed on the basis of feature level information, then an impairment at the level of the retino-centric feature representation should be reflected in impaired performance on this task. If there were a deficit at this level of representation, possible outcomes include decreased overall accuracy or the finding of a display size effect, whereby response times increase with increasing display size.

Stimuli

Displays of 2, 4, and 6 items were prepared. Half of the displays included one target X among distractor Os. The elements of each display appeared within an imaginary 3 × 3 grid:

```
* * *      O O
* * *    X O O
* * *    O
```

The stimuli subtended an angle of 2° and were displayed randomly either at centre or to the right or left of fixation. Maximum eccentricity was 2.5° and at least one element in each display was presented in the most eccentric column. Stimuli were displayed in green letters on a black background presented on an Amdek Video 300 monochrome monitor controlled by an I.B.M. P.C.

Procedure

In all the experiments described in this paper the stimuli were presented well within the area of macular sparing as indicated by perimeter testing results. Furthermore, in order to reduce the possibility of eye movements that could bring a stimulus into the blind visual field, displays were presented randomly at different locations with exposure durations of 250msec. or less.

Each trial in the visual search experiment began with a warning tone. This was followed by a fixation point ":" that was displayed for 750msec. The stimulus was then displayed for 250msec. The subjects were asked to press a key as quickly as possible if an X was present.

HR participated in 2 practice sessions consisting of a total of 300 trials before data from 3 experimental sessions were collected. The control subject GR participated in 2 experimental sessions while EE took part in one. GR was a right-handed male 5 years older than HR with corrected to normal acuity. EE was a right-handed female 10 years older than HR matched for acuity on the basis of modulation transfer function data. Both were high-school graduates.

Results

As can be seen in Fig. 6, HR's reaction-time results indicate that target-present trials with six-item displays were consistently processed more slowly than two- and four-item displays. An analysis of variance indicated that HR showed a significant main effect of display size in each of the three sessions she was tested (session 1: $F[2,240] = 5.63$, $P < 0.004$; session 2: $F[2,160] = 3.56$, $P < 0.03$; session 3: $F[2,160] = 7.08$, $P < 0.001$). Error rates on target-present trials, ranging from 0–2%, were not correlated with display size and were comparable to the error rates obtained for the normal subjects: 1–5%.

The performance of the control subjects (see Fig. 6), revealing no significant main effect of display size ($F[2,496] = 2.23$, $P > 0.1$), were consistent with that reported in the literature for similar experiments. This

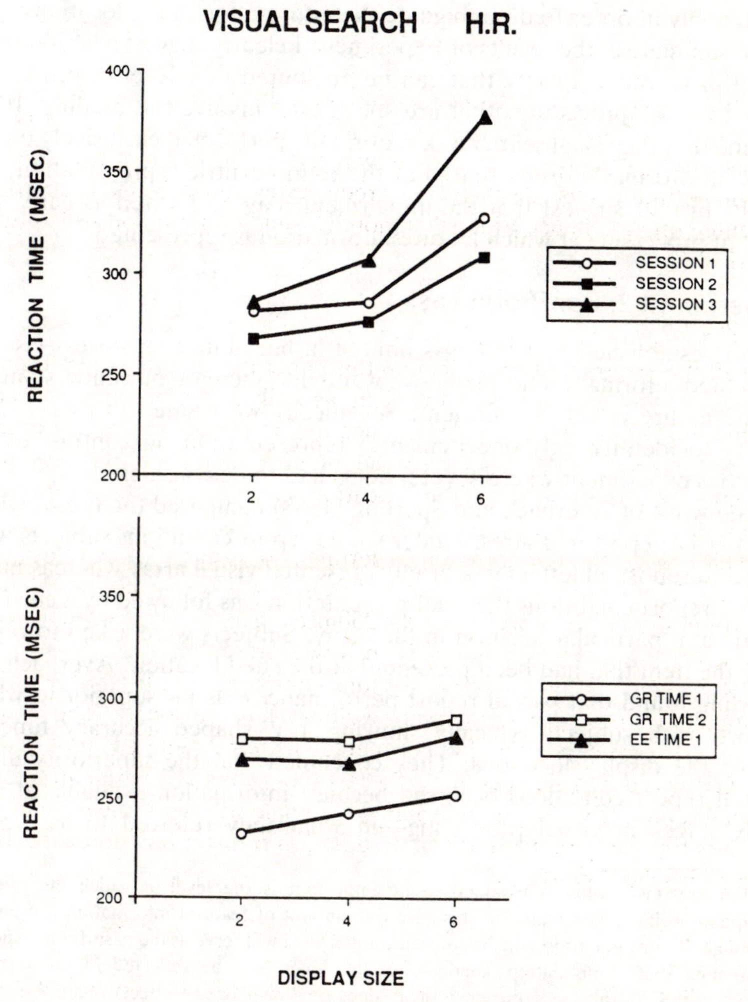

FIG. 6 The relationship between reaction time and display size for HR and two normal control subjects in a task where subjects were required to search for an X among Os.

indicated that the display characteristics were such that the items could be processed in parallel by normal subjects.

At a general level, the finding of a display size effect for HR indicates that her ability to process items in a nonreading task was impaired. More specifically, however, although overall accuracy was not affected, it would appear that HR's ability to make a detection decision on the basis of information from a feature level of representation was not normal. Within the theory of visual search that we have summarised, the finding of a display size effect is an indication that, at least on some trials, attentional resources were allocated sequentially to the different display locations, presumably in order to disambiguate the information at the locations.

To summarise, the results of Experiment 1 clearly suggest a limitation in visual processing capacity that can be attributed to a level of processing prior to those procedures that are specifically involved in reading. If we assume that the visual search task is normally performed exclusively on the basis of information represented at the retino-centric representation, the results further suggest that the impairment may be located as early as a level of processing at which feature information is represented.[2]

Experiment 2: Bar Probe Task

Having established that HR was limited in her ability to process visually presented information normally, we wanted to increase our understanding of the nature of the impairment. Specifically we wanted to assess HR's ability to identify only one item in a representation, in contrast to the previous experiment where several items had to be considered.

The work of Averbach and Sperling (1968) compared the use of whole and partial report measures. Under whole report conditions subjects were asked to report all letters in a briefly presented visual array whereas under partial report conditions the brief presentation was followed by a cue (e.g. a bar) at a particular location in the array. Subjects were asked to report only the item that had been presented at the cued location. Averbach and Sperling found that partial report performance was far superior to whole report, with subjects typically showing a W-shaped accuracy function across the display locations. They concluded that the superiority under partial report conditions occurred because information available at very early stages in visual processing—in what they referred to as "iconic

[2]For any task, what is assumed to be important is the level at which the relevant manipulation has taken place (in this case the amount of featural information presented). Although we may not know which representational level will serve as the basis for a response, we assume that manipulations made at earlier levels will be reflected in the response characteristics (in this case, presence or absence of a display size effect) regardless of the representational level at which a response decision is actually made.

memory"—is lost during the course of the whole report. Consequently partial report, requiring that only one item be identified, was thought to be a more accurate measure of the information available at early stages of visual processing.

In the case of HR this seemed a useful method for discovering the integrity of information at any particular location in the visual field given that, in this paradigm, information should not be lost in the course of examining the representations of the other items in the display. Thus, a uniform deficit at a retino-centric level of feature representation might be expected to result in impaired performance at all positions in a display. As a consequence, HR would show the normal W-shaped function shifted downwards. Such a result could be taken to indicate an overall reduction in early processing capacity across the visual field.

Stimuli

Equal numbers of high- and low-frequency words, pseudowords, and random strings ranging in length from 3 to 7 letters were presented blocked by length (total n = 500) in a counterbalanced manner. Stimuli were presented in upper case and subtended an angle of 2.5° to 5.5° depending upon stimulus length. They were displayed on a monochrome Amdek Video 300 monitor controlled by an I.B.M. P.C.

Procedure

At the beginning of each block the subject was informed of the length of the arrays to be presented in the block. Stimuli were presented on the left side of the screen. On each trial 2 "+" signs, displayed for 150msec., marked the length and position of the coming stimulus. This provided subjects with the information necessary to allow fixation at the point each subject considered most effective and was designed to allow HR to fixate appropriately in light of her field cut. Each stimulus was displayed for 250msec. From 1–16msec after stimulus offset an underline was displayed under one of the letter positions for 150msec. Subjects were asked to report verbally the letter that had appeared over the underline cue.

Results

All subjects showed a difference in accuracy when performance with orthographically regular strings (words + pseudowords) was compared to performance with random letter strings—GR: 77%/58% ($\chi^2 = 12.95$, $P < 0.001$); EE: 79%/60% ($\chi^2 = 16.80$, $P < 0.001$); HR: 36%/25% ($\chi^2 = 4.5$, $P < 0.05$). The finding of superior performance with orthographically regular strings is typically reported in similar paradigms (see

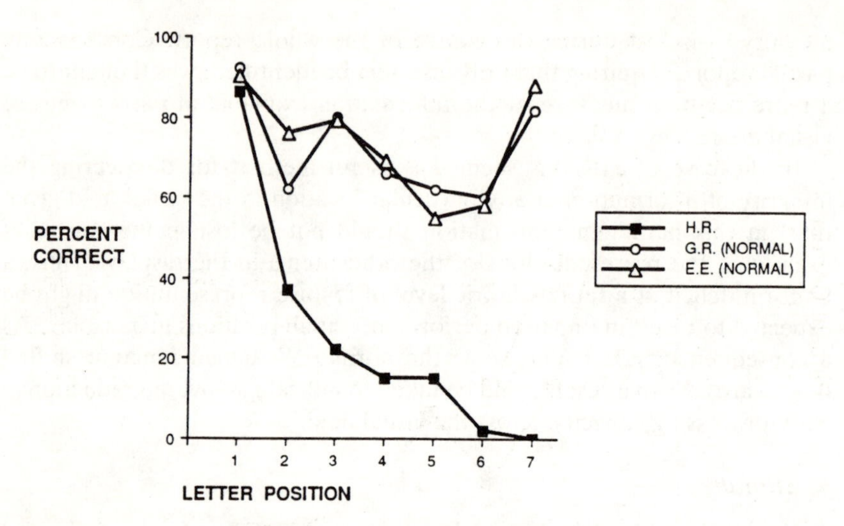

FIG. 7 Accuracy of report in a bar probe task according to the position of the target letter within the string. Results are collapsed across stimulus type and length.

Baron & Thurston, 1973; Gibson, Pick, Osser, & Hammond, 1962; Reicher, 1969; among others, for reports with normal subjects, and Bub et al., 1989, for a report of the performance of a letter-by-letter reader). However, as we mentioned earlier, the implications of such a finding are not obvious and it will not be considered further at this time. Instead, as can be seen in Fig. 7, the data have been presented collapsed across stimulus type and length.

HR's overall accuracy was 33%, very significantly inferior to that of the control subjects: 74% and 72% ($\chi^2 = 223.5$, $P < 0.001$). However, the results were different from those predicted by the hypothesis that HR's impairment could be attributed to a reduction in processing capacity across the visual field. That is, HR's performance did not correspond to the typical W-shaped function shifted downward: instead her accuracy declined steeply across display positions.

It is important to note that this occurred in spite of the fact that presumably only one item in the display had to be identified. Recall that it was precisely because of the requirement that only one item must be identified that, for normal subjects, a partial report paradigm resulted in relatively uniform performance across display positions (except for what are thought to be local effects of crowding or lateral inhibition).

For the sake of simplicity, in Fig. 8 we have presented performance only with three- and seven-letter strings, although performance was comparable with all string lengths. We can see that the accuracy function was similar for both lengths. In addition, it should be noted that, except for the first

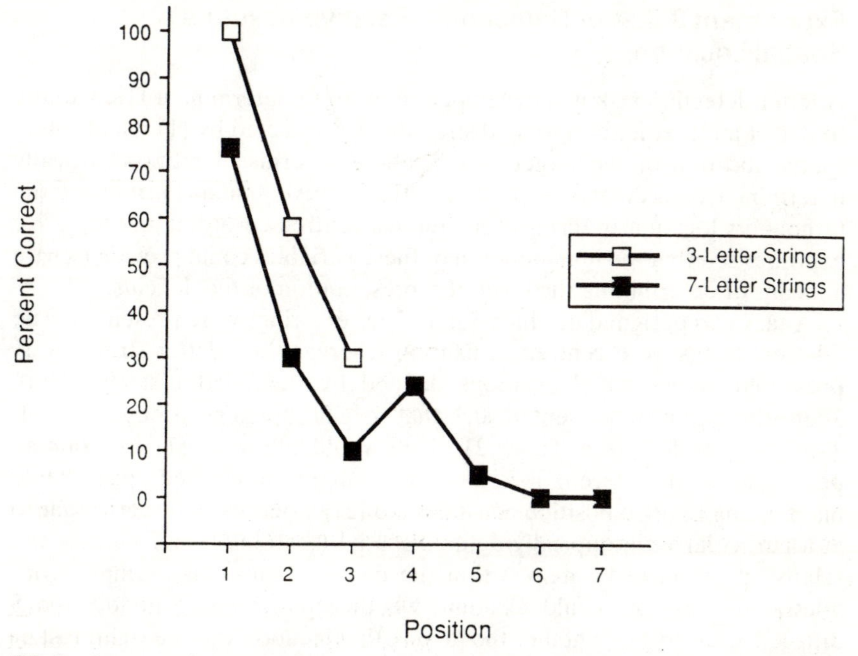

FIG. 8 Accuracy of report for three- and seven-letter strings in the bar probe task according to the position of the letter within the string. Results are collapsed across stimulus type.

position of the three-letter strings, HR's performance was not comparable to that of the normal subjects. This raises the possibility that processing was impaired even at initial display positions. Certainly a striking impairment is evident by the second position.

The shape of the accuracy function suggests a left-to-right *gradient* of decreasing processing efficiency across display positions. This is not easily explained by a *uniform* impairment across a retino-centric feature representation. Instead we found that HR's performance was affected by the position of the target: within any given string, items further to the right were responded to with decreased accuracy. However, it is not possible to conclude, on the basis of the results obtained thus far, whether such a gradient is present at the retinocentric or the stimulus-centred representation. That is, performance may be impaired on the right because items at this location are presented on the right side of retinotopically defined space. Alternatively, it could be that the rightward items are reported with reduced accuracy because they correspond to the right portion of the stimulus and similar results would be obtained independently of the actual location on the screen (and hence retinotopic location) at which the stimulus is presented. Either or both of these accounts would be compatible with the obtained pattern of results.

Experiment 3: Letter Detection—Relative/absolute Spatial Location

A letter detection task was developed in order to determine if HR's ability to detect a target letter among distractors was affected by (1) the absolute spatial location of the target—its location in terms of retino-centrically determined co-ordinates—and/or (2) the relative spatial location of the target—its location in terms of a stimulus-centred co-ordinate frame. We hypothesised that the manipulation of these variables could provide us with a means of determining the level of representation of the deficit/s.

A task was designed in which 3- and 7-letter strings were presented. The 7-letter strings were centred at fixation whereas the 3-letter strings were presented across the 7 positions defined by the 7-letter string. Thus, 3-letter strings were presented such that they occupied positions 1–3, 2–4, 3–5, 4–7, or 5–7 (see Table 2). This would allow us (1) to examine performance at different locations (1–7) in retino-centred space while maintaining relative position constant and (2) to determine if performance at a particular retinotopically defined spatial location was affected by the relative position of an item within the display. Thus, for example, with 3-letter displays we could examine whether performance at location 5 differed according to whether the item at that location was the rightmost or leftmost item of the stimulus.

Stimuli

K, X, Z, N, or Y served as target letters. The distractors were D, J, G, R, B, and P. A target was present among distractors on half of the trials (total n = 280). Half of the stimuli contained 7 letters and half 3 letters. Stimuli were presented randomly with a maximum eccentricity of approxi-

TABLE 2
Presentation Positions for Stimuli in Experiment 3

Position	*1*	*2*	*3*	+ *4*	*5*	*6*	*7*
7-letter stimulus	D	K	J	G	R	B	P
3-letter stimulus	D	K	J				
		D	K	J			
			D	K	J		
				D	K	J	
					D	K	J

Note: All stimuli were displayed on the same row: the two-dimensional extension in this table is just for illustrative purposes.

mately 2.5°. Stimuli were displayed in white letters on a black background on a N.E.C. Multisync colour monitor controlled by an I.B.M. A.T.

Procedure

On each trial the target letter was presented at the central fixation position for 150msec. Subjects had been instructed that they were to look for this letter in the subsequent stimulus display. Upon offset of the target letter, a stimulus was displayed for 250msec. Subjects were asked to press a key as quickly as possible if the target letter was present in the string.

Results

HR's performance was inferior to that of the normal control subject with both 3-letter (70%/97%; $\chi^2 = 16.86$, $P < 0.001$) and 7-letter strings (55%/95%; $\chi^2 = 28.25$, $P < 0.001$) (see Table 3). The accuracy function with 7-letter strings, as was the case in the previous experiment, showed a relatively steep left-right slope. Once again performance was below normal even on the first position of 7-letter strings.

The data from the 3-letter stimuli can be analysed to determine the contribution of relative and absolute location on detection accuracy. This can be done most economically by collapsing across performance on the 2 sets of 3-letter strings presented to the left of fixation and the 2 sets presented to right (see Fig. 9).

The fact that performance at each of the 3 relative positions is better with strings presented to the left than with strings presented to the right

TABLE 3
Accuracy Results for Experiment 3 for HR and GR (Normal Control Subject)

Position	*1*	*2*	*3*	*4*	*5*	*6*	*7*
7 Letters							
HR	83%	80%	80%	50%	40%	40%	17%
GR	100%	70%	90%	100%	100%	100%	100%
3 Letters							
HR	100%	100%	50%				
GR	100%	100%	100%				
HR		100%	100%	50%			
GR		100%	100%	100%			
HR			100%	100%	25%		
GR			100%	100%	75%		
HR				75%	25%	33%	
GR				100%	100%	100%	
HR					100%	33%	0%
GR					100%	83%	100%

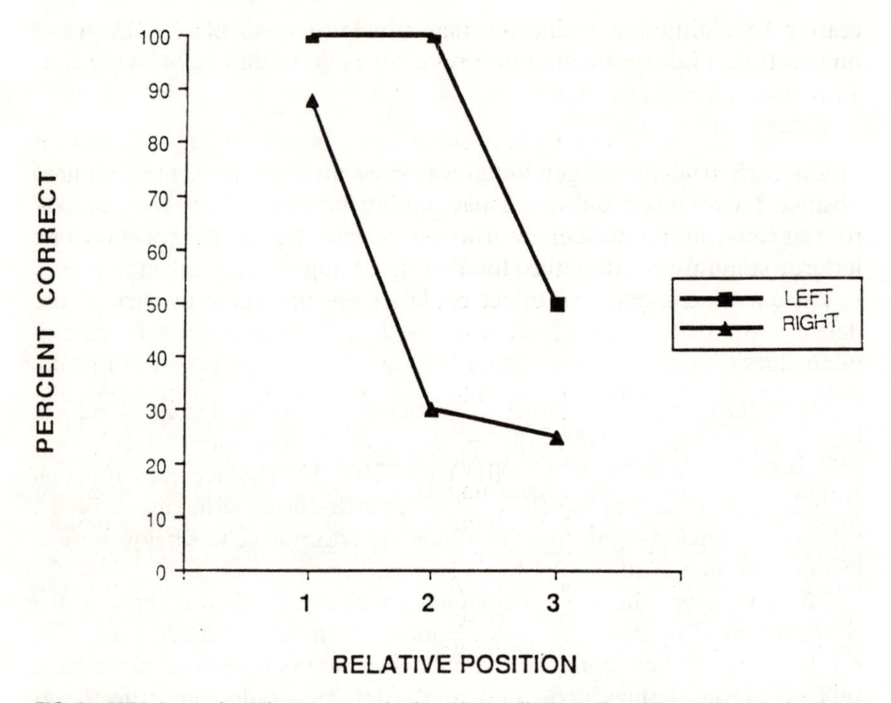

FIG. 9 HR's letter detection accuracy in three-letter displays. Results are presented collapsing across the two sets of displays presented to the left of fixation and the two sets presented to the right.

reflects the contribution of *absolute* spatial location. These results are consistent with those obtained with the 7-letter strings and point to an impairment that affects the left of a retino-centrically defined space more than it does the right.

In addition, there is a striking effect of *relative* position with accuracy systematically lowest at the rightmost position in each 3-letter stimulus. This effect occurs regardless of whether the stimuli are presented to the right or to the left of fixation. The effect of relative position is *independent* of absolute spatial position. This can be seen if we compare performance at relative position 3 of stimuli presented to the left side of retino-centric space, with performance at relative position 1 of stimuli presented to the right. In terms of the deficit in retino-centrically defined space, all positions in stimuli presented to the left should be *better* than all positions of stimuli presented to the right. However, we see that position 3 of stimuli presented to the (relatively intact) left is far *inferior* to position of 1 of stimuli presented to the (relatively damaged) right.

The results of this experiment, along with those of the previous experiment, clearly support the hypothesis of a left-to-right gradient of processing difficulty at a retino-centric level of representation. We were, however, less certain of the interpretation of the relative position effect. Two possibilities came to mind:

1. The relative position effect could represent a *left-right* gradient of processing efficiency across a *stimulus-centred* space, similar to the gradient observed across retino-centric space. With such a deficit, the level of performance with any given item would be affected (as was observed) by its relative position within the stimulus; alternatively,
2. The relative position effect could simply be a consequence of the deficit at the *retino-centric* level of representation. That is, because ease of item identification decreases from left-right across the retino-centrically defined representation it is possible that, in order to identify items, the patient allocated all visual/attentional resources *sequentially* to one location at a time. If HR began at the left and proceeded to the right of each stimulus, then information regarding items later in the sequence would be processed later and, as a consequence, may have decayed before identification was possible. In this case the relative position effect could be considered a *serial position effect*. According to the serial position hypothesis we would also expect to see the observed result—performance should vary with left-right position within the string.

Thus, it was not clear if the observed relative position effect reflected an impairment at a stimulus-centred level of representation or, alternatively, if it resulted from the serial processing of items whose retino-centric representation was degraded. Experiment 3, therefore, although providing additional evidence in support of a deficit to a retino-centric level of representation, also raised some questions regarding the nature of the observed effect of relative spatial position on performance.

Experiment 4A: Horizontal/Vertical Letter Detection

In order to disentangle the two possible explanations for the relative position effect we used a letter detection task to compare performance with stimuli that have a left–right spatial extent—horizontally displayed strings of three letters—with stimuli that do not—vertically displayed strings of equal size.

According to the serial position hypothesis, which proposes that the relative position effect is the result of the patient's allocation of resources sequentially to each item in a string, we should expect performance to be *equivalent* for horizontally and vertically presented strings presented at comparable locations in retino-centrically defined space. Equivalent performance is expected because both display types contain an equal number of items. Thus, regardless of orientation or the order in which items are processed, if items are processed sequentially, on every trial the item processed third will have a greater probability than the item processed first of not being identified. Over a number of trials this should result in comparable *overall* performance with both vertically and horizontally presented stimuli.

In contrast, according to the hypothesis that attributes the relative position effect to a left-right gradient of processing efficiency at the level of a stimulus-centred representation, we should expect: (1) overall performance to be worse with horizontally vs. vertically presented strings because only the horizontal strings would be affected by a left-right gradient of processing efficiency across a stimulus-centred representation; and (2) that the horizontally presented stimuli themselves should demonstrate an effect of the left-right gradient with accuracy at relative position 1 superior to accuracy at position 3.

Stimuli

Three points were selected around which the display of the stimuli was organised: the centre of the screen, 1.6° to the right of centre and 1.6° to the left (see Fig. 10). Three-letter stimuli were displayed vertically either beginning or ending at each of these points, for a total of six stimulus display positions for vertical strings. Horizontally displayed stimuli also either began or ended at each of these points, for a total of four stimulus display positions for horizontal strings. This arrangement allowed us to compare performance on vertically and horizontally presented stimuli that shared display positions.

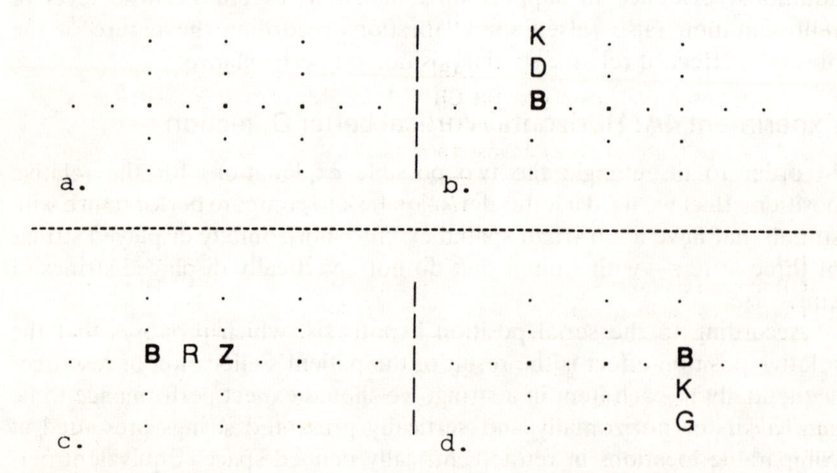

FIG. 10 Horizontal and vertical display positions for the three-letter strings presented in Experiments 4a and 4b. **a.** The displays were organised around the boldface positions, the points indicate display locations. **b–d** illustrate examples of possible displays.

The same target and distractor stimuli were used in this experiment as were used in the previous one. Stimuli for target and nontarget trials were identical for both horizontal and vertical displays. An equal number of target and nontarget trials were presented (total n = 360) probing each display position an equal number of times. Stimuli were displayed with white letters on a black background on a N.E.C. Multisync colour monitor controlled by an I.B.M. A.T.

Procedure

On each trial the target letter for the trial was presented in the centre of the screen for 1500msec. A 3-letter stimulus was then presented for 200msec. Subjects were asked to press a key as quickly as possible if the target was present in the display. HR, as well as the normal control subject, GR, and a reading-impaired control subject, PS,[3] were each tested twice.

Results

Given that, at this point, our principal concern is with examining effects of relative rather than absolute position, performance can be collapsed across display positions for vertical and horizontal strings separately. The two most eccentric positions to the right and left of the rightmost and leftmost horizontal displays respectively, have been omitted from all analyses as there were no vertical strings presented at these eccentricities.

Table 4 presents accuracy results with vertical and horizontal target-present displays for the three subjects. For HR, an ANOVA of the accuracy results revealed a main effect of orientation, indicating that her

TABLE 4
Letter Detection Accuracy for HR, GR (Normal Control), and PS (Reading-impaired Control) in Vertically and Horizontally Displayed 3-letter Strings (Results are Collapsed across Display Positions)

Subject	*Horizontal Displays*	*Vertical Displays*
HR	76% (73/96)	86% (185/216)
GR (normal control)	96% (92/96)	84% (181/216)
PS (reading-impaired control)	99% (95/96)	98% (212/216)

[3]PS, a right-handed male, was 48 years old at the time of testing. He had suffered a head injury 2 years earlier that resulted in the evacuation of a right frontal hematoma. C.T.-scan results indicated extensive left temporal damage as well as lesser right temporal damage. His speech was fluent except for a selective naming deficit for animals and vegetables (see Hillis & Caramazza, in press). Lexical decision and reading were affected with reading errors consisting predominantly of visually similar words or nonword regularisation responses.

accuracy was significantly lower with horizontal vs. vertical displays ($F[1,310] = 4.32$, $P < 0.04$). In contrast, the normal control subject showed superior performance with horizontally presented strings. Superior performance with horizontal displays was not unexpected given that the vertical displays involved greater eccentricities than the horizontal ones. Performance on the vertical displays, therefore, could have been affected by the normal reduction in acuity at more eccentric locations. The reading-impaired control was essentially at ceiling with both horizontal and vertical displays.

The *serial* position explanation of the relative position effect obtained in the previous experiment attributed left/right differences to a need to process stimuli sequentially due to a reduction in processing capacity at the retino-centric level of representation. Such an account would have predicted equivalent performance with vertical and horizontal stimuli. However, the hypothesis that the effect of relative position resulted from a left-right gradient of processing efficiency at the level of a *stimulus-centred representation* predicted the inferior performance with the horizontally displayed stimuli that was obtained. This hypothesis also predicted a further, more specific, result: horizontal stimuli should not only result, on average, in worse performance than vertical stimuli, but horizontal stimuli should also reveal a "stimulus internal" left-right performance decrement.

In Fig. 11 we have presented the results obtained with horizontal and vertical stimuli collapsed across different display positions. This allows us

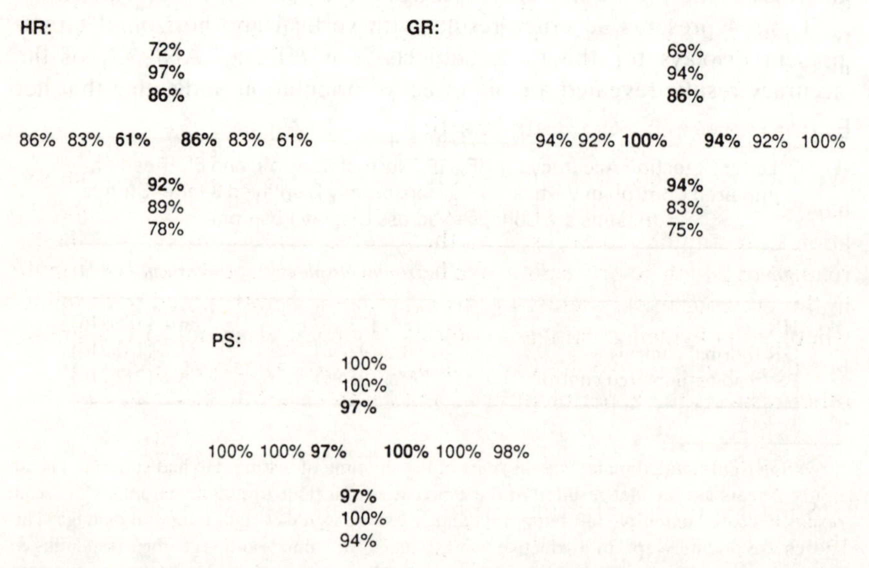

FIG. 11 Letter detection accuracy at different relative positions with horizontal and vertical displays.

to observe the effect of relative position for the horizontal stimuli. HR showed a significant effect of relative position for horizontally displayed stimuli ($F[1,94] = 6.46$, $P < 0.01$) whereas the control subjects did not. That is, stimuli on the right of a horizontal display were responded to with lower accuracy than stimuli on the left, even though they were presented to the same retinotopic locations.

This can be seen by comparing the results obtained at the locations represented in bold typeface. These results represent performance with letters presented at the same positions on the screen—at identical positions in terms of absolute, retino-centred space. They differ, however, in terms of type of display (horizontal/vertical) and relative position. Thus, relative position 3 of horizontal stimuli can be compared to relative position 1 of horizontal stimuli as well as with top and bottom positions of vertical stimuli. We see that for the control subjects there were no differences among the four results. For HR, on the other hand, performance was comparable for all positions except for relative position 3 of the horizontal strings. This is just the result one would expect if a stimulus-centred representation were damaged more on the right side than on the left.

In sum, the account which attributed left/right differences to sequential processing was not upheld since performance was not comparable on vertical and horizontal strings. Instead, HR's performance in this experiment can be best understood as reflecting a gradient of impairment across a stimulus-centred level of representation. This impairment is accompanied by a left-right decrement in processing efficiency at the level of the retino-centric representation that was revealed by the preceding experiments.

Experiment 4B: Horizontal/Vertical Bar Detection

We have assumed that the levels of representation and processing that we have described, although necessarily involved in developing a representation of a stimulus to be used by the reading system, are not specific to reading or language processing. We have, however, used only letter stimuli in the previous experiments. In this experiment we attempted to examine whether the evidence gathered could be obtained using nonletter stimuli. For these purposes we used horizontal and vertical bars as stimuli. In all other respects the experiment was identical to Experiment 4.

Stimuli

Stimuli consisted of strings of three bars—horizontal and/or vertical—that could be displayed either horizontally or vertically. Horizontal and vertical bars were presented equally often as targets. On a target-present trial, for example, a horizontal target would be presented followed by a three-item display in which a horizontal bar was presented along with two vertical bars. A target-absent trial could consist of, for example, a horizontal bar target followed by a stimulus containing three vertical bars. Bars were approximately the same height and width as the letter stimuli used in previous experiments. However, they differed from the letter stimuli in that the thickness of the bars was of one pixel whereas letter stimuli were drawn with lines of two pixel thickness. This resulted in the bars appearing to be somewhat fainter than the letter stimuli.

Procedure

Procedures were identical to those in the previous experiment; only HR was tested on this task.

Results

Figure 12 presents overall accuracy results as well as position-specific results for this experiment. We see results comparable to those reported for the previous experiment. Overall accuracy was significantly inferior for horizontal strings ($F[1,339] = 8.49$, $P < 0.004$). We can see that horizontal strings revealed a clear effect of relative position such that performance at the third position of 3-letter strings was strikingly impaired ($F[2,99] = 8.34$, $P < 0.004$). In addition, if we compare performance at the same display locations we see again that detection ability at position 1 of horizontal strings and the top and bottom positions of vertical strings was at a comparably high level, whereas performance at the third positions of horizontal displays was significantly impaired.

Thus, the results of Experiment 4b confirm the notion that the levels of processing and representation illuminated by HR's performance are not specific to the processing of alphanumeric symbols but are involved in the representation of spatially arrayed stimuli more generally.

HR:

93%
Overall Accuracy: 97%
95%

Horizontal 89%
Vertical 96% 95% 100% 71% 95% 100% 71%

100%
100%
89%

FIG. 12 Overall bar detection accuracy and accuracy at different relative positions for horizontal and vertical displays.

DISCUSSION

We will begin with a review of the principal findings in this case which we will group according to whether they are related to lexical or prelexical processing:

Nonlexical Processing

1. An effect of display size was observed in a "feature" search task;
2. Clear effects of absolute spatial position were documented in letter detection and bar probe tasks;
3. A relative spatial position effect was observed that could not be attributed to a serial position effect;
4. The effects of relative spatial position were also documented using nonletter stimuli.

Lexical Processing

1. HR demonstrated a marked effect of letter length in reading consistent with her claim that she could only read words letter-by-letter;
2. No effects were uncovered that indicated semantic processing of words that had not been explicitly identified;
3. Neither written nor oral spelling performance revealed spatial position effects.

We have argued that HR's performance on tasks assessing nonlexical visual/perceptual processing can be understood as resulting from impairments at the level of the retino-centric feature representation as well as at the level of the stimulus-centred letter shape representation. Specifically, the finding that accuracy in letter detection (Experiments 2 & 3) is affected by the absolute spatial location of an item has been interpreted as indicating an impairment to the retino-centric level of representation. The additional finding, that detection accuracy is further affected by the position of an item (letter or bar) relative to the stimulus of which it is a part (Experiments 4a and b), has been understood as indicating an impairment to a processing stage at which shapes are represented in a stimulus-centred co-ordinate frame.[4]

---

[4]Riddoch, Cleton, Fery, & Humphreys (this issue) claim that a stimulus-centred level of representation is not required to account for results such as these. They seem to argue that the "stimulus-centred level of representation" actually corresponds to the area of distribution of attention to a retino-centric level of representation. It is not clear whether such a proposal can account for effects of relative position that are independent of effects of absolute (retinotopically determined) position. If it can, then it is not clear that it is actually different from a proposal that includes a stimulus-centred level of representation. We have argued that there is a representational level at which the *co-ordinate frame* in which an item is represented is determined by the relationship among the parts of an item and that this co-ordinate system is independent of a retinotopically defined co-ordinate frame. We have not, however, determined whether or not an item must be the focus of attention in order for the relative positions of the parts of the item to become relevant.

In the framework outlined in the Introduction, another representational level is presented—the word-centred graphemic level. At this level of representation, location and display-specific characteristics of the stimulus have been abstracted away and an abstract, canonically oriented representation of graphemes has been computed. Caramazza and Hillis (1990) describe the performance of patient NG who, they concluded, demonstrated an impairment at this representational level. They found that NG substituted or deleted the right-hand portion of words (PEACH → pea or pearl) regardless of the specific form of presentation (horizontal, mirror-reversed, vertical) or the modality of input or output (reading, written spelling to dictation, oral spelling, etc.). Thus, for example, she read TƎMOƆ as comet and, in oral spelling, spelled huge H,U,G. These results could only be attributed to a deficit at an abstract level of representation at which the spatial organisation of a representation depends entirely on the co-ordinates of the canonical form.

In contrast, HR did not show a spatially determined distribution of errors in oral or written spelling; instead her errors were almost entirely phonologically plausible renderings of the word. These results indicate that, in contrast to NG, for HR the word-centred representational level was not affected (see also Ellis et al., 1987; and Behrmann, Moscovitch, Black, & Mozer, in press for an apparently similar dissociation between impaired stimulus-centred and intact word-centred levels of processing).

The fact that the performance of both HR and NG can be accounted for within this framework gives us greater confidence in its accuracy. These results indicate that different representational levels can be damaged independently. In fact, many of the apparent contradictions and confusions that have arisen in the discussion of the nature of spatial deficits can be attributed to attempts to characterise the performance of the different patients in terms of only one representational level. When their performance is considered within this richer and more articulated processing theory, many of these confusions disappear (see Caramazza & Hillis, 1990, for a detailed discussion of what they consider to be "psuedo-paradoxical" results in this literature). The fact that this theory can resolve a number of these longstanding confusions further adds to its credibility.

Implications for Accounts of Letter-by-letter Reading

Given the finding, in the case of HR, of an impairment to prelexical processes and because, presumably, processing at these levels must be accomplished successfully in order to ensure normal access to the lexicon, it is clear that we cannot rule out that the letter-by-letter reading performance in HR is the result of a deficit to visual/perceptual processes prior to lexical access. Although a number of reports now indicate that letter-by-letter readers may suffer from prelexical impairments, whether or not other patients who demonstrate letter-by-letter reading performance suffer from impairments at similar levels of processing will be known only when they are studied with that possibility in mind. On the basis of the evidence presented in this paper we would conclude, therefore, that unless prelexical processing impairments are ruled out in specific patients, the claim that the deficit underlying letter-by-letter reading is post-perceptual is clearly unwarranted.

However, in order to provide an *explanatory* account of the letter-by-letter reading performance we must be able to relate the impairment documented at prelexical processing levels to the observed letter-by-letter performance. That is, we should be able to describe the relationship between the spatial deficits described for HR and the specific form of her reading impairment.

We can think of each processing level as a space on which information is represented or, alternatively, as a set of processors, each dedicated to processing a spatial location. At any given spatial location (for each of these representational levels) information may be more or less available—more or less difficult to process, more or less "noisy". Thus, in this context, damage can be thought of, in a general manner, as the introduction of noise at particular locations in representational space. The amount and distribution of the noise, beyond that which is normal, is determined by the location and extent of the damage to the space or processors.[5]

Consequently, a patient's performance on a task will depend on the extent of the damage at the absolute or relative location at which a stimulus is presented as well as the requirements of the task. For example, a task that requires a patient to discriminate an X among Os may be able to be performed more accurately than the discrimination of a K among Ps and Rs. In addition we will assume that, as is generally the case with difficult discriminations, the allocation of greater resources or attention to a particular location can help to increase discriminability—increase the signal-to-noise ratio. Because of this, cues or the serial allocation of resources may result in improved performance (see Riddoch & Humphreys, 1987 for a discussion of performance improvements for "neglect" patients under cued conditions).

---

[5]Alternatively, damage can be considered to affect not the information presented at certain locations in representational space, but instead the ability to attend to or allocate attention to certain spatial locations. At the level of detail at which theories of attention and representation are currently articulated, it is not apparent to us that it is possible to distinguish between alternatives such as these. All the arguments we present are applicable to either hypothesis.

In the case of HR we have argued that the results obtained suggest a left–right gradient of processing difficulty in which performance is often not at a normal level even at the first position of a string. This is illustrated in Fig. 13, where we have presented the results recorded on the various experiments described in this report with both three- and seven-letter strings. If this is an accurate reflection of the gradient of processing difficulty, then we can speculate that in the case of HR, where damage extends across a representation, processing resources (perhaps what is commonly referred to as attention) may be allocated sequentially to each location within a representation in order to identify (increase the signal/noise ratio) what has been presented to each location. In reading this would result in what we observe as letter-by-letter reading.

The sequential allocation of resources apparently results in the relatively accurate identification of the letters at each location (as noted earlier, letter misidentifications occurred only approximately 4% of the time). This relatively accurate representation of the stimulus is then, presumably, used to access the lexicon. However, HR's reading performance (see Table 4), even if we disregard those occasions in which letter misidentifications occurred, was not normal—in particular, a number of visually similar word responses and regularisation errors were made.

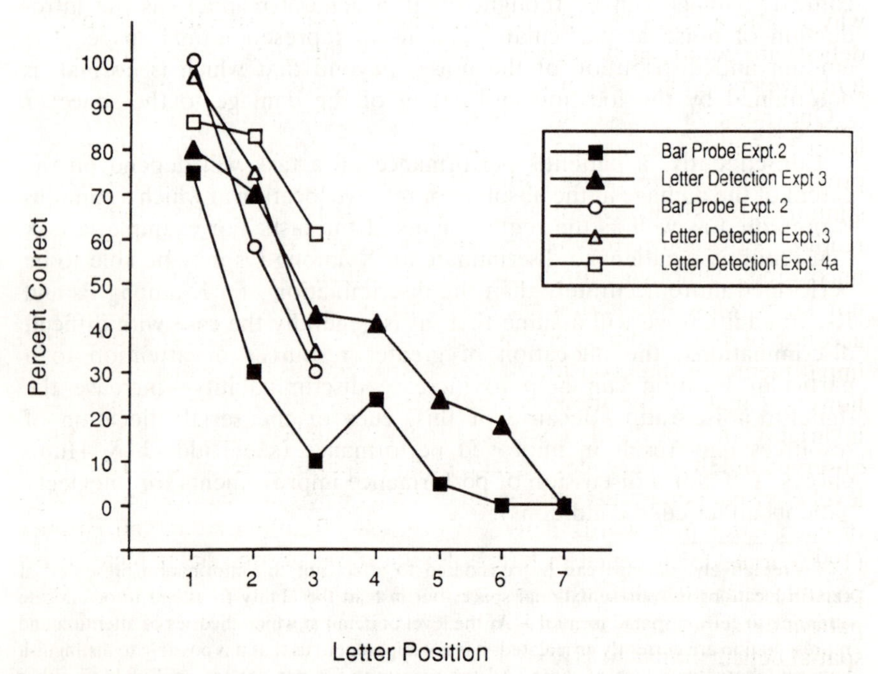

FIG. 13 HR's letter detection accuracy for three- and seven-letter strings in a number of experiments.

Patterson and Kay (1982) noted that some letter-by-letter readers were able to read correctly all words once letter-by-letter identification had taken place whereas others, similar to HR, continued to produce some incorrect responses. They concluded that although both groups suffered from a deficit that required serial letter identification, the latter patients suffered from an additional lexical deficit that rendered certain lexical representations unavailable even when the constituent letters had been identified correctly. HR's reading errors after correct letter-by-letter identification can be explained in a similar manner or, alternatively, they may reflect an additional deficit at other representational and processing levels.

What is important to note is that the *letter-by-letter performance* that is the focus of interest in this report is accounted for with the explanation provided earlier regarding deficits at both the retino- and stimulus-centred representational levels. The additional observation of *reading errors* may need to be accounted for in other ways that do not reflect on the adequacy of the account provided for the letter-by-letter behaviour.

Spatial Deficits and Reading Performance

We are left, nonetheless, with one of the questions with which we started: why is HR a letter-by-letter reader whereas other patients with spatial deficits are described as neglect dyslexics? For this question we have only a tentative and ad hoc response. Nonetheless it is worth considering.

One possibility, of course, is that in HR the spatial deficit and the letter-by-letter reading are unrelated. Although the spatial deficit can provide us with interesting information regarding the processing of visual stimuli, it does not bear on the question of letter-by-letter reading. The reading performance may be due to an additional deficit that we have not uncovered. Although entirely possible, we will argue that as long as we do not know what this additional deficit might be *and* we can provide an account of the reading performance in terms of the spatial processing impairment, we shall consider it more parsimonious to do so. We are not, however, making the more general claim that letter-by-letter reading is invariably the result of a spatial processing deficit similar to the one observed in HR. There may, in fact, be a number of different deficits at the level of visual/perceptual processing that may result in the serial processing of each letter in a word. Thus, for example, Reuter-Lorenz and Brunn (1990) argue for a deficit in letter identification. On the other hand, it is possible that the difficulty in *simultaneous* letter identification of the patient described by Kay and Hanley (this issue) may actually result from a spatial deficit similar to HR's.

Although it would appear to be the case that HR and "neglect" patients (such as those described by Behrmann et al., in press; Caramazza & Hillis,

1990; Ellis et al., 1987) suffer from spatially determined deficits, it is interesting to note that the slopes observed in letter detection tasks (Fig. 12) are markedly different from the distribution of errors in reading produced by the "neglect" patients, for whom performance is essentially normal until the centre position of a word and then drops off from the centre position. Of course, the *reading* results of the neglect patients can only be compared with the *letter detection* results reported for HR if we assume (a perhaps unwarranted assumption) that the reading performance of neglect patients reflects the availability of information at different spatial locations—the same assumption made in our interpretation of HR's letter detection performance. Based on this assumption it would appear that HR and these neglect patients may have different underlying processing efficiency or "noise" distributions. Thus, it is possible that neurological impairment may result in different damage functions across a given level of representation.

In the case of HR, we have argued that damage extends across a representation, resulting in the sequential allocation of processing resources to each location within a representation in order to identify what has been presented to each location. In the case of neglect dyslexia, however, if information is normally available until approximately the centre of a representation, then parallel processing may proceed as usual based on the available information. This would result in the one-sided deletion and substitution errors observed in the reading of these patients.

In sum, we are suggesting that although HR and "neglect" patients both have spatial deficits, they may differ in the shape and slope of the underlying processing efficiency function. In Fig. 14 we have presented an example of hypothetical underlying functions that might occur at any of the representational levels. Also important to note in this discussion is that the extent to which a patient will be impaired at a particular spatial location will depend not only on the extent of damage at that location but also on the task demands. We can think of different tasks as having different thresholds at which the information necessary to perform the task becomes available. In this manner, the detection of an X among Os may require a lower threshold than reading or the detection of a K among Ps and Rs. In addition there may be an awareness threshold below which a person will be unaware that a stimulus has been presented; it may be that for many neglect patients information is available below this threshold and, as a consequence, the patients claim to be unaware that a stimulus has been presented to a certain location.

This proposal should not be taken to mean that the *cause* of the processing efficiency function is necessarily the same for neglect patients and HR. In neglect patients the step-like dissociation of performance on items left vs. right of centre is striking. Such a dissociation, and as a

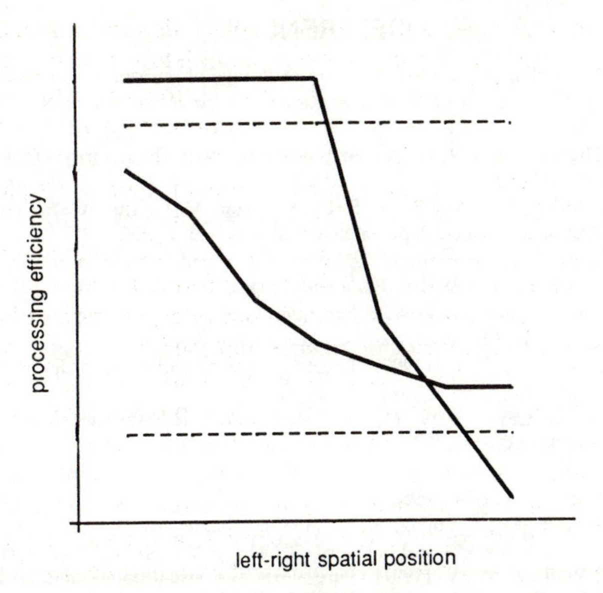

FIG. 14 The solid lines represent hypothetical processing efficiency functions for patients with spatial deficits. The dashed lines represent hypothetical threshold values for different tasks.

consequence the corresponding processing efficiency function, may in fact result from different underlying causes. From the point of view of those processes that are affected by the efficiency function at any particular level of representation, these causal differences may be irrelevant. They are certainly irrelevant at the gross level of description at which the theory is currently articulated.

In conclusion, we have identified a spatial deficit in a patient that can be attributed to impairment at both retino-centric and stimulus-centred levels of representation. We have proposed an account of the relationship between these deficits and the letter-by-letter reading performance observed in the patient. These findings demonstrate that previous post-perceptual explanations of letter-by-letter reading were clearly premature. Furthermore, we have suggested a framework within which we can understand HR's performance and that of other patients with spatial deficits. This framework has allowed us to speculate on the reasons why such patients may differ in their reading performance. Clearly this is only a beginning, but it is our hope that this work will serve to guide future questions.

Manuscript received 7 March 1990
Revised manuscript received 15 June 1990

REFERENCES

Averbach, E. & Sperling, G. (1968). Short-term storage of information in vision. In R. N. Haber (Ed.), *Contemporary theory and research in visual perception*. New York: Holt, Rinehart, & Winston.

Baron, J. & Thurston, I. (1973). An analysis of the word superiority effect. *Cognitive Psychology*, *4*, 207–228.

Behrmann, M., Moscovitch, M., Black, S. E., & Mozer, M. C. (in press). Perceptual and conceptual factors in neglect: Personal and extrapersonal. *Brain*.

Bub, D. N., Black, S., & Howell, J. (1989). Word recognition and orthographic context effects in a letter-by-letter reader. *Brain and Language*, *36*, 357–376.

Bub, D. N. & Bruemmer, A. (1988). *Pure alexia—A functional interpretation of a disconnection syndrome*. Montreal, Canada: Academy of Aphasia.

Caramazza, A. & Hillis, A. E. (1990). Levels of representation, co-ordinate frames, and unilateral neglect. *Cognitive Neuropsychology*, *7*, 391–445.

Duncan, J. & Humphreys, G. W. (1989). Visual search and stimulus similarity. *Psychological Review*, *96*, 433–458.

Egeth, H., Jonides, J., & Wall, S. (1972). Parallel processing of multi-element displays. *Cognitive Psychology*, *3*, 647–698.

Ellis, A. W., Flude, B. M., & Young, A. W. (1987). "Neglect dyslexia" and the early visual processing of letters in words and nonwords. *Cognitive Neuropsychology*, *4*(4), 439–464.

Farah, M. J. & Wallace, M. A. (1991). Pure alexia as a visual impairment: A reconsideration. *Cognitive Neuropsychology*, *8*, 313–334.

Friedman, R. B. & Alexander, M. P. (1984). Pictures, images, and pure alexia: A case study. *Cognitive Neuropsychology*, *1*(1), 9–23.

Gibson, E. J., Pick, A. D., Osser, H., & Hammond, M. (1962). The role of grapheme-phoneme correspondence in the perception of words. *American Journal of Psychology*, *75*, 554–570.

Hillis, A. & Caramazza, A. (in press). The reading process and its disorders. In D. I. Margolin (Ed.), *Cognitive neuropsychology in clinical practice*. Oxford: Oxford University Press.

Kay, J. & Hanley, R. (1991). Simultaneous form perception and serial letter recognition in a case of letter-by-letter reading. *Cognitive Neuropsychology*, *8*, 249–273.

Kinsbourne, M. & Warrington, E. K. (1962). A variety of reading disability associated with right-hemisphere lesions. *Journal of Neurology, Neurosurgery, and Psychiatry*, *25*, 334–339.

Marr, D. (1982). *Vision*. New York: W. H. Freeman & Co.

Monk, A. F. (1985). Co-ordinate systems in visual word recognition. *Quarterly Journal of Experimental Psychology*, *37(A)*, 613–625.

Patterson, K. & Kay, J. (1982). Letter-by-letter reading: Psychological descriptions of a neurological syndrome. *Quarterly Journal of Experimental Psychology*, *34A*, 411–441.

Reuter-Lorenz, P. A. & Brunn, J. L. (1990). A prelexical basis for letter-by-letter reading: A case study. *Cognitive Neuropsychology*, *7*, 1–20.

Riddoch, M. J., Humphreys, G. W., Cleton, P., & Fery, P. (1990). Interaction of attentional and lexical processes in neglect dyslexia. *Cognitive Neuropsychology*, *7*, 479–517.

Riddoch, M. J. & Humphreys, G. (1987). Perceptual and action systems in unilateral visual neglect. In M. Jeannerod (Ed.), *Neurophysiological and neuropsychological aspects of spatial neglect*. Amsterdam: Elsevier.

Riecher, G. M. (1969). Perceptual recognition as a function of meaningfulness of stimulus material. *Journal of Experimental Psychology*, *81*, 274–280.

Shallice, T. & Saffran, E. (1986). Lexical processing in the absence of explicit word identification: Evidence from a letter-by-letter reader. *Cognitive Neuropsychology*, *3*(4), 429–458.

Treisman, A. (1988). Features and objects: The fourteenth Bartlett Memorial Lecture. *Quarterly Journal of Experimental Psychology*, *40A*, 201–237.

Warrington, E. K. & Shallice, T. (1980). Word-form dyslexia. *Brain*, *103*, 99–112.

COGNITIVE NEUROPSYCHOLOGY, 1991, *8* (3/4) 313–334

Pure Alexia as a Visual Impairment: A Reconsideration

Martha J. Farah and Marcie A. Wallace
Carnegie Mellon University, Pittsburgh, U.S.A.

We contrast two types of explanation for the syndrome of pure alexia: the visual impairment hypothesis, according to which the reading difficulty is just the most obvious manifestation of an impairment in visual perception; and the word form hypothesis, according to which the reading difficulty results from damage to reading-specific mechanisms. We argue that the word form hypothesis cannot account for certain findings in the literature on pure alexia, and that the visual impairment hypothesis is consistent with the available data. In addition, we present two new studies in support of the visual impairment hypothesis. In the first study, a pure alexic patient was found to be impaired on tests that assess the specific type of visual impairment hypothesised to underlie pure alexia. He was not impaired on the less specific tests that had been used previously to argue that perception is intact in pure alexia. In the second study, the additive factors method was used to identify the locus of impairment during reading in the same pure alexic patient. An interaction was found between the visual quality of the words and the length of the words. This implies that the abnormal word length effect in pure alexia (i.e. the letter-by-letter reading strategy) originates in the same processing stage as the visual quality effect, that is, in visual perception. Finally, we attempt to generalise about which kinds of processes make use of dedicated brain hardware and which do not, and suggest that the visual impairment hypothesis of pure alexia is more consistent with this generalisation than is the word form hypothesis.

Requests for reprints should be made to Martha J. Farah, Department of Psychology, Carnegie-Mellon University, Pittsburgh, PA 15213, U.S.A.

This research was supported by O.N.R. contract N0014-89-J3016, N.I.H. grant NS23458, and N.I.H. R.C.D.A. K04NS01405 and NIMH training grant 5T32 MH19102. We would like to thank Robin Rochlin for assistance in data collection, and the following readers and reviewers for helpful suggestions: Marlene Behrmann, Alfonso Caramazza, Max Coltheart, Glyn Humphreys, Karalyn Patterson, Jane Riddoch. Eric Siéroff, and Saul Sternberg. We would also like to thank TU for his help with this project.

EXPLANATIONS OF PURE ALEXIA AND LETTER-BY-LETTER READING

Patients with pure alexia are impaired at reading, despite intact comprehension of spoken language and intact ability to produce written language. To the extent that these patients can read at all, they appear to do so letter-by-letter, earning them the alternative label "letter-by-letter readers". The letter-by-letter strategy may be obvious, as when they name the letters aloud as they read, or it may be apparent only after examination of their reading latencies, which show a characteristic linear increase with the number of letters in the word.

There have been three general types of hypothesis put forth in neuropsychology to explain pure alexia. The first is the disconnection account, originally proposed by Dèjerine (1892), and more recently championed by Geschwind (1965). According to this account, reading consists of associating visual information in occipital cortex with language representations in posterior language areas. This is done by way of the left angular gyrus, adjacent to Wernicke's area, which is hypothesised to contain stored multimodal associations linking the visual and sound patterns of printed words. Thus, pure alexia results from any lesion that disconnects the visual cortex from the left angular gyrus. The neuropathology of pure alexia is generally consistent with this hypothesis (e.g. Damasio & Damasio, 1983; Greenblatt, 1983), often involving a left occipital lesion (causing blindness in the right visual field) and damage to the adjacent splenium (disconnecting left visual field information from the left hemisphere). Despite the anatomical support for this interpretation of pure alexia, it is not an altogether satisfying explanation. For one thing, although it is not in any way *inconsistent* with the letter-by-letter reading strategy of pure alexic patients, it is also not *explanatory* of this highly characteristic feature of the syndrome. It is, of course, possible that disconnection may contribute to some cases of pure alexia. Nevertheless, because they do not offer an explanation for letter-by-letter reading, disconnection accounts will not be discussed further here.

According to a second type of hypothesis, pure alexia results from an impairment in visual perception, which is not limited to the perception of printed words during reading but is merely most obvious in this context. Although low-level visual perception (e.g. acuity, colour and depth perception, length and orientation discrimination) are believed to be normal in pure alexia, it has been claimed by some that shape recognition is impaired, especially when *multiple* shapes must be recognised rapidly or in parallel. This hypothesis was first put forth by Kinsbourne and Warrington (1962). They studied the visual perception of three pure alexics and found that their tachistoscopic recognition thresholds for single forms (letters or simple pictures) were within normal limits, but that their thresholds departed dramatically from those of normals when more than one form had to be recognised. In an ingenious series of experiments, they found that the visual processing "bottleneck" in these patients was determined solely by the number of separate forms to be recognised. Spatial factors such as size, position, and separation of the stimuli had no effect. They therefore concluded that these patients had a disorder of simultaneous form perception, or "simultanagnosia", and that this disorder was the cause of their alexia: because they could recognise only one letter at a time, they were forced to read letter by letter.

Levine and Calvanio (1978) replicated and extended the findings of Kinsbourne and Warrington with three new cases of what they termed "alexia-simultanagnosia". Among the novel results of their study were three findings that helped to pinpoint the locus of processing impairment more precisely than the original Kinsbourne and Warrington studies. First, Levine and Calvanio demonstrated that the difficulty with multiple stimuli is present even when the task does not involve naming the stimuli but merely judging whether two of the stimuli in an array are identical or not. This implies that the limitation is truly affecting perception per se, and not the process of labelling the percept. Second, subjects made more errors in this matching task when the letters in the display were visually similar (e.g. OCO, as opposed to OXO), again implicating a visual locus for the processing breakdown. Finally, Levine and Calvanio contrasted the effects of position cues presented just before and just after the stimulus array on subjects' performance. If shape recognition per se is limited to just one item, then the pre-cue should improve performance because it allows the subject to recognise the one item that has been cued, but the post-cue should not, because it comes after the stimulus array has disappeared and thus cannot guide selective perception. In contrast, if the bottleneck is occurring after shape recognition, in some short-term memory buffer or labelling process, then the post-cues should also help. Levine and Calvanio found that subjects were helped by the pre-cues: if they knew in advance *which* letter (indicated by its position) from a multi-letter array they were to report, they could do so accurately, even with the other letters present. However, if the cue came after perceptual processing has been completed it did not help, again implicating visual recognition per se as the locus of impairment.

More recently, several other studies have uncovered additional evidence of visual impairment in pure alexics. Although these studies were not designed to characterise the precise nature of the visual impairment, they do add some degree of confirmation to the hypothesis that visual impairment plays a role in pure alexia. Patterson and Kay (1982) examined the nature of the errors made by four pure alexic patients in identifying individual letters during reading and found that they were strongly dependent on visual similarity. This is what one would expect if visual perception were at fault in these patients and is consistent with the observations of Levine and Calvanio (1978) of their alexic patients, who also made predominantly visual errors.

Friedman and Alexander (1984) assessed the recognition of tachistoscopically presented verbal and nonverbal visual material with a pure alexic subject. When the tasks involved simple stimulus detection, discriminating the orientation of lines presented individually, or recognising which of two letters was presented individually, the pure alexic's thresholds were within the range of the normal subjects'. In contrast, when the task involved recognising more complex visual stimuli, either verbal (words) or nonverbal (line drawings), pure alexic's thresholds were elevated with respect to the normal subjects' thresholds. Friedman and Alexander (1984, p. 9) conclude that "pure alexia is the behavioural manifestation of a deficit in the speed of visual identification, which is not specific to orthographic material."

Three groups of investigators have examined the performance of pure alexic subjects in letter-matching tasks, in which pairs of letters must be judged "same" or "different" as quickly as possible. Although slightly different experimental designs were used in each case, all three were found to have difficulty with this relatively simple visual task (Bub, Black, & Howell, 1989; Kay & Hanley, this vol.; Reuter-Lorenz & Brunn, 1990). The two patients who were shown letters of differing case were particularly impaired at cross-case matching, in which the subject cannot rely at all on low-level physical stimulus features to perform the task (Kay & Hanley, in press; Reuter-Lorenz & Brunn, 1990). In addition, performance seemed keenly sensitive to the number of stimuli to be recognised within a particular amount of time: Kay and Hanley's and Reuter-Lorenz and Brunn's cases performed better when the two letters were presented sequentially, with a half second between them. Bub et al. found that their subject was disproportionately slowed in his judgements of simultaneously presented letters by the occurrence of another letter 200msec. before the pair to be compared.

To summarise the second type of hypothesis, pure alexia is just the most obvious manifestation of a disorder of visual perception that is not limited to verbal material. This visual disorder consists of a slowed or diminished ability to recognise multiple or complex visual stimuli. Word recognition demands just this ability (see, e.g., Johnston & McClelland, 1980, for evidence that individual letters must be recognised in order for word recognition to take place). Because these patients cannot recognise multiple letters at once, they adopt a strategy of reading one letter at a time.

In contrast, a third type of hypothesis explains pure alexia in terms of disruption to reading-specific processes. Warrington and Shallice (1980) suggested that normal reading requires that the individually recognised letters be grouped into recognisable higher-order units, corresponding to morphemes and/or whole words. They term these higher-order visual representations "word forms" and hypothesise that pure alexic patients have sustained damage to the word form system. This explains why their ability to recognise words seems to be mediated solely by recognising a single letter at a time. Because these patients have no word forms to match against the (normally perceived) letters of the word, they use their knowledge of spelling to identify words from the individual letters, therefore spelling them out.

The evidence presented by Warrington and Shallice for damaged word forms in pure alexia is of two kinds. First, they attempt to show that their pure alexic patients have good or at least adequate visual perception of letters and words, ruling out a visual perceptual locus for the impairment. The specific tests of visual perception that they used will be discussed later. By a process of elimination, they argue, this strengthens the support for a higher-order, reading-specific locus of impairment. Second, they showed that these patients had much more difficulty reading script than print. One characteristic of script writing is that the individual letters are less distinctive than individual printed characters, and therefore recognition of words in script relies more on overall word form than the recognition of printed words. Thus, the greater impairment with script is consistent with a word form deficit. Of course, it should be noted that this is also consistent with the hypothesis of visual impairment, and for the same reason, namely that individual letters are visually less distinctive in script than in print.

Patterson and Kay (1982) proposed a modification of the word form hypothesis, according to which the word form system is intact, but that its input from letter recognition systems is limited to one letter at a time. This hypothesis can account for all of Warrington and Shallice's data. In fact, both versions of the word form hypothesis are compatible with all of the data collected by Warrington and Shallice and Patterson and Kay, and both groups acknowledge this (Patterson & Kay, 1982; Shallice, 1984, chapter 4). Patterson and Kay's reasons for preferring their alternative include several indirect and, in their words, "intuitive" considerations. One of the most compelling is their observation (1982, p. 433) that for some patients "enormous effort was required to identify letters; but, once that had been achieved, moving from letters to the word was virtually automatic". This is the opposite of what one would expect if the word forms themselves were damaged.

RECONSIDERING THE HYPOTHESIS OF VISUAL IMPAIRMENT

The word form hypothesis was an extremely influential one, and seems to have eclipsed the hypothesis of visual impairment, if discussions of pure alexia in recent neuropsychology textbooks are an indication (e.g. Ellis & Young, 1988; McCarthy & Warrington, 1990). We will argue that the hypothesis of visual impairment has been discarded prematurely. This argument has three parts: first, a review of some recent data that are problematic for the word form hypothesis but not for the visual impairment hypothesis; second, a critique of the evidence used by Warrington, Shallice, Patterson, and Kay to reject the visual impairment hypothesis; and third, new data implicating visual impairment as the cause of the reading disturbance in a pure alexic subject.

Recent evidence suggests that at least some pure alexic patients do have access to word form information during reading. Bub et al. (1989) and Reuter-Lorenz and Brunn (1990) assessed the ability of two pure alexic subjects to recognise letters in the contexts of words and nonwords. In normal subjects, letters are perceived more quickly and accurately in word contexts because of top-down support from competing word form representations, and this phenomenon is known as the "word superiority effect". The effect cannot be attributed to guessing the identity of a letter based on the partial or full perceptions of the other letters in the word, because it can be demonstrated even in a forced-choice task in which both of the letter choices make a word. For example, if the stimulus word is "cap", and the choices for the final letter are "p" and "t", subjects will be more successful at choosing "p", even though "t" would also make a word, than if the letter string had been "dat" and the same choice of final letters given. The pure alexic subjects of Bub et al. and Reuter-Lorenz and Brunn showed the word superiority effect. Furthermore, the alexics' word superiority effects were of roughly the same magnitude as the control subjects'. The ability of higher-order, multi-letter patterns to affect the encoding of individual letters in a word demonstrates rather directly that such higher-order multi-letter patterns, or word forms, are available in pure alexia. It is not inconsistent with the visual impairment hypothesis, as the word superiority effect is believed to influence visual recognition of words *at the letter level* (McClelland & Rumelhart, 1981).

Two cases of pure alexia have not shown word superiority effects (Behrmann, Black, & Bub, in press; Kay & Hanley, this vol.). One possible conclusion from this variability is that pure alexia can be caused by different underlying impairments, and that these latter two cases are caused by impairment or inaccessibility of the word form system. However, there is a second possibility, according to which visual impairment underlies all cases of pure alexia, and the word superiority effect is absent in some cases because of encoding strategies adopted as a result of the visual impairment. Johnston and McClelland (1974) showed that the word superiority effect is greatly diminished or abolished in normal subjects when they attempt to read the letter in a particular position, rather than distributing their attention across all letter positions. Of course, letter-by-letter reading consists of just this strategy: first reading the letter in the first position, then reading the letter in the second, and so on. The available evidence from the pure alexic subjects suggests that it is the presence versus absence of the letter-by-letter strategy while performing the experimental task, rather than the presence versus absence of word form knowledge, that determines whether pure alexics will show a word superiority effect.

In the two cases that showed a word superiority effect, analysis of their accuracy as a function of letter position indicated that they had abandoned the letter-by-letter strategy in the context of the experiment. Although they required much longer exposure durations than normal subjects to attain the same overall level of performance, consistent with diminished visual recognition capacity, the *profile* of performance over letter positions was normal: accuracy was highest in the first and last letter positions, and lower in the middle letter positions, consistent with a normal strategy of distributing attention over all letter positions (and the normal advantage for end letters). The two cases who did not show a word superiority effect did not abandon their letter-by-letter reading strategy in the experiment: Berhmann et al.'s case and Kay and Hanley's case both showed a gradient of performance across letter positions, with best performance in the first position, next best in the second, and so on. Even within one case, there is a correlation between the profile of performance across letter positions and the word superiority effect: in one variant of the experiment, Bub et al.'s case failed to show the word superiority effect, and also showed the left-to-right gradient in accuracy over letter positions.

"Implicit" reading is another source of evidence on the availability of word forms in pure alexia. Pure alexics can sometimes make accurate lexical decisions about words that they are unable to identify explicitly (i.e. read aloud). For example, Shallice and Saffran's (1986) case performed far above chance in discriminating words from pseudowords when the letter strings were presented too quickly for him to read them aloud. He also performed above chance in certain categorisation tasks, in which he was to decide whether a word named something from a particular semantic category, such as living things. Landis, Regard, and Serrat (1980) and Grossi, Fragassi, Orsini, De Falco, and Sepe (1984) report cases of pure alexia in which words presented too briefly to be read could be matched with their corresponding pictures or objects. Coslett and Saffran (1989) describe several cases in which lexical decision, categorisation, and picture matching of briefly presented unread words were all relatively preserved. These findings might seem to imply that at least some word form information is available in pure alexia. However, not all cases tested have shown implicit reading ability. Patterson and Kay (1982) and Warrington and Shallice (1980) failed to find evidence of implicit reading in their cases.

As with the word superiority effect, the differences between cases in implicit reading ability can be interpreted in two ways. On the one hand, there could be different forms of pure alexia with different underlying causes. Some cases of pure alexia could be caused by destruction of the word form system, and in these cases we would not expect to find implicit reading ability. On the other hand, it is possible that all pure alexia is caused by a visual impairment, and the presence versus absence of implicit reading abilities depends upon the subjects' strategies for encoding briefly presented letter strings. Shallice and Saffran's case (1986, p. 435) described his strategy for performing lexical decision as "a process of looking at the whole length of the word and finding a combination of letters which can't be right, or looking at the whole word and seeing that it looked sensible", a description that contrasts with the letter-by-letter strategy he used for explicit word identification. Coslett and Saffran (1989) report that they encouraged their subjects to look at the whole word and not to attempt to explicitly identify it using a letter-by-letter strategy. They remark (p. 355) that "it was our impression that when subjects attempted to use a letter-by-letter strategy, as they all did initially, there was no convincing evidence of better than chance performance on lexical decision and categorization tasks" and that the onset of reliable implicit reading effects was accompanied by a reduction in accuracy for reporting the initial letter of the strings, consistent with the abandonment of the letter-by-letter strategy. They point out that previous failures to find implicit reading occurred in tasks in which explicit word identification was also required, encouraging a letter-by-letter strategy. They also showed that with longer exposure durations, subjects performed *worse* on the implicit reading tasks, presumably because the letter-by-letter strategy became viable. It may be for similar reasons that Landis et al.'s (1980) case lost his implicit reading ability as he regained his ability to identify words explicitly letter-by-letter, and that most cases with implicit reading are particularly slow or inaccurate at letter-by-letter reading.

In sum, the presence of the word superiority effect and implicit reading abilities in some pure alexic patients suggests that word form information is available in at least some cases. The absence of these phenomena in other cases does not necessarily imply that a loss of word form information underlies the pure alexia in these cases. Strategy differences, for which there is some independent evidence, could account for the absence of these phenomena in subjects with intact word form representations.

The visual impairment hypothesis was rejected by proponents of the word form hypothesis on the grounds of the good performance of their subjects on tests of visual perception. However, it is a neuropsychological truism that abilities such as visual perception are composed of many distinct and dissociable subprocesses, and it therefore follows that patients who pass certain tests of visual perception with flying colours could be severely impaired on others. Let us examine the tests of visual perception that Warrington, Shallice, Patterson, and Kay administered to their patients, and consider whether these tests tapped the specific ability described by proponents of the visual impairment hypothesis.

Warrington and Shallice (1980) carried out several different tests of visual perception with a mildly alexic case, RAV. This subject required less than 2secs. to read 3- and 4-letter words and only 3secs. to read 7- and 8-letter words. For purposes of comparison, other cases reviewed by Shallice (1988) required as much as 17secs. on average to read 3- and 4-letter words, and close to 50secs. on average to read 7- and 8-letter words. On 2 standard tests of reading he scored well: on the Schonell graded word reading test he performed "at a high level" (98%), and on the Nelson reading test he obtained a reading I.Q. of 121. Thus, his impairment was evident only in the slowness with which he read most text. Warrington and Shallice also administered a few of their visual tests to a second case, JDC, who was more impaired than RAV. Patterson and Kay (1982) replicated some of Warrington and Shallice's results with their case, TP, whose severity is in the middle range of the cases reviewed by Shallice (1988).

Both Warrington and Shallice (1980) and Patterson and Kay (1982) assessed the effects of visual angle and number of distracting characters on their subjects' ability to recognise alphanumeric characters. Displays such as "6STOP4" were shown tachistoscopically, with instructions to read the digits in the first and last position. For both Warrington and Shallice's case, RAV, and Patterson and Kay's case, TP, performance was unaffected by the number of intervening letters. Similarly, RAV was able to read the central letter in a tachistoscopic display of five letters, and his ability to read two briefly presented letters, although not perfect, was unaffected by how far apart they were spaced. Does this mean that these patients did not have an impairment in the rapid recognition of multiple characters? No, because these tasks did not require the recognition of the distractor characters, and the characters to be recognised were in positions known by the subject in advance. As mentioned earlier, Levine and Calvanio (1978) demonstrated that "alexic-simultanagnosics" are unaffected by distractor letters when the position of the letter to be reported was known in advance. Therefore, on the hypothesis that pure alexics suffer from the type of visual impairment described by Kinsborne, Warrington, Levine, and Calvanio, they would not be predicted to show detrimental effects of number of distracting letters in the tasks just described. Furthermore, Kinsbourne and Warrington (1962) demonstrated that spatial separation amongst the stimuli to be recognised has no effect on ease of recognition, again predicting that the separation manipulation would not affect the performance of RAV and TP even according to the visual impairment hypothesis. In a different type of task, Warrington and Shallice gave RAV, and the more impaired JDC, an array of 25 letters to read aloud without time pressure. They report that RAV completed the task flawlessly, and JDC made only 3 errors; time to complete the task is not reported. As before, this finding is consistent with the visual impairment hypothesis: Kinsbourne and Warrington stressed the idea that the relevant visual impairment involves *rapid* visual encoding, and this predicts that, given sufficient time, pure alexics could recognise many stimuli arbitrarily.

Warrington and Shallice also present the results of three tachistoscopic "whole report" tasks with RAV. When shown 3 letters simultaneously for 50msec. (unmasked), RAV made only 8 errors out of 40 trials. When shown 4 digits simultaneously for 100msec. (unmasked), RAV made 5 errors out of 20 trials. Finally, when shown strings of 5 letters that were either randomly chosen or were statistical approximations to English for 100msec. (unmasked), RAV reported 53% of the random letters and 72% of the letters in strings approximating English. Although these levels of performance are above those of the alexics studied by Kinsbourne and Warrington (1962) and Levine and Calvanio (1978), RAV is an extremely mild alexic and would therefore be expected to show only mild visual impairment. Furthermore, the absence of control data makes it difficult to determine whether these findings confirm or disconfirm the hypothesis that RAV has a mild visual impairment. Although Warrington and Shallice point out that his performance is roughly equivalent to the mean performance of left hemisphere damaged patients tested in the same task by Warrington and Rabin (1971), the latter patients viewed the stimuli for less time (50msec.), which would make the task harder.

Finally, Warrington and Shallice cite the good performance of their patients on various clinical tests involving picture interpretation as evidence against visual impairment. Their patients were tested with the Peabody picture vocabulary test, the W.A.I.S. picture completion test, and the W.A.I.S. picture arrangement test. Although JDC performed well below average on all three of these tests, RAV performed well, rating "high average range" on the two W.A.I.S. subtests. Once again, these tests are probably not the appropriate ones for detecting the relevant form of visual impairment: with the exception of picture arrangement, which involves sequencing simple scenes, they do not require that multiple objects be recognised simultaneously or rapidly.

In the following two experiments we attempt to test the visual impairment hypothesis more directly, in a single case of letter-by-letter reading. The tasks are selected to assess the specific visual ability hypothesised to be impaired, namely, the ability to recognise multiple objects rapidly. This ability is tested with verbal and nonverbal materials in the paper and pencil visual perception tasks of Experiment 1, and with verbal materials during reading in Experiment 2.

EXPERIMENT 1

In this experiment, we assessed the visual perception of a pure alexic patient using a set of paper and pencil tests designed specifically to test the rapid recognition of multiple visual forms. For purposes of comparison, we also administered the two W.A.I.S.-R. subtests used by Warrington and Shallice (1980) to assess visual perception in their pure alexic subjects.

Methods

Subject

TU is a 51-year-old right-handed man. He is a high school graduate who, until the time of his illness, worked as a safety inspector for the railroad. Approximately one year prior to the testing reported here a left occipital arterial venous malformation ruptured and bled. An intraventricular haematoma was evacuated and the A.V.M. resected. Residual neurological problems aside from alexia included mild right hemiparesis, right homonymous hemianopia, anomia, and memory impairment. There was no neglect apparent on clinical examination, and no evidence of visual agnosia in picture naming. Aural language comprehension, writing and spelling were intact. In contrast, reading was extremely slow and laborious, and appeared to be accomplished in a letter-by-letter manner. Irregular words were read about as successfully as regular words and his occasional errors seemed to result from the misidentification of individual letters within a word. Three weeks after surgery, a C.T.-scan showed a lesion in the left temporal lobe.

Materials and Procedure

The three "perceptual speed" subtests from the Ekstrom, French, and Harman (1976) kit of factor-referenced cognitive tests were administered. These tests, and their relevance to the issue of visual impairment in pure alexia, are described here.

Finding A's Test. The materials for this test consist of columns of words, 41 words per column, of which 5 words in each column contain the letter "a". The subject's task is to draw a line through each word that contains an "a". The subject is told that there are 5 such words per column and that speed is important. For our subject, we elaborated on these instructions by pointing out that he did not need to read the words, and that the *only* objective was to find the "a's" as quickly as possible. Practice is given with 3 columns of 21 words each. The score is the number of words marked correctly in 2 2-minute sessions. Figure 1a shows the practice trials from this test.

Number Comparison Test. The materials for this test consist of pairs of multidigit numbers (3–9 digits each). The subject's task is to indicate whether the 2 numbers in the pair are identical or differ by one digit. The subject is told to go as quickly as possible without sacrificing accuracy, and that the score will be the number correct minus the number wrong obtained in 2 1½-minute sessions. Practice is given with 16 pairs of numbers. Figure 1b shows the practice trials from this test.

Identical Pictures Test. Each item in this test consists of a geometric figure or picture on the left, with 4 similar stimuli in a row to the right. One of these stimuli is identical to the figure or picture on the left, and the subject's task is to place a check under that one. The subject is told to go as quickly as possible without sacrificing accuracy, and that the score will be

(a)

1	2	3	4	5
cider	~~east~~	stripe	insert	defend
bough	blind	coarse	court	settle
fudge	chord	govern	pearl	lodge
greet	~~solar~~	perfect	bridle	oaken
~~fault~~	spoon	special	recess	crown
~~leap~~	piece	consist	soapy	quest
count	rinse	mostly	able	glimpse
shore	~~drawn~~	shrink	pledge	every
~~easel~~	fleet	pencil	refuse	break
define	sense	hinder	better	where
entire	uncle	solace	patrol	thorn
ghost	white	keeper	judge	pause
knife	~~coach~~	night	defect	hence
hedge	south	clock	trust	short
~~petal~~	period	picnic	other	person
scope	miller	smart	straw	warm
ripen	~~slogan~~	finger	noisy	juice
under	height	useful	defer	enter
~~heard~~	event	slowly	field	ordeal
quite	bond	meant	mend	nurse
jump	west	quick	skill	cool

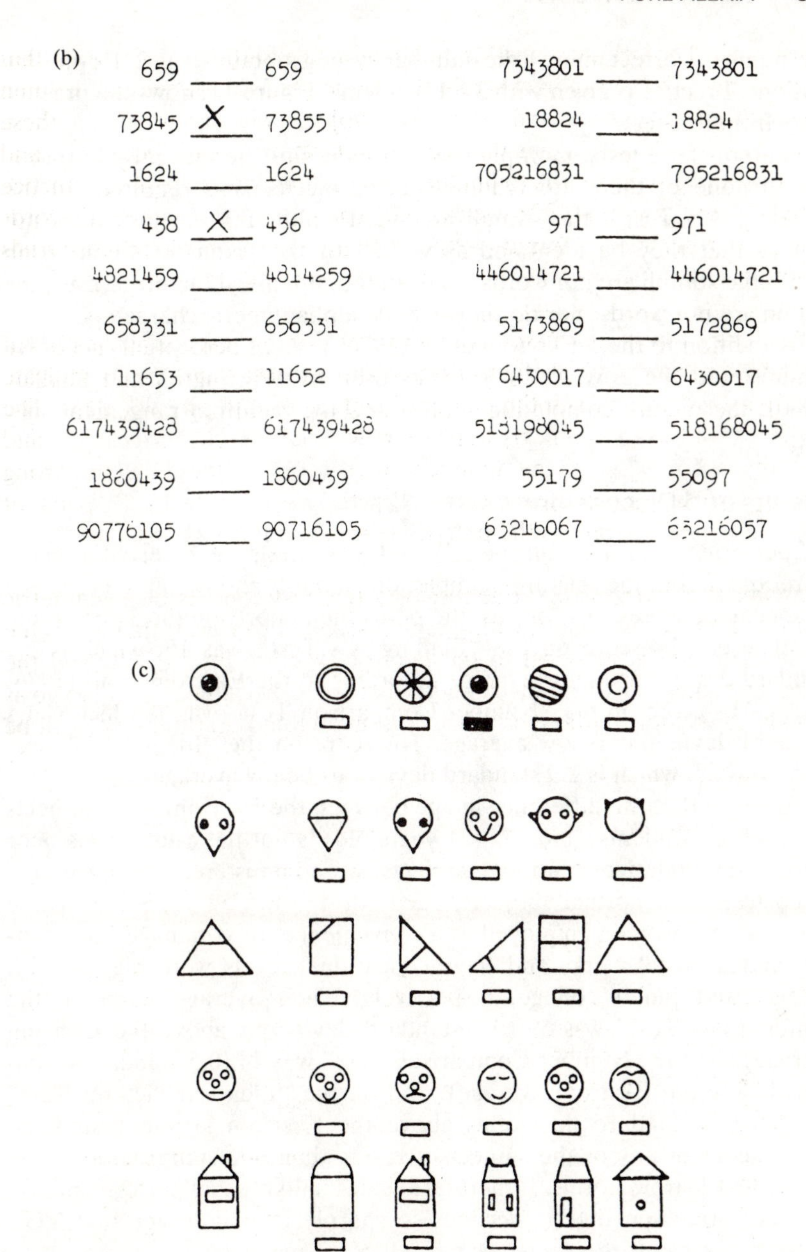

FIG. 1 Practice items from the three tests of "perceptual speed" in the kit of factor-referenced cognitive tests (Ekstrom et al., 1976): (a) the Finding A's Test; (b) the Number Comparison Test; (c) the Identical Pictures Test.

the number correct minus the number wrong obtained in 2 1½-minute sessions. Practice is given with 3 sets of items. Figure 1c shows the practice trials from this test.

In all of these tests, multiple visual stimuli must be recognised rapidly, and in none of them are reading-specific mechanisms required. In the "Finding A's Test", the stimuli are words, although the task does not require that they be identified as words. In the "Number Comparison Test", the stimuli are not words at all. In the "Identical Pictures Test", the stimuli are not words, nor do they include alphanumeric characters.

In addition to the 3 Ekstrom et al. (1976) tests of perceptual speed, we administered the 2 W.A.I.S. subtests used by Warrington and Shallice (1980): the picture completion subtest and the picture arrangement subtest.

Results and Discussion

TU performed normally on the 2 W.A.I.S. subtests: he received a scaled score of 10 on the picture completion subtest and 9 on the picture arrangement subtest. In contrast, he performed poorly on the 3 perceptual speed tests. His score on the "Finding A's Test" was 15, which is 2.1 standard deviations below average according to the Ekstrom et al. (1976) norms. His score on the "Number Comparison Test" was 7, which is 4.1 standard deviations below average. His score on the "Identical Pictures Test" was 27, which is 2.9 standard deviations below average.

To verify that the difference in age between the Ekstrom et al. subjects (high school students) and TU (51 years old) is not the cause of his poor performance relative to normal subjects, we administered the perceptual speed tests to 3 normal subjects, aged 48, 55, and 59 years old. These subjects were women employed as a convenience store manager, a secretary, and a postal clerk, and their educational levels were high school, college, and junior college, respectively. Their average score on the "Finding A's Test" was 59 (0.8 standard deviations above the Ekstrom average), on the "Number Comparison Test" was 24 (0.5 standard deviations below the Ekstrom average), and on the "Identical Pictures Test" was 59 (0.5 standard deviations above the Ekstrom average), and the lowest score of any of the subjects was less than one standard deviation below the Ekstrom norms. It therefore seems unlikely that performance on the perceptual speed tests declines so sharply in middle age that TU's performance can be explained as a result of normal ageing.

In TU, at least, pure alexia is accompanied by an impairment in the rapid recognition of multiple stimuli, whether the stimuli be words, letters, numbers, or geometric forms and pictures. The dissociation observed between TU's adequate performance on the W.A.I.S. picture completion and picture arrangement subtests and his poor performance on the Ekstrom et al. (1976) perceptual speed tests confirms that the former are not sensitive tests of the ability to recognise multiple stimuli rapidly, and that the adequate performance of previously described subjects on these tests cannot be used to argue against the existence of a visual impairment in these subjects.

EXPERIMENT 2

The results of Experiment 1, as well as those of Kinsbourne and Warrington (1962), Levine and Calvanio (1978), and others cited earlier, are of a correlational nature. That is, they show that subjects who have pure alexia also have an impairment in the rapid recognition of multiple visual forms. The present experiment was designed to assess the role of visual impairment in causing the characteristic letter-by-letter strategy *during reading*. It is based on the "additive factor method" of Sternberg (1969), according to which two experimental factors or manipulations that affect the same internal processing stage will have interactive effects when applied simultaneously, whereas if they affect different processing stages they will have additive effects.

The two factors under study in this experiment are word length and visual quality. According to the visual impairment hypothesis, word length affects the reading latencies of pure alexics because each additional letter taxes their visual recognition abilities. In other words, *the additional time required for each additional letter is filled with visual processing, and the locus of the word length effect is therefore visual.* According to the word form hypothesis, word length affects the reading latencies of pure alexics because they are forced to spell the words in order to recognise them. Their visual recognition of the letters is hypothesised to be no different from that of a normal person. Therefore, *the additional time required for each additional letter is not filled with visual processing, but with some combination of letter naming, short-term auditory memory processing, and access to long-term spelling knowledge, and the locus of the word length effect is therefore post-visual.*

The visual quality of the stimulus is a factor that affects visual perception, but not the post-perceptual processes of name retrieval, short-term auditory memory, or spelling. Therefore, the two hypotheses make different predictions about the effects of combining word length and visual quality manipulations. Specifically, the visual impairment hypothesis predicts an interaction between these two factors, as they are both hypothesised to affect the same processing stage. The word form hypothesis predicts no interaction (i.e. additivity) because the two factors are hypothesised to affect different processing stages.

Methods

Subject

TU served again as a subject in this experiment.

Materials

Eighty words each of length 3, 4, 5, 6, and 7 letters were selected from the Francis and Kuçera (1982) word listings, such that the frequencies of the words in each list were roughly yoked.[1] The 80 words of each length were divided into 4 lists each, yielding a total of 20 word lists with approximately equal mean word frequencies. The lists were printed in a 14 point bold "Geneva" typefont using a Macintosh computer and laser printer. Half of the lists of each word length were masked with a random line-segment pattern. Examples of unmasked and masked words are shown in Fig. 2. As a result, 2 lists of each word-length were unmasked, and 2 lists were masked.

Procedure

The 20 lists were presented in the following order: 3-letter—masked; 6-letter—unmasked; 7-letter—masked; 4-letter—unmasked; 5-letter—masked; break; 3-letter—unmasked; 6-letter—masked; 7-letter—unmasked; 4-letter—masked; 5-letter—unmasked; break; followed by the same order backwards (i.e. 5-letter—unmasked; 4-letter—masked; etc.). For each list, the page was placed in front of the subject with a cover over it. When the cover was removed, the subject was instructed to read each

point

moral

until

FIG. 2 Examples of unmasked and masked words.

---

[1]For the 30 lowest frequency words in each list (39–73 occurrences per million), the words in each yoked set differed by no more than one occurrence per million. For the 30 middle frequency words (82–171 occurrences per million), the words in each yoked set differed by no more than 6 occurrences per million. For the 20 highest frequency words (183–419 occurrences per million) the words in each yoked set differed by no more than 12 occurrences per million.

word as quickly as possible, without stopping for comments until the end of the list. Errors were corrected immediately. If a word was not read after a repeat attempt, he was told to go on to the next word. The session was videotaped for later transcription and timing.

Results and Discussion

Latencies for each word were recorded by stop-watch from the videotape. Latencies for errors (i.e. words read incorrectly) were not included in the analyses to be reported. There were an average of 1.5 errors per unmasked list and 3.5 errors per masked list. There was no particular trend in errors as a function of word length. Outlier latencies were also excluded from the analyses. A latency was considered an outlier if it was more than 2.5 standard deviations from the mean of the latencies from the same list. This criterion was applied iteratively, until a set of latencies were all within 2.5 standard deviations of their mean. There were an average of 0.5 outlier latencies per unmasked list and 1.5 per masked list, again showing no trend as a function of word length.

The resultant means from the 10 conditions of interest are shown in Fig. 3. Two important aspects of the results are immediately apparent. First, each factor had an effect. Reading latency shows the classic increase with word length. This function begins to flatten out at the longer word

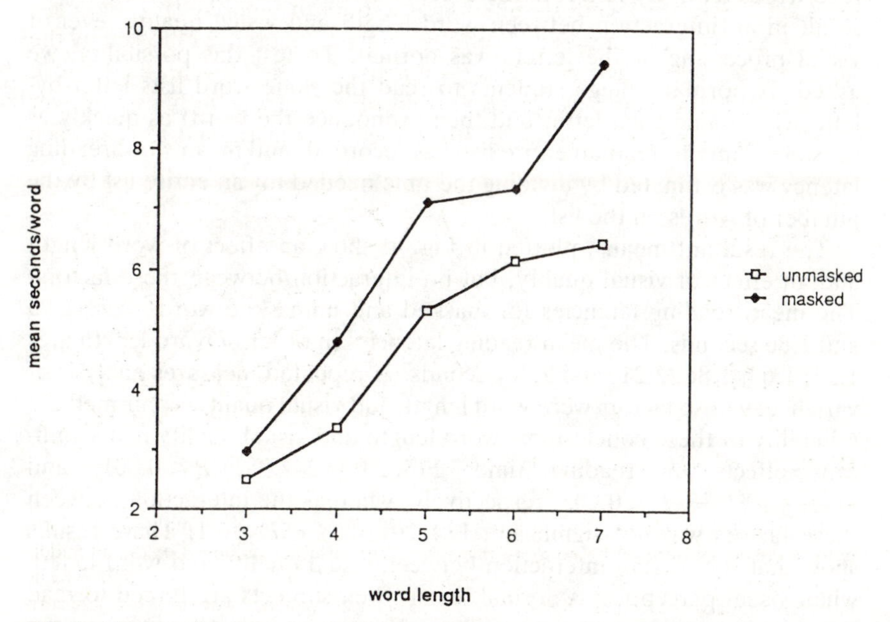

FIG. 3 Mean reading latencies of TU for unmasked and masked words of length 3, 4, 5, 6, and 7 letters.

lengths, as the likelihood of correctly guessing a word before all letters have been read increases. The mean reading latencies, in order of word length, are: 2.73, 4.08, 6.22, 6.75, and 7.95 seconds. Visual degradation also had an effect on reading latency. The mean reading latencies for unmasked and masked words are 4.76 and 6.33 seconds, respectively. Second, there appears to be an interaction between word length and visual quality, such that the effects of word length were exacerbated by the masking manipulation, as predicted by the visual impairment hypothesis. The mean reading latencies for the unmasked words, in order of word length, are: 2.50, 3.36, 5.33, 6.15, and 6.46 seconds. The mean reading latencies for the masked words, in order of word length, are: 2.95, 4.80, 7.10, 7.34, and 9.44 seconds, respectively.

The reliability of these effects was assessed by a 2-way analysis of variance whose factors were word length (3, 4, 5, 6, 7 letters) and visual quality (masked, unmasked). As expected, word length had a significant effect; $F(4, 310) = 47.24$, $P < 0.001$, as did visual quality: $F(1, 310) = 26.74$, $P < 0.001$. The interaction between word length and visual quality, predicted by the visual impairment hypothesis, was also significant: $F(4, 310) = 4.46$, $P < 0.002$.

Is it possible that the word form hypothesis is able to account for the interaction between word length and visual quality? Perhaps the need to read words letter-by-letter, in the absence of word forms, would somehow result in an interaction between word length and visual quality, even if visual processing of the letters was normal. To test this possibility, we asked six normal college students to read the same word lists letter-by-letter (i.e. name each letter and then pronounce the word) as quickly as possible. Time to read an entire list was recorded, and mean word reading latency was estimated by dividing the time needed for an entire list by the number of words on the list.

The resultant means, plotted in Fig. 4, show an effect of word length and an effect of visual quality, but no interaction between these factors. The mean reading latencies for masked and unmasked words were 1.93 and 1.86 seconds. The mean reading latencies in order of word length are: 1.35, 1.60, 1.86, 2.21, and 2.46 seconds. A repeated measures analysis of variance, whose factors were word length and visual quality, confirmed the reliability of these conclusions: word length and visual quality had significant effects on reading time: $F(4, 20) = 244.95$, $P < 0.001$, and $F(1, 5) = 31.75$, $P < 0.005$, respectively, whereas the interaction between these factors was not significant: $F(4, 20) = 1.19$, $P > 0.1$. These results show that there is no interaction between visual quality and word length when visual perception is normal, even when subjects are forced to read letter-by-letter. This conclusion is consistent with other findings on the effects of visual noise on multiple character recognition. For example,

Pashler and Badgio (1985) found that, in naming the highest digit present in an array, subjects took longer to respond the more digits were present, and when the digits were visually degraded, but there was no interaction between these two effects. How might one account for the performance of TU and the control subjects without postulating that TU's impairment is visual? There is an alternative explanation in terms of cascade models of stage processing (McClelland, 1979). According to such an account, the additivity observed in the normal subjects is the result of a superadditive interaction between word length and visual quality operating on different stages arranged in cascade, and a subadditive interaction between those same factors resulting from an increasing opportunity for top-down facilitation of perception by word forms with increasing word length and visual degradation. If TU's word forms were damaged, this would "unmask" the superadditive interaction by eliminating the subadditive influences of word forms. However, there are two difficulties with this account. First, it requires that the sizes of the two interactions being fortuitously equal, in order to produce the additivity found in normal subjects. Second, Pashler and Badgio showed that additivity is obtained even when there is no opportunity for top-down support from word forms.

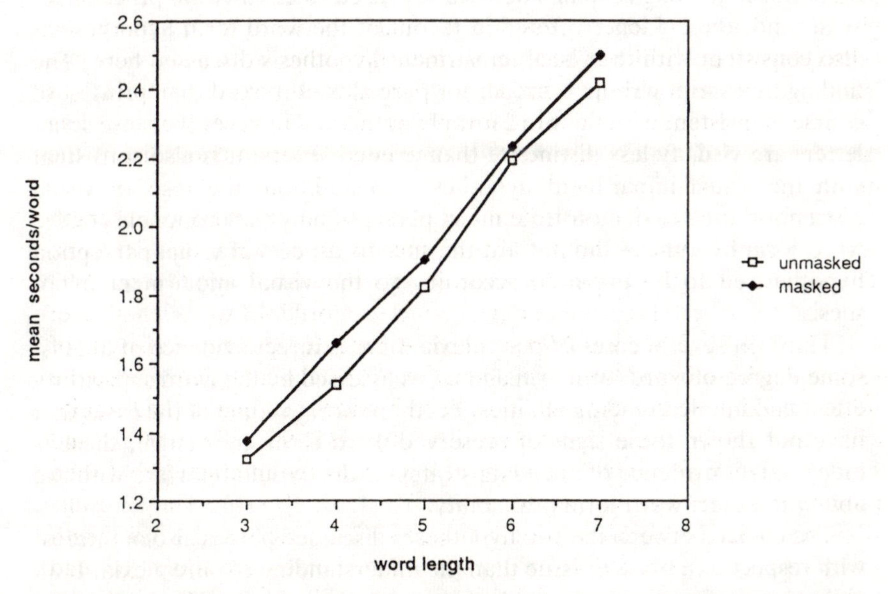

FIG. 4 Mean reading latencies of six normal subjects, reading letter-by-letter as quickly as possible, for unmasked and masked words of length 3, 4, 5, 6, and 7 letters.

GENERAL DISCUSSION

The letter-by-letter reading strategy of pure alexic patients has been explained in two very different ways. According to one account, it results from damage to *reading-specific* mechanisms, specifically those that relate the perceived letters of the word to stored representations of word form. According to the other account, it results from damage to mechanisms that are normally required for reading, but not only for reading; specifically, the visual ability to recognise multiple shapes rapidly.

Although we must remain open to the possibility that there is more than one underlying cause of pure alexia in different patients, the available evidence is most consistent with the hypothesis of visual impairment. We will recapitulate this evidence briefly here.

First, there is a variety of different evidence suggesting that pure alexics have an impairment in rapidly recognising multiple shapes. This includes the findings of Kinsbourne, Warrington, Levine, and Calvanio, that pure alexic patients have a specific impairment in recognising multiple shapes, either alphanumeric or entirely nonverbal, when presentations are brief. It also includes the ubiquitous clinical observation of visual errors in letter identification by these patients. Finally, it includes our finding that a pure alexic patient was impaired on paper and pencil tests of rapid shape identification, with verbal and nonverbal materials, and that the locus of his abnormally long reading latencies appeared to be in visual processing.

Second, the evidence offered in favour of the word form hypothesis is also consistent with the visual impairment hypothesis discussed here. The finding that script writing is harder for pure alexics to read than print is, of course, consistent with the word form hypothesis. However, because script letters are visually less distinctive than printed letters, it is also consistent with the visual impairment hypothesis. In addition, the tests of visual perception used to demonstrate intact perception by the proponents of the word form hypothesis did not test the specific aspects of visual perception hypothesised to be impaired according to the visual impairment hypothesis.

Third, in several cases of pure alexia there is direct evidence of at least some degree of word form availability, as assessed by the word superiority effect and implicit reading abilities. Furthermore, in some of the cases that have not shown these signs of preserved word form knowledge, there is independent evidence of encoding strategies that would interfere with the ability to detect word form availability.

The choice between the two hypotheses discussed here is also of interest with respect to a broader issue than the understanding of pure alexia. If an ability can be impaired selectively and permanently by focal brain damage, this suggests that this ability is normally performed using *dedicated hard-*

ware, that is, some relatively local part of the brain that is required for that ability and is not required for any other abilities. There are many examples in neuropsychology of processes that may be impaired selectively and permanently by focal brain damage and thus appear to depend upon dedicated hardware. Colour vision, skilled movement, learning, and sentence parsing are all in this category. In contrast, some of the abilities that cognitive psychologists study do not seem to fit this pattern. We do not see *selective* impairments in chess or physics problem-solving, and hence we may conclude that these abilities do not depend on dedicated hardware.

What is the difference between the kinds of abilities for which we use dedicated hardware and the kinds for which we apparently do not? Colour vision, skilled movement, learning, and sentence parsing are all abilities that are evolutionarily old, shared by all members of the species, and innate. Chess and physics problem-solving are very recent, performed by only a small fraction of the species, and acquired through instruction. Although we know of no reason *why* this distinction should be co-extensive with whether or not an ability makes use of dedicated hardware, the examples listed here, and all of the others that we could think of, are consistent with this generalisation. In terms of evolutionary history, prevalence, and acquisition, reading is much more like chess than like colour vision. Therefore, we would like to suggest that the visual impairment hypothesis of pure alexia is preferable a priori to hypotheses that postulate damage to reading-specific mechanisms. It remains to be seen whether all cases of pure alexia, as well as other dyslexias, can be explained without postulating damage to reading-specific mechanisms.

Manuscript received 15 February 1990
Revised manuscript received 20 June 1990

REFERENCES

Behrmann, M., Black, S., & Bub, D. N. (in press). The evolution of letter-by-letter reading. *Brain and Cognition*.

Bub, D. N., Black, S., & Howell, J. (1989). Word recognition and orthographic context effects in a letter-by-letter reader. *Brain and Language*, *36*, 357–376.

Coslett, H. B. & Saffran, E. M. (1989). Evidence for preserved reading in "pure alexia". *Brain*, *89*, 327–359.

Damasio, A. R. & Damasio, H. (1983). The anatomic basis of pure alexia. *Neurology*, *33*, 1573–1583.

Déjerine, J. (1892). Contribution à l'étude anatomoclinique et clinique des differentes variétés de cécité verbale. *Mémoires de la Société de Biologie*, *4*, 61–90.

Ekstrom, R., French, J. W., & Harman, H. H. (1976). *Manual for kit of factor-referenced cognitive tests*. Princeton, N.J.: Educational Testing Service.

Ellis, A. W. & Young, A. W. (1988). *Human cognitive neuropsychology*. Hillsdale, N.J.: Lawrence Erlbaum Associates Inc.

Friedman, R. B. & Alexander, M. P. (1984). Pictures, images, and pure alexia: A case study. *Cognitive Neuropsychology*, *1*, 9–23.
Geschwind, N. (1965). Disconnexion syndromes in animals and man. Part II. *Brain*, *88*, 585–645.
Greenblatt, S. H. (1983). Localisation of lesions in alexia. In A. Kertesz (Ed.), *Localisation in neuropsychology*. New York: Academic Press.
Grossi, D., Fragassi, N. A., Orsini, A., De Falco, F. A., & Sepe, O. (1984). Residual reading capacity in a patient with alexia without agraphia. *Brain and Language*, *23*, 337–348.
Johnston, J. C. & McClelland, J. L. (1974). Perception of letters in words: Seek and ye shall not find. *Science*, *184*, 1192–1194.
Johnston, J. C. & McClelland, J. C. (1980). Experimental tests of a hierarchical model of word identification. *Journal of Verbal Learning and Verbal Behaviour*, *19*, 503–524.
Kay, J. & Hanley, R. (in press). Simultaneous form perception and serial letter recognition in a case of letter-by-letter reading. *Cognitive Neuropsychology*.
Kinsbourne, M. & Warrington, E. K. (1962). A disorder of simultaneous form perception. *Brain*, *85*, 461–486.
Kuçera, H. & Francis, W. N. (1967). *Computational analysis of present-day American English*. Providence: Brown University Press.
Landis, T., Regard, M., & Serrat, A. (1980). Iconic reading in a case of alexia without agraphia caused by brain tumour: A tachistoscopic study. *Brain and Language*, *11*, 45–53.
Levine, D. N. & Calvanio, R. (1978). A study of the visual defect in verbal alexia-simultanagonosia. *Brain*, *101*, 65–81.
McCarthy, R. A. & Warrington, E. K. (1990). *Cognitive neuropsychology: A clinical introduction*. New York: Academic Press.
McClelland, J. L. (1979). On the time relations of mental processes: An examination of systems of processes in cascade. *Psychological Review*, *86*, 287–300.
McClelland, J. L. & Rumelhart, D. E. (1981). An interactive activation model of context effects in letter perception. *Psychological Review*, *88*, 375–407.
Pashler, H. & Badgio, P. (1985). Visual attention and stimulus identification. *Journal of Experimental Psychology: Human Perception and Performance*, *11*, 105–121.
Patterson, K. E. & Kay, J. (1982). Letter-by-letter reading: Psychological descriptions of a neurological syndrome. *Quarterly Journal of Experimental Psychology*, *34A*, 411–441.
Reuter-Lorenz, P. A. & Brunn, J. L. (1990). A prelexical basis for letter-by-letter reading: A case study. *Cognitive Neuropsychology*, *7*, 1–20.
Shallice, T. (1988). *From neuropsychology to mental structure*. New York: Cambridge University Press.
Shallice, T. & Saffran, E. M. (1986). Lexical processing in the absence of explicit word identification: Evidence from a letter-by-letter reader. *Cognitive Neuropsychology*, *3*, 429–458.
Sternberg, S. (1969). The discovery of processing stages: Extensions of Donders' method. *Acta Psychologica*, *30*, 276–315.
Warrington, E. K. & Rabin, P. (1971). Visual span of apprehension in patients with unilateral cerebral lesions. *Quarterly Journal of Experimental Psychology*, *23*, 423–431.
Warrington, E. K. & Shallice, T. (1980). Word-form dyslexia. *Brain*, *103*, 99–112.

INDEX